The Labor Market Impact of Forced Displacement

The Labor Market Impact of Forced Displacement

Jobs in Host Communities in Colombia, Ethiopia, Jordan, and Uganda

Jan von der Goltz, Kirsten Schuettler,
Julie Bousquet, and
Tewodros Aragie Kebede

WORLD BANK GROUP

Contents

Boxes

Figures

Maps

Acknowledgments

Work on this report was led by Jan von der Goltz and Kirsten Schuettler, under the supervision of Federica Saliola and Ian Walker, and with invaluable advice and support from Paolo Verme. The core team consisted of Julie Bousquet, Jan von der Goltz, Tewodros Aragie Kebede, Jean-Francois Maystadt, Kirsten Schuettler, and Svein-Erik Stave. The extended team included Lukas Delgado-Prieto, Juan Miguel Gallego, Andrés García-Suaza, Anna Gasten, Mark Kadigo, Juan Diego Mayorga, Angie Mondragón-Mayo, Mira Saidi, Colette Salemi, Alexander Sarango Iturralde, Carlos Sepúlveda, and Huafeng Zhang.

Data collection for this report was led by the Fafo Research Foundation for the World Bank, in partnership with Departamento Administrativo Nacional de Estadística and Universidad del Rosario in Colombia, the Policy Studies Institute in Ethiopia, and Bishop Stuart University in Uganda.

Production of the report was supported by Amy Lynn Grossman, Aldo Morri, and Sasha Romanova, with guidance from Alexandra Humme.

The team especially thanks our colleague Norbert Schady for his advice and guidance and is indebted to our colleagues Paola Elice and Paolo Verme. We are also grateful to Emily Reilly and Ciara Silke of the UK Foreign, Commonwealth and Development Office (FCDO) for their consistent support and guidance. The work has benefited greatly from peer review comments received at different stages from our colleagues Caroline Bahnson, Johannes Hoegeveen, Eric Mvukiyehe, Caglar Ozden, Abla Safir, and Tara Vishvanath, as well as from Ziad Ayoubi (United Nations High Commissioner for Refugees, UNHCR); Howard Standen (FCDO); Jan Stuhler (Universidad Carlos III de Madrid); and Carlos Vargas-Silva (University of Oxford). Our colleagues Dina Abu-Ghaida, Aziz Atamanov, Alfredo Manfredini Bohm, Carole Chartouni, Maria Davalos, Gabriel Demombynes, Andreas Eberhard, Maddalena Honorati, Rada Nawwaf Nafe Naji, Benjamin Reese, and Andrea Vermehren counseled the team on country context and policy dialogue.

Contributions to the report's chapters are as follows: Kirsten Schuettler led chapter 1, with inputs from Jan von der Goltz. Kirsten Schuettler led chapter 2, with inputs from Julie Bousquet, Jan von der Goltz, and Svein-Erik Stave. Julie Bousquet and Jan von der Goltz led chapter 3, with inputs from Anna Gasten, Mark Marvin Kadigo, Jean-Francois Maystadt, and Kirsten Schuettler. Jan von der Goltz led chapter 4, with inputs from Julie Bousquet, Tewodros Aragie Kebede, Kirsten Schuettler, and Svein-Erik Stave. Core and extended team members provided comments and research assistance.

Special topics 1 and 2 summarize results from working papers commissioned for this study. The core team wrote the special topics. Authorship of working papers is acknowledged separately.

This report is part of the "Building the Evidence on Protracted Forced Displacement: A Multi-Stakeholder Partnership" program that is funded by the UK government, is managed by the World Bank, and was established in partnership with the UNHCR to expand the global knowledge on forced displacement by funding quality research and disseminating results for the use of practitioners and policy makers. This report does not necessarily reflect the views of the UK government, the World Bank, or the UNHCR.

Main Messages

The overall labor market effects of hosting refugees are modest, or even positive, in the countries studied, although some host country workers can be adversely affected even as others enjoy new opportunities.

- On average, and in a context of aid and government investments, host community workers are in nearly all instances unaffected or benefit from the opportunities brought by the arrival of refugees.

- However, in important instances, groups of host workers face adversity from greater labor market competition, while others benefit. Those who lose out are sometimes, but not always, vulnerable groups.

- Effective policies are needed to assist harmed host workers. Because overall effects tend to be mild and some groups benefit, such policies are likely to be feasible.

Refugees find ways to work even in host countries that restrict labor market access, but policies have important repercussions on how refugees participate in the labor market.

- Many refugees face significant financial challenges, so they must find ways to work, even in restrictive policy environments.

- Refugees often face difficulties in finding good jobs, even in liberal policy environments, and therefore must rely on unearned income from humanitarian aid or remittances.

- Labor market integration policies help shape the kind of work refugees do and the quality of jobs they can access.

Policies to integrate refugees into the economy affect which groups of host workers face competition and which gain opportunities, but competition may not start with these policy choices.

- Greater labor market access for refugees will usually expose some groups of host workers to increased competition in the labor market.

- However, more open access may also lessen competition for other groups of host workers. Granting refugees the legal right to work can reduce competition for host workers in informal jobs, for instance, while granting freedom of movement can reduce competition in localities near camps.

In host countries in which self-employment is a major source of jobs, two policy goals are key: helping refugees access capital and helping hosts seize new market opportunities.

- In many host economies, most people engage in self-employment and household market activities. In such labor markets, access to capital and land is critical for refugees, who often lose assets during displacement.

- In the meantime, the demand boost that refugees bring to local consumer markets can offer important opportunities for self-employed host workers. Policies should support them in seizing these opportunities.

In host communities in which economic activities are less diversified, it is difficult for refugees to bring skills that complement those of hosts.

- In high-income economies, refugees and hosts can expect better job outcomes when skills among the two groups complement each other.

- However, labor markets are less diversified in many lower-income countries, and a few common activities provide livelihoods for most people. Refugees therefore often find themselves doing the same types of work as host workers.

- In these environments, refugees' access to capital and refugees' traditions, networks, and perceptions may determine their work more than their skills.

Hosts' attitudes toward refugees may depend on worries about job competition, both in localities where there is significant competition and in localities where there is less.

- Policies to welcome refugees into local economies will be sustainable only if they are acceptable to host workers.

- Experimental evidence from Ethiopia and Uganda shows that host workers' views of refugees depend on whether there are concerns about job competition, regardless of the actual degree of competition.

- To promote welcoming attitudes, policy needs to provide effective support to host workers, communicate well about the labor market participation of refugees, and encourage opportunities for personal interaction and perspective-taking.

Globally, most refugees live in low- and middle-income economies. Policies designed for high-income countries may not be appropriate for these labor markets.

- Low- and middle-income countries harbor three times as many refugees as high-income countries.

- Effective policy must reflect and be tailored to job markets in host countries.

- Policy analysis must especially take account of the self-employment and informal activities many hosts depend on.

Thoughtful policy toward greater economic integration can improve refugee livelihoods while ensuring job opportunities for hosts.

- Although some host workers face greater competition, hosting refugees also brings important opportunities, and policies can compensate those adversely affected.

- At the same time, greater economic integration can make a profound difference for refugees and allow them to rebuild their lives.

- Policies based squarely in the realities of host country labor markets can balance these two goals.

Executive Summary

This report helps provide an understanding of how displacement affects job outcomes in host communities in low- and middle-income countries and identifies ways to support better job opportunities for hosts and refugees. Forced displacement is at its highest since World War II, with 37.8 million refugees displaced internationally as of mid-2022. For many refugees, displacement has lasted a long time, and—because few refugees have returned to their homes in recent years—policies focus on how to integrate them into the economies of host communities. This policy direction, in turn, raises questions and concerns about the potential negative effects on job prospects for host workers. Public debate tends to focus on refugees who settle in high-income countries, yet low- and middle-income countries host three of every four refugees. This report looks at job outcomes for hosts and refugees in these economies and seeks to identify policy directions to support both refugee and host workers.

Despite much recent research on how forced displacement affects job outcomes, significant knowledge gaps remain. To promote confident policy making, this report focuses on addressing two particularly important gaps by doing the following:

- *Providing systematic empirical evidence that compares how forced displacement and policy toward economic integration affect job outcomes across different countries and contexts.* Effects on job outcomes vary with factors such as the structure of the host labor market, the political economy and regulatory setting, the number and geographical distribution of displaced people, and their capabilities as employed or self-employed workers. However, most evidence is limited to single-country case studies using idiosyncratic data and methods. This report focuses on enabling comparisons.

MAP ES.1 Analysis and data collection for this report

JORDAN
3% share of all refugees
hosted in low- and middle-income countries

- Harmonized secondary data analysis
- Jordan Compact work permit analyzed

COLOMBIA
11% share of all refugees
hosted in low- and middle-income countries

- New nationwide primary data
- Harmonized secondary data analysis
- PEP and PPT analyzed

UGANDA
6% share of all refugees
hosted in low- and middle-income countries

- New Isingiro and Kampala primary data
- Harmonized secondary data analysis
- Listing experiment conducted

ETHIOPIA
4% share of all refugees
hosted in low- and middle-income countries

- New Addis Ababa and Jijiga primary data
- Harmonized secondary data analysis
- Listing experiment conducted

Source: Original map for this report.
Note: PEP = Special Permanence Permit; PPT = Temporary Protection Permit.

- *Strengthening the understanding of the mechanisms through which hosting displaced workers affects job outcomes to better inform policy making.* Numerous mechanisms have been proposed, including skills complementarities between workers, aid and public investment flows, changes to market demand, and factors that facilitate or limit the ability of host workers to adapt. However, lack of data limits how well these issues can be studied to inform policy.

This report studies job outcomes in host communities in Colombia, Ethiopia, Jordan, and Uganda. These four countries are all among the top host countries worldwide, and together they account they for 24 percent of refugees or other people in need of international protection who live in low- or middle-income countries. Map ES.1 shows the economies included and explains what analytical work was done in each of them. They were chosen with an eye toward allowing for comparisons across contexts that can inform policy. They represent both low-income countries (Ethiopia and Uganda) and middle-income countries

> *Colombia, Ethiopia, Jordan, and Uganda are all among the top host countries worldwide, and together they account for 24 percent of refugees or other people in need of international protection who live in low- or middle-income countries.*

(Colombia and Jordan) as well as, within each income group, one country with a more liberal labor market access regime for refugees (Colombia and Uganda) and another that has opened up more cautiously (Ethiopia and Jordan); table ES.1 provides an overview of these characteristics. After studying how displacement affects job outcomes in host communities within each country, the report offers comparative perspectives.

To facilitate clearer comparisons between countries, this report uses a harmonized approach to analyze how forced displacement has changed job outcomes in each of the four host countries. The report relies on standard research methods but places special emphasis on applying them consistently across the four countries. This harmonized approach limits variations in the analytical process to highlight differences in country context. The goal is to facilitate more compelling qualitative comparisons of forced displacement repercussions across economies than previous studies allow. The analysis shows results for the entire labor force as well as for important groups of workers. Because job outcomes are complex, the report further considers a range of outcome measures, including welfare proxies, measures of labor market participation and job quality, and proxies for structural economic shifts.

TABLE ES.1 Characteristics of displacement, case study countries

Characteristic	Ethiopia	Uganda	Colombia	Jordan
Registered refugees and asylum seekers	0.9 million refugees (1 percent of host population) from Eritrea, South Sudan, and Sudan	1.5 million refugees (3 percent of host population) from Burundi, Democratic Republic of Congo, Somalia, and South Sudan	2.9 million Venezuelans in need of international protection (5 percent of host population)	0.7 million Syrian refugees (7 percent of host population) out of 3 million Iraqi, Palestinian, and Syrian refugees
Residence time (median)	Addis Ababa: 4 years Jijiga: 31 years	Kampala: 4 years Isingiro: 9 years	4 years	8–9 years
Policies toward labor market participation and freedom of movement	• Previously highly restrictive (must live in camps, not allowed to work) • Since 2010, out-of-camp policy for Eritrean refugees; informal work around camps supported since 2012; since 2016, further out-of-camp and work permits planned	• Refugees allowed to work and move freely (but services limited to settlements) • Allocation of land in settlements, but size and quality of plots decreasing with time	• Venezuelans allowed to move freely • Introduction of a residence permit for Venezuelans including right to work in 2017 (PEP) and a longer residence permit in 2021 (PPT)	• Syrian refugees allowed to move freely • Introduction of Jordan Compact granting work permits to Syrian refugees in 2016
Camps and settlements; urban versus rural	About 90 percent of refugees in camps; 10 percent in Addis Ababa (mostly Eritreans)	90 percent of refugees in rural settlements; 7 percent in Kampala	No camps or settlements; about 90 percent of Venezuelans in urban areas	About 26 percent of Syrian refugees in camps; about 71 percent in urban areas

Source: Original table for this report.
Note: PEP = Special Permanence Permit; PPT = Temporary Protection Permit.

Labor markets are diverse, and refugees and their hosts engage with the market and with each other in complex ways. To inform policy choices, this report explores in detail the conduits through which host and refugee workers affect each other's job outcomes. In Ethiopia and Uganda, novel data sets designed and collected for this report are used to compare hosts and refugees in select labor markets in a way that national data do not usually permit. The report offers additional perspectives on Colombia and Jordan using labor market data collected for this report in Colombia and rich publicly available data in Jordan.

"Special Topic 1: The Impact of Work Permits on Job Outcomes for Hosts and Refugees" summarizes new results from studies commissioned for this report on how three well-known work permit schemes in the two middle-income countries affect job outcomes among hosts. These schemes include the Jordan Compact, which created access for Syrian refugees to some formal sector jobs in selected industries, and Colombia's Special Permanence Permit and Temporary Protection Permit, two large permit programs to regularize Venezuelan refugee access to formal jobs. The study of the Temporary Protection Permit relies on novel data collected for this report, and results on the Jordan Compact and the Temporary Protection Permit are new additions to the literature.

Although the report focuses on actual job impacts, "Special Topic 2: The Role of Perceived Labor Market Competition in Shaping Attitudes toward Refugees" studies the role of perceptions. An inflow of refugees affects host communities in many ways other than through the labor market. Thus, studies have assessed effects on prices, public services such as education or health, natural resources, and environmental degradation. All these repercussions influence public perceptions and attitudes toward refugees, which, in turn, affect social cohesion and public support for refugee policies. At the same time, public perceptions related to displacement may differ from actual measured effects. Against this backdrop, the report commissioned a framing experiment in the two low-income focus countries to explore whether and how perceived and actual labor market competition shape host and refugee perceptions of each other.

Summary of empirical results
How does forced displacement affect job outcomes for hosts?

Across the four economies studied, overall effects on jobs in refugee-hosting communities are modest or even positive. In each of the four economies, displacement leads to no aggregate change in proxy variables for welfare in host communities, or sometimes even leads to gains: in low-income countries, average consumption increased about 3 percent with a doubling of the number of refugees hosted (figure ES.1). Similarly, despite concerns over potential job competition, there is little evidence of overall adverse effects on employment in host communities. Importantly, these results come in the context of significant international support to host countries; it is not clear what the impact of displacement would have been without support. Overall, the results are broadly in line with the existing empirical literature: although certain groups of host workers can face greater labor competition, hosting refugees affects host workers less negatively than often expected.[1]

However, hosting refugees changes labor markets, and even where the aggregate effect of hosting displaced workers is positive, some groups of workers experience declines in consumption, earnings, or activity levels; that is, in some cases, although there are "winners" in refugee-hosting communities, there are also people who lose. For instance, in Uganda, urban workers in host communities experienced an estimated 4 percent decline in consumption (within the statistical margin of error), offset by a 3 percent gain among rural workers. In Colombia, although there is no robust effect on overall employment, youth employment is estimated to have decreased by 1 percentage point with a doubling of the number of refugees hosted (figure ES.1).

Shifts in sector and type of activity are modest and often mirror changes in consumption and income among workers engaged in the different activities. This correspondence indicates that host workers adapt to opportunities and challenges arising from hosting displaced groups. In Colombia and Uganda, sectoral shifts into agriculture of 1 percentage point of all employment are seen alongside benefits to those active in agriculture. In Jordan, the data show a shift of 2 percentage points from wage employment, where mean earnings declined, into temporary work, where mean earnings increased. Across countries, these structural shifts are typically small, which is perhaps unsurprising given that even large refugee inflows are of relatively modest size compared with the size of the overall host labor force.

In the four economies analyzed, host workers in the agriculture sector often benefit as displaced persons increase consumer demand for food. Ethiopian and Ugandan farmers record significant consumption gains, alongside an increase in market-oriented farming activities in Uganda. Gains are also seen in Colombia and Jordan, but they are statistically within the margin of error. The preponderance of positive effects in agriculture—more clearly observed in economies more open to refugee participation—points to the importance of how increased product market demand improves job outcomes for some in lower-income countries.

Comparative analysis does not yield many predictions about which groups are likely to enjoy opportunities and which are likely to face competition, underscoring the importance of tracking local impacts. Across many groups of workers studied, there are few clear patterns of positive and adverse impacts beyond the patterns of adaptation and opportunity in agriculture. Vulnerable groups of

FIGURE ES.1 How does forced displacement affect job outcomes for hosts?

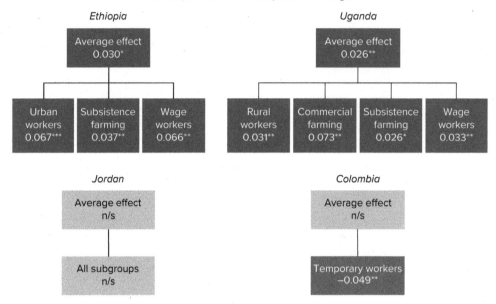

a. Effects on hosts' consumption or earnings

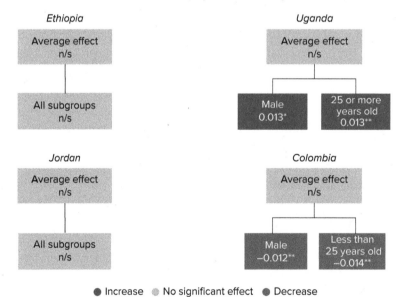

b. Effects on the employment rate among hosts

● Increase ● No significant effect ● Decrease

Source: World Bank.
Note: n/s = not significant.
*$p < .05$, **$p < .01$, ***$p < .001$

workers, such as younger workers and women, are sometimes affected more, but not in all instances. Similarly, although the report cannot conclusively analyze distributional impacts, it finds no evidence that households with low asset wealth are systematically more affected than those who are better off. With few general patterns in distributional impacts, policy must rely on effective analysis of local contexts. Chapter 5 provides guidance on job analysis to help identify risks of competition as well as opportunities.

What effect do work permit schemes have on hosts' and refugees' job outcomes?

Many legal, social, and economic factors determine the degree to which refugees are active in the economy. One important dimension that attracts much policy attention is the right to work, often granted through formal work permits. Despite their prominence, work permits are not always decisive for participation in low- and middle-income countries. For instance, where most economic activity is informal, finding paid work without a permit is possible; and, where most jobs are in self-employment, permits may matter little in the absence of access to capital. However, at least in middle-income countries, work permits can facilitate access to good formal sector jobs. Perhaps as important, even in lower-income economies with little formal work, permit programs can put refugee workers on an equal footing with hosts in the informal sector and raise their bargaining power and ability to defend their rights.

Work permit policies show little overall effect on host workers' earnings, but they change which workers face competition.

Work permit policies show little overall effect on host workers' earnings, but they change which workers face competition. Jordan's work permit program was associated with small effects on job outcomes for hosts in its early days— some positive and some adverse—while two programs in Colombia showed no adverse effects. In its first year, the Jordan Compact—the first program to allow limited loosening of Jordan's stringent policy toward refugee participation in the formal labor market—is estimated to have increased formal wage earnings for host workers by 4 percent, albeit with a slight drop in the share of formal employment of 1 percentage point. Notably, there is no evidence of adverse aggregate effects on employment or unemployment rates, nor on overall earnings. The two permit programs studied in Colombia substantially expanded access to formal jobs in labor markets in which many refugees were already informally active. Neither is associated with perceptible adverse aggregate job outcomes for hosts across a range of activity, earnings, and formality indicators, in line with the results of a previous study on the first residence permit in Colombia (Bahar, Ibáñez, and Rozo 2021).

For displaced workers, the more generous work permit program in Colombia led to large wage gains, shifts into wage work, and earnings increases for those who remained self-employed. The second, longer-term permit program in Colombia illustrates the promise such programs hold for improving job outcomes for refugees. Refugees who received permits reported large wage gains of about one-third, echoing results of an earlier study of the first residence permit program (Ibáñez et al. 2022). Further, access to work permits clearly expanded refugees' choices in the labor market. Refugees who received their first permit through this second program (rather than switching from a previous permit) showed a large shift out of self-employment of 12 percentage points, whereas those who remained self-employed saw large gains in earnings of about one-third and one-quarter, respectively.

In what ways does refugee participation in the economy shape job outcomes for hosts?

Policy shapes refugee participation but does not completely determine it: many refugees work even in restrictive labor markets, and many refugees depend on unearned income even in countries with liberal refugee work policies. However, policy restrictions on refugee participation in the economy clearly have significant effects in middle-income labor markets, and they are at least partially effective even in highly informal labor markets, such as Ethiopia and Uganda. Among the localities studied, refugees are far more likely to work where there are relatively liberal rules. However, a substantial number of refugees work even in more restrictive labor markets. For instance, refugee labor force participation in the two localities studied in Ethiopia is 42 percent—far below the 64 percent participation for host workers, but substantial in the context of relatively restrictive policies. Conversely, refugees depend heavily on unearned income even in less restrictive labor markets: 57 percent of refugees in Kampala, for instance, rely primarily on unearned income compared with 8 percent of host workers.

Many refugee households draw upon unearned income, and many consume in local markets, highlighting opportunities that arise for hosts from higher market demand. Across the low-income labor markets studied, refugees are far less likely to be active and employed than hosts (figure ES.2). Displacement itself is the most obvious reason for low activity among refugees, rather than differences in demographics, education, or other characteristics. At the same time, many refugee households use earned or unearned income to buy local goods and services. Thus, many refugee households are solely consumers in their host economies, but even those that compete in the labor market contribute to market demand.

Refugee constraints push them toward vulnerable and lower-income jobs, creating specific patterns of competition and opportunities for hosts.

FIGURE ES.2   In what ways does the refugee labor market situation shape job outcomes for hosts?

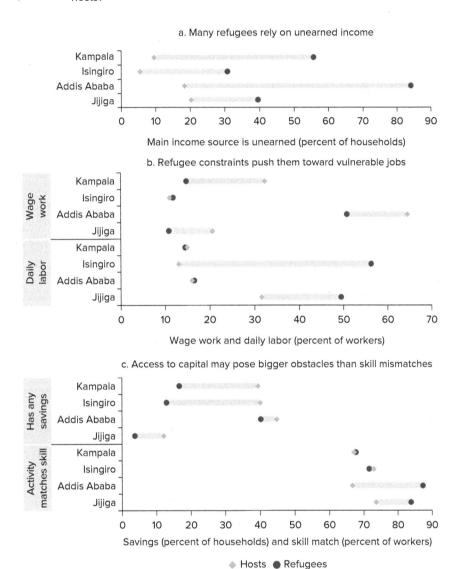

a. Many refugees rely on unearned income

Main income source is unearned (percent of households)

b. Refugee constraints push them toward vulnerable jobs

Wage work and daily labor (percent of workers)

c. Access to capital may pose bigger obstacles than skill mismatches

Savings (percent of households) and skill match (percent of workers)

◆ Hosts   ● Refugees

Source: World Bank based on data collected for this report.

Across the economies studied, refugees face more constraints than hosts and are more likely to work in vulnerable jobs. Consistently, refugees are less active in the kinds of jobs most hosts hold, even when their activity profiles before displacement are similar to those of hosts. Thus, they are less likely to hold wage jobs where such jobs are common or to be self-employed (including as farmers) where this kind of work is the chief income source for hosts.

Conversely, vulnerable daily labor plays a greater role for refugees than for hosts (figure ES.2), as does informal work in middle-income countries. This is the case even in the more liberal labor markets studied, although the large benefits refugees derive from the work permit programs in Colombia show that policies play an important role in shaping refugee outcomes. The limited range of job choices is usually reflected in lower earnings; in the low-income labor markets and in Jordan, median refugee earnings can be as low as half that of hosts.

Few refugees bring assets when displaced, and refugee households have lower savings and accumulate assets more slowly, likely hampering their ability to establish self-employment. Across contexts, refugees report lower asset wealth (sometimes by very wide margins), lower savings, more debt, and more limited access to formal lending. In Kampala, for instance, there is a gap of 0.15 standard deviation in an index of asset wealth, gaps of 26 percentage points in savings and debt (figure ES.2), and a 16-percentage-point difference in use of formal borrowing. In low-income countries, accumulating savings is slow and difficult, and the ability to bring some household assets when seeking refuge may have decisive implications for future work. However, only about one in seven refugee households in Ethiopia and Uganda had the opportunity to sell assets when first displaced, and far fewer brought cash savings. Further, there is little evidence that refugees catch up to hosts in accumulating assets. These facts suggest that refugees face considerable additional barriers to establishing self-employed activities, a key source of jobs and incomes, particularly in low-income labor markets.

Self-employed refugees in Ethiopia and Uganda invest less than hosts, hire fewer workers from outside their households, contend with additional obstacles, and tend to have lower revenue. In these two low-income countries, refugees with self-employed activities outside of agriculture invest less than hosts in business activities, with a gap of up to 40 percent in Uganda. Whereas most self-employed workers rely on savings or loans from family and friends, only hosts borrow from formal lenders. Hosts and refugees share key business concerns—access to funding, finding customers, and transporting goods—but refugees face additional obstacles, such as harassment, that reflect the harshness of the business environment. Those self-employed in agriculture face greater challenges in accessing land and are much less likely to produce for the market—by a margin of 30 percentage points in Uganda's rural Isingiro district, for instance.

Among refugee workers, skills match with jobs surprisingly well, but the degree of matching may have a lower bearing on job quality in lower-income countries than in wealthier economies. Refugees and hosts across the four economies largely report similarly good skill matches, and overlap between top skills and current activities is substantial. This is not to say that skills always match, especially for women, but there is little indication of an additional gap for refugees. It is possible, however, that, even where the overall activity apparently matches, the specific tasks refugees carry out may match their skills less well. Furthermore, it is worth recalling that refugees in the study localities tend to have lower revenues and work more precarious jobs, arguably more important dimensions of job quality than skill matches. In addition, language is a significant barrier for many refugees, limiting their ability to perform well even in jobs that match their other skills.

How does labor market competition influence attitudes?

Hosts' and refugee workers' perceptions of, and attitudes toward, each other affect job outcomes for both groups. Attitudes can directly shape market interactions, such as decisions to hire workers or to buy from particular suppliers. They also indirectly determine support among hosts for the economic integration of refugees. Because working matters so much—not just for welfare, but also for identity—it is likely that attitudes and perceptions in turn depend on whether hosts and refugees compete in the labor market or whether hosting refugees provides opportunities.

> *Host workers exhibit prejudicial attitudes toward refugees only when they are trained in the same occupation. Thus, job competition—and even worries about potential competition—may shape hosts' attitudes.*

In Ethiopia and Uganda, hosts who view refugees as competitors are more likely to hold prejudicial attitudes, and fear of job competition may shape attitudes as much as actually experiencing competition. Evidence from four labor markets in these countries shows that hosts exhibit prejudicial attitudes toward refugees only when they are trained in the same occupations and, thus, represent potential labor market competitors. Remarkably, the study found that this is particularly the case in two labor markets where there is limited actual competition between refugees and hosts, suggesting that worries over possible competition may influence attitudes as much as, or more than, actually experiencing competition. Refugees are not prone to similar biases toward hosts; indeed, in the study localities, refugees sometimes view their hosts more favorably than they view fellow refugees.

Policy implications
What policies can support better host job outcomes?

Distributional changes demand policy attention even where displacement or work permit schemes cause few changes in overall employment outcomes for hosts. The four countries studied all experienced substantial refugee inflows, but there has been little change in aggregate participation and unemployment.

Similarly, estimated effects from large work permit schemes on jobs for hosts are limited. However, there are gains for some groups of workers and adverse effects on others, notably in the short term. Sometimes the adverse effects are borne by particularly vulnerable groups of workers, but this is not systematically the case. Policy makers should direct their attention toward assisting workers who encounter disruption and vigilantly tracking whether vulnerable groups are affected. Quick and effective support is critical to welfare, fairness, social stability and, ultimately, sustaining policies to help refugees rebuild their livelihoods.

With support from the international community and small economywide effects, host workers can be directly compensated for any harm caused to them from competition. Absence of economywide adverse effects from hosting refugees and granting work permits should not blind policy makers to the fact that some groups of workers may face greater labor market competition. However, limited or even positive aggregate effects suggest that policies can focus on compensating those affected, help them adapt, and boost overall demand for labor where competition has increased. Low- and middle-income countries need ongoing support from the international community to accomplish this. Indeed, the favorable effects found in this study come in the context of such aid and might not have been achievable without it. The goal of compensation should be to restore or improve job opportunities for hosts, not to provide permanent income support. Temporary support is, however, a proven policy option. Cash transfers or, in wealthier economies, unemployment insurance payments can help workers weather temporary losses of opportunity and fund investments in new activities (whether for supplies, training, job search, or travel).[2]

The arrival of displaced workers presents opportunities that deserve as much policy attention as concerns about labor market competition. Public discourse tends to focus on potential adverse effects on jobs for hosts. Far less attention is paid to opportunities from the arrival of additional consumers and from aid and investment that often accompany refugee flows. This analysis shows potential for important gains in host communities. Policy should not only seek to limit potential harm to hosts but also consider how best to help workers and businesses seize these opportunities.

To seize these opportunities, host country policy makers need to foster a favorable business environment and invest resources wisely for hosts and refugees alike. In addition to sector-specific policies, a beneficial business and investment climate can help businesses seize the opportunities created by refugee inflows. Investments in infrastructure and facilitating access to finance in host communities can also help. Host communities in Tanzania provide an example of long-term gains due to such investments: the infrastructure built continues to reduce transportation costs and yield benefits even after refugees returned (Maystadt and Duranton 2019).

Structural changes in host communities reflect a "move toward opportunity" that policies can support by improving access to capital or by funding retraining or mobility. Analysis of the four economies studied here shows that host workers make significant efforts to adapt to the arrival of refugee workers. Overall, there is a "move to opportunity" toward sectors and activities likely to experience increased demand and less competition. Policy can seek to facilitate such shifts. In low-income countries, policies can support self-employed workers in making small investments to change their activities. In higher-income economies, support is likely to involve access to capital and finance for firms; improving the investment climate, particularly in sectors where new opportunities arise; and providing training opportunities for workers. Supporting workers' geographic mobility can also help facilitate adaptation, including policies to support affordable housing at new destinations, align minimum wages to the cost of living, provide information, and counter discrimination against internal migrants.

The agriculture sector is often well-positioned to provide additional opportunities for host communities, and public investment can help seize these openings. Across the four countries analyzed, agriculture workers in host communities benefit from the influx of refugees. It is intuitive that refugees increase demand for food and that opportunities for producers arise in food markets. At the same time, the food sector can also help employ refugees. Policies should consider investments to help local communities benefit from such opportunities. Low-income countries often have a well-defined pipeline of productivity-enhancing investments in search of financing, which is likely to include support to individual farmers to adopt technology, add cash crops, or process their products before taking them to market. Higher-income economies often focus on targeting support to competitive value chains. Support to cooperatives and investment in infrastructure are further priorities in most economies.

Policies designed to broaden refugee labor market access should consider the likely distributional effects and how they may increase or reduce competition for different host groups. The two countries in this study with more liberal refugee policies (Colombia and Uganda) do not show worse outcomes than those with more restrictive policies. The introduction of work permit programs did not lead to substantial adverse effects on hosts. Still, all policy choices affect distributional outcomes, and more or less liberal policy regimes will affect different groups differently. Policies that restrict access to formal jobs for refugees will raise competition for vulnerable workers in the informal sector, whereas labor market competition may shift toward formal jobs in countries issuing work permits to refugees. Liberalizing access to land or capital may increase competition among self-employed workers but may lessen it among daily laborers.

Policies for better job outcomes for refugees

Refugee support must carefully consider the type of activities in which there is demand for labor and for self-employment, and sectors in need of product supply. Conditions vary enormously in host labor markets, especially with income levels and between urban and rural areas. For instance, schemes to promote access to formal jobs are likely more appropriate in urban or higher-income labor markets with more demand for wage workers. In agricultural areas, access to land and capital is crucial. Elsewhere, focusing on lowering barriers to self-employment might best support refugee workers.

To help refugees establish and succeed in self-employment, policies need to alleviate the substantial capital constraints refugees face. Both displacement itself and barriers to earning good incomes disadvantage refugees in building capital, especially in low-income economies where accumulating savings is already very difficult. Lack of access to capital is a severe obstacle in labor markets where self-employment is a major economic activity. It also limits the ability of refugees to take more risks when setting up an economic activity or to wait for better jobs and invest in job searching. Policies should seek to alleviate these capital constraints. Understanding the viable avenues that exist for refugees to access capital is vital. For instance, in low-income markets where even hosts rarely borrow outside the family, borrowing may be especially hard for refugees. In such economies, small recurrent cash transfers have a successful track record in helping refugees rebuild some assets or fund job searching. Promising evidence on economic inclusion programs suggests that providing refugees with larger cash grants may have more sustained impacts than cash transfers. In higher-income economies, policies can help refugees start firms by improving their access to finance, for instance, through loan guarantees or psychometric credit scoring. Legally allowing refugees to create businesses also promotes formal firm creation and growth, as seen in Colombia (Bahar, Cowgill, and Guzman 2022).

Skill matches may help refugees improve their livelihoods but perhaps not in obvious ways, so policies need to be based on careful assessment. Refugee skill gaps may not be based on having less education; they could—as in this study—be due to the lack of language or practical skills. Further, skill matches may be less relevant than in higher-income markets, both because most jobs in lower-income labor markets are in a smaller number of common activities and because the skill gap between host and refugee workers is typically (though not always) less wide. Policy makers must determine whether refugees are well equipped to find a niche among workers who carry out common activities. In addition, capacity to invest may be more important to success than skills match. Evidence shows that training programs not combined with cash provision or access to finance will likely not succeed, at least in the short term and in low-income settings.

In labor markets with significant formal employment and vigorous labor demand, work permits and acceptance of credentials are important tools for supporting refugees. Although policy attention to the repercussions of work permits on hosts is warranted, it should not be forgotten that refugees stand to benefit substantially from work permit programs, especially where having a work permit gives a refugee a realistic chance of obtaining a higher-earning, formal job with better working conditions. This report cautions against applying approaches from high-income countries to low- and middle-income countries. However, host countries with vigorous labor demand should consider evidence from high-income countries showing that refugees benefit when quickly allowed to work and when their educational and professional credentials are readily accepted.

Even in labor markets with little demand for formal workers, work permits can empower refugee workers by providing a potent and visible signal that they have a right to work, thus promoting their bargaining power and reducing their vulnerability. In economies where informality and self-employment are common, this signaling may be the most important function of a work permit scheme. Therefore, policy makers should seek additional ways to send the same message, for instance, by creating programs in which permits are easy to obtain and not tied to formal work, or through government communications campaigns targeting workers and employers. In addition, because work permits alone are unlikely to facilitate job access in such labor markets, policy attention needs to address other obstacles refugees face in lower-income economies, such as access to land and capital for self-employment.

Investing in host communities and promoting contact with, and information about, refugees can soften negative views toward displaced workers. Supportive attitudes from hosts are important to the well-being of refugees and to their success in building lives while living in displacement. This report's findings suggest it is important to address concerns about actual or potential labor market competition. Policy discourse increasingly acknowledges the importance of providing job support to host communities alongside the displaced, but worries about competition can shape perceptions even when there is little actual competition. Experimentation is needed to identify effective approaches. Emerging evidence suggests that promoting contact between hosts and refugees can change attitudes, although questions remain. Other initiatives that have improved attitudes in some settings include raising awareness of the situation refugees find themselves in, or directly encouraging listeners to empathize with refugees by imagining themselves being in a similar situation.

Priorities for future work to inform policy

To inform policy, future work should ask how aid, market demand, access to capital, and freedom of movement shape job outcomes; study distributional impacts; and ask what promotes welcoming host attitudes. Policy will benefit from a clearer understanding of how aid to host communities facilitates adaptation to new competition and opportunities. Rising market demand remains less well understood than labor market competition, and further research can help shape more effective policy to help host workers seize opportunities. In lower-income economies in particular, constraints to accessing capital are critical barriers for host and refugee workers, and further work on effective ways to facilitate access would be fruitful. In addition to studying the longer-term impacts of work permits, future research would need to verify the impact of granting refugees freedom of movement. Further, expanding the investigation of impacts along the income distribution and in localities that host particularly large numbers of refugees is warranted. Finally, concerns about job competition clearly help shape attitudes toward refugees, and policy will benefit from a better understanding of how such concerns relate to actual competition, and how they are most effectively addressed.

Notes

1 | For an overview of the literature see, for instance, Verme, and Schuettler (2021). Additional references are provided in chapter 1 of the full report.

2 | A full discussion of the literature related to this and other support modalities is provided in chapter 5 of the full report.

References

Bahar, Dany, Bo Cowgill, and Jorge Guzman. 2022. "Legalizing Entrepreneurship." NBER Working Paper 30624, National Bureau of Economic Research, Cambridge, MA.

Bahar, Dany, Ana María Ibáñez, and Sandra V. Rozo. 2021. "Give Me Your Tired and Your Poor: Impact of a Large-Scale Amnesty Program for Undocumented Refugees." *Journal of Development Economics* 151: 102652.

Ibáñez, Ana María, Andrés Moya, María Adelaida Ortega, Sandra V. Rozo, and Maria José Urbina. 2022. "Life out of the Shadows. The Impacts of Regularization Programs on the Lives of Forced Migrants." Policy Research Working Paper 9928, World Bank, Washington, DC.

Maystadt, Jean-François, and Gilles Duranton. 2019. "The Development Push of Refugees: Evidence from Tanzania." *Journal of Economic Geography* 19 (2): 299–334.

Verme, Paolo, and Kirsten Schuettler. 2021. "The Impact of Forced Displacement on Host Communities: A Review of the Empirical Literature in Economics." *Journal of Development Economics* 150: 102606.

Abbreviations

ACS	adaptive cluster sampling
ARRA	Agency for Refugee and Returnee Affairs (Ethiopia)
CARA	Control of Alien Refugees Act (Uganda)
DANE	Departamento Administrativo Nacional de Estadística (National Administrative Department of Statistics) (Colombia)
EA	enumeration area
ERSS/ESS	Ethiopia Socio-economic Survey
EU	European Union
FE	fixed effects
GEIH	Gran Encuesta Integrada de Hogares (Large Integrated Household Survey) (Colombia)
GDP	gross domestic product
HHR-LMS	Harmonized Host and Refugee Labor Market Survey, Ethiopia and Uganda
ILO	International Labour Organization
IV	instrumental variable
JLMPS	Jordan Labor Market Panel Surveys
LIC	low-income country
LSMS	Living Standards Measurement Study
LSMS-ISA	Living Standards Measurement Study–Integrated Studies on Agriculture
MIC	middle-income country
MoU	memorandum of understanding
OCP	out-of-camp policy
ODA	official development assistance

OLS	ordinary least squares
PEP	Permiso Especial de Permanencia (Special Permanence Permit) (Colombia)
PM	Encuesta Pulso de la Migración (Colombia)
PPS	probability proportionate to size
PPT	Permiso por Protección Temporal (Temporary Protection Permit) (Colombia)
RUMV	Registro Administrativo de Migrantes Venezolanos (Administrative Registry of Venezuelan Immigrants) (Colombia)
SSRJ	Survey of Syrian Refugees in Jordan
UNHCR	United Nations High Commissioner for Refugees
UNPS	Uganda National Panel Survey

1. State of Knowledge

Study background and objectives

Although much policy attention goes toward refugees who settle in high-income countries, three of every four of the world's refugees and other people in need of international protection are hosted in low- and middle-income countries.[1] For many of these refugees, displacement has lasted a long time: on average, refugees have resided outside of their home countries for more than 10 years (Devictor and Do 2017). The number of new and existing refugees dwarfs the number of returns and resettlements.

Where forced displacement is protracted, the promotion of employment opportunities for refugees and host communities is the lynchpin of development-led interventions. When refugees are displaced for longer periods, humanitarian aid is not an appropriate or effective way of ensuring a dignified life of reasonable economic opportunity. The focus instead shifts toward development interventions. The discourse on the humanitarian-development nexus, the Comprehensive Refugee Response Framework, and the Global Compact on Refugees all highlight that, in such protracted displacement situations, labor market access is imperative for refugees. Regaining and establishing livelihoods are primary objectives of forcibly displaced people that will allow them to rebuild their lives if they cannot return home or resettle elsewhere. In addition, when refugees participate in the labor market and become self-reliant, the need for financial support from host countries and the international community declines.

Policies and interventions to facilitate refugees' labor market participation have gained traction over the past decade in low- and middle-income countries. Some countries, such as Uganda, have long histories of facilitating the labor market participation of refugees. More generally, refugee policies, including access to labor markets, have become more liberal over time in low- and middle-income countries (Blair, Grossman, and Weinstein 2022). Despite many structural, policy, and institutional constraints, internationally promoted employment strategies and compacts have begun to be defined and implemented in countries such as Colombia, Ethiopia, Jordan, and Türkiye in the past decade. In addition to these policy-level shifts, multilateral organizations and bilateral donors have increased their funding for job interventions for refugees (Schuettler 2020).

The impacts of the labor market participation of forcibly displaced workers on job outcomes for hosts as well as the efficacy of policies to facilitate participation are contested (Becker and Ferrara 2019; Verme and Schuettler 2021). What is agreed is that impacts and policy outcomes can vary in relation to the structure of the economy, preexisting labor market conditions, the number and geographic distribution of displaced people, their capabilities as employed or self-employed workers, and the political economy and regulatory setting. At the same time, outcomes will vary depending on the type of novel job promotion policies and more classic job support interventions implemented for those forcibly displaced and their host communities (Schuettler and Caron 2020).

Four significant gaps in knowledge need to be filled:

- First, as yet, there is limited systematic empirical evidence across different countries and contexts on the direct and secondary impacts of forced displacement on labor markets, such as labor force participation, employment and unemployment rates, wages, skills mix, substitution effects and segmentation, and the size of formal and informal employment and employment in different sectors. Evidence is limited to single-country case studies, and the data, identification strategies, and empirical specifications vary greatly (Verme and Schuettler 2021).

- Second, there is even less understanding of the mechanisms, transmission channels, and factors that explain these impacts, such as aid, investment, and entrepreneurial strategies; regulatory environment; productivity; market demand and capacity; skills complementarities and gaps; and adaptation mechanisms of locals (such as moving geographically or switching occupations). Many papers also lack data on refugee characteristics and labor market participation in the same locations as locals, which could help explain impacts. Especially in low-income countries, effects are likely to be highly localized because of high transportation costs and markets that are not well integrated.

- Third, there is no comprehensive research on which interventions and strategies work (or do not work), including policies such as job compacts, preferential market access, and liberalized work permit provision.

- Finally, although there is no lack of reports and surveys containing data on host populations' perceptions of refugees, few studies have used rigorous economic methodologies to analyze relationships between hosts' perceptions and refugees' interactions and impacts on local labor markets, including through experimental designs.

These gaps in knowledge are strongly related to a lack of empirical data of a nature that can be used to fully apply rigorous research methodologies. Attempts at carrying out rigorous analyses are often limited by weaknesses of the available data, such as small samples; data that cover only displaced or only host populations; data collected by using sample frames not designed for the purpose of impact analysis (for example, national labor force statistics that are not representative for refugee populations and have very small samples in the remote areas where refugees reside); and a lack of administrative or panel data, notably in low- and middle-income countries.

This study provides empirical evidence to contribute to filling some of these prominent knowledge gaps. Although no single study can hope to close all the critical knowledge gaps identified above, this report (and its associated publications) attempts to advance what is known about these issues.

- First, it offers a harmonized analysis of the impact of displacement on job outcomes for hosts in four countries, using consistent methods to isolate as much as possible the influence of context-specific factors on outcomes.

- Second, it uses new data from four labor markets in two countries to allow the mechanisms through which displacement affects hosts' labor market outcomes to be assessed using a detailed side-by-side analysis of the labor market activities of these two groups of workers, and of their interactions. Most existing studies of the labor market impacts of forced displacement are based on surveys typically covering either host or refugee populations separately or not covering them in the same geographic areas and including limited data on labor markets and work. Even though labor force surveys are fairly standardized, data units, definitions, collection strategies, and geographic coverage vary across countries and make comparisons challenging. Thus, to facilitate assessments of contextual factors that influence labor market outcomes in different countries, the study makes an attempt to harmonize the collection of a set of key labor market outcomes across three of the four case study countries.

- Third, the study uses consistent methods in two countries to analyze the impact of work permit programs on job outcomes for hosts and displaced workers, including through new data. These include the Jordan Compact, which created access for Syrian refugees to some formal sector jobs in selected industries, and Colombia's Special Permanence Permit (Permiso Especial de Permanencia, or PEP) and Temporary Protection Permit (Permiso por Protección Temporal, or PPT), two large permit schemes to regularize Venezuelan migrants and their access to jobs. The analysis of the work permit impacts complements a review of the impact of different job support modalities, as well as their cost, done in companion pieces to this report (Barberis et al. 2022; Schuettler and Caron 2020).

- Finally, the report conveys results from an experiment designed to help assess the role of perceptions on labor market outcomes for the displaced. In addition to job outcomes, an inflow of refugees also potentially affects prices, public services such as education or health, natural resources, and environmental degradation in host communities. These impacts influence public perceptions and attitudes toward refugees, which, in turn, affect social cohesion and public support for refugee policies. At the same time, how impacts are perceived may differ from actual, measured effects. Against this backdrop, a framing experiment was included in the surveys in Ethiopia and Uganda to explore whether and how perceived and actual labor market competition shapes host and refugee perceptions of each other.

Case study countries

The report's work is anchored in the study of four countries: Colombia, Ethiopia, Jordan, and Uganda. Together, these countries host a quarter of all refugees in low- and middle-income countries (box 1.1). These economies were selected on the basis of their suitability for answering the policy questions asked in this report. Thus, they represent both low- and middle-income countries as well as, within each of these income groups, a more restrictive and a more generous environment with respect to policies, regulatory frameworks, and interventions related to access to labor markets for the displaced. In addition, the secondary data available for each country allowed for a harmonized assessment of impacts, and the state of the country-focused literature was such that a comparison could be enriched with related findings, but also left substantial questions of context and mechanisms behind impacts open to exploration through primary data.

A common feature of the selected case study countries is that refugees have been officially allowed to work in various ways. In Uganda, all refugees have had legal access to the labor market for more than two decades. In Colombia, Venezuelans were granted legal access to the labor market in July 2017 and

BOX 1.1   To what extent do the economies studied in this report reflect the diversity of low- and middle-income countries that host refugees?

Low- and middle-income countries host three of every four refugees displaced worldwide. Although most of these countries host some refugees, a relatively small number of countries accounts for most hosted refugees. Thus, the six host countries with the largest refugee populations account for half of all refugees living in low- and middle-income countries, and four of every five refugees displaced in such countries live in the 15 countries that host the largest number of refugees.

Figure B1.1.1 shows how different low- and middle-income countries contribute to giving refuge to the displaced, focusing on those countries that each host at least 2 percent of all refugees in low- and middle-income countries. Among them, the four countries chosen for this study are

home to between 3 percent and 11 percent of refugees in low- and middle-income countries, and they include the countries that host the second- and fourth-largest numbers of refugees in the developing world. Together, the four countries account for nearly one of every four refugees displaced in low- and middle-income countries (24 percent). The two low-income countries analyzed—Ethiopia and Uganda—together account for 44 percent of all refugees hosted in low-income countries.

As explained in chapter 2, middle- and low-income country labor markets differ in important ways. This study, therefore, includes two countries in each income group to reflect these qualitative differences. Ethiopia and Uganda share important structural

FIGURE B1.1.1   The middle- and low-income countries that host the most refugees

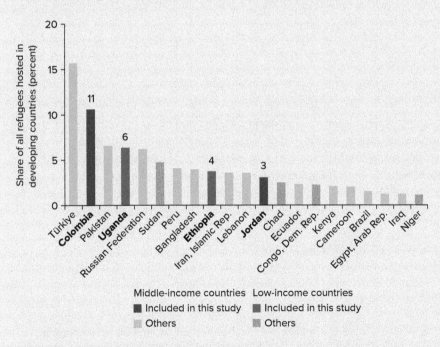

Source: United Nations High Commissioner for Refugees 2022 data on refugees and other persons in need of international protection; World Development Indicators 2021 Atlas gross national income per capita.

(continued)

BOX 1.1 To what extent do the economies studied in this report reflect the diversity of low- and middle-income countries countries that host refugees? (*continued*)

characteristics with other large low-income host nations, all of which are also located in Africa. In total, the region hosts nearly all refugees who live in low-income countries. Despite their idiosyncratic features, Colombia and Jordan both have labor markets with characteristics typical of middle-income countries; notably, the numbers of the unemployed are much higher than in lower-income countries, especially in the cities and among youth; paid work for others plays a far greater role compared with self-employment; and human capital is higher.

Like other host countries, the case study countries reflect a range of more and less generous policies toward the participation of refugees in the labor market. Policies toward participation of refugees have become more generous over time in many developing countries (Blair, Grossman, and Weinstein 2022), including the ones studied here, as discussed in chapter 2. However, gradations remain. Data from the Center for Global Development's *2022 Global Refugee Work Rights Report* (Ginn et al. 2022) reflect this

range. Roughly half of those developing countries for which data were available had at least an intermediate score for access to work permits and ability to conduct informal self-employed activities, whereas half scored lower. Scores for freedom of movement were a bit more favorable, with half of all developing countries at least at an intermediate score. The four countries included in this study reflect this diversity (if not its extremes), with a range of scores from intermediate-low to intermediate-high in each policy dimension.

Of all refugees worldwide, about 30 percent live in camps and about 60 percent live in urban areas. The countries studied here reflect this diversity of living situations, including countries where no, some, or nearly all refugees live in camps, and conversely most, many, or only a few refugees live in urban areas. Similarly, the regions selected for primary data collection in Ethiopia and Uganda include areas in and around camps, rural settlements, and urban areas (refer to chapter 4 for an in-depth discussion)

---

can now obtain a 10-year residence permit. In Jordan, and to a lesser degree in Ethiopia, a large number of refugees has obtained de jure access to certain sectors of the labor market as part of international agreements, that is, so-called compacts, through which the two host countries have committed to granting work permits to a specific number of refugees in exchange for access to international export markets and international financial support. One particular aspect of interest in the countries selected for this study is the effect of granting work permits to refugees on the informal labor market in which most refugees obtain work—whether legally or illegally.

Data sources

The report uses existing household and labor market surveys collected among host populations as well as data on the number and location of refugees in the four countries. Three of the data sets collected among hosts are individual-level panel data sets. The Ethiopian Socio-Economic Survey is a panel survey with three waves collected as part of the Living Standards Measurement Studies over the period 2011–16. For Uganda, the report uses three waves covering the period 2009–12 of the Living-Standards Measurement Study—Integrated Studies on Agriculture data set, which is derived from the Uganda National Panel Survey. For Jordan, the Jordan Labor Market Panel Surveys collected in 2010 and 2016 are used. In Colombia, the study relies on the Gran Encuesta Integrada de Hogares (Large Integrated Household Survey), a monthly repeated cross-section survey, from 2015 to 2019. For refugees' locations, the study uses existing data from the United Nations High Commissioner for Refugees in Ethiopia and Uganda, and from the censuses in Colombia and Jordan. Further, the study draws upon data on work permits from the Jordan Department of Statistics and on residence permits (including work permits) from Colombia's National Office of Migration (Migración Colombia).

New primary data from quantitative labor market surveys were collected in Colombia, Ethiopia, and Uganda (map 1.1 illustrates this data collection effort and other analysis conducted for the report). The design of these surveys was guided by the intent to complement existing data on hosts and refugees in such a way as to allow for the analysis of questions that are hard to approach with available data. For Ethiopia and Uganda, the goal of data collection was to allow an in-depth comparison of hosts and refugees to be made regarding their job

MAP 1.1 Analysis and data collection for this report

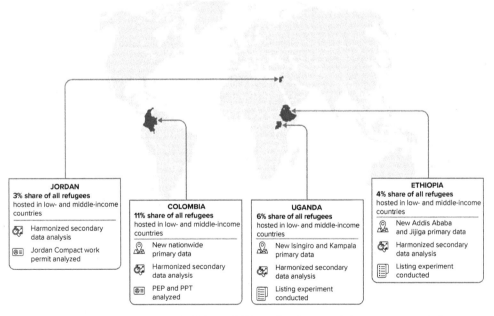

Source: United Nations High Commissioner for Refugees 2022 data for refugees and other persons in need of international protection.
Note: PEP = Permiso Especial de Permanencia (Special Permanence Permit); PPT = Permiso por Protección Temporal (Temporary Protection Permit).

activities and interactions, side by side in the same labor markets. In Colombia, the goal was to collect additional labor market information within an ongoing series of high-frequency surveys at a point that would support analysis of the impact of a new, generous work permit program. During the design and piloting of the questionnaires, qualitative data were collected in Ethiopia and Uganda to inform the survey data collection and analysis.

The surveys in Ethiopia and Uganda covered refugees and hosts in selected locations within each country. In Ethiopia, the capital, Addis Ababa, was covered, as were, in the Somali region of Ethiopia, Jijiga city, Kebribeyah town, and Kebribeyah refugee camp. In Uganda, the survey covered three locations: the capital city Kampala, as well as Isingiro district, and the Nakivale refugee settlement in the southwest of the country. Using maps of the selected enumeration areas (EAs) provided by the Ethiopian Central Statistical Service and the Ugandan Bureau of Statistics, the study team listed all households in the selected EAs using door-to-door visits before drawing the sample. The EAs were selected using probability proportionate to the size, where size is measured by the number of households. In addition, in Addis Ababa and Kampala, the study used adaptive cluster sampling to capture additional refugee households. Adaptive cluster sampling is useful for capturing rare populations (Thompson 1990), but no other study so far seems to have used this technique to sample refugees (Eckman and Himelein 2022). Using the listing of households in the initial EAs in the two cities, those EAs with 10 percent or more refugee households were identified, and all of their neighboring EAs were listed. The exercise served as the basis for random sampling of both refugee and host households in both cities.

In Ethiopia and Uganda, the study team developed two structured questionnaires aimed at capturing information related to labor market outcomes and variables that can help explain them. The first questionnaire was administered to household heads and included questions on demographic profile, education, and labor market participation of all household members; household economy; and living standard measures for the household. The second questionnaire was administered to a randomly selected individual of the household and included the following survey modules: background and skills, labor market participation, and job characteristics; mobility history; social network; experimental component; social integration and perception; and subjective well-being. The questionnaire development process included a pilot exercise to refine and finalize both the content of the questionnaire and field implementation procedures.

In Colombia, similar labor market–related questions were included in the Pulso de la Migración survey. The National Statistical Administrative Department conducted four rounds of the survey by phone among displaced Venezuelans and Colombians who returned from República Bolivariana de Venezuela between July 2021 and April 2022. The survey is representative at the national level; its sample was selected from the first-semester respondents of the cross-sectional household survey Gran Encuesta Integrada de Hogares's migration module.

Structure of the report

The executive summary of this report describes the scope of analytical work carried out and summarizes the main findings and their policy implications. Chapter 1 summarizes what job impacts should be expected based on economic theory and existing empirical studies. Chapter 2 provides a comparative overview of the refugee population, refugee policy, and the host economy and labor market in each of the four countries. Chapter 3 provides an assessment of impacts on the labor market outcomes of hosts based on secondary data using a harmonized methodology. "Special Topic 1: The Impact of Work Permits on Jobs Outcomes for Hosts and Refugees" discusses the effect of work permit schemes in Colombia and Jordan. Chapter 4 uses the primary data collected to discuss in detail the labor market outcomes and interactions of hosts and refugees. "Special Topic 2: The Role of Perceived Labor Market Competition in Shaping Attitudes toward Refugees" reports findings on the relationship of refugees' and hosts' perceptions and labor market competition. Chapter 5 concludes with a discussion of how the report's lessons can help guide labor market analysis with the goal of informing refugee policy, distills policy tools to improve job outcomes for hosts and refugees, and defines avenues for future research.

Economic theory

Standard labor market models of migration predict short-term losses from a refugee influx for host workers through greater labor supply. With no labor market models developed specifically for forced displacement, models that explore the impact of migration on labor markets are the most useful theoretical touchstone for this investigation. This section introduces the standard model of migration impacts, asks when its predictions may not hold, and discusses how adjustments in the labor market could change outcomes.

The standard model

In the simplest, canonical model of a closed economy, one type of labor, and a constant-returns-to-scale production function, an inflow of workers changes the ratio of labor to capital and thus its price. This is usually modeled as a short-run impact: over the longer run, firms are expected to reinvest gains, leading to an increase in labor demand (Borjas 2014). A consequence of the arrival of migrant or displaced workers is thus distributional because wealth may shift away from workers toward firms (from labor to capital). When the model assumes an open economy, capital will flow in from outside, responding to its increased marginal productivity, and labor-to-capital ratios will equalize more quickly. The simpler models often assume that labor demand is downward sloping, that is, the lower the wages the higher the demand for labor by firms, and that the labor supply is inelastic, that is, that the labor supply curve is vertical and the number of workers supplying labor does not change even if the wage changes. If the latter assumption is dropped, an influx of refugee workers will lead not only to a decrease in wages but also to changes in employment, unemployment, and, potentially, labor force participation. Even more sophisticated models take into account that labor supply elasticities might also be heterogeneous and vary between different types of workers who have different reservation wages (Dustmann, Schonberg, and Stuhler 2016). As a result, impacts will not be the same for all workers.

When models include different types of labor, the effect of the supply shock on the labor market outcomes of workers depends on the skill composition of migrant or displaced workers and their hosts. If migrant workers have a high degree of substitutability with hosts, immigration or displacement will tend to decrease host wages. By contrast, if migrants have a high degree of complementarity with hosts, immigration may raise productivity and increase wages. This logic holds for the entire labor market, but also for subgroups: those groups that experience the largest supply shifts of substitutable (complementary) labor supply lose (win) not only in absolute terms but also relative to the ones that experience smaller shifts. Here again, the refugee inflow will thus have distributional impacts. The refugee inflow will change relative wages and, potentially, employment if immigrants increase the amount of only certain skill groups in the labor force but not of others.

Conditions under which the assumptions of the standard model might not hold

Like migrants, refugees cannot be assumed to be perfect substitutes for native workers, even if they share important characteristics. Migrants and natives of the same age, and who share similar work experience and education, might still differ in significant ways in their labor market engagement. Importantly, they often do not possess the same language, social, and cultural skills. Employers might not value domestic and foreign-earned credentials and experience in the same way, leading to downgrading between and within occupations (Dustmann, Schonberg, and Stuhler 2016; World Bank 2018). Migrants' legal status also influences what types of jobs they are able to do (Card and Peri 2016).

Migrants and natives who have the same education and experience on paper can thus not be assumed to be perfect substitutes under these conditions. When occupational downgrading happens, they might not even compete with natives in their same education or occupational group (Dustmann, Frattini, and Preston 2013; Lebow 2024). As a result, the impacts of displacement on hosts' labor market outcomes measured in empirical investigations hinge upon the degree of substitution that is assumed (Card and Peri 2016).

A migrant or refugee inflow influences the labor market through an increase not only in labor supply but also in labor demand. Although the canonical model is a partial equilibrium model that looks at migrants as workers first, migrants and refugees are also consumers and, potentially, investors and employers. A second conduit through which forced displacement is expected to affect labor market outcomes is therefore a positive shock to demand for goods and services through the arrival of additional consumers in the market. Such demand effects have an impact on labor market outcomes where goods and services have a domestic component and the displaced are able to partic-ipate in the market.[2] Where such a demand shock is observed, it changes the price of goods and services, encouraging producers of goods and services with a domestic component to raise output and putting upward pressure on wages. How strongly and quickly these changes materialize depends on the elasticity of the supply of goods and services. Whether this demand effect outweighs a potential labor supply effect on labor market outcomes is ambiguous in the model. Further, in contrast to typical labor migrant inflows, refugee shocks are often accompanied by an increase in international aid or social services pro-vided by the government, as well as by investment in infrastructure such as roads, airports, or service infrastructure near camps (Verme and Schuettler 2021). Both can raise labor demand in the local labor market and affect the local prices of goods produced by self-employed workers. Food aid can be expected to have different impacts on local markets than cash support. Finally, if refugees bring capital, they may become employers, thus also affecting labor demand (and further raising output in the long term as a result of the addi-tional capital available). They also bring human capital and networks, which can increase firms' productivity.

In labor markets where self-employment prevails, product market demand and capital ownership are key to welfare impacts. The standard model is written for labor markets characterized by firms and employees. However, in lower-income labor markets, many jobs are in self-employment and household activities. Applying the models to such labor markets requires some reinter-pretation. For the self-employed, incomes will tend to rise if displaced groups generate additional market demand for goods and services. Incomes will tend to drop when displaced workers start self-employed activities that are substi-tutable for those in which hosts are active (a positive supply shock in prod-uct markets). Capital ownership by the displaced is a key prerequisite for their labor market participation. The standard model's predictions about skill complementarity and substitutability among employees hold analogously for self-employed workers.[3]

Refugees differ from labor migrants, which influences the types and magnitudes of effects predicted by the models. The decision to migrate is typically modeled as the result of a comparison of expected welfare in the origin and destination countries, net of expected migration costs (Borjas 1987; Roy 1951; Sjaastad 1962). In contrast to labor migrants, refugees self-select on the basis of their need for safety, not their ability to maximize income. Whereas labor migrants aim for destinations where they believe there will be labor market demand and a higher premium for their skills, refugees tend to move with little preparation to the closest place where they can be safe—with less regard for labor demand and skill complementarities in host countries. As a result, compared with migrant workers who tend to move with the business cycle, refugees can be expected to have skills that are less complementary to those of hosts and to be more likely to arrive in times of low labor demand, which can lead to stronger competition between refugees and hosts. Over time, however, refugees can also adapt to the local labor market and acquire location-specific human capital (such as language skills) just like labor migrants, which leads to occupational upgrading.

The framework conditions for refugee participation in the labor market also differ from those for labor migrants, further altering impacts. First, refugees often arrive in large groups, leading to a large increase in consumer demand and labor supply in a short period. Second, refugees' access to labor markets is normally more restricted than that for immigrant workers, which might lead to more concentrated effects (for example, in and around camps and settlements if refugees are not allowed to move and settle freely or focused on the informal sector if refugees are not legally allowed to work). Restrictions also influence how quickly the labor supply may increase. Third, refugee populations usually receive humanitarian aid or other types of external support, which might lead to increased economic activity and to more employment opportunities in refugee areas.

Potential labor market adjustments that diminish impacts of a refugee inflow

The canonical model does not take into account that the downward pressure on wages and employment after the arrival of refugee workers is expected to decline in the longer term because of labor market adjustments. The primary effects of a refugee inflow are increases in labor supply and, neglected by the canonical model, consumer demand. As secondary effects, capital will flow in and firms will increase their output in response to the cheaper labor and increased demand, expanding employment opportunities. Additional adjustments include changes in internal migration patterns of natives, occupational changes of natives, and adaptation of firms. Each is discussed in turn.

In addition to accepting lower wages or becoming unemployed, host workers can also decide to move geographically. Host workers may be more mobile than refugee workers, if refugee workers see their ability to freely move and settle restrained and lack the necessary assets and networks to move. Host workers may move to other cities or localities in such situations to avoid competition and wage drops from labor supply shocks. However, it is worth noting that, in many low-income countries, the major cities provide labor markets for asset-poor low-skilled workers that cannot be easily found elsewhere. Conversely, firms can benefit from higher labor supply and consumer demand by relocating to areas most favored by immigrants.

Displaced groups with complementary skills are expected to affect labor market outcomes for hosts less than groups with skills that are substitutes. When displacement causes a large increase in labor supply concentrated in certain occupations, hosts may seek to downgrade or upgrade to other occupations that demand lower or higher skills, or to move vertically within the same skill group to a job in a sector with less competitive pressure from displaced workers. They may also opt to drop out or join the labor force later to pursue further education.

Firms may respond to an increased labor supply by changing their capital and labor mix. Existing firms that can employ labor at lower wages are discouraged from investing in labor-saving technology; others have an incentive to adapt the product mix and start new businesses in labor-intensive activities. The former effect is most likely to arise when there is an inflow of workers whose activities are relatively easily replaced by machinery, that is, typically, low-skilled manual laborers. In contrast, immigration of highly skilled workers may be less likely to create incentives against automation (Borjas 2014).

State of empirical knowledge

The number of empirical studies of the impacts of refugees on host communities has drastically increased over the past decade, but methodological challenges and gaps remain. The first empirical study in the field of economics is from 1990, and until 2011 an average of only one or two studies was published per year (Verme and Schuettler 2021). Since the conflict in the Syrian Arab Republic erupted in 2011, the pace of empirical work has increased dramatically, and at present a much larger number of empirical studies addressing the impacts of refugees on host communities is available. Impacts on labor market outcomes of hosts are among the types of impacts most studied. However, significant gaps in knowledge, as well as methodological challenges, remain. In particular, these difficulties include (1) incorporating contextual factors that mediate impacts in both economic models and empirical studies; (2) convincingly addressing the "endogeneity" of displacement to job outcomes (that is, the fact that places to which refugees are displaced may be systematically different in job outcomes from other places, regardless of displacement); and (3) using comparable methodologies, empirical specifications, and definitions across studies so that results can be compared across contexts. Box 1.2 discusses measurement challenges that arise in the empirical estimation of the standard model.

Existing studies of the impacts of refugees on host labor market outcomes show large variations in results, both between contexts and in many cases even within the same setting. A range of contextual factors influences the types and magnitude of the impacts of displacement on job outcomes for hosts, making empirical analyses complex and challenging to compare. These factors include the structure of the host economies, refugee and labor market policies, characteristics of refugee populations, and the degree of international support and government investments following the inflow of refugees. Such factors could explain why impacts seem to vary considerably across contexts. Furthermore, the effects of forced displacement are dynamic and change over time. Theory predicts and the evidence generally confirms that effects turn more positive over time as a result of various adaptation processes in the labor market. The timing of when an inflow study measures impacts might thus also influence results. Average results and results for certain subgroups in the labor market also do not necessarily match. Different subgroups in the labor market are affected differently, depending on context. Unfortunately, the fact that studies use different data, definitions, time horizons, identification strategies, and empirical specifications makes it difficult to say whether the different results are due to differences in measurement or differences in actual impacts resulting from context. Studies also often lack the data needed to explore the role of contextual factors and mechanisms that could help explain differences in results.

Impacts are less negative than expected

In general, studies show that impacts on labor market outcomes are less negative than standard economic models anticipate. According to a review of 59 empirical economic studies of the impacts of refugees on host populations, 76 percent of the 446 results on employment showed nonsignificant or positive impacts on employment rates among the host populations (79 percent when weighted by the impact factor[4] of the journal in which they were published). Half of the employment results came from middle-income countries and a quarter each from high-income and low-income countries. Among the 322 results on wages, 72 percent were positive or nonsignificant (unweighted and

BOX 1.2   How to measure the impact of migration and forced displacement

There is no agreement among researchers about how to measure the impact of immigrants or refugees on local populations. Studies use very different research designs and empirical specifications (see Verme and Schuettler 2021).

One important area of disagreement is how to model the independent shock or treatment variable, that is, the migrant or refugee inflow. Some researchers compare areas that are more or less affected by migrant or refugee inflows. Others measure the shifts in different groups of workers (the so-called skill-cell approach). And some researchers combine the two (Dustmann, Schonberg, and Stuhler 2016). How to measure the relative shift in supply in different types of labor has been particularly debated and shown to change the direction of estimated effects (Borjas 2014; Card and Peri 2016).

A key debate about how impacts should be measured focuses on a case in a high-income country: the sudden arrival of a large number of Cubans in Miami, Florida, after the so-called Mariel boatlift in 1980. The first study of the event by Card (1990) found no impact, which was later confirmed by other studies using different methodologies (Angrist and Krueger 1999; Clemens and Hunt 2019; Peri and Yasenov 2019). While confirming no significant effect on employment or unemployment (overall or for any subgroup) and no impacts on wages overall nor for all low-skilled workers, Borjas (2017) and Borjas and Monras (2017) find that the relative wages of a certain subgroup of low-skilled individuals were negatively affected. The definition of this subgroup and the ability of the data to measure impacts on this subgroup have been contested by other researchers (Clemens and Hunt 2019; Peri and Yasenov 2019). The debate thus revolves around the assumed substitutability between different types of workers (in this case, dropouts and high school graduates), which affects who is assumed to experience impacts and how strongly the impacts are likely to diffuse (Card and Peri 2016).

In addition to the question of the correct independent variable, researchers struggle with addressing endogeneity. Compared with economic migrants, refugees leave their countries and settle in areas because of factors that differ from those influencing natives' economic outcomes, especially when governments decide where refugees should be settled. Nevertheless, possible endogeneity can still bias results. Areas receiving more refugees can have closer ties to the countries of origin or be more prosperous. Their growth path might also change compared with before the inflow because of additional factors associated with the refugee inflow, for example, if they are closer to the border (and thus are affected by conflict spillovers) or benefit from an aid inflow or government investments. To address endogeneity, most researchers have used instrumental variables or tried to exploit policies that randomly place refugees in certain areas. Instrumental variables approaches used to address endogeneity have their own limitations. They assume that there is a third variable that influences the outcome of interest only through its impact on the independent variable (exclusion restriction). By using this variable to predict expected values of the independent variable and substituting these predictions for the independent variable itself, the endogeneity issues noted above are assumed to be circumvented. However, the instrumental variables typically used in the forced displacement literature have come under scrutiny (Goldsmith-Pinkham, Sorkin, and Swift 2020) (for a more detailed discussion, refer to chapter 3 of this report).

Beyond the conceptual disagreements over how best to measure the independent variable and how to address endogeneity, research designs and empirical specifications also differ because of data constraints. These data constraints are more severe in low- and middle-income countries. The sample size of existing surveys covering hosts and refugees in the areas where refugees reside is usually insufficient. Panel data or even administrative data (which allow for more rigorous, causal analysis because the same individuals are followed over time) including refugees are particularly rare. Chapter 3 discusses what is feasible with the available data in the four case study countries covered by this report.

weighted by the journal's impact factor) (Verme and Schuettler 2021). Two-thirds of the wage results were from middle-income countries and one-third from high-income countries. Results included in the review covered average results among hosts as well as results for specific subgroups of workers. Wages are a useful indicator for labor market impacts only in middle- and high-income labor markets. In low-income countries, where self-employment is much more prevalent and the population usually has several sources of income, the fewer existing studies often use consumption as a proxy for income. These studies also tend to find positive or nonsignificant impacts on consumption (Kreibaum 2016; Maystadt and Duranton 2019; Maystadt and Verwimp 2014), but not in all cases (Depetris-Chauvin and Santos 2017).

These actual impacts also do not align with the perceptions of the host populations. In a first study comparing results with perceptions, Kreibaum (2016) finds that, among hosts in Uganda, perceptions of their own economic well-being were negative whereas the actual average impact on welfare as measured by consumption and public service provision was positive. Similarly, although Loschmann, Bilgili, and Siegel (2019) find positive impacts on the type of labor market activities and an increase in household assets among Rwandans living closer to refugee camps, they do not find an impact on the subjective perception of those Rwandans about their household's economic situation.

Who experiences negative impacts?

Although no impacts or even positive impacts are found surprisingly often, the literature shows that there may be losses for subgroups of workers or where inflows are large relative to the labor market's size. As models that allow for more than one type of labor predict, many empirical studies find that there are groups who benefit, groups that are not affected, and groups that lose out. Impacts are heterogeneous and affect subgroups in the labor market differently. The inflow thus has distributional impacts within the host community that are important to understand from a development policy perspective. Such adverse consequences may arise more broadly when inflows are very large relative to the size of the labor market.

Studies from low- and middle-income countries identify some groups that are more often negatively affected—young and less-experienced workers, less-educated workers, workers in the informal sector, and immigrant workers (Lebow 2024; Malaeb and Wahba 2023; Verme and Schuettler 2021). The negative impacts on these already disadvantaged groups in host labor markets seem to occur most frequently where refugees are not allowed to work. Accordingly, relatively privileged groups tend to benefit disproportionately from the positive impacts of displacement events. Land and business owners and other employers, workers in the formal sector, and medium- or highly skilled workers make up the majority of these groups. Better-off host community women might benefit from better availability of childcare (Pedrazzi and Peñaloza-Pacheco 2023; Ruiz and Vargas-Silva 2018b). However, studies do not always agree on which subgroups are affected and what the magnitudes of the impacts are.

Studies show mixed effects on employment in the informal and formal sectors. In Türkiye, where much research has been conducted, several studies have shown significant negative effects from Syrian refugees on employment in the informal sector (Altındağ, Bakış, and Rozo 2020; Ceritoglu et al. 2017; Del Carpio and Wagner 2015; Tumen 2016). These results align with potentially greater competition for such jobs from refugee workers. At the same time, the same studies have shown no or positive effects on the employment of hosts in the formal sector caused by "occupational upgrading" (that is, a move toward more-qualified jobs by host workers who experience greater competition in less-qualified jobs and to more communication-related tasks if refugees do not speak the local language) and an increase in the number of formal jobs. In Jordan, however, no significant negative employment effects have been observed in the informal sector for Jordanian workers (Fakih and Ibrahim 2016; Fallah, Krafft, and Wahba 2019); and, in Colombia, results are mixed (see the section "Evidence for the four case study countries"). Other than leading to direct displacement, the labor supply shock also influences changes in formal versus informal employment because of firms substituting informal for formal labor and changes in the ratio of informal and formal firms in the economy (as the former become more competitive because of the increase in labor supply) (Altındağ, Bakış, and Rozo 2020; Delgado-Prieto 2022; Rozo and Winkler 2021).

Studies from host areas with very high inflows of refugees into local labor markets indicate that local workers are negatively affected above certain thresholds of absorption. Even where many refugees arrive in a labor market, and even if studies measure impacts in areas of the host country where inflows are highest, refugees still make up a comparatively small share of workers. This low concentration might explain why so few studies find overall negative effects. However, large and sudden inflows of refugees reaching a certain proportion of local labor markets (10 to 15 percent) may indeed negatively affect employment in the short term (Aydemir and Kirdar 2017; Braun and Mahmoud 2014). However, some studies have also shown that refugee workers mainly start competing with other refugee workers or previous immigrant workers, not native workers, when the share of refugees in the labor market reaches a certain level. Examples of this mechanism come from both the high- and middle-income economies of Germany (Gehrsitz and Ungerer 2022), Colombia (Bonilla-Mejía et al. 2020; Lebow 2024), and Jordan (Malaeb and Wahba 2023).

What reasons explain why displacement may have no or positive impacts on hosts?

Some empirical studies find that an influx of refugees can positively affect local business activity and new firm creation, which again creates new employment opportunities. As noted in the section "Economic theory," the growth of the number of consumers in refugee-hosting areas and the inflow of aid and investments, combined with the availability of cheaper labor, can lead to increased economic activity and new employment opportunities. Additionally, displaced persons may bring physical capital with them as well as human capital, and they may have new networks that complement those among hosts—although displacement can also diminish capital and rend networks. The few existing studies looking at demand-side developments find that the arrival of Syrian refugees in Türkiye led to increased production, profits, and sales for existing firms along with new firm creation, notably including firms co-owned by Syrian refugees (Altındağ, Bakış, and Rozo 2020; Cengiz and Tekguc 2022). Evidence for Colombia shows a positive impact on formal firm creation from the introduction of residence and work permits (Bahar, Cowgill, and Guzman 2022).

In particular, most studies from refugee camp settings show significant positive effects on the income and welfare of host populations in surrounding areas due to the increase in available resources and demand. Refugee camps are often placed in remote areas with few resources. The inflow of refugees increases demand, and additional resources become available through aid, investments, and the money that refugees bring with them. Simulations performed by Taylor et al. (2016) find that camps in Rwanda where refugees were given cash aid (as opposed to in-kind support) increased the net real income in the host area surrounding the camps by US$200–US$253 annually. In the Turkana region of Kenya, researchers looking at the economic welfare impacts of camps in the surrounding area concluded that the negative impacts of the increased competition were vastly outweighed by the economic opportunities provided by the camp and the increased demand generated by refugees (Alix-Garcia et al. 2018). Positive effects on household consumption and welfare among the native populations around camps are also documented in Rwanda, Tanzania, and Uganda (Kreibaum 2016; Loschmann, Bilgili, and Siegel 2019; Maystadt and Verwimp 2014), even if not everyone wins among the local population. Such positive impacts may persist over time when permanent infrastructure is created, for example, roads that reduce transportation costs (Maystadt and Duranton 2019).

Empirical papers observe some of the adaptation mechanisms described in the "Economic theory" section that generally lead to less negative impacts over time. These adjustments are usually interpreted as diluting the actual impact of the inflow. Many empirical studies seek to measure the impact of displacement without adaptations, and thus try to account for adaptive mechanisms, but do not study them directly. At the same time, however, these adjustments could be facilitated by policy to attenuate negative impacts, and the aim should be to understand them better to design such policies. One mechanism found by papers on Denmark, Greece, Tanzania, and Türkiye is the occupational upgrading of locals, including more communication-intensive jobs that refugees cannot do if they do not speak the language, increasing complementarities between refugees and hosts (Akgunduz and Torun 2020; Ceritoglu et al. 2017; Del Carpio and Wagner 2015; Foged and Peri 2016; Murard and Sakalli 2018; Ruiz and Vargas-Silva 2015). Papers on Colombia (Caruso, Gomez Canon, and Mueller 2021; Lebow 2022) and Jordan (Fallah, Krafft, and Wahba 2019) do not, however, find any or much evidence of occupational upgrading in the aftermath of the inflow. Changes in internal migration patterns among native workers to avoid high competition areas are another adaptive mechanism observed in relation to refugee influxes in some but not all contexts, with lower in-migration more prevalent than higher out-migration (Akgunduz, Aldan, and Bagir 2021; Bonilla-Mejía et al. 2020; Bryant and Rukumnuaykit 2013; Caruso, Canon, and Mueller 2021; El-Mallakh and Wahba 2021; Lebow 2022). When refugees are allowed to move freely, their geographic dispersion also dilutes impacts, as a simulation for Kenya shows (Sanghi, Onder, and Vemuru 2016). Very few studies have analyzed and observed whether existing firms change the labor and capital mix they employ, for example, by introducing capital-intensive changes that reduce labor force needs later than firms in non-refugee-receiving areas, or substituting refugee workers for capital (Akgunduz and Torun 2020; Lewis et al. 2004). No evidence seems to exist so far on more-labor-intensive firms entering areas with high refugee inflows.

What do we know about refugees' labor market outcomes?

The analysis of refugee characteristics and labor market outcomes is seldom combined with their labor market impacts. On the one side, many studies measuring impacts on labor market outcomes of hosts provide data only on refugee numbers and settlements but not on their characteristics and actual labor market participation. On the other side, a separate set of studies explore the labor market outcomes of refugees. Because of inadequate data availability in low- and middle-income countries, only some are able to compare the outcomes with hosts and with outcomes before displacement.

Empirical results confirm that refugees have different characteristics than hosts and other labor migrants, but how they differ depends on the context. Who decides to flee is shaped by conflict dynamics (who is targeted by conflict parties; who has more or less to lose by leaving) as well as the destination country (how safe and costly is the journey; who has networks) (Ibáñez 2014; Schon 2019). As a result of these factors, for example, Syrian refugees in Europe are more likely to be male and more educated than the Syrian average before the war, whereas in countries neighboring Syria, refugees are less educated and there is a higher likelihood of female-headed households (Schuettler and Do 2023).

Refugee displacement is typically accompanied by a loss of physical, human, and social capital. Existing data for refugees from low- and middle-income countries such as Ethiopia, Iraq, Jordan, Lebanon, and Uganda show that refugees have fewer assets than hosts and owned more assets before their displacement (Krishnan et al. 2020; Mejia-Mantilla et al. 2019; Pape, Petrini, and Iqbal 2018). Refugees lack networks at destination, which are important for labor market integration (Schuettler and Caron 2020). Because of traumatic events before their displacement or during their journey to their new destination, refugees usually also have worse mental health than the host population, even though the studies find strong variation in the levels of incidence because contextual factors and the methodologies used differ (Bogic, Njoku, and Priebe 2015; Porter and Haslam 2005). How refugees are received at destination, whether they are socially isolated and not allowed to work (Hussam et al. 2022), or whether they receive mental health support (Acarturk et al. 2016; Knaevelsrud et al. 2015; Neuner et al. 2008), can reinforce or attenuate these mental health effects.

Refugees tend to fare worse than hosts and other labor migrants on the labor market, but outcomes can improve over time if the conditions are favorable. Because of data availability, the more rigorous evidence comes from high-income countries.[5] The cross-sectional data from low- and middle-income countries provide similar results but are not able to track changes over time. The data show that refugees tend to participate less in the labor market, have lower employment rates, face more precarious working conditions, and rely more on unearned income (aid or remittances) at their destination (Fallah, Krafft, and Wahba 2019; Fix et al. 2019; Krishnan et al. 2020; Mejia-Mantilla et al. 2019; Pape, Petrini, and Iqbal 2018).

Evidence for the four case study countries

Existing empirical studies disagree to different extents on the direction and size of impacts and how different types of workers are affected in each of the four case study countries. The two studies on Uganda both find positive impacts on consumption but disagree on which channels are responsible for these positive impacts (D'Errico et al. 2022; Kreibaum 2016). The two studies on Ethiopia contradict each other not only in the mechanisms at play but also in the results (Belayneh 2020; Walelign, Wang Sonne, and Seshan 2022). In Jordan, two studies find limited impacts on host labor market outcomes (Fakih and Ibrahim 2016; Fallah, Krafft, and Wahba 2019), which is corroborated by two studies showing the out-migration of Jordanians in affected areas and impacts on migrant workers instead of Jordanians (El-Mallakh and Wahba 2021; Malaeb and Wahba 2023). Many more studies have been published on Colombia, all finding negative effects on wage levels but of very different orders of magnitude (Caruso, Gomez Canon, and Mueller 2021; Delgado-Prieto 2022; Lebow 2022, 2024; Lombardo and Peñaloza-Pacheco 2021; Peñaloza-Pacheco 2022).

Empirical studies from Uganda find overall positive impacts on consumption of host populations surrounding refugee settlements in rural areas but do not agree on which types of workers are affected in what ways. D'Errico et al. (2022) find that proximity to refugee settlements in the northwest and southwest of the country increases the consumption of the host population. They find significant reductions in the average value of crop sales and increases in participation in paid employment and in wage income for host households living closer to the refugee households, indicating a shift toward wage employment and away from work on their own land as an important adaptation mechanism. They do not find any impacts on self-employment income in agricultural and nonagricultural activities. Like D'Errico et al. (2022), Kreibaum (2016) finds that proximity to refugee settlements in the southwest part of the country increases the monthly consumption of the host population around the settlements. She finds clear negative impacts on consumption only for those depending on unearned income (potentially consistent with price increases in consumer markets), and negative consumption impacts for the wage-employed that are significant only in some specifications. She also finds that hosts benefit from improved access to private primary schools. Interestingly, as noted previously, the local host population does not see these improvements but rather perceives that the presence of refugees decreases their well-being.

The studies for Ethiopia find both positive and negative effects and put forward contradicting mechanisms that explain these effects. Walelign, Wang Sonne, and Seshan (2022) show that refugee inflows to camps benefit host communities by creating jobs in which people engage as secondary occupations, diversifying their income sources. The refugee inflows also lead to higher demand for livestock products, perhaps because refugees are usually provided with cereals as in-kind humanitarian aid, increasing agricultural commercialization of livestock products but not of crops. The refugee presence also decreases the distance to markets, potentially because of the creation of new markets from increased demand. Male-headed households were more likely to benefit than female-headed households. Negative effects were mainly observed in the Gambela region on Ethiopia's western border with South Sudan, where the refugee population is the largest, and larger than the host population. At the same time, Belayneh (2020) shows that hosting refugees crowds out some types of paid work for others among hosts in rural Ethiopia, but he detects no significant effects for urban areas. He finds that only temporary (casual) labor activities are crowded out by refugees, and only on the extensive margin (that is, a reduction in the number of hosts doing this type of work rather than a reduction of hours worked among those who continue to do it), but he finds no effect of hosting refugees on more regular salaried work. Furthermore, he finds no effects of refugees on self-employment in nonfarm activities among host populations. Through these channels and an increase in agricultural input prices, the refugee inflow reduces food consumption expenditure per capita in rural areas but has no impact on wealth. In addition to finding contradicting results about which subgroups are affected, the papers also differ in their explanations of how these impacts might come about, which hinge on the data they have.

Empirical studies from Jordan generally show limited effects of Syrian refugees on labor market outcomes for the Jordanian host population. Fakih and Ibrahim (2016) find no relationship between refugee inflows and trends in employment, unemployment, or labor force participation in the most affected governorates in Jordan. Similarly, Fallah, Krafft, and Wahba (2019) find that Jordanian hosts in areas with a high share of refugees do not have worse labor market outcomes compared with those in areas less exposed to refugees. They find no difference in unemployment and employment, likely because of increased labor demand. When using panel data, they find a shift in the type of work done by Jordanians who are more exposed to the refugee influx: formality and hourly (but not monthly) wages increase, and some move from the private to the public sector. Confirming another adaptation mechanism, El-Mallakh and Wahba (2018) find an increased probability of Jordanians migrating out of regions with a higher concentration of Syrian refugees. Although Jordanians seem to adapt and are not negatively affected, Malaeb and Wahba (2023) show that labor market outcomes of immigrant workers in Jordan worsened after the arrival of Syrian refugees: they were more likely to work informally and work fewer hours, and had lower wages in areas with high numbers of Syrian refugees, indicating that Syrian refugees in Jordan compete with other immigrant groups rather than with the host population.

Empirical studies of the labor market impacts of Venezuelans displaced in Colombia generally show negative effects on wage levels but vary in the magnitudes found. The studies usually find that less-skilled Colombians in the informal sector are mostly affected by these negative wage effects (Caruso, Gomez Canon, and Mueller 2021; Delgado-Prieto 2022; Lebow 2022, 2024; Lombardo and Peñaloza-Pacheco 2021; Peñaloza-Pacheco 2022). The size of the negative wage effects varies between studies, perhaps in line with differences in the empirical specifications employed, notably if an instrumental variable was used and how the shock variable (that is, the inflow from República Bolivariana de Venezuela) was defined (Lebow 2022). Some studies find negative effects on labor force participation (Bonilla-Mejía et al. 2020; Caruso, Gomez Canon, and Mueller 2021; Lebow 2022; Pedrazzi and Peñaloza-Pacheco 2023), and employment (Bonilla-Mejía et al. 2020; Delgado-Prieto 2022; Peñaloza-Pacheco 2022

Pedrazzi and Peñaloza-Pacheco 2023), overall or only for different subgroups. Results on unemployment (Bonilla-Mejía et al. 2020; Lebow 2022; Peñaloza-Pacheco 2022) and hours worked (Caruso, Gomez Canon, and Mueller 2021; Delgado-Prieto 2022; Lebow 2022; Pedrazzi and Peñaloza-Pacheco 2023) are mixed. Changes in occupation skill groups and out-migration of Colombians (Caruso, Gomez Canon, and Mueller 2021; Lebow 2022) seem small and do not significantly contribute to diminishing negative wage effects, whereas deterrence of internal migration might or might not play a more important role (Bonilla-Mejía et al. 2020; Caruso, Gomez Canon, and Mueller 2021).

The effects on host job outcomes observed from the inflow of Venezuelans in need of international protection resemble those found in studies that assess the impact of internal displacement in Colombia. Two studies with this focus find negative short-run effects on wages for hosting populations (Calderón-Mejía and Ibáñez 2016; Morales 2018). They indicate that the negative effects are greater for low-skilled workers and for women, particularly in the informal sector. Morales (2018) also finds that host populations migrate out of areas with high shares of internally displaced persons.

The introduction of a residence permit for displaced Venezuelans shifted impacts. In a study analyzing the labor market effects of the PEP policy allowing permit holders from República Bolivariana de Venezuela to work and access social services, Bahar, Ibáñez, and Rozo (2021) find "negligible effects" on hosts' formal employment, primarily affecting highly educated and female workers in the short run. This result seems to be due to an increase in the formal employment of Venezuelans after the introduction of the PEP (Ibáñez et al. 2022). Before the introduction of the PEP, the Venezuelan inflow mainly negatively affected low- and medium-skilled women whereas it increased the labor force participation rate of highly skilled women because of better availability of childcare (Pedrazzi and Peñaloza-Pacheco 2023). Consistent with these results, Lombardo et al. (2022) find that the PEP diminished the negative impacts on Colombians in lower-paid jobs because it reduced the magnitude of occupational downgrading among Venezuelans.[6] With regard to overall economic activity, studies find that the inflow increased exports, potentially because of a decline in low-skilled wages and the ability to hire workers with the required skills (Lombardo and Peñaloza-Pacheco 2021). They also find that the inflow increased informality, conceivably because firms substituted formal workers for informal workers in line with lower wages (Delgado-Prieto 2022), and that the PEP raised formal firm formation (Bahar, Cowgill, and Guzman 2022).

In addition to the need to resolve inconsistent results within countries, the evidence on the four case study countries also shows the need to better understand differences in results across countries. Results vary across the case study countries, running from positive impacts (Uganda) to no impacts (Jordan) to negative impacts (Colombia). These differences in results between case study countries are not surprising, given the differences in refugee inflows, host country economies, and labor markets, as well as country policies. Given the lack of consistent methods, it is, however, hard to tease out what drives impacts. In addition, because most of the studies have data only on refugee numbers but not on their characteristics, and lack a larger sample size in the same location as hosts, they cannot explore the interaction between refugees and hosts to explain impacts.

Notes

1 | United Nations High Commissioner for Refugees calculation based on data from mid-2022.

2 | In recent years, refugees in camps have been encouraged to participate in local markets as consumers, with organizations providing vouchers and cash assistance to them. This strategy recognizes the potential role of the displaced as consumers in local markets.

3 | In new business creation, there can also be upstream and downstream benefits for local hosts that are complementary to the refugee businesses.

4 | Impact factors measure to what degree research published in a journal is cited in other research. They thus reflect how influential research is and perhaps, ultimately, the quality of the research in each journal.

5 | Based on Schuettler and Caron (2020), for Canada, European countries, and the United States: Anders, Burgess, and Portes (2021); Aslund, Forslund, and Liljeberg (2017); Bakker, Dagevos, and Engbersen (2017); Baum, Lööf, and Stephan (2018); Baum et al. (2020); Connor (2010); Cortes (2004); Evans and Fitzgerald (2017); Fasani, Frattini, and Minale (2022); Lens, Marx, and Vujic (2019); Ortensi and Ambrosetti (2022); Ruiz and Vargas-Silva (2018a); Sarvimaki (2017); and Spadarotto et al. (2014).

6 | Pointing in the same direction, using a model that allows for imperfect substitutability between Venezuelans and Colombians, Lebow (2024) also estimates that, without occupational downgrading among Venezuelans, negative wage impacts for low-skilled Colombian workers would decrease.

References

Acarturk, C., E. Konuk, M. Cetinkaya, I. Senay, M. Sijbrandij, B. Gulen, and P. Cuijpers. 2016. "The Efficacy of Eye Movement Desensitization and Reprocessing for Post-Traumatic Stress Disorder and Depression among Syrian Refugees: Results of a Randomized Controlled Trial." *Psychological Medicine* 46 (12): 2583–93.

Akgunduz, Yusuf Emre, Altan Aldan, and Yusuf Kenan Bagir. 2021. "Immigration and Inter-Regional Job Mobility: Evidence from Syrian Refugees in Turkey." Working Paper 1461, Economic Research Forum, February. https://ideas.repec.org//p/erg/wpaper/1461.html.

Akgunduz, Yusuf Emre, and Huzeyfe Torun. 2020. "Two and a Half Million Syrian Refugees, Tasks and Capital Intensity." *Journal of Development Economics* 145: 102470.

Alix-Garcia, Jennifer, Sarah Walker, Anne Bartlett, Harun Onder, and Apurva Sanghi. 2018. "Do Refugee Camps Help or Hurt Hosts? The Case of Kakuma, Kenya." *Journal of Development Economics* 130: 66–83.

Altındağ, Onur, Ozan Bakış, and Sandra V. Rozo. 2020. "Blessing or Burden? Impacts of Refugees on Businesses and the Informal Economy." *Journal of Development Economics* 146: 102490.

Anders, Jake, Simon Burgess, and Jonathan Portes. 2021. "The Long-Term Outcomes of Refugees: Tracking the Progress of the East African Asians." *Journal of Refugee Studies* 34 (2): 1967–98.

Angrist, Joshua D., and Alan B. Krueger. 1999. "Empirical Strategies in Labor Economics." In *Handbook of Labor Economics*, Vol. 3, edited by Orley Ashenfelter and David Card, 1277–366. Amsterdam: Elsevier.

Aslund, Olof, Anders Forslund, and Linus Liljeberg. 2017. "Labour Market Entry of Non-Labour Migrants—Swedish Evidence." Working Paper 2017:15, Institute for Evaluation of Labour Market and Education Policy, Uppsala, Sweden.

Aydemir, Abdurrahman B., and Murat G. Kirdar. 2017. "Quasi-experimental Impact Estimates of Immigrant Labor Supply Shocks: The Role of Treatment and Comparison Group Matching and Relative Skill Composition." European Economic Review 98: 282–315.

Bahar, Dany, Bo Cowgill, and Jorge Guzman. 2022. "Legalizing Entrepreneurship." Working Paper 30624, National Bureau of Economic Research, Cambridge, MA.

Bahar, Dany, Ana María Ibáñez, and Sandra V. Rozo. 2021. "Give Me Your Tired and Your Poor: Impact of a Large-Scale Amnesty Program for Undocumented Refugees." *Journal of Development Economics* 151: 102652.

Bakker, Linda, Jaco Dagevos, and Godfried Engbersen. 2017. "Explaining the Refugee Gap: A Longitudinal Study on Labour Market Participation of Refugees in the Netherlands." *Journal of Ethnic and Migration Studies* 43 (11): 1775–91.

Barberis, Virginia, Laura Brouwer, Jan von der Goltz, Timothy Hobden, Mira Saidi, Kirsten Schuettler, and Karin Seyfert. 2022. "Cost-Effectiveness of Jobs Projects in Conflict and Forced Displacement Contexts." Jobs Working Paper 72, World Bank, Washington, DC.

Baum, C. F., H. Lööf, and A. Stephan. 2018. "Refugee Immigrants, Occupational Sorting and Wage Gaps." Working Paper Series in Economics and Institutions of Innovation 473, Royal Institute of Technology, CESIS-Centre of Excellence for Science and Innovation Studies, Stockholm.

Baum, Christopher F., Hans Lööf, Andreas Stephan, and Klaus F. Zimmermann. 2020. "Occupational Sorting and Wage Gaps of Refugees." GLO Discussion Paper 562 [rev.], Global Labor Organization, Essen.

Becker, Sascha O., and Andreas Ferrara. 2019. "Consequences of Forced Migration: A Survey of Recent Findings." *Labour Economics* 59: 1–16.

Belayneh Ayenew, Ashenafi. 2020. *Welfare Impact of Hosting Refugees in Ethiopia.* Policy Research Working Paper 9613, World Bank, Washington, DC.

Blair, Christopher W., Guy Grossman, and Jeremy M. Weinstein. 2022. "Forced Displacement and Asylum Policy in the Developing World." *International Organization* 76 (2): 337–78.

Bogic, Marija, Anthony Njoku, and Stefan Priebe. 2015. "Long-Term Mental Health of War-Refugees: A Systematic Literature Review." *BMC International Health and Human Rights* 15 (1): 1–41.

Bonilla-Mejía, Leonardo, Leonardo Morales, Didier Hermida-Giraldo, and Luz Florez. 2020. "The Labor Market of Immigrants and Non-Immigrants: Evidence from the Venezuelan Refugee Crisis." Borradores de Economia, Banco de la Republica de Colombia. https://econpapers.repec.org/paper/bdrborrec/1119.htm.

Borjas, George J. 1987. "Self-Selection and the Earnings of Immigrants." *American Economic Review* 77(4): 531–53.

Borjas, George J. 2014. *Immigration Economics.* Cambridge, MA: Harvard University Press.

Borjas, George J. 2017. "The Wage Impact of the Marielitos: A Reappraisal." *ILR Review* 70 (5): 1077–110.

Borjas, George J., and Joan Monras. 2017. "The Labour Market Consequences of Refugee Supply Shocks." *Economic Policy* 32 (91): 361–413.

Braun, Sebastian, and Toman Omar Mahmoud. 2014. "The Employment Effects of Immigration: Evidence from the Mass Arrival of German Expellees in Postwar Germany." *Journal of Economic History* 74 (1): 69–108.

Bryant, John, and Pungpond Rukumnuaykit. 2013. "The Labour Market Impacts of Immigration to Developing Countries: Evidence from a Registration Campaign in Thailand." *Journal of Development Studies* 49 (6): 785–800.

Calderón-Mejía, Valentina, and Ana María Ibáñez. 2016. "Labour Market Effects of Migration-Related Supply Shocks: Evidence from Internal Refugees in Colombia." *Journal of Economic Geography* 16 (3): 695–713.

Card, David. 1990. "The Impact of the Mariel Boatlift on the Miami Labor Market." *ILR Review* 43 (2): 245–57.

Card, David, and Giovanni Peri. 2016. "Immigration Economics by George J. Borjas: A Review Essay." *Journal of Economic Literature* 54 (4): 1333–49.

Caruso, German, Christian Gomez Canon, and Valerie Mueller. 2021. "Spillover Effects of the Venezuelan Crisis: Migration Impacts in Colombia." *Oxford Economic Papers* 73 (2): 771–95. doi:10.1093/oep /gpz072.

Cengiz, Doruk, and Hasan Tekguc. 2022. "Is It Merely a Labor Supply Shock? Impacts of Syrian Migrants on Local Economies in Turkey." *ILR Review* 75 (3): 741–68.

Ceritoglu, E., H. Yunculer, H. Torun, and S. Tumen. 2017. "The Impact of Syrian Refugees on Natives' Labor Market Outcomes in Turkey: Evidence from a Quasi-Experimental Design." *IZA Journal of Labor Policy* 6 (1): 1–28.

Clemens, Michael A., and Jennifer Hunt. 2019. "The Labor Market Effects of Refugee Waves: Reconciling Conflicting Results." *ILR Review* 72 (4): 818–57.

Connor, Phillip. 2010. "Explaining the Refugee Gap: Economic Outcomes of Refugees versus Other Immigrants." *Journal of Refugee Studies* 23 (3): 377–97.

Cortes, Kalena E. 2004. "Are Refugees Different from Economic Immigrants? Some Empirical Evidence on the Heterogeneity of Immigrant Groups in the United States." *Review of Economics and Statistics* 86 (2): 465–80.

Del Carpio, Ximena V., and Mathis C. Wagner. 2015. "The Impact of Syrian Refugees on the Turkish Labor Market." Policy Research Working Paper 7402, World Bank, Washington, DC.

Delgado-Prieto, Lukas. 2022. "Immigration, Wages, and Employment under Informal Labor Markets." Center for Open Science, Charlottesville, VA. https://www.dropbox.com/s/udld8y6oh58fq8r /Col_Immigration_LADP_2022.pdf?dl=0&unfurl=1.

Depetris-Chauvin, Emilio, and Rafael J. Santos. 2017. "The Impacts of Internal Displacement Inflows on Host Communities in Colombia." KNOMAD Working Paper 27, World Bank, Washington, DC.

D'Errico, Marco, Rama Dasi Mariani, Rebecca Pietrelli, and Furio Camillo Rosati. 2022. "Refugee-Host Proximity and Market Creation in Uganda." *Journal of Development Studies* 58 (2): 213–33.

Devictor, Xavier, and Quy-Toan Do. 2017. "How Many Years Have Refugees Been in Exile?" *Population and Development Review* 43 (2): 355–69.

Dustmann, Christian, Tommaso Frattini, and Ian P. Preston. 2013. "The Effect of Immigration along the Distribution of Wages." *Review of Economic Studies* 80 (1): 145–73, https://doi.org/10.1093/restud /rds019.

Dustmann, Christian, Uta Schonberg, and Jan Stuhler. 2016. "The Impact of Immigration: Why Do Studies Reach Such Different Results?" *Journal of Economic Perspectives* 30 (4): 31–56.

Eckman, Stephanie, and Kristen Himelein. 2022. "Innovative Sample Designs for Studies of Refugees and Internally Displaced Persons." In *Migration Research in a Digitized World: Using Innovative Technology to Tackle Methodological Challenges*, IMISCOE Research Series, edited by Steffen Potzschke and Sebastian Rinken, 15–34. Cham: Springer International Publishing. doi:10.1007 /978-3-031-01319-5_2.

El-Mallakh, Nelly, and Jackline Wahba. 2021. "Upward or Downward: Occupational Mobility and Return Migration." *World Development* 137 (January): 105203.

Evans, William N., and Daniel Fitzgerald. 2017. "The Economic and Social Outcomes of Refugees in the United States: Evidence from the ACS." Working Paper 23498, National Bureau of Economic Research, Cambridge, MA.

Fakih, Ali, and May Ibrahim. 2016. "The Impact of Syrian Refugees on the Labor Market in Neighboring Countries: Empirical Evidence from Jordan." *Defence and Peace Economics* 27 (1): 64–86. doi:10.1080/10242694.2015.1055936.

Fallah, Belal, Caroline Krafft, and Jackline Wahba. 2019. "The Impact of Refugees on Employment and Wages in Jordan." *Journal of Development Economics* 139: 203–16. doi:10.1016/j.jdeveco .2019.03.009.

Fasani, Francesco, Tommaso Frattini, and Luigi Minale. 2022. "(The Struggle for) Refugee Integration into the Labour Market: Evidence from Europe." *Journal of Economic Geography* 22 (2): 351–93.

Fix, J. R., U. J. Pape, F. K. Appler, T. P. Beltramo, F. N. P. Nimoh, L. A. R. Rivera, F. Schmieding, and N. M. Kariuki. 2019. *Understanding the Socioeconomic Conditions of Refugees in Kenya: Volume A–Kalobeyei Settlement: Results from the 2018 Kalobeyei Socioeconomic Survey*. Washington, DC: World Bank Group.

Foged, Mette, and Giovanni Peri. 2016. "Immigrants' Effect on Native Workers: New Analysis on Longitudinal Data." *American Economic Journal: Applied Economics* 8 (2): 1–34.

Gehrsitz, Markus, and Martin Ungerer. 2022. "Jobs, Crime and Votes: A Short-Run Evaluation of the Refugee Crisis in Germany." *Economica* 89 (355): 592–626.

Ginn, T., R. Resstack, H. Dempster, E. Arnold-Fernandez, S. Miller, M. Guerrero Ble, and B. Kanyamanza. 2022. *Replication Data for: 2022 Global Refugee Work Rights Report.* doi:10.7910/DVN/CKNNVT.

Goldsmith-Pinkham, Paul, Isaac Sorkin, and Henry Swift. 2020. "Bartik Instruments: What, When, Why, and How." *American Economic Review* 110 (8): 2586–624.

Hussam, Reshmaan N., Erin M. Kelley, Gregory V. Lane, and Fatima T. Zahra. 2022. "The Psychosocial Value of Employment: Evidence from a Refugee Camp." *American Economic Review* 112 (11): 3694–724.

Ibáñez, Ana María. 2014. "Growth in Forced Displacement: Cross-Country, Sub-National and Household Evidence on Potential Determinants." In *International Handbook on Migration and Economic Development,* edited by Robert E. B. Lucas. Edward Elgar Publishing, 2014.

Ibáñez, Ana María, Andrés Moya, María Adelaida Ortega, Sandra V. Rozo, and Maria José Urbina. 2022. "Life Out of the Shadows: Impacts of Amnesties in the Lives of Refugees." Working Paper, World Bank, Washington, DC. https://openknowledge.worldbank.org/handle/10986/36967.

Knaevelsrud, Christine, Janine Brand, Alfred Lange, Jeroen Ruwaard, Birgit Wagner. 2015. "Webbased Psychotherapy for Posttraumatic Stress Disorder in War-Traumatized Arab Patients: Randomized Controlled Trial." *Journal of Medical Internet Research* 17 (3): e3582.

Kreibaum, Merle. 2016. "Their Suffering, Our Burden? How Congolese Refugees Affect the Ugandan Population." *World Development* 78: 262–87.

Krishnan, Nandini, Flavio Russo Riva, Dhiraj Sharma, and Tara Vishwanath. 2020. "The Lives and Livelihoods of Syrian Refugees in the Middle East." Policy Research Paper Working Paper 9327, World Bank, Washington, DC.

Lebow, Jeremy. 2022. "The Labor Market Effects of Venezuelan Migration to Colombia: Reconciling Conflicting Results." *IZA Journal of Development and Migration* 13 (1): 1–49.

Lebow, Jeremy. 2024. "Immigration and Occupational Downgrading in Colombia." *Journal of Development Economics* 166: 103164 https://doi.org/10.1016/j.jdeveco.2023.103164.

Lens, Dries, Ive Marx, and Suncica Vujic. 2019. "Double Jeopardy: How Refugees Fare in One European Labor Market." *IZA Journal of Development and Migration* 10 (1).

Lewis, Ethan. 2004. "How Did the Miami Labor Market Absorb the Mariel Immigrants?" Working Paper 04-3, Federal Reserve Bank of Philadelphia, Philadelphia, PA.

Lombardo, Carlo, Julian Martinez-Correa, Leonardo Peñaloza-Pacheco, and Leonardo Gasparini. 2022. "The Distributional Effect of a Migratory Exodus in a Developing Country: The Role of Downgrading and Regularization." Working Paper 4573, Asociación Argentina de Economía Política.

Lombardo, Carlo, and Leonardo Peñaloza-Pacheco. 2021. "Exports 'Brother-Boost': The Trade-Creation and Skill-Upgrading Effect of Venezuelan Forced Migration on Colombian Manufacturing Firms." Working Paper 0283, CEDLAS, Universidad Nacional de La Plata. https://www.econstor.eu /handle/10419/250372.

Loschmann, Craig, Ozge Bilgili, and Melissa Siegel. 2019. "Considering the Benefits of Hosting Refugees: Evidence of Refugee Camps Influencing Local Labour Market Activity and Economic Welfare in Rwanda." *IZA Journal of Development and Migration* 9 (1): 5. doi:10.1186/s40176-018-0138-2.

Malaeb, Bilal, and Jackline Wahba. 2023. "Impact of Syrian Refugees on Male Immigrants' Labor Market Outcomes in Jordan." *International Migration Review* 1–32. doi:10.1177/01979183221149015.

Maystadt, Jean-Francois, and Gilles Duranton. 2019. "The Development Push of Refugees: Evidence from Tanzania." *Journal of Economic Geography* 19 (2): 299–334. doi:10.1093/jeg/lby020.

Maystadt, Jean-Francois, and Philip Verwimp. 2014. "Winners and Losers among a Refugee-Hosting Population." *Economic Development and Cultural Change* 62 (4): 769–809.

Mejia-Mantilla, Carolina, Besufekad Alemu, Johanna Fajardo, and Nobuo Yoshida. 2019. "Informing the Refugee Policy Response in Uganda. Results from the Uganda Refugee and Host Communities 2018 Household Survey." World Bank, Washington, DC.

Morales, Juan S. 2018. "The Impact of Internal Displacement on Destination Communities: Evidence from the Colombian Conflict." *Journal of Development Economics* 131: 132–50.

Murard, Elie, and Seyhun Orcan Sakalli. 2018. "Mass Refugee Inflow and Long-Run Prosperity: Lessons from the Greek Population Resettlement." Discussion Paper 2005, Centre for Research and Analysis of Migration, Department of Economics, University College London.

Neuner, Frank, Patience Lamaro Onyut, Verena Ertl, Michael Odenwald, Elisabeth Schauer, and Thomas Elbert. 2008. "Treatment of Posttraumatic Stress Disorder by Trained Lay Counselors in an African Refugee Settlement: A Randomized Controlled Trial." *Journal of Consulting and Clinical Psychology* 76 (4): 686.

Ortensi, Livia Elisa, and Elena Ambrosetti. 2022. "Even Worse than the Undocumented? Assessing the Refugees' Integration in the Labour Market of Lombardy (Italy) in 2001–2014." *International Migration* 60 (3): 20–37.

Pape, Utz Johann, Benjamin Petrini, and Syedah Aroob Iqbal. 2018. "Informing Durable Solutions by Microdata: A Skills Survey for Refugees in Ethiopia." World Bank, Washington, DC.

Pedrazzi, Julian, and Leonardo Peñaloza-Pacheco. 2023. "Heterogeneous Effects of Forced Migration on the Female Labor Market: The Venezuelan Exodus in Colombia." *Journal of Development Studies* 59 (3): 324–41. doi:10.1080/00220388.2022.2139609.

Peñaloza-Pacheco, Leonardo. 2022. "Living with the Neighbors: The Effect of Venezuelan Forced Migration on the Labor Market in Colombia." *Journal for Labour Market Research* 56 (1): 1–32.

Peri, Giovanni, and Vasil Yasenov. 2019. "The Labor Market Effects of a Refugee Wave: Synthetic Control Method Meets the Mariel Boatlift." *Journal of Human Resources* 54 (2): 267–309.

Porter, Matthew, and Nick Haslam. 2005. "Predisplacement and Postdisplacement Factors Associated with Mental Health of Refugees and Internally Displaced Persons: A Meta-Analysis." *JAMA* 294 (5): 602–12.

Roy, Andrew Donald. 1951. "Some Thoughts on the Distribution of Earnings." *Oxford Economic Papers* 3 (2): 135–46.

Rozo, Sandra V., and Hernan Winkler. 2021. "Is Informality Good for Business? The Impacts of Inflows of Internally Displaced Persons on Formal Firms." *Journal of Human Resources* 56 (4): 1141–86.

Ruiz, Isabel, and Carlos Vargas-Silva. 2015. "The Labor Market Impacts of Forced Migration." *American Economic Review* 105 (5): 581–6.

Ruiz, Isabel, and Carlos Vargas-Silva. 2018a. "Differences in Labour Market Outcomes between Natives, Refugees and Other Migrants in the UK." *Journal of Economic Geography* 18 (4): 855–85.

Ruiz, Isabel, and Carlos Vargas-Silva. 2018b. "The Impact of Hosting Refugees on the Intra-Household Allocation of Tasks: A Gender Perspective." *Review of Development Economics* 22 (4): 1461–88. doi:10.1111/rode.12383.

Sanghi, Apurva, Harun Onder, and Varalakshmi Vemuru. 2016. "Yes" In My Backyard? The Economics of Refugees and Their Social Dynamics in Kakuma, Kenya. Washington, DC: World Bank.

Santamaria, Julieth. 2022. "'When a Stranger Shall Sojourn with Thee': The Impact of the Venezuelan Exodus on Colombian Labor Markets." Working Paper 020046, Alianza EFI. https://ideas.repec.org/p/col/000561/020046.html.

Sarvimaki, Matti. 2017. *Labor Market Integration of Refugees in Finland*. VATT Research Report 185, VATT Institute, Helsinki.

Schon, Justin. 2019. "Motivation and Opportunity for Conflict-Induced Migration: An Analysis of Syrian Migration Timing." *Journal of Peace Research* 56 (1): 12–27.

Schuettler, Kirsten. 2020. *Jobs Interventions for Refugees and Internally Displaced Persons*. Washington, DC: World Bank. https://openknowledge.worldbank.org/handle/10986/34767.

Schuettler, Kirsten, and Laura Caron. 2020. "Jobs Interventions for Refugees and Internally Displaced Persons." Jobs Working Paper 47, World Bank, Washington, DC.

Schuettler, Kirsten, and Quy-Toan Do. 2023. "Outcomes for Internally Displaced Persons and Refugees in Low and Middle-Income Countries." Policy Research Working Paper 10278, World Bank, Washington, DC.

Sjaastad, Larry A. 1962. "The Costs and Returns of Human Migration." *Journal of Political Economy* 70 (5, Part 2): 80–93.

Spadarotto, Claudio, Maria Bieberschulte, Katharina Walker, Michael Morlok, and Andrea Oswald. 2014. "Erwerbsbeteiligung von anerkannten Fluechtlingen und vorlaeufig Aufgenommenen auf dem Schweizer Arbeitsmarkt." KEK-CDC Consultants and B, S, S. on Behalf of the Federal Office of Migration.

Taylor, J. Edward, Mateusz J. Filipski, Mohamad Alloush, and Ernesto Gonzalez-Estrada. 2016. "Economic Impact of Refugees." *Proceedings of the National Academy of Sciences of the United States of America* 113 (27): 7449–53.

Thompson, Steven K. 1990. "Adaptive Cluster Sampling." *Journal of the American Statistical Association* 85 (412): 1050–9. doi:10.2307/2289601.

Tumen, Semih. 2016. "The Economic Impact of Syrian Refugees on Host Countries: Quasi-Experimental Evidence from Turkey." *American Economic Review* 106 (5): 456–60.

Verme, Paolo, and Kirsten Schuettler. 2021. "The Impact of Forced Displacement on Host Communities: A Review of the Empirical Literature in Economics." *Journal of Development Economics* 150: 102606. doi:10.1016/j.jdeveco.2020.102606.

Walelign, Solomon Zena, Soazic Elise Wang Sonne, and Ganesh Seshan. 2022. "Livelihood Impacts of Refugees on Host Communities." Policy Research Working Paper 10044, World Bank, Washington, DC.

World Bank. 2018. *Moving for Prosperity: Global Migration and Labor Markets*. Washington, DC: World Bank.

2. The Context for Labor Market Engagement of Refugees

Introduction

This chapter provides an overview of the demographic, social, economic, and political factors that shape the labor market impact of forced displacement in the four case study countries. The impact of displacement on labor market outcomes for hosts is shaped by the actual participation of refugees in the labor market. In turn, participation hinges on important factors, namely (1) the characteristics of refugees, the size and speed of the refugee inflow, and where and how they reside in the country; (2) the policies and regulations governing residence, right to work, and freedom of movement, as well as the social environment, attitudes, and perceptions of hosts; and (3) the host economy and the structure of the labor market. This chapter provides an overview of what is known about these three key factors in the four countries included in this study.

Many of the issues noted here are then explored in more conclusive detail in chapter 4, relying on primary data collected for this report.

The factors that shape the labor market impact of forced displacement share commonalities but also exhibit great differences between the four case study countries. Across the four countries, refugee inflows vary in how recent they are; whether they are concentrated in urban or rural areas; whether the displaced live in camps, settlements, or alongside hosts in their communities; and the level of education among refugees. The policy environments share a common dynamic in that the rules have become more liberal over time in all four case study countries, but openness to refugee labor market participation ranges widely. At the same time, the host country labor markets are quite typical of middle- or low-income country labor markets, allowing for some peculiarities. In all countries, job growth and quality are insufficient to keep up with new entrants in the labor market.

The chapter is structured as follows: First, it presents the refugee populations and their main characteristics. Second, it discusses the policies, regulations, and overall social environment that mediate refugee participation in the labor market. Third, it provides an overview of the host economies and labor market conditions.

The refugee populations and their characteristics

The refugee inflows vary between the four case study countries with regard to size, duration, origin, and concentration as well as individual characteristics of refugees (table 2.1). The refugee inflows are more recent in Colombia and Jordan and have been protracted in Ethiopia and Uganda. Refugees tend to be geographically concentrated, either in urban areas (Colombia, Jordan) or in rural areas (Ethiopia, Uganda). They make up between 1 percent and 7 percent of the overall host population, but a much higher percentage in localities where many refugees settle, particularly in those countries where many still live in camps or settlements. They have higher dependency ratios (Ethiopia, Jordan, Uganda) and are younger than hosts (in all countries) but have similar gender ratios. With the exception of Colombia, they have a lower level of education than hosts, even if in some cases only slightly. In Colombia and Jordan, they generally speak the same language as their hosts, whereas in Ethiopia and Uganda, this is not always the case.

TABLE 2.1 Summary comparison of refugees population characteristics, case study countries

Characteristics	Ethiopia	Uganda	Colombia	Jordan
Registered refugees and asylum seekers	0.9 million (1 percent of host population)	1.5 million (3 percent of host population)	2.9 million displaced Venezuelans (5 percent of host population)	0.7 million Syrian refugees (7 percent of host population) out of 3 million refugees (30 percent of host population)
Origin	South Sudan (46 percent), Somalia (29 percent), Eritrea (18 percent), Sudan (5 percent)	South Sudan (60 percent), Democratic Republic of Congo (30 percent), Somalia (4 percent), Burundi (3 percent)	República Bolivariana de Venezuela	Syrian Arab Republic (22 percent), Iraq (2 percent), Palestinian refugees (75 percent)
Main inflows	Since late 1980s; increased inflows since 2010	Since 1950; recent spikes in South Sudanese refugees 2016–17, Congolese refugees 2017–19	2016–19, 2021–present	2012–14
Residence time (median)	Addis Ababa: 4 years Jijiga: 31 years	Kampala: 4 years Isingiro: 9 years	4 years	8–9 years
Camps, settlements	About 90 percent of refugees in camps; 10 percent in Addis Ababa (mostly Eritreans)	90 percent of refugees in rural settlements; 7 percent in Kampala	No camps or settlements; about 90 percent of Venezuelans in urban areas	About 26 percent of Syrian refugees in camps; about 71 percent in urban areas
Working-age population	In Addis Ababa, 74 percent of refugees are working age (versus 67 percent of hosts) and 46 percent in Jijiga (same as hosts)	Similar share of working-age refugees and hosts: about 67 percent in Kampala and 49 percent in Isingiro	70 percent of Venezuelans and 66 percent of hosts are working age	52 percent of refugees are working age compared with 61 percent of hosts
Level of education	Slightly lower than hosts	Overall lower than hosts but higher in Kampala	Initially higher than hosts, now similar	Lower than hosts
Language	Depends on refugees group and where they settled	Depends on refugees group and where they settled	Same as hosts (different dialect)	Same as hosts (different dialect)

Source: Original table for this report.

Syrian refugees in Jordan

Jordan has welcomed refugee populations from various conflicts in the region since 1948. As of 2021, the country hosted more than 3 million registered refugees.[1] Of these, 2.3 million are Palestinian refugees registered with the United Nations Relief and Works Agency, most of whom have been in Jordan for a very long time.[2] Most Palestinian refugees who arrived after the 1948 Palestinian-Israeli war have obtained citizenship in Jordan, but this is not the case for those who arrived after the Six-Day War between Israel and its neighboring Arab states in 1967. As of 2019, about 414,000 Palestinian refugees still lived in refugee camps in Jordan.[3] They have not benefited from the legal changes that have been introduced to assist the Syrian refugee population in Jordan; for example, they do not have the same rights as Syrians in accessing the Jordanian labor market (see the section in this chapter "Policies governing the labor market participation of refugees"). Another refugee population living in Jordan is the Iraqis, who arrived from the Gulf War in 1991 and from the US invasion of Iraq in 2003. Although an estimated 500,000 (often quite well-off) Iraqis settled in Jordan after the 2003 invasion (FAFO 2007), relatively few registered with the United Nations High Commissioner for Refugees (UNHCR). There are still 67,000 Iraqi refugees registered with UNHCR in Jordan, of whom 90 percent live in Amman.[4] Neither of these long-settled groups is the focus of the analysis in this report.

Most recently, Jordan has since 2011 hosted significant numbers of refugees displaced from the Syrian Arab Republic. In 2022, about 670,000 Syrian refugees were registered with UNHCR in Jordan (figure 2.1), whereas estimates based on the latest national census from 2015 indicate that about 1.3 million Syrians live in the country. UNHCR numbers suggest that arrivals increased exponentially in the early years after the beginning of the conflict in Syria in 2011 (figure 2.1). However, the inflow has subsequently slowed: since 2014, the number of registered refugees living in Jordan has stabilized at more than 600,000, with only a slow increase, of about 50,000, between 2014 and 2022.

Nearly all Syrian refugees live in the northwestern part of Jordan. Among the approximately 670,000 registered Syrian refugees, about 90 percent live in four governorates since 2012: Mafraq (24 percent in 2016), Irbid (21 percent), Zarqa (17 percent), and Amman (28 percent) (map 2.1). These governorates are relatively close to the Syrian border in the northwest of the country, and they contain the largest cities in Jordan. The remaining roughly 10 percent are located in the eastern and southern governorates of the country, and the number is gradually declining in governorates more toward the south.

The share of Syrian refugees living in camps has declined compared with the early days of the Syrian conflict, and today about 80 percent live outside of camps. In the first couple of years of refugee influx from Syria, most of the refugees were settled in refugee camps. However, since 2014, the share of those

FIGURE 2.1 Syrian refugee population in Jordan, total and by selected governorates, 2012–22

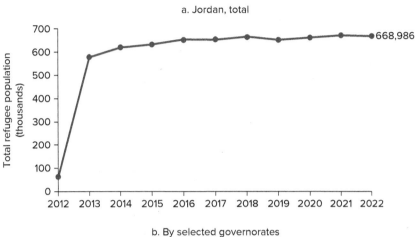

a. Jordan, total

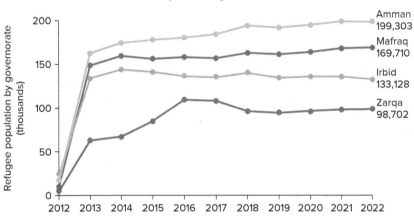

b. By selected governorates

Source: Original figure for this report based on data from United Nations High Commissioner for Refugees (UNHCR) reports on registered Syrians in Jordan at the governorate level, annually 2012–22: UNHCR 2012a, 2014a, 2015b, 2016a, 2017a, 2018a, 2019b, 2020, 2021c, 2022b; UNHCR, "Total Registered Syrian Refugees" (https://data.unhcr.org/en/situations/syria/location/36).
Note: The total number of Syrian refugees was compiled from the data available at the governorate level. An exception is 2013: due to lack of data availability, data at the governorate level were estimated based on the total number of Syrian refugees in 2013 and numbers for 2014 at governorate levels. For 2012, the figure for Amman was adjusted up by 926 refugees to fit the total number of refugees given.

living in refugee camps has been relatively stable at about 20 percent.[5] In 2022, more than 130,000 registered refugees lived in five refugee camps, located in Mafraq, Zarqa, and Irbid. The largest one, Zaatari Camp in Mafraq, hosts more than 80,000 Syrian refugees. Azraq and Emirati Jordanian Camp in Zarqa host about 44,000 and 7,000, respectively, whereas the two smallest camps, in Irbid (Cyber City and King Abdullah Park), host 1,000 Syrian refugees in total.[6]

MAP 2.1   Distribution of Syrian refugees in Jordan, by governorate, December 2016

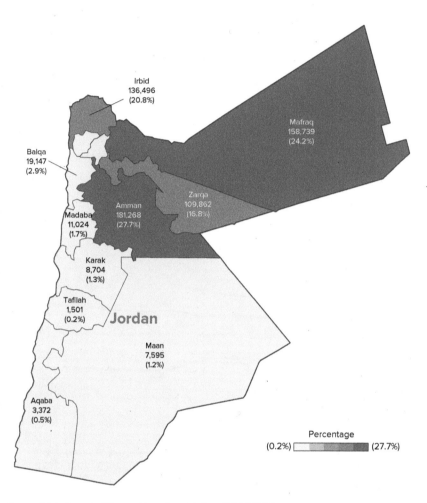

Source: Original map for this report based on data from UNHCR 2016a.

Among the 80 percent of all registered Syrian refugees living outside camps, 37 percent live in Amman, 25 percent in Irbid, 16 percent in Mafraq, and 9 percent in Zarqa.

About half of the Syrian refugee population living in Jordan comes from Daraa Governorate in southern Syria, which shares a border with Jordan. Traditionally, and before the conflict erupted in Syria, there had always been strong social and economic interaction between people in Daraa and people in the northern governorates of Jordan, where most of the refugees live today (Tiltnes, Pedersen, and Zhang 2019). Daraa is known for its agricultural production. Syrian men in Daraa also worked in construction and services before the war (World Bank 2020). Informality was higher in Daraa compared with other parts of Syria (World Bank 2020).

The Syrian refugee population is much younger than the Jordanian host population and, as a result, the dependency ratio is higher.[7] Only 52 percent of refugees were working age in 2018 compared with 61 percent of hosts (Tiltnes, Pedersen, and Zhang 2019). Among the Syrian refugee population, a slightly greater share of those living in camps consists of children and teenagers under age 18, compared with the Syrian refugee population living outside camps. In addition, a slightly greater share of Syrian refugees living outside camps consists of individuals older than age 60 compared with those living inside camps. Similar to the host population, the gender distribution among the Syrian refugee population in Jordan is quite even, among both those in camps and those living elsewhere.[8]

Education and literacy levels of Syrian refugees are much lower than those of Jordanian hosts. More than one in four Syrian refugees older than age 20 had not completed any education level in 2017/2018, compared with about 10 percent of Jordanians; only 5 percent had completed education above secondary level (12 years of schooling), compared with about 30 percent of Jordanians. Furthermore, the literacy rate among Syrian refugees was about 72 percent compared with nearly 100 percent among Jordanians. Among the Syrian refugees older than age 50, only 45 percent were literate (Tiltnes, Pedersen, and Zhang 2019).[9]

Venezuelans displaced in Colombia

An estimated 2.9 million Venezuelans in need of international protection were in Colombia as of the end of 2022, in addition to internally displaced Colombians and Colombian returnees from República Bolivariana de Venezuela.[10] In the 1970s, Colombians had fled to República Bolivariana de Venezuela to avoid violent conflict in their homeland; and, in the 1990s, Colombians accounted for 77 percent of all immigrants in República Bolivariana de Venezuela. In 2015, this flow of migrants reversed, and large numbers of Venezuelans started entering Colombia, together with returning Colombians, because of worsening insecurity and the economic situation and instability in República Bolivariana de Venezuela. Beginning in 2016, these numbers started to rise exponentially, from 54,000 to 404,000 at the end of 2017, 1.2 million in 2018, and 1.8 million in 2019. Numbers rose strongly again after August 2021 to nearly 2.9 million at the end of 2022 (figure 2.2). A third of all Venezuelans in need of international protection were in Colombia. They made up about 5 percent of Colombia's population in 2022. Colombia has very few refugees and asylum seekers from other nations; however, the country has more than 7.7 million internally displaced people who have fled their homes because of the conflict within Colombia between the government and nonstate armed groups. In addition, since the Venezuelan crisis, about 845,000 Colombians have returned from República Bolivariana de Venezuela.[11]

FIGURE 2.2 Venezuelan population in Colombia, total and by selected departments, 2018–22

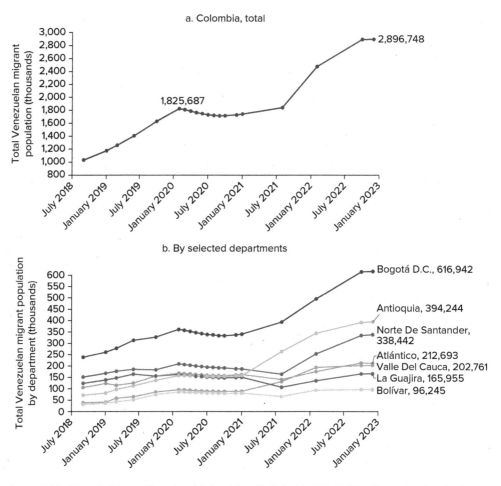

Source: Original figure for this report based on data from Migración Colombia 2018–22 (https://www.migracioncolombia .gov.co/infografias).
Note: The total number of Venezuelans was compiled from the data available at the department level.

The impact of the inflow is geographically concentrated, notably in urban areas given that displaced Venezuelans do not live in camps or settlements. Only three departments and the capital, Bogotá (out of 32 departments in total), hosted more than half of all Venezuelans in 2022 (map 2.2). Since the beginning of the inflow, northern departments at the border with República Bolivariana de Venezuela have seen high numbers, but over time numbers have strongly increased in Bogotá and in the western part of the country as migrants resettled. At the beginning of 2022, 88 percent were found in urban areas, and about half lived in only eight cities, led by Bogotá, which hosted about half a million alone (making up more than 6 percent of its population).[12]

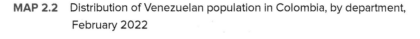

MAP 2.2 Distribution of Venezuelan population in Colombia, by department, February 2022

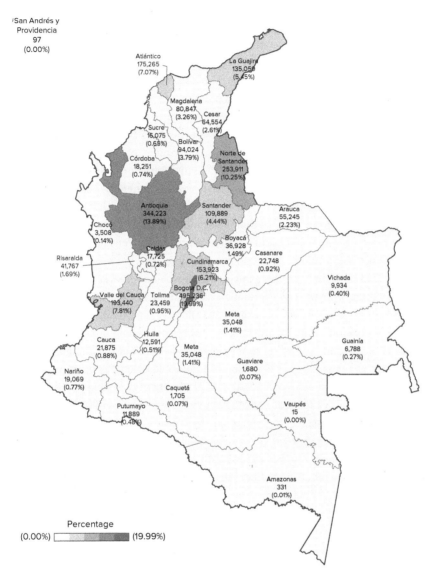

Source: Original map for this report based on data from Migración Colombia (https://www.migracioncolombia .gov.co/infografias-migracion-colombia/infografias-2022).

Displaced Venezuelans are younger and more are of working age compared with the host population. About 70 percent of Venezuelans and 66 percent of hosts are of working age, according to the Gran Encuesta Integrada de Hogares (Large Integrated Household Survey, or GEIH). GEIH data show that Venezuelans are, on average, 30 years old, compared with 36 years for hosts. This average difference between the working-age population of natives and Venezuelans has been consistent both before and after the massive inflow.

According to GEIH data, the gender composition of Venezuelans in Colombia is balanced and men and women have a similar age structure. For families who did not travel together, the man migrated first in three out of four cases, according to the first round of the 2021 Colombia Departamento Administrativo Nacional de Estadística (National Administrative Department of Statistics, or DANE) Encuesta Pulso de la Migración (Migration Pulse Survey, or PM). Men are more likely to move to Colombia for work than women, whereas women are more likely to migrate for family reunification (DANE and Ladysmith 2021). According to labor market surveys, just like their male counterparts, Venezuelan women are younger, on average, than Colombians (23 years old for Venezuelan women and 35 for Colombian women). About 40 percent of Venezuelan women are not married but live with their partner; this percentage is not greater than 25 percent for Colombian women. The economic crisis and migration seem to reduce the number of children Venezuelan women in Colombia have (Holloway et al. 2022).

The education level of working-age Venezuelan migrants is similar to that of Colombians. According to data from the PM, Venezuelans in the labor force were about as likely as Colombians to have no or only primary education (26 percent of Venezuelans compared with 21 percent of Colombians). GEIH data show that, whereas a third of Venezuelans in Colombia before 2017 had tertiary education, most Venezuelans arriving during 2018 and 2019 had only secondary education. As a result, in 2016 Venezuelan migrants were more likely to have tertiary education than hosts, but were slightly less likely in 2019. At the same time, Venezuelans were much more likely than hosts to have secondary education in 2019—67 percent of Venezuelans compared with 50 percent of hosts.

Refugees in Uganda

Since World War II, Uganda has hosted many different groups of refugees, while also expelling some populations and facing significant internal displacement. The country's history of hosting refugees goes back to the early 1940s, when the British temporarily settled Polish refugees in the country (Watera et al. 2017). Uganda's role in hosting refugees from neighboring African countries began in 1955 with the influx of nearly 80,000 refugees from the civil war in Sudan. In 1959, Congolese and Rwandese refugees were settled in the western part of Uganda. Since then, the country has hosted large numbers of refugees from conflicts and natural disasters in many African countries, including

Burundi, Democratic Republic of Congo, Eritrea, Ethiopia, Kenya, Mozambique, Senegal, Sierra Leone, Somalia, South Africa, Sudan, and Zimbabwe (Easton-Calabria 2021; Watera et al. 2017). During that time, however, Idi Amin expelled Ugandans of Indian descent in 1972 and Kenyans in 1969–70. In addition to refugees, up to 1.8 million people were internally displaced within Uganda during 1997 to 2005 because of the conflict between the Ugandan government and the Lord's Resistance Army (IDMC 2012). Most of them have returned or resettled elsewhere since the signing of a cease-fire agreement in 2006.[13]

In 2022, Uganda was the largest host country in Sub-Saharan Africa, with nearly 1.5 million refugees and asylum seekers from countries in the region.[14] From the 1960s until 2013, the total annual refugee population in Uganda was relatively stable at 100,000–300,000. By end of 2017, this number had increased significantly, mainly resulting from a massive increase of South Sudanese refugees between 2016 and 2017 (figure 2.3). In addition, the number of refugees from the Democratic Republic of Congo doubled from about 200,000 to 400,000 between 2017 and 2019. At the end of 2022, the total number of refugees and asylum seekers in Uganda stood at nearly 1.5 million. Refugees were mainly from South Sudan (60 percent), the Democratic Republic of Congo (30 percent), Somalia (4 percent), and Burundi (3 percent) in 2022.

Other than those living in Kampala, refugees in Uganda are hosted in districts in the north and southwestern regions of the country, where they live in settlements. Such settlements, as defined by UNHCR, are usually established in an "uninhabited or sparsely-populated area, with a view to creating new self-supporting rural communities that ultimately will form part of the economic and social system of the area" (Idris 2017, 3). The three districts hosting most of the refugees in the northern part of the country in 2022 were Adjumani (208,000), Arua (198,000), and Yumbe (190,000) (map 2.3). In the southwestern part, the districts of Isingiro (175,000), Kyegegwa (119,000), and Kamwenge (90,000) hosted the largest refugee populations. Because the refugee settlements in general are located in sparsely populated areas of the country where plots of agricultural land are available, the refugees make up a significant part of the total population in most of these areas. In four districts, refugees made up the majority of the population in 2023 (Obongi, Adjumani, and Madi Okollo in the West Nile subregion and Lamwo in the Northern region). They made up about 30 percent of the total population in Isingiro and 7 percent in Kampala.[15]

Refugees settle in line with geographic proximity, and kinship, ethnic, and language ties. The vast majority of South Sudanese refugees live in settlements in the northwestern part of Uganda, whereas the vast majority of refugees from the Democratic Republic of Congo live in settlements in the southwestern part. Rwandese refugees live mainly in the southernmost settlements of Uganda, whereas about two-thirds of the Somali refugees in Uganda live in the urban capital of Kampala (Mejia-Mantilla et al. 2019). Of the approximately 120,000 refugees living in Kampala in 2022, about one-third of them come from Somalia

FIGURE 2.3   Refugee population in Uganda, total and by selected districts, 2009–22

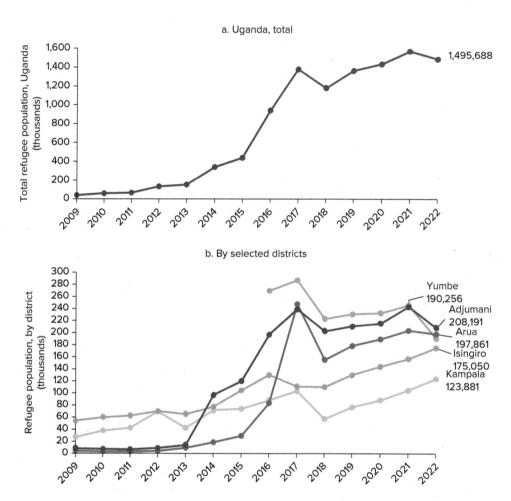

Source: Original figure for this report based on data from Office of the Prime Minister of Uganda and the United Nations High Commissioner for Refugees (with settlement data further described in Maystadt et al. 2020). *Note:* A biometric refugee verification exercise conducted in 2018 corrected numbers downwards (Office of the Prime Minister, UNHCR, and WFP 2018).

and one-third from the Democratic Republic of Congo. About 20 percent come from Rwanda, while the remaining proportion consists of refugees from Burundi and South Sudan.[16] The Nakivale refugee settlement, located in Isingiro, is the oldest refugee settlement in Uganda, having been established in 1959, and it has received different waves of refugees over time. In 2022, about 60 percent of the refugees in Isingiro were from the Democratic Republic of Congo, 20 percent from Burundi, and the rest from Rwanda and Somalia.

MAP 2.3 Distribution of refugees in Uganda, by districts, 2022

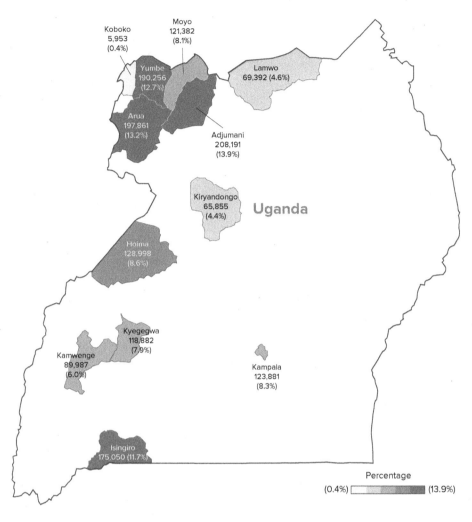

Source: Original map for this report based on data from the Office of the Prime Minister of Uganda and the United Nations High Commissioner for Refugees.

In a refugee settlement such as Nakivale, like their surrounding hosts in rural Uganda, a lower share of refugees is part of the working population compared with Kampala. According to the Harmonized Host-Refugee Labor Market survey (HHR-LMS) collected for this report in Uganda, about 48 percent of refugees in Isingiro are working age, whereas about 67 percent are of working age in Kampala. The same holds for hosts. The median age of the head of refugee households is 36 in Kampala (38 for hosts) compared with 42 in Isingiro (45 for hosts).

The number of female-headed households is higher among refugees, and their households are slightly larger. The number of female-headed households among refugees in Kampala and Isingiro is 10 percentage points higher than among hosts (HHR-LMS Uganda). Nationwide, the gap is even higher as a result of the even higher incidence of female-headed households among refugees in the West Nile region (Mejia-Mantilla et al. 2019). Whereas the median household size among the refugees living in Kampala is five people, the corresponding figure for the refugee population living in Nakivale in the Isingiro area is seven people. The average household size for Ugandan nationals is slightly lower compared with refugee households, with six people for those living in Isingiro and four in urban Kampala (HHR-LMS Uganda).

Refugees in Kampala have higher education levels than hosts, although not in the West Nile and southwest regions. In Uganda, 41 percent of host and 35 percent of refugee household heads completed some primary school (Mejia-Mantilla et al. 2019). In Kampala, refugee heads of households are more educated than hosts, but in the West Nile and southwest regions, a higher percentage have never attended any formal schooling compared with hosts (Mejia-Mantilla et al. 2019). As a result, refugees have a similar level of literacy as hosts in Kampala but a lower level than hosts in Isingiro. In Kampala, two-thirds of refugee heads of household completed secondary school, compared with 40 percent for hosts. In the West Nile and southwest regions, this is the case for only 4 percent of refugee heads and 11 percent and 7 percent of hosts, respectively (Mejia-Mantilla et al. 2019).

Refugees in Ethiopia

Ethiopia has a complex history of migration and refugee flows, from being the origin of millions of refugees and internally displaced persons to being a transit country and hosting large refugee populations. At the peak of the civil war and drought in 1980, 2.5 million Ethiopians were refugees (Adugna 2021). In 2020, an estimated 280,000 Ethiopians were still refugees or asylum seekers.[17] Since November 2020, the numbers increased again because of the conflict in the northern Tigray region between the federal government and Tigray People's Liberation Front leaders. More than 50,000 new refugees fled the country in the first two months after the start of the conflict,[18] and about 4 million Ethiopians were internally displaced by the end of 2022.[19] Some of the largest numbers of internally displaced persons live in the Somali region, in refugee camps in Fafan (Jijiga) and Liban, as well as in and around Tigray.[20] In addition to being a country of origin, Ethiopia has become a transit country, notably for migrants and refugees from Eritrea and Somalia. Mostly moving irregularly, these migrants aim to eventually reach the Gulf Cooperation Council Countries, South Africa, or Europe (Adugna 2021).

In 2022, Ethiopia was the third-largest refugee hosting country in Africa, with more than 880,000 registered refugees and asylum seekers, predominantly from Eritrea, Somalia, and South Sudan.[21] The number of refugees in

Ethiopia grew strongly in the late 1980s and then again after 2010 (Adugna, Rudolf, and Getachew 2022; figure 2.4). The last large inflow of refugees came with the start of the conflict in South Sudan in 2013, with South Sudanese refugees making up nearly half of all refugees in Ethiopia in 2022. Because of this large inflow, the number of camps more than doubled. Most refugees live in the 24 refugee camps established across five regional states and jointly run by UNHCR and Ethiopia's Refugees and Returnees Service (formerly the Agency for Refugee and Returnee Affairs, or ARRA). More than 70,000 others resided outside of camps in the capital, Addis Ababa, in 2022 (map 2.4). The number of

FIGURE 2.4   Refugee population in Ethiopia, total and by selected regions, 2012–22

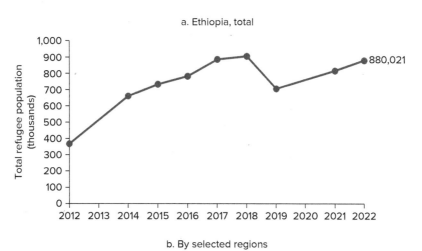

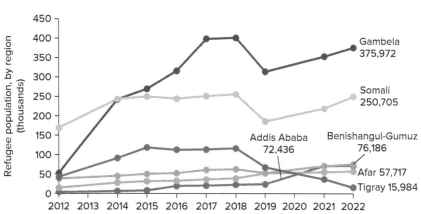

Source: Original figure for this report based on data from the United Nations High Commissioner for Refugees (UNHCR): UNHCR 2012b, 2014b, 2015a, 2016b, 2017b, 2018b, 2019c, 2021b, 2022c.
Note: The total number of refugees was compiled from the data available for each region.

refugees in the capital doubled in 2021, when two refugee camps in the northern Tigray region were closed because of the conflict and the mostly Eritrean refugees moved to Addis Ababa.[22] Of the 880,000 refugees in Ethiopia in 2022, 46 percent came from South Sudan, 29 percent from Somalia, 18 percent from Eritrea, and 5 percent from Sudan.[23]

The location of refugees differs by country of origin given that they mostly reside close to the border with their origin country. Gambela in the west (43 percent) and Somali in the east (29 percent) hosted the largest numbers of refugees in 2022, followed by Benishangul-Gumuz (9 percent) and Addis Ababa (8 percent) (map 2.4). South Sudanese refugees are mostly located in camps around the city of Gambela in the west, with some also living in the Benishangul-Gumuz region and the Southern Nations, Nationalities, and Peoples' Region.[24] Most Sudanese refugees settled in the Benishangul-Gumuz region in western Ethiopia. Somali refugees primarily live in the Somali region, in three camps (Aw-barre, Kebribeyah, and Sheder) in the Fafan (Jijiga) zone in the northern

MAP 2.4 Distribution of refugees in Ethiopia, by region, 2022

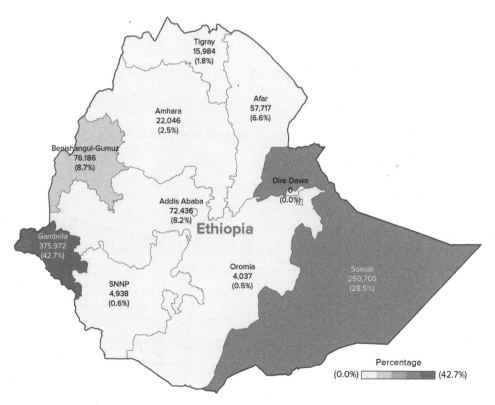

Source: Original map for this report based on data from the United Nations High Commissioner for Refugees.
Note: SNNP = Southern Nations, Nationalities, and Peoples.

part of the region, and five camps (Bokolmanyo, Buramino, Hilaweyn, Kobe, and Melkadida) in the Liben zone in the southeast of the region. Somali refugees arrived in Jijiga in several waves with the eruption of a civil war in 1991. As of November 2022, the registered refugee population in Jijiga stood at 45,000 persons, fairly evenly distributed across the three camps.[25] Eritrean refugees are mostly hosted in the northern part of the Tigray and Afar regions and account for the vast majority of the out-of-camp refugees and the majority of the registered refugees in Addis Ababa. Small refugee groups of other nationalities live throughout the country.

The working-age population of refugees is lower in Jijiga than in the capital. Only 61 percent of refugees in Jijiga are of working-age compared with 81 percent of hosts according to the primary data collected for this report (HHR-LMS Ethiopia). The opposite is true in Addis Ababa, where 74 percent of refugees are working age compared with 67 percent of hosts. The lower percentage of working-age refugees in Jijiga means that those who can work are likely to have to support a larger number of nonworking family members compared with refugees in Addis Ababa, making it more difficult to achieve self-reliance. Across all regions, women and girls account for about half of both the refugee and host populations. About 60 percent of the refugees are children.[26]

Refugees have lower levels of education than hosts in nearly all regions. At the national level, about 40 percent of both the refugee and the host community working-age population have no education. Education levels are higher in the capital than in the rest of the country. Ethiopian hosts, however, have a higher number of average years of education in nearly all regions hosting refugees, including the Somali region (World Bank 2018b). Hosts are also more likely than refugees to have attained secondary education (19 percent versus 13 percent) as well as university education (6 percent versus 2 percent) (World Bank 2018b). The educational attainment of refugees differs by nationality. Eritreans are the most likely to have some education, followed by South Sudanese and Sudanese. About 60 percent of Somali refugees do not have any education (World Bank 2018b). As a result, refugees in Addis Ababa, who are mostly Eritreans, are more likely than hosts to have more than primary education and to be literate, whereas the opposite is true in Jijiga, according to primary data gathered for this report (HHR-LMS Ethiopia).

Policies governing the labor market participation of refugees

The policy environment has become more liberal over time in all four case study countries, but openness to refugee labor market participation varies (table 2.2). Whereas Uganda implemented a policy promoting the self-reliance of refugees

TABLE 2.2 Summary comparison of key policies toward the labor market participation of refugees, case study countries

Policy	Ethiopia	Uganda	Colombia	Jordan
Recognized as refugees	Yes	Yes	No	Registered by UNHCR
1951 Geneva Refugees Convention signed	Yes (with reservations)	Yes (with reservations)	Yes	No
Right to work	Only very few	Yes	With residency permit (PEP or PPT) accessible for most Venezuelans	With work permit (between 36,000 and 62,000 issued per year 2016–2021)
Right to move freely	De jure only, very few out of camp before 2019; planned to expand to 10 percent of refugees population	Yes, but services limited to settlements	Yes	Yes, but those in camps need to request movement passes
Access to social services	In camps	In settlements	With residency permit (PEP or PPT)	Inside and outside of camps

Source: Original table for this report.
Note: PEP = Special Permanence Permit; PPT = Temporary Protection Permit; UNHCR = United Nations High Commissioner for Refugees.

two decades ago, the other three countries only recently implemented policy changes to facilitate refugees' labor market access. Colombia has gone furthest with a residency permit valid for 10 years that provides refugees with the same access to the labor market and social services as Colombians. Jordan has opened parts of its labor market and made work permits more accessible. Since 2016, Ethiopia has opened its labor market to some refugees and allowed more refugees to move out of camps.

The Jordan Compact

Although it does not legally recognize refugees, Jordan allows UNHCR to determine refugee status and protect refugees. Despite hosting large numbers of refugees, Jordan is not party to the 1951 Geneva Convention on the Status of Refugees or the 1967 Protocol on the Status of Refugees, and Jordanian law makes limited reference to asylum seekers and refugees. Jordan also refers to Syrian refugees as "visitors," "guests," or "Arab brothers," none of which have any legal meaning under domestic laws, leading Syrian refugees to fall under the overall foreigners' law (ILO 2015a; Zetter and Ruaudel 2016). However, Jordan has had a memorandum of understanding (MoU) with UNHCR since 1998 (renewed in 2003 and 2014) and has been a member of the UNHCR Executive Committee since 2006. The MoU gives UNHCR the right to determine the refugee status of asylum seekers in Jordan, and an obligation to provide for their protection. The MoU is based on the 1951 Geneva Convention on the Status of Refugees and the 1967 Protocol on the Status of Refugees and ensures that refugees have many of the same rights with regard to protection in Jordan as those defined in the convention (Francis 2015; ILO 2015a).

Unlike Iraqis who entered Jordan after 1998, Syrians entering the country since 2011 as asylum seekers or who are UNHCR-registered refugees are not given residency rights, which has made it difficult for them to become legally employed in Jordan. Without a residency permit, Syrian refugees outside of camps were treated like migrant workers (ILO 2015a; Zetter and Ruaudel 2016). According to Jordanian labor law, migrant workers can obtain jobs in occupations open to non-Jordanians only if they have competencies that are not available in Jordan or if the demand for labor is higher than the existing supply for the occupation. Sectors open for non-Jordanian workers include manufacturing, construction, agriculture, care work, and the food industry; most professions such as engineering, teaching, or the medical professions, as well as sectors such as sales, hairdressing, driving, and others, are closed (ILO 2015b). Even in the sectors that are open to migrant workers, a quota system defines the maximum percentage of foreign workers who can work in each of these sectors. These quotas range from 5 percent to 70 percent, depending on the sector (ILO 2015b). As a result, only between less than 3,000 and less than 6,000 Syrian refugees were issued work permits until the end of 2015, resulting in a high degree of informal employment among Syrians in Jordan (ILO 2015a, 2015b, 2017).

In February 2016, labor market access for Syrian refugees in Jordan changed significantly when the international community and Jordan signed the so-called Jordan Compact. The idea behind the compact is that the international community, including the European Union (EU), the United States, and the World Bank, provides Jordan with major grants and concessional loans as well as an exemption from EU trade barriers to stimulate investment and jobs in Jordan. In exchange, Jordan provides access to education and legal work opportunities to Syrian refugees by providing 200,000 work permits (Barbelet, Hagen-Zanker, and Mansour-Ille 2018; Stave, Kebede, and Kattaa 2021). The Jordanian government limited the issuance of work permits to sectors of the economy open to migrant workers. Refugees from countries other than Syria cannot apply for permits (Stave, Kebede, and Kattaa 2021).

Important barriers to accessing work permits, on both the demand side and the offer side, resulted in relatively low uptake. The initial low uptake was explained by information frictions because neither employers nor refugees knew about the work permits and how to proceed; entry costs requiring both sides to pay some fee; administrative burdens tied to the demands of the work permits; the fear and reluctance of refugees to be formally linked to an employer, to leave more flexible informal employment, and to lose social assistance; the fact that many refugees had a portfolio of several jobs that could not easily be formalized; and a mismatch between the aspirations and needs of Syrian refugees and the opportunities in sectors open to them, notably in the manufacturing sector (Amjad et al. 2017; Barbelet, Hagen-Zanker, and Mansour-Ille 2018). In addition, those living in camps were required to request movement passes to leave the camps (Ginn et al. 2022).

The slow uptake of work permits by Syrians at the beginning of the compact led the government of Jordan to make several adjustments to the initial regulations. Two months after the signature of the compact, the government waived the application fees for work permits. To address the concern that work permits tied refugees to one employer, and to speed up permit issuance in line with the commitments made, permits began to be issued through cooperatives in the agricultural sector in October 2016, and then in the construction sector in June 2017. Refugees valued the flexibility and ease of obtaining work permits in agriculture, and requested them for work in other sectors (Ait Ali Slimane and Al Abbadi 2023). As a next step, beginning in the fall of 2018, Syrian refugees were able to apply for flexible work permits in any open sector without being sponsored by an employer, and they could move freely between employers within the sector for which the permit is issued. Beginning in mid-2017, Syrian refugees in camps were allowed to apply for work permits and to work outside of camps. At the end of 2018, Syrians were allowed to open and operate home-based businesses, which was particularly important for women (Stave, Kebede, and Kattaa 2021). As a result of these adjustments to the policies regulating Syrian refugees' access to work in Jordan, 62,000 work permits were issued in 2021, including 31,000 flexible ones (figure 2.5).

FIGURE 2.5 Number of work permits issued to Syrian refugees in Jordan per year, 2016–21

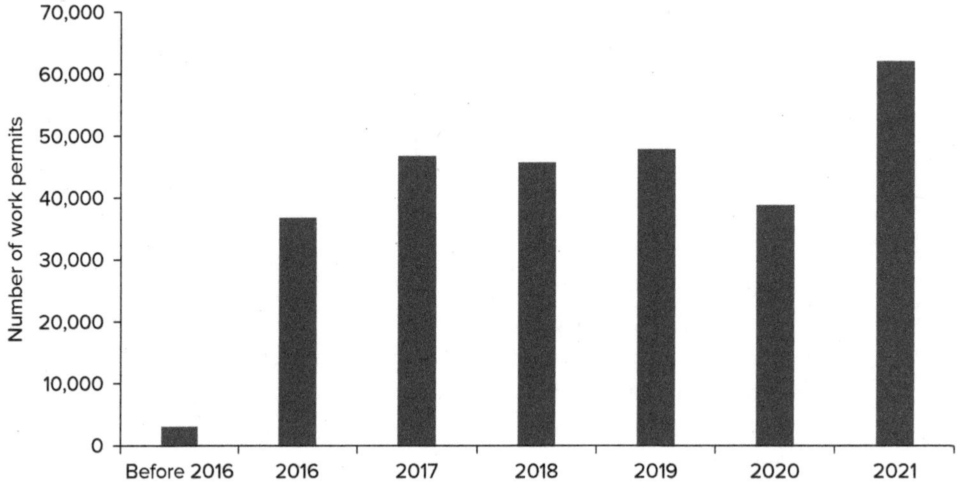

Source: Stave, Kebede, and Kattaa 2021; UNHCR 2022b.

The Special and Temporary Residence Permits in Colombia

Venezuelans are not recognized as refugees in Colombia, even though UNHCR considers them to be persons in need of international protection. Colombia ratified the 1951 Geneva Convention on the Status of Refugees and the 1967 Protocol on the Status of Refugees as well as the regional Cartagena Declaration on Refugees. A national decree governs the application procedure for recognition of refugee status, for which the Ministry of Foreign Affairs of Colombia is in charge. The Cartagena Declaration extends the definition of refugee to include persons "who have fled their country because their lives, safety or freedom have been threatened by generalized violence, foreign aggressions, internal conflicts, massive violation of human rights or other circumstances have seriously disturbed public order." Nevertheless, Venezuelans in Colombia are officially considered to be immigrants, not refugees.

In response to the massive inflow of Venezuelans after 2016, the Colombian government created a residence permit called Permiso Especial de Permanencia (Special Permanence Permit, or PEP) in July 2017. The PEP residence permit was renewable every two years and allowed Venezuelans to remain temporarily in Colombia, move and settle freely in the country, join the formal labor force, and access public services, such as education, health, and childcare. Applicants had to meet the following conditions: Venezuelan nationality, passport stamped when entering Colombia (dropped in August 2018), in Colombia when the PEP decree was issued, no judicial record, and no expulsion or deportation order. PEP residence permits were granted in nine rounds between July 2017 and the end of 2021 and benefited 737,488 Venezuelans (figure 2.6).

In 2018, the government allowed Venezuelans with irregular legal status to apply for the PEP if they had been in the country when the PEP decree was issued. Many Venezuelans ended up being undocumented, given that they entered the country through unofficial crossing points because they lacked a valid passport or had overstayed the 180 days Venezuelans are allowed to visit Colombia on a tourist visa. As a first step, to estimate the number of Venezuelans in the country, the government established the Registro Administrativo de Migrantes Venezolanos (Administrative Registry of Venezuelan Immigrants, or RUMV) in April 2018. The Colombian government allowed irregular migrants who had previously registered with the RUMV to apply in July 2018 and at the same time increased the coverage of registration stations; consequently, 2018 had the highest number of permits granted (figure 2.6).

In January 2021, the Colombian government announced a new residence permit called Permiso por Protección Temporal (Temporary Protection Permit, or PPT). The PPT was created as a reaction to the continued unresolved economic situation in República Bolivariana de Venezuela and the often irregular entry of more Venezuelans. It grants the same rights as the PEP, but with a longer period—10 years—until expiration, meaning longer-term

FIGURE 2.6 Total number of PEPs granted in Colombia per year, 2017–21

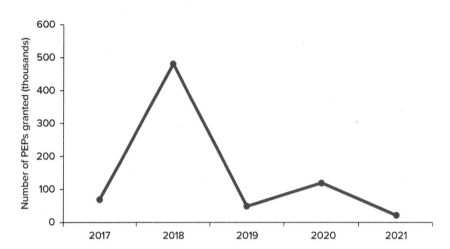

Source: Original figure for this report based on data from Migración Colombia (https://public.tableau.com /app/profile/migraci.n.colombia/viz/PermisoEspecialdePermanencia-PEP/Inicio).
Note: Data through end of 2021. PEP = Permiso Especial de Permanencia (Special Permanence Permit).

security for those with the previous residency permit. Those who arrived after the PEP decree was issued and were thus unable to access the PEP could now apply. Only those who arrived in Colombia after January 2021 and did not have their passport stamped when entering are not allowed to apply. The registration phase of this new temporary residence permit was launched in May 2021. By October 2022, about 1.5 million PPT had been delivered to displaced Venezuelans.[27]

With the PPT, nearly all Venezuelans gained legal access to the labor market and to social services identical to those afforded to Colombians, whereas fewer than half had had access in 2019–20. Thanks to the opening of the PEP to irregular migrants who had been in Colombia before July 2017, only about 5 percent of Venezuelans were irregular as of mid-2018. This number started to rise again, reaching 57 percent at the end of 2019 and continuing at a similar level through January 2021.[28] With the introduction of the PPT, only 10 percent of Venezuelans were still irregular as of December 2022 (figure 2.7).

These policy changes are remarkable in a context of deteriorating acceptance of the inflow. The Gallup Migration Acceptance Index in Colombia declined steeply between 2016 and 2019.[29] Together with Ecuador and Peru, which also received large numbers of displaced Venezuelans, Colombia was in the top three countries that saw the largest decline in the index over this period (Esipova, Ray, and Pugliese 2020).

FIGURE 2.7   Changes in the number of Venezuelans with irregular status after the introduction of the PPT in Colombia, 2021

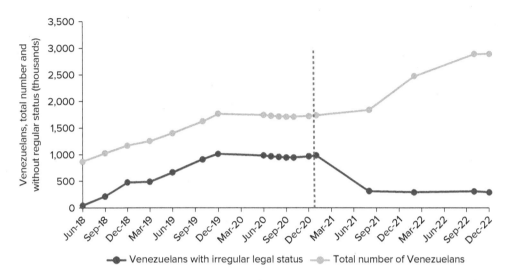

Source: Original figure for this report based on data from Migración Colombia 2018–22 (https://www.migracioncolombia .gov.co/infografias).
Note: Data through February 2022. PPT = Permiso por Protección Temporal (Temporary Protection Permit). The grey dashed line marks the date of the announcement of the PPT in January 2021.

The Self-Reliance Strategy in Uganda

Early refugee policies in Uganda were highly restrictive, even if they were not always fully enforced. In 1960, following the Control of Refugees from the Sudan Ordinance of 1955, Uganda introduced the Control of Alien Refugees Act (CARA), which was the first legal regulation addressing the influx of refugees after the country's independence in 1962. CARA was a restrictive policy prioritizing political control of refugees rather than protection and rights (Vemuru et al. 2016). When Rwandan refugees entered Uganda in the early 1960s, they were primarily confined to designated camps in the southwestern part of the country, and Sudanese refugees escaping from violence in southern Sudan were confined to camps in the northern part of the country (IRRI 2018). In 1976, Uganda ratified the 1951 Geneva Convention on the Status of Refugees and the 1967 Protocol on the Status of Refugees, although with several reservations; and, in 1987, the country ratified the 1969 Organization of African Unity Refugee Convention. The restrictive regulations of CARA, such as the restrictions on refugees' freedom of movement, contradicted Uganda's obligations under these conventions (IRRI 2018; Vemuru et al. 2016). However, restrictions under CARA were not fully enforced, and usually implemented only in periods of mass inflows (Sharpe and Namusobya 2012; Vemuru et al. 2016).

The policy that Uganda has become internationally acclaimed for, the Self-Reliance Strategy for refugees, was introduced in 1999 and later complemented by support for host communities. The Self-Reliance Strategy was implemented as part of a global humanitarian-development nexus initiative by UNHCR. It aimed to make refugees independent of humanitarian aid by allocating land to them and providing them free access to health and education services by integrating refugees and hosts into the same national public systems (IRRI 2018). In 2003, Uganda's Self-Reliance Strategy was adjusted through the Development Assistance to Refugee-Hosting Areas policy to ensure more benefits such as public services and other development interventions for the local host populations, who mainly provided support to refugees but were seeing little benefit in return (Hovil 2001; Zetter and Ruaudel 2016). Uganda continued to promote the economic inclusion of refugees while supporting their surrounding host communities (IRRI 2018). In 2016, Uganda became a pilot country of the UNHCR Comprehensive Refugee Response Framework, which promotes the inclusion of refugees in host communities and provides reliable support for hosts. Uganda also introduced the Refugee and Host Population Empowerment Strategy, which aims to harmonize the refugee response in Uganda by integrating refugee programming into the national development plan to the benefit of refugees and hosts. The government of Uganda has agreed with the international community that 30 percent of all nonfood international refugee assistance will directly target host communities (UN Country Team and World Bank 2017).

With the new Self-Reliance Strategy, the former camps were meant to become self-reliant settlements and refugees were given access to land and, later, the right to work and freedom of movement. The refugee camps in Uganda were renamed "settlements" to indicate the policy shift and the transformation of refugees from receivers of humanitarian aid into self-reliant communities. Refugees in the settlements were provided with plots of land for residential and agricultural purposes, in addition to food and cash assistance, which was to be gradually reduced into full self-reliance in five years (IRRI 2018). Refugees living outside of the settlements, however, were not eligible for assistance. Replacing the 1960 Control of Alien Refugees Act, the National Refugees Act in 2006 and the National Refugee Regulations in 2010 enshrined the policy changes into law. They granted all refugees in Uganda access to land (but not ownership) in the settlements, the right to own and sell movable property and to lease immovable property, the same right to work and start a business as the most favored foreigners living in the country, freedom of movement, and access to essential public services in the settlements.[30] The plots of land were provided by the local host populations, which, in turn, benefited from the development of schools and health centers in the communities, serving both the refugees and the host populations.

Despite the rights provided to refugees by Uganda's Self-Reliance Strategy, most refugees are still tied to living in settlements in practice, mainly because humanitarian assistance and social services are still primarily being provided in the settlements, with insignificant support given to urban refugees. In addition, job opportunities for refugees in urban centers are limited. Refugees living in cities also risk being legally classified as economic migrants rather than refugees, and they lack official refugee status unless they have been registered in the settlements (IRRI 2018). Refugees also face administrative barriers in obtaining the necessary work permit stamp, which requires possessing Convention travel documents (UNHCR 2021d). Refugees residing in settlements also need to obtain permits to leave and return to the settlements (Vemuru et al. 2016).

Refugees in settlements in Uganda are offered plots of land for shelter and for cultivation, to allow them to grow food for subsistence and for market sale. Over time, the size of the plots has been reduced because of the declining availability of land as refugee numbers have increased. In Nakivale, the plots for cultivation are now supposed to be 50 meters by 50 meters, but have ended up being only 30 meters by 30 meters, or even smaller (Betts et al. 2019; Development Pathways 2020; UNHCR and UN-Habitat 2020). At the same time, the quality, fertility, and proximity to market of available land has worsened. Because refugees do not have secure land ownership and lack formal paperwork to enforce agreements regarding land, they may prioritize the next harvest over investing in maintaining or increasing the land's quality (Betts et al. 2016; Schuettler and Caron 2020). Newcomers are less likely to get access to any plot of arable land. About 80 percent of the Congolese households that arrived before 2012 have access to land compared with just 17 percent of those that arrived after 2012 (Betts et al. 2019).

In many settlement areas across Uganda, the self-reliance policy has led to tensions between local host populations and refugees. Hosts and refugees compete over scarce resources in the settlement areas, particularly around land and collection of firewood. Tensions between refugees and host communities also arise when hosts perceive that refugees can access resources that the host community cannot, notably education and training (Gumisiriza 2018; Vemuru et al. 2016). Evidence also indicates that Ugandan employers might discriminate against refugees, and are unaware of refugees' rights to work and to move freely (Loiacono and Silva Vargas 2019).

The slow opening of the labor market in Ethiopia

For many years, Ethiopia has hosted refugees with an open-door policy. Those seeking asylum from Eritrea, from south and central Somalia, South Sudan, Sudan, and the Republic of Yemen are automatically recognized as refugees without having to go through a status determination procedure (being so-called prima facie refugees). The government also regularly grants refugee status to asylum seekers from other countries (Graham and Miller 2021). The refugee response in Ethiopia brings together 50 operational partners, including the government of Ethiopia's Refugees and Returnees Service (formerly ARRA), supported by UNHCR together with other UN agencies and international and national nongovernmental organizations (UNHCR 2019a).

The country did not grant refugees the right to work and severely limited their labor market access, but tolerated some informal work, and even supported it after 2012. The 1995 constitution limits the right to work to citizens. Ethiopia has ratified the 1951 Geneva Convention on the Status of Refugees and the 1967 Protocol on the Status of Refugees, but it holds reservations regarding, among other things, the right for refugees to engage in wage-earning employment (Article 17 of the 1951 convention). Further, and in contradiction of the constitution, the 2004 Refugee Proclamation allowed the government to restrict refugees' residence and movement to specific areas. In effect, the government required all refugees to live in camps and limited their ability to move freely, did not allow them to work, and imposed restrictions on other key rights for economic inclusion, including property and land ownership and access to financial services (Graham and Miller 2021). As a result, most refugees could only work informally in the limited markets in and around camps and were not able to farm or be pastoralists. In practice, such informal livelihoods were tolerated—and after 2012 even supported through government-sanctioned livelihoods programs implemented by international organizations within the refugee camps and the surrounding host communities (Adugna et al. 2022; Zetter and Ruaudel 2016). In the Jijiga area, for example, UNHCR supports refugees and the host communities in their economic activities, in addition to providing food aid and cash-based assistance.

Since 2010, refugees who have Ethiopian sponsors have been able to leave camps but not to work—a change that in practice has been limited to a relatively few Eritrean refugees. In 2010, the government introduced an out-of-camp policy (OCP) that allowed refugees to apply for permits to live outside camps. The policy originally applied only to Eritrean refugees because of the close cultural ties and existing networks with Ethiopians and the perception that opening it to other origin countries posed more security risks (Samuel Hall Consulting 2014). Although the OCP was extended in 2019 to other nationalities, it continued in practice to be offered only to Eritreans (UNHCR 2022a). To apply for an out-of-camp permit, refugees must be sponsored by a relative who is an Ethiopian citizen and who signs an agreement with Ethiopia's Refugees and Returnees Service (formerly ARRA) that they can cover the refugee's living expenses. After a sponsor is obtained, the Refugees and Returnees Service (formerly ARRA) conducts a vetting process to verify the relative's ability to support the refugee. Some refugees, however, have also been allowed to move out of camp because of support received through remittances from relatives abroad (Samuel Hall Consulting 2014). Even if allowed to reside outside of camps, OCP beneficiaries are still not granted the right to work. As of 2018, there were almost 20,000 OCP beneficiaries, about 2 percent of all refugees in the country at that time (Talukder et al. 2021). Until 2020, about 28,000 Eritrean refugees had managed to fulfill the requirements and move to cities (Adugna et al. 2022). After the conflict in Tigray broke out, additional Eritreans from the camps fled to Addis Ababa (UNHCR 2021e).

At the Leaders' Summit on Refugees in New York in September 2016, the Ethiopian government made nine pledges to increase the economic and social inclusion of refugees in the country (ARRA 2018; United Nations 2016): (1) expand the OCP to 10 percent of the total refugee population; (2) provide work permits to refugees and to those with a permanent residence identification within the bounds of domestic laws; (3) provide work permits to refugee graduates in the fields of work permitted to employ foreign workers; (4) make irrigable land available to 100,000 people, including refugees and host communities, subject to availability of external finance; (5) build industrial parks with international partners and set aside 30 percent of jobs in these parks for refugees; (6) provide driver's licenses, allow refugees to open bank accounts, and provide birth certificates for those born in Ethiopia; (7) increase school enrollment for refugees; (8) expand and enhance the provision of basic social services for refugees; and (9) allow local integration, that is, obtention of Ethiopian nationality, for refugees who have lived in Ethiopia for 20 years or more.

Subsequently, Ethiopia piloted the UNHCR Comprehensive Refugee Response Framework and signed the Ethiopia Jobs Compact—international initiatives that supported the economic inclusion of refugees—and made additional pledges during the Global Refugee Forum 2019. Together with Uganda and 13 other countries, Ethiopia began to pilot the Comprehensive Refugee Response Framework in 2017 to include refugees in host communities and to support host communities in a coordinated way. Ethiopia has made progress on registering of refugees and including them in education and health services, as well as on improving the legal framework (Graham and Miller 2021). However, the rollout of livelihood and job-creation schemes has been slower not only because of the lack of necessary international funding, but also because of poor coordination frameworks and the absence of grassroots stakeholder participation (Binkert et al. 2021). To support Ethiopia's pledge in New York on providing jobs to refugees, a Job Compact, inspired by the Jordan Compact, was signed between the government of Ethiopia and international partners (the European Investment Bank; the EU; the UK Foreign, Commonwealth and Development Office; and the World Bank). The international partners pledged to create jobs for refugees and Ethiopians

by financially supporting Ethiopia's industrialization and employment policies. During the Global Refugee Forum 2019, Ethiopia made four additional
pledges to promote refugee economic and social inclusion, complementing
the pledges made in 2016 (UNHCR 2021a).

The 2019 Refugee Proclamation included policies to expand refugees'
social and economic inclusion, and the government operationalized them
through three directives, but implementation has been slow. The 2019 Refugee
Proclamation revised the 2004 Refugee Proclamation and the existing OCP. To
implement the new Refugee Proclamation, the government issued three directives regarding the right to work, to move freely, and to appeal against the implementation of policies and services. The government planned to allow almost
75,000 eligible refugees to live out of camps, in addition to those refugees who
already had OCP status. Between 2019 and 2021, nearly 50,000 out-of-camp
permits were issued (UNHCR 2021a). Further, the government aimed to provide work permits to 30,000 refugees; however, between 2019 and 2022 only
2,800 work permits were issued to refugees (UNHCR 2022d) and the speed of
implementation has not quickened in the following couple of years. The work
permits are limited to (1) employment in projects funded by the international
community for refugees and hosts, and (2) employment in positions that cannot be filled by hosts—the same conditions applied to other foreigners (Federal
Democratic Republic of Ethiopia 2019; Ginn et al. 2022). Regarding the Global
Refugee Forum commitments, Ethiopia, together with international partners,
has created economic opportunities through agricultural and livestock value
chains for 7,000 refugees and 10,000 host community members as of 2021
(out of a target of up to 90,000 overall) (UNHCR 2021a).

Economy and labor market characteristics

The case study countries are typical examples of labor markets in middle-
and low-income countries, with some peculiarities (table 2.3 illustrates
these patterns).[31] Colombia and Jordan both have labor markets typical of
middle-income countries. Compared with low-income countries, they have
higher numbers of unemployed, notably in cities; rely more on paid work
for others (whether regular salaried work or daily labor); and have greater
human capital. In Colombia, employment is strongly dependent on the service sector, and urbanization rates are particularly high. Jordan stands apart
in that it has a very low labor force participation rate, high employment in
the public sector, and a large number of migrant workers who are allowed
to work in specific, low-skilled segments of the labor market. Ethiopia and
Uganda are classic low-income country labor markets, with lower skills, productivity, and earnings; much employment in the agricultural sector; most

TABLE 2.3 Summary comparison of main economy and labor market characteristics, case study countries

Characteristics	Ethiopia	Uganda	Colombia	Jordan
Income level, 2021	Low	Low	Upper middle	Upper middle
GDP per capita, 2021 (current US$)	925	884	6,104	4,100
GDP growth average, 2012–21 (percent)	8.6	4.5	2.9	2.0
Human Capital Index, 2020	0.4	0.4	0.6	0.6
Women, Business and the Law score, 2023	76.9	81.3	84.4	46.9
Proportion of informal employment in total employment, 2021 (percent)	85	95	63	52
Important immigrant or displaced populations not considered in this study	About 4 million IDPs	Small numbers	High number of IDPs; earlier migrants from Venezuela, R.B., and Colombians who returned from Venezuela, R.B.	40 percent of the employed are immigrants from Asia and MENA; 2.3 million are Palestinian refugees
Overall labor force participation rate (percent of total population ages 15+), 2021	78 (women: 72)	68 (women: 64)	65 (women: 52)	39 (women: 14)
Employment-to-population ratio, 2021 (percent)	76	66	55	31
Unemployment rate, 2021 (percent)	4	3	14	19

Source: Original table for this report based on data from World Bank, World Development Indicators (https://databank .worldbank.org/source/world-development-indicators) and International Labour Organization Department of Statistics, ILOSTAT, "Statistics on the Informal Economy" (https://ilostat.ilo.org/topics/informality/) and "ILO SDG Explorer: Employment by Sex, Economic Activity, and Age Group" (https://www.ilo.org/shinyapps/bulkexplorer58/?lang=en&id=SDG_0831_SEX _ECO_RT_A/).
Note: GDP = gross domestic product; IDP = internally displaced person; MENA = Middle East and North Africa.

other jobs in commerce and personal services; and a nearly completely informal job market. In Ethiopia, employment in the industrial sector increased between 2013 and 2022. In all four countries, gross domestic product (GDP) and job growth are insufficient to keep up with the number of new entrants into the labor market. In Colombia and Jordan, and recently in Ethiopia, large groups of other immigrant or displaced populations compete with refugees in the labor market.

Jordan: Low participation and a highly segmented labor market

Among the lowest range of upper-middle-income countries in 2021,[32] Jordan has an economy that relies significantly on services and remittances, and most employment is in wage jobs, many of which are informal. With GDP per capita of about US$4,100 in 2021, Jordan was just above the threshold of the World Bank's definition of an upper-middle-income country. The service sector contributes 61 percent of GDP; industry accounts for 23 percent; and agriculture makes a minor contribution (5 percent). Remittances from Jordanian workers abroad, particularly in other Arab countries, are also a significant contributor to GDP, accounting for about 11 percent. Sector shares in employment are not dissimilar but reflect lower productivity in services, with services contributing 73 percent of employment, industry 24 percent, and agriculture 3 percent in 2019. Among the employed, 73 percent are in wage employment, and an additional 11 percent work as temporary laborers; 62 percent of these jobs are informal.[33] Self-employment plays a much smaller role.

The influx of Syrian refugees to Jordan came during a period of stagnant GDP growth and low investment. Amid weak investment, GDP has grown only about 2 percent, on average, between 2012 and 2021, with negative growth in 2020; and GDP growth per capita has been negative in all years since 2013 except 2021. During the same period, foreign direct investment also declined steadily, and constituted only 1.7 percent of GDP in 2020. Furthermore, the Jordanian economy is quite dependent on official development assistance (ODA). In 2021, ODA was equivalent to about 44 percent of gross capital formation in the country. Jordan benefited from 10 percent of bilateral, country-allocable ODA to refugee situations in 2018–19, even higher than the approximately 7.5 percent of refugees worldwide that Jordan hosts when including Palestinian refugees (Hesemann, Desai, and Rockenfeller 2021). In general, job creation and employment in Jordan have been highly associated with economic growth, and unemployment rates have steadily increased alongside the weak economic performance of the past decade (Winkler and Gonzales 2019).

Jordan has a low labor force participation rate, particularly among women, even in comparison with other Arab countries. The total labor force participation rate at the end of 2021 stood at a mere 39 percent, compared with a world average of 59 percent and more than 40 percent in neighboring Arab countries, according to estimates by the International Labour Organization (ILO). For Jordanian women, the participation rate is as low as 14 percent, even if they are more skilled than their male peers. Compared with men, a larger share of female workers is employed in the public sector and in formal jobs in the private sector, similar to the general situation in other Arab countries (Winkler and Gonzales 2019). With a Women, Business and the Law score well below the global average and similar to that of Syria, Jordan has differences in laws, regulations, and social norms between men and women, as well as other barriers such as lack of safe transportation and childcare, that likely explain the low female participation rate (Winkler and Gonzales 2019; World Bank 2018a, 2023b).

Unemployment rates are also high in Jordan by international comparison. The ILO estimates, that, at the end of 2021, the total unemployment rate for Jordanian workers was nearly 20 percent, compared with a world average of

6 percent and about 15 percent in neighboring Arab countries. As mentioned, unemployment rates have increased steadily during the past decade—by 7 percentage points since 2012—along with poor economic development in the country. Unemployment rates are particularly high among women, workers with advanced education, and youth (40 percent of the labor force ages 15–24 according to ILO estimates in 2021). In general, the high unemployment rates among the former two groups are related to scarcity of jobs that job seekers consider to be suitable, that is, public sector jobs or formal high-skill jobs Jordanian workers typically hold in the private sector. Conversely, many young Jordanian men with low education compete with immigrant and Syrian workers for low-skill jobs in the informal labor market.

The public sector is a very important employer and provides particularly attractive jobs; the private sector, by contrast, is sluggish. About 40 percent of all employed Jordanians work in the public sector, which is characterized by higher wages than the private sector and by formal employment (Winkler and Gonzales 2019). At the same time, the private sector has a very large number of small-scale enterprises and a few large and old enterprises, with a "missing middle" of medium-sized businesses. This is a well-known pattern in economies that lack dynamism, whereby few small businesses are able to grow over time. The vast majority of all enterprises in the private sector employ fewer than nine people, and in total these micro enterprises employ about half of all workers in the private sector (World Bank 2016a). These micro enterprises are also much more likely to be informal (World Bank 2016b). More than 50 percent of Jordanian workers work informally, reflective of the fact that most private sector employment in Jordan is informal. The proportion is even higher for non-Jordanians (Razzaz 2017).

Even before the arrival of Syrian refugees, immigrants accounted for nearly half of all employed workers in Jordan. The Jordanian labor market is characterized by a high degree of segmentation between workers of different nationalities, gender, and education levels, and between those employed in the formal and informal private sector and the public sector (Winkler and Gonzales 2019). With respect to nationalities, even before the arrival of Syrian refugees, the labor force reflected a remarkable balance between Jordanians, who, with a very low labor force participation rate constitute only about half of the employed (about 1.4 million workers), and immigrant workers, who account for more than 40 percent of the employed in the country (1.2 million workers). In addition, an estimated 250,000 Syrians were employed in the Jordanian labor market in 2017–2018 (Tiltnes, Pedersen, and Zhang 2019).

The Jordanian labor market is strongly protected by regulations defining the sectors in which immigrant workers can work (see the section titled "The Jordan Compact"). These regulations are mainly based on demand for labor in sectors that are less popular among Jordanians, who are generally more educated and have higher ambitions than immigrant workers in terms of the employment they seek. The public sector is practically closed to immigrant workers, meaning that almost all migrant workers work in the private sector. The largest shares of documented immigrant workers are people from South Asian and Southeast Asian countries, mainly women, working in the Qualified Industrial Zones and as domestic workers; Egyptians working in the agricultural sector; and workers from other Arab countries working in various service sectors. However, estimates indicate that only a portion of the immigrant workers in Jordan are registered and that most unregistered immigrants are informally employed in the service sector (Razzaz 2017).

Colombia: Reliance on the service sector and low formal wage employment

Colombia's middle-income economy grew significantly in the years leading up to the Venezuelan crisis. An upper-middle-income country, Colombia recorded GDP per capita of US$6,104 in 2021. Between 2000 and 2019, Colombia's GDP per capita grew by an average of 2.5 percent per year, leading to a clear decline in extreme poverty (Carranza et al. 2022). Building on its strong performance, Colombia was able to join the Organisation for Economic Co-operation and Development in 2020.

Even though the economy rebounded quickly after the COVID-19 (coronavirus) pandemic, inequality remains high. The COVID-19 pandemic caused a contraction in GDP of about 7 percent in 2020 and a rise in the share of people living below the national poverty line from 36 percent to 45 percent, but the economy rebounded with nearly 11 percent growth in 2021. Partly because of the pandemic, Colombia has one of the highest levels of income inequality worldwide (World Bank 2021a). Although Colombia hosted more than 6 percent of all refugees worldwide, it received only about 1 percent of all bilateral country-allocable ODA to refugee situations in 2018–19 (Hesemann, Desai, and Rockenfeller 2021).

The labor force participation rate is higher than in Jordan and the service sector provides most employment. In line with typical middle-income indicators, the employment rate in Colombia was 55 percent in 2021, and the labor force participation rate was 65 percent, according to modeled ILO estimates. Labor force participation is 25 percentage points higher for men than for women. Among workers, about 64 percent were employed in services and commerce in 2021, 20 percent in the industrial sector, and 16 percent in agriculture. Although the contribution to GDP was somewhat higher for the industrial sector (25 percent) than its contribution to employment in 2021, it was somewhat lower for agriculture (8 percent) and services (58 percent). A lack of diversification in employment and the strong reliance on service sectors makes the labor market vulnerable to shifts in internal demand (Carranza et al. 2022).

Colombia's labor productivity in services is lower than that of other countries at a similar level of income (Carranza et al. 2022).

Self-employment plays a more important role than in Jordan, and informality is even higher. Among those employed, about half were in wage employment in 2019, about a third were self-employed outside of agriculture, 12 percent were temporary workers, and 9 percent were self-employed in agriculture, according to GEIH data. Self-employment thus makes up a more important part of employment in Colombia than in Jordan. As in Jordan, levels of informality are high, with nearly two in three jobs informal (63 percent) in 2021. Access to formal employment is notably difficult for those with less than high school education (Carranza et al. 2022).

Unemployment began to rise after 2015, parallel with the inflow from República Bolivariana de Venezuela, and then strongly increased as a result of the COVID-19 pandemic. Although unemployment had consistently fallen since 2009, reaching 8 percent in 2015, it began to slowly rise even though the economy was still growing before the pandemic hit. It has been argued that the arrival of displaced Venezuelans contributed to this increase (Carranza et al. 2022). The increase drastically accelerated with the pandemic: the unemployment rate rose to 15 percent in 2020 (26 percent for youth), from 10 percent in 2019 (20 percent for youth). It declined slowly in 2021 to 14 percent and then 11 percent in 2022, but remains higher for youth (22 percent). At the same time, women and youth labor force participation decreased. Unemployment was higher for women than for men (14 percent versus 9 percent in 2022) and slightly higher for those with intermediate education compared to those with basic or advanced education. Nearly double the share of young women than young men are not in education, employment, or training (32 percent compared with 17 percent). Job opportunities are notably limited in rural areas, and Colombia has a high rate of urbanization (Carranza et al. 2022). Overall, territorial inequalities are high (World Bank 2021a).

Uganda: Low-income labor market with labor force growing nearly as fast as the economy

Uganda is a low-income country with GDP per capita of US$884 in 2021. Although the country experienced strong growth in the 2000s, recent economic growth has slowed considerably. With a less supportive external environment, fewer reforms promoting growth, and shocks such as droughts and then the COVID-19 pandemic, growth since 2011 has barely been above the high annual population growth rate of 3 percent (World Bank, IFC, and MIGA 2021).[34] As a result, per capita real GDP growth halved to 1 percent, on average, in the past 10 years. According to the latest official estimates, extreme poverty remained high in 2019/20; and, as in 2012/13, about a third of the population lived below the national poverty line, mostly in rural areas (World, IFC, and MIGA 2021). The Kampala subregion has the lowest poverty rate of all regions (World Bank, IFC, and MIGA 2021). Poor access to basic services contributed further to multidimensional poverty. Children born in Uganda today are likely to be only 38 percent as productive when they grow up as they could be if they enjoyed complete education and full health (World Bank 2021b).

The country's high poverty incidence reflects a labor market in which most available work is very low in productivity, mostly in agriculture, and informality is high. The labor force participation rate was nearly 70 percent (with a 7 percentage point higher participation rate for men than for women) and the unemployment rate negligible at 3 percent in 2021, but the quality of jobs is low. Nearly three in four jobs were in agriculture in 2019, but because of weak productivity the sector contributes only about a quarter of GDP.[35] Employment in services is slightly higher than 20 percent, and only about 6 percent are employed in the industrial sector. Of those employed, 95 percent were in informal employment in 2021 (99 percent in agriculture and 88 percent outside of agriculture).[36] Only a privileged few benefit from access to high-skill and formal employment, mainly found in the public sector and among the few large enterprises in the country. The public sector employs less than 2 percent of the workforce, and employees in the sector tend to hold on to their jobs until retirement (Merotto 2020).

In 2018/19, about 50 percent of the working-age population was in paid employment (with a 20 percentage point difference between men and women) and about 33 percent was engaged in subsistence farming. Whereas those in paid employment increased by 8 percentage points compared with 2011/12, those in subsistence farming decreased by a similar percentage (World Bank 2022). Households whose head switched from the agricultural to the nonagricultural sector benefited from the highest consumption growth, but opportunities to switch are not widely available (World Bank 2022). Spatial inequalities are increasing. Youth still predominantly join the agricultural sector (Merotto 2020). The share of youth not in education, employment, or training is 14 percent, with a higher share of women than men.

Ethiopia: High economic growth but still low-quality employment

Land-locked Ethiopia is a low-income country, with a GDP per capita of US$925 in 2021. GDP has been growing steadily at an annual average of nearly 9 percent between 2012 and 2021, making it one of the fastest-growing economies worldwide. As a result, GDP per capita has increased by nearly 6 percent over the same period, the highest increase among the four case study countries in this report. However, the GDP growth rate declined from 8.6 percent in 2019 to 5.6

in 2021, likely because of the COVID-19 pandemic and the conflict in Tigray, as well as floods and the worst locust outbreak in 70 years, which have particularly affected the Somali region.

Ethiopia has seen substantial success in growing its small industrial sector, with a doubling of the value added of the sector from 2013 to 2022. Still, industry remains a small employer, accounting for 9 percent of all jobs in 2019. With about 20 percent of jobs in the service sector, agriculture remains by far the most important source of employment and provides livelihoods for about 66 percent of workers, even if its share in GDP is similar to that of services. The employment share of agriculture, however, has declined by over 10 percentage points from 2010 to 2022, whereas the number of jobs in services increased. Agriculture in Ethiopia is particularly often exposed to severe weather events such as droughts (World Bank 2016b).

Those employed mainly work in more precarious types of employment, mostly in the informal sector. The labor force participation rate is 78 percent and is higher for men (85 percent) than women (72 percent). It is slightly higher in rural areas (66 percent) compared with urban areas (62 percent), but lower in the Somali region (51 percent). Those employed are mainly self-employed and contributing family members, with 85 percent of employment considered vulnerable. Only 14 percent of the labor force are employees, with a stark difference between urban and rural areas. Among those working in 2021, 85 percent were in informal employment, with a much higher share in agriculture (95 percent) than outside of agriculture (67 percent).[37] Seventy-five percent of workers had low-skill jobs in 2021, a decline of just 3 percentage points since 1999 (Chapman and Vinez 2023).

About a quarter of Ethiopia's population lives below the poverty line, reflecting the poor productivity of job activities. Although overall poverty rates have declined (from 44 percent of the population living below the national poverty line in 2000 to 30 percent in 2011, to 24 percent in 2016), poverty remains particularly high in rural areas, and real consumption did not grow for the poorest 20 percent of the rural population from 2005 to 2016 (Bundervoet et al. 2020). Poverty reduction and job creation have been slow because of infrastructure and human capital deficits and limited private sector growth and investment (World Bank 2016b). Literacy levels are low, even compared with other low-income countries, and even lower for women (44 percent compared with 59 percent of men in 2017) (World Bank 2023a). The country also suffers from shortages of housing in urban areas and tensions over land. Although Ethiopia is still predominantly rural, estimates show that it is urbanizing rapidly, with an urban population that is expected to triple by 2034, growing by more than 5 percent each year (World Bank 2015).

Notes

1 | World Bank DataBank, "Refugee Population by Country or Territory of Asylum—Jordan," https://data
.worldbank.org/indicator/SM.POP.REFG?locations=JO.

2 | United Nations Relief and Works Agency for Palestine Refugees in the Near East (UNRWA), "Where
We Work—Jordan," https://www.unrwa.org/where-we-work/jordan.

3 | UNRWA, "Where We Work—Jordan."

4 | ReliefWeb, "Registered Iraqis in Jordan (15 November 2019)," https://reliefweb.int/report/jordan
/registered-iraqis-jordan-15-november-2019.

5 | United Nations High Commissioner for Refugees (UNHCR), Operational Data Portal: Syria Regional
Refugee Response Jordan, https://data.unhcr.org/en/situations/syria/location/36.

6 | UNHCR, Operational Data Portal: Syria Regional Refugee Response Jordan.

7 | UNHCR, Operational Data Portal: Syria Regional Refugee Response Jordan.

8 | UNHCR, Operational Data Portal: Syria Regional Refugee Response Jordan.

9 | World Bank DataBank, World Development Indicators, https://databank.worldbank.org/source/world
-development-indicators.

10 | The Colombian government considers Venezuelans arriving in Colombia since 2016 due to the
deteriorating political, economic and security situation in Venezuela as migrants (not refugees).
UNHCR initially referred to Venezuelans arriving in Colombia as *Venezuelans displaced in
Colombia* and, since 2022, as *Venezuelans in need of international protection*. All three terms are
used interchangeably in this report.

11 | UNHCR, Operational Data Portal: Colombia, https://data.unhcr.org/en/country/col.

12 | Migración Colombia, Distribución de Venezolanos en Colombia, https://www.migracioncolombia.gov
.co/infografias-migracion-colombia/infografias-2022.

13 | Internal Displacement Monitoring Centre (IDMC), "Country Profile: Uganda," https://www.internal
-displacement.org/countries/uganda.

14 | As Uganda has a very high recognition rate for asylum-seekers, the term *refugee* is used in the
remainder of this chapter to encompass both those who are already recognized as refugees as well as
those who are awaiting a decision.

15 | Own calculations based on refugee (September 2023) and host population (2021–22) data from
UNHCR, https://data.unhcr.org/fr/country/uga.

16 | Harmonized Host-Refugee Labor Market survey (HHR-LMS) Uganda and UNHCR, "Refugee
Statistics and Verification —Uganda."

17 | UNHCR, "Refugee Data Finder," https://www.unhcr.org/refugee-statistics/download/?url=DzMr82.

18 | UNHCR, Operational Data Portal: Ethiopia Situation – Tigray Emergency Response, https://data
.unhcr.org/en/working-group/284?sv=0&geo=160.

19 | IDMC, "Ethiopia," https://www.internal-displacement.org/countries/ethiopia.

20 | UNHCR, Operational Data Portal: Ethiopia, https://data.unhcr.org/en/country/eth.

21 | As the number of asylum seekers is very small compared to the number of refugees in Ethiopia (2,217 compared to 877,804 in 2022), the term refugees is used in this chapter for both groups.

22 | UNHCR, Operational Data Portal: Ethiopia. These numbers do not include the apparently significant numbers of undocumented refugees, mainly Somalis, living in Addis Ababa (Moret, Baglioni, and Efionayi-Mader 2006; Zetter and Ruaudel 2016).

23 | UNHCR, "Ethiopia," https://www.unhcr.org/countries/ethiopia.

24 | The description of the location of the different refugee groups in Ethiopia is based on Graham and Miller (2021), and World Bank (2018b).

25 | UNHCR, Operational Data Portal: Horn of Africa, Somalia Situation, https://data.unhcr.org/en/situations/horn/location/172.

26 | UNHCR, "Ethiopia."

27 | Data from Migración Colombia.

28 | World Bank staff calculations based on data from Migración Colombia.

29 | The index ranges from 0 to 9. The 2016 value for Colombia was 6.1, compared with 4.0 in 2019.

30 | "Uganda: The Refugee Act 2006," https://www.refworld.org/docid/4b7baba52.html, and "Uganda: The Refugees Regulations, 2010," https://www.refworld.org/docid/544e4f154.html.

31 | Unless otherwise noted, all data in this section are from the World Bank's World Development Indicators. Labor force participation rate, employment to population ratio, and unemployment rates are modeled International Labor Organization estimates, for ages 15 and older from the International Labour Organization Department of Statistics, ILOSTAT, "ILO SDG Explorer: Employment by Sex, Economic Activity, and Age Group," https://www.ilo.org/shinyapps/bulkexplorer58/?lang=en&id=SDG_0831_SEX_ECO_RT_A/. The proportion of informal employment in total employment is from ILOSTAT, "Statistics on the Informal Economy," https://ilostat.ilo.org/topics/informality/.

32 | Jordan was moved to lower-middle-income status in June 2023.

33 | World Bank staff calculations based on Jordan Labor Market Panel Surveys 2016 and ILOSTAT, "Statistics on the Informal Economy."

34 | World Bank, "The World Bank in Uganda," https://www.worldbank.org/en/country/uganda.

35 | Different data sources do not align with regard to a potential change in those employed in agriculture over the past decade (World Bank, IFC, and MIGA 2021).

36 | ILOSTAT, "Statistics on the Informal Economy."

37 | ILOSTAT, "Statistics on the Informal Economy."

References

Adugna, Fekadu, Markus Rudolf, and Mulu Getachew. 2022. "A Matter of Time and Contacts: Trans-Local Networks and Long-Term Mobility of Eritrean Refugees." *Journal of Ethnic and Migration Studies* 48 (18): 1–19. doi:10.1080/1369183X.2022.2090155.

Adugna, Girmachew. 2021. "Once Primarily an Origin for Refugees, Ethiopia Experiences Evolving Migration Pattern." Migration Policy Institute. https://www.migrationpolicy.org/article/ethiopia -origin-refugees-evolving-migration.

Ait Ali Slimane, Meriem, and Shereen Al Abbadi. 2023. "Six Years after the Jordan Compact: The Effect of Labour Market Policies on Syrians' Economic Integration." *Forced Migration Review.* https://www .fmreview.org/sites/fmr/files/FMRdownloads/en/issue71/aitalislimane-alabbadi.pdf.

Amjad, Renad, Jaafar Aslan, Emma Borgnäs, Divya Chandran, Elizabeth Clark, Alessandro Ferreira dos Passos, Jaiwon Joo, and Ola Mohajer. 2017. "Examining Barriers to Workforce Inclusion of Syrian Refugees in Jordan." Better Work Discussion Paper 25, International Labour Organization and International Finance Corporation, Geneva. https://labordoc.ilo.org/discovery /delivery/41ILO_INST:41ILO_V2/1267879410002676.

ARRA (Agency for Refugee and Returnee Affairs). 2018. "Road Map for the Implementation of the Federal Democratic Republic of Ethiopia Government Pledges and the Practical Application of the CRRF in Ethiopia." ARRA, Addis Ababa. https://data.unhcr.org/en/documents/details/62655.

Barbelet, Veronique, Jessica Hagen-Zanker, and Dina Mansour-Ille. 2018. "The Jordan Compact: Lessons Learnt and Implications for Future Refugee Compacts." Policy Briefing, Overseas Development Institute, London.

Betts, Alexander, Louise Bloom, Josiah Kaplan, and Josiah Naohiko. 2016. "Protracted Refugee Camps." In *Refugee Economies: Forced Displacement and Development*, edited by Alexander Betts, Louise Bloom, Josiah Kaplan, and Naohiko Omata. Oxford, UK: Oxford University Press. doi:10.1093/acpr of:oso/9780198795681.003.0006.

Betts, Alexander, Imane Chaara, Naohiko Omata, and Olivier Sterck. 2019. "Refugee Economies in Uganda: What Difference Does the Self-Reliance Model Make?" Oxford Department of International Studies, Oxford, UK. https://www.rsc.ox.ac.uk/publications/refugee -economies-in-uganda-what-difference-does-the-self-reliance-model-make.

Binkert, Eva, Merlin Flaig, Lukas Frucht, Jorn Gravingholt, Jannis Konig, Jana Kuhnt, Philipp Lendle, Abdirahman A. Muhumad, and Katharina Potinius. 2021. "Local Governments and the Sustainable Integration of Refugees in Ethiopia." Discussion Paper 21/2021, German Institute of Development and Sustainability, Bonn.

Bundervoet, Tom, Arden Jeremy Finn, Shohei Nakamura, Berhe Mekonnen Beyene, Pierella Paci, Nataliya Mylenko, and Carolyn Turk. 2020. "Ethiopia Poverty Assessment: Harnessing Continued Growth for Accelerated Poverty Reduction." World Bank, Washington, DC. https://documents.worldbank .org/en/publication/documents-reports/documentdetail/992661585805283077/ethiopia -poverty-assessment-harnessing-continued-growth-for-accelerated-poverty-reduction.

Carranza, Eliana, William David Wiseman, Andreas Eberhard-Ruiz, and Ana Lucia Cardenas Martinez. 2022. *Colombia Jobs Diagnostic: Structural Challenges for the Creation of More and Better Jobs.* Washington, DC: World Bank. http://openknowledge.worldbank.org/handle/10986/37403.

Chapman, Emily Weedon, and Margaux Vinez, eds. 2023. *Working Today for a Better Tomorrow in Ethiopia: Jobs for Poor and Vulnerable Households.* International Development in Focus. Washington, DC: World Bank. doi:10.1596/978-1-4648-2020-5.

DANE (Departamento Administrativo Nacional de Estadística) and Ladysmith. 2021. *Población migrante venezolana en Colombia, un panorama con enfoque de género.* Statistical Note. Bogota. https:// www.dane.gov.co/files/investigaciones/notas-estadisticas/jul-2021-nota-estadistica-poblacion -migrante-venezolana-panorama-con-enfoque-de-genero.pdf.

Development Pathways. 2020. "Analysis of Refugee Vulnerability in Uganda." Working Paper. https://www .developmentpathways.co.uk/publications/analysis-of-refugee-vulnerability-in-uganda/.

Easton-Calabria, Evan. 2021. "Uganda Has a Remarkable History of Hosting Refugees, but Its Efforts Are Underfunded." *The Conversation,* August 26, 2021. https://theconversation.com/uganda -has-a-remarkable-history-of-hosting-refugees-but-its-efforts-are-underfunded-166706.

Esipova, Neli, Julie Ray, and Anita Pugliese. 2020. "World Grows Less Accepting of Migrants." *Gallup,* September 23, 2020. https://news.gallup.com/poll/320678/world-grows-less-accepting-migrants .aspx.

FAFO. 2007. "Iraqis in Jordan: Their Number and Characteristics." FAFO. http://www.dos.gov.jo/dos _home_e/main/Iraqis%20in%20Jordan.pdf.

Federal Democratic Republic of Ethiopia. 2019. "Agency for Refugees and Returnees Affairs Directive to Determine the Procedure for Refugees Right to Work." https://www.refworld.org/pdfid /60a503084.pdf.

Francis, Alexandra. 2015. *Jordan's Refugee Crisis*. Washington, DC: Carnegie Endowment for International Peace.

Ginn, T., R. Resstack, H. Dempster, E. Arnold-Fernandez, S. Miller, M. Guerrero Ble, and B. Kanyamanza. 2022. *2022 Global Refugee Work Rights Report*. Washington, DC: Center for Global Development. https://www.cgdev.org/publication/2022-global-refugee-work-rights-report.

Graham, Jimmy, and Sarah Miller. 2021. "From Displacement to Development: How Ethiopia Can Create Shared Growth by Facilitating Economic Inclusion for Refugees." Center for Global Development, Washington, DC.

Gumisiriza, Pius. 2018. "Challenges and Emerging Issues Affecting the Management of Refugees in Uganda." *Ugandan Journal of Management and Public Policy Studies* 15 (1): 40–55.

Hesemann, J., H. Desai, and Y. Rockenfeller. 2021. "Financing for Refugee Situations 2018–19." OECD Publishing, Paris. https://www.oecd.org/dac/conflict-fragility-resilience/docs/financing -refugee-situations-2018-19.pdf.

Holloway, Kerrie, Alexander Alegría Lozada, Megan Daigle, and Rocío Murad. 2022. "Changing Gender Norms in Displacement. Venezuelans in Bogota, Cucuta and Pasto, Colombia." HPG Working Paper, ODI, London. https://cdn.odi.org/media/documents/Changing_gender_norms_revSep22 .pdf.

Hovil, Lucy. 2001. "Refugees and the Security Situation in Adjumani District, Uganda." Refugee Law Project Working Paper, Makerere University. https://www.refugeelawproject.org/files/working _papers/RLP.WP02.pdf.

IDMC (Internal Displacement Monitoring Centre). 2012. "Uganda: Need to Focus on Returnees and Remaining IDPs in Transition to Development." Norwegian Refugee Council, Geneva. https:// www.internal-displacement.org/publications/uganda-need-to-focus-on-returnees-and -remaining-idps-in-transition-to-development.

Idris, Iffat. 2017. "Effectiveness of Various Refugee Settlement Approaches." K4D Helpdesk Report. GSDRC, University of Birmingham. https://assets.publishing.service.gov.uk/media/5a5f337eed915 d7dfea66cdf/223-Effectiveness-of-Various-Refugee-Settlement-Approaches.pdf.

ILO (International Labour Organization). 2015a. *Access to Work for Syrian Refugees in Jordan: A Discussion Paper on Labour and Refugee Laws and Policies*. Beirut: ILO Regional Office for Arab States. https://www.ilo.org/wcmsp5/groups/public/---arabstates/---ro-beirut/documents/publication /wcms_357950.pdf.

ILO (International Labour Organization). 2015b. "Work Permits for Syrian Refugees in Jordan." ILO Regional Office for Arab States, Beirut. https://www.ilo.org/wcmsp5/groups/public/---arabstates /---ro-beirut/documents/publication/wcms_422478.pdf.

ILO (International Labour Organization). 2017. *Work Permits and Employment of Syrian Refugees in Jordan: Towards Formalising the Work of Syrian Refugees*. Beirut: ILO Regional Office for Arab States. https://webapps.ilo.org/wcmsp5/groups/public/---arabstates/---ro-beirut/documents /publication/wcms_559151.pdf.

IRRI (International Refugee Rights Initiative). 2018. "Uganda's Refugee Policies: The History, the Politics, the Way Forward." Rights in Exile Policy Paper, International Refugee Rights Initiative, Kampala.

Loiacono, Francesco, and Mariajose Silva Vargas. 2019. "Improving Access to Labour Markets for Refugees: Evidence from Uganda." International Growth Center Report C-43445-UGA-1. https://www.theigc .org/sites/default/files/2019/10/Loiacono-and-Vargas-2019-final-paper_revision.pdf.

Maystadt, Jean-François, Valerie Mueller, Jamon Van Den Hoek, and Stijn van Weezel. 2020. "Vegetation Changes Attributable to Refugees in Africa Coincide with Agricultural Deforestation." *Environmental Research Letters* 15 (4). https://doi.org/10.1088/1748-9326/ab6d7c.

Mejia-Mantilla, Carolina, Besufekad Alemu, Johanna Fajardo, and Nobuo Yoshida. 2019. *Informing the Refugee Policy Response in Uganda. Results from the Uganda Refugee and Host Communities 2018 Household Survey*. Washington, DC: World Bank Group.

Merotto, Dino. 2020. "Uganda: Jobs Strategy for Inclusive Growth." Policy Note, World Bank, Washington, DC. http://openknowledge.worldbank.org/handle/10986/33342.

Moret, Joelle, Simone Baglioni, and Denise Efionayi-Mader. 2006. "The Path of Somali Refugees into Exile: A Comparative Analysis of Secondary Movements and Policy Responses." SFM Studies 46, Swiss Forum for Migration and Population Studies, Neuchatel.

Office of the Prime Minister (OPM), UNHCR, and World Food Programme (WFP). 2018. Joint Press Release. "OPM and UNHCR complete countrywide biometric refugee verification exercise." https://data.unhcr.org/en/documents/details/66545.

Razzaz, Susan. 2017. *A Challenging Market Becomes More Challenging.* Beirut: ILO Regional Office for Arab States. https://www.ilo.org/wcmsp5/groups/public/---arabstates/---ro-beirut/documents /publication/wcms_556931.pdf.

Samuel Hall Consulting. 2014. "Living Out of Camp: Alternative to Camp-Based Assistance for Eritrean Refugees in Ethiopia." Norwegian Refugee Council, Oslo.

Schuettler, Kirsten, and Laura Caron. 2020. "Jobs Interventions for Refugees and Internally Displaced Persons." Working Paper, World Bank, Washington, DC. https://openknowledge.worldbank.org /handle/10986/33953.

Sharpe, Marina, and Salima Namusobya. 2012. "Refugee Status Determination and the Rights of Recognized Refugees under Uganda's Refugees Act 2006." *International Journal of Refugee Law* 24 (3): 561–78. doi:10.1093/ijrl/ees036.

Stave, Svein Erik, Tewodros Aragie Kebede, and Maha Kattaa. 2021. *Impact of Work Permits on Decent Work for Syrians in Jordan.* Beirut: ILO Regional Office for Arab States. https://www.ilo.org /wcmsp5/groups/public/—arabstates/—robeirut/documents/publication/wcms820822.pdf.

Talukder, Md. Noorunnabi, Abdullah Al Mahmud Shohag, Eashita Haque, Md. Irfan Hossain, and Joseph Falcone. 2021. "Economic Opportunities for Refugees: Lessons from Five Host Countries." Population Council, Dhaka. https://knowledgecommons.popcouncil.org/cgi/viewcontent .cgi?article=2585&context=departments_sbsr-pgy.

Tiltnes, Age, Jon Pedersen, and Huafeng Zhang. 2019. *The Living Conditions of Syrian Refugees in Jordan.* Fafo-Report 2019:04. Oslo: Fafo. https://www.fafo.no/images/pub/2019/20701.pdf.

United Nations. 2016. "New York Declaration for Refugees and Migrants: Public Summary Document." United Nations, New York. https://refugeesmigrants.un.org/sites/default/files/public_summary _document_refugee_summit_final_11-11-2016.pdf.

UN Country Team and World Bank. 2017. "ReHoPE—Refugee and Host Population Empowerment Strategic Framework—Uganda." https://reliefweb.int/report/uganda/rehope-refugee-and -host-population-empowerment-strategic-framework-uganda-june-2018-0.

UNHCR (United Nations High Commissioner for Refugees). 2012a. "Statistical Report on UNHCR Registered Syrians Registered from 01 March 2011." https://data.unhcr.org/en/documents /details/36331.

UNHCR (United Nations High Commissioner for Refugees). 2012b. "Ethiopia Refugee populations by Region as of 30 Sept. 2012." https://data.unhcr.org/en/documents/details/31677.

UNHCR (United Nations High Commissioner for Refugees). 2014a. "External Statistical Report on Registered Syrians in Jordan as 20 December 2014." https://data.unhcr.org/en/documents /details/43064.

UNHCR (United Nations High Commissioner for Refugees). 2014b. "UNHCR Ethiopia Data Infographic Map (December 2014)." https://data.unhcr.org/en/documents/details/29838.

UNHCR (United Nations High Commissioner for Refugees). 2015a. "Ethiopia—Refugees and Asylum-Seekers, 31 Dec 2015." https://data.unhcr.org/en/documents/details/30610.

UNHCR (United Nations High Commissioner for Refugees). 2015b. "External Statistical Report on UNHCR Registered Syrians." https://data.unhcr.org/en/documents/details/44362.

UNHCR (United Nations High Commissioner for Refugees). 2016a. "External Statistical Report on UNHCR Registered Syrians as of 31 December 2016." UNHCR, Geneva. https://data.unhcr.org/en /documents/details/52802.

UNHCR (United Nations High Commissioner for Refugees). 2016b. "UNHCR Ethiopia Infographics November 2016." https://data.unhcr.org/en/documents/details/53024.

UNHCR (United Nations High Commissioner for Refugees). 2017a. "Syrian Refugees in Jordan-Admin Level1—End of December 2017." https://data.unhcr.org/en/documents/details/61513.

UNHCR (United Nations High Commissioner for Refugees). 2017b. "UNHCR Ethiopia Operation: Population Breakdown as of 30 October 2017." https://data.unhcr.org/en/documents/details/61133.

UNHCR (United Nations High Commissioner for Refugees). 2018a. "Infographic—Syrian Refugees in Jordan—December 2018." https://data.unhcr.org/en/documents/details/67611.

UNHCR (United Nations High Commissioner for Refugees). 2018b. "UNHCR Ethiopia Infographics August—December 2018." https://data.unhcr.org/en/documents/details/66334.

UNHCR (United Nations High Commissioner for Refugees). 2019a. "Ethiopia Country Refugee Response Plan." UNHCR, Geneva.

UNHCR (United Nations High Commissioner for Refugees). 2019b. "Jordan: Statistics for Registered Syrian Refugees (as of 15 December 2019)." https://data.unhcr.org/en/documents/details/73053.

UNHCR (United Nations High Commissioner for Refugees). 2019c. "UNHCR Ethiopia Infographics as of October 31, 2019." https://data.unhcr.org/en/documents/details/72204.

UNHCR (United Nations High Commissioner for Refugees). 2020a. "Jordan: Statistics for Registered Syrian Refugees (as of 31 December 2020)." https://data.unhcr.org/en/documents/details/84052.

UNHCR (United Nations High Commissioner for Refugees). 2021a. "Ethiopia GRF Pledge Progress Report." UNHCR, Geneva. https://globalcompactrefugees.org/sites/default/files/2021-12 /Ethiopia%20GRF%20Pledge%20Progress%20Report.pdf.

UNHCR (United Nations High Commissioner for Refugees). 2021b. "Ethiopia Refugees and Asylum Seekers Population as of 30 November 2021." https://data.unhcr.org/en/documents/details/90203.

UNHCR (United Nations High Commissioner for Refugees). 2021c. "Jordan: Statistics for Registered Syrian Refugees (as of 31 December 2021)." https://data.unhcr.org/en/documents/details/90313.

UNHCR (United Nations High Commissioner for Refugees). 2021d. "Knowledge Brief: Improving Employment Outcomes for Refugees." UNHCR, Geneva. https://data.unhcr.org/ar/documents /details/88388.

UNHCR (United Nations High Commissioner for Refugees). 2021e. "UNHCR Regains Access to Tigray Refugee Camps, Calls for Emergency Funds to Scale Up Assistance." https://www.unhcr.org /news/briefing/2021/8/611232a04/unhcr-regains-access-tigray-refugee-camps-calls-emergency -funds-scale-assistance.html.

UNHCR (United Nations High Commissioner for Refugees). 2022a. "Ethiopia: Refugee Policy Review Framework Country Summary as at 30 June 2020." UNHCR, Geneva. https://reliefweb.int /report/ethiopia/ethiopia-refugee-policy-review-framework-country-summary-30-june -2020-march-2022.

UNHCR (United Nations High Commissioner for Refugees). 2022b. "Jordan Issues Record Number of Work Permits to Syrian Sefugees." Press Release, January 25, 2022. https://www.unhcr.org/news /news-releases/jordan-issues-record-number-work-permits-syrian-refugees.

UNHCR (United Nations High Commissioner for Refugees). 2022c. "Ethiopia Refugees and Asylum seek-ers statistics as of 30 November 2022." https://data.unhcr.org/en/documents/details/97597.

UNHCR (United Nations High Commissioner for Refugees). 2022d. Annual Results Report Ethiopia. https://reporting.unhcr.org/sites/default/files/2023-06/EHGL%20Ethiopia.pdf.

UNHCR (United Nations High Commissioner for Refugees) and UN-Habitat. 2020. *Nakivale Settlement Profile. Isingiro District, Uganda*. Nairobi: UN-Habitat; Geneva: United Nations High Commissioner for Refugees.

Vemuru, Varalakshmi, Yonatan Y. Araya, Endeshaw Tadesse, Charles Kalu Kalumiya, Dismas Nkunda, Faisal Buyinza, Joseph Okumu, and Karoline Klose. 2016. "An Assessment of Uganda's Progressive Approach to Refugee Management." World Bank, Washington, DC. https://documents1.worldbank .org/curated/en/259711469593058429/pdf/107235-WP-PUBLIC.pdf.

Watera, Winnie, Claire Seremba, Ivan Otim, Donnas Ojok, Bernard Mukhone, and Anna Hoffmann. 2017. "Uganda's Refugee Management Approach within the EAC Policy Framework." Konrad-Adenauer -Stiftung, Bonn.

Winkler, Hernan, and Alvaro Gonzales. 2019. "Jobs Diagnostic Jordan." Technical Report Issue No. 18, World Bank, Washington, DC. https://documents1.worldbank.org/curated/en/681161574 097516931/pdf/Jobs-Diagnostic-Jordan.pdf.

World Bank. 2015. "Ethiopia Urbanization Review: Urban Institutions for a Middle-Income Ethiopia." World Bank, Washington, DC. https://openknowledge.worldbank.org/entities/publication /d5929a56-ffd3-5985-b90e-aaa0e429d6a7.

World Bank. 2016a. "Jordan—Promoting Poverty Reduction and Shared Prosperity: Systematic Country Diagnostic." Report No. 103433-JO. World Bank, Washington, DC.

World Bank. 2016b. *Priorities for Ending Extreme Poverty and Promoting Shared Prosperity: Systematic Country Diagnostic*. Washington, DC: World Bank. http://documents.worldbank.org/curated /en/913611468185379056/Ethiopia-Priorities-for-ending-extreme-poverty-and-promoting-shared -prosperity-systematic-country-diagnostic.

World Bank. 2018a. *Hashemite Kingdom of Jordan—Understanding How Gender Norms in MNA Impact Female Employment Outcomes*. Washington, DC: World Bank Group. http://documents .worldbank.org/curated/en/859411541448063088/HashemiteKingdomofJordanUnderstanding HowGenderNormsinMNAImpactFemaleEmploymentOutcomes.

World Bank. 2018b. "A Skills Survey for Refugees in Ethiopia." World Bank, Washington, DC. https:// documents1.worldbank.org/curated/en/996221531249711200/pdf/128185-WP-PUBLIC-P162987 -SkillsReport.pdf.

World Bank. 2020. *The Mobility of Displaced Syrians: An Economic and Social Analysis*. Washington, DC: World Bank. https://openknowledge.worldbank.org/entities/publication/f6ff609b -42eb-53df-947f-00a0c23f78c1.

World Bank. 2021a. *Building an Equitable Society in Colombia*. Washington, DC: World Bank.

World Bank. 2021b. *The Human Capital Index 2020 Update: Human Capital in the Time of COVID-19.* Washington, DC: World Bank.

World Bank. 2022. *Uganda Poverty Assessment: Strengthening Resilience to Accelerate Poverty Reduction.* Washington, DC: World Bank.

World Bank. 2023a. "Ethiopia Gender Landscape." World Bank, Washington, DC. http://documents .worldbank.org/curated/en/099953006302216890/IDU05a085a280489c046c80a61a090d4b72e57e9.

World Bank. 2023b. *Women, Business and the Law.* Washington, DC: World Bank. https://openknowledge .worldbank.org/server/api/core/bitstreams/b60c615b-09e7-46e4-84c1-bd5f4ab88903/content.

World Bank, IFC (International Finance Corporation), and MIGA (Multilateral Investment Guarantee Agency). 2021. *Uganda Systematic Country Diagnostic Update.* World Bank, Washington, DC. http://hdl.handle.net/10986/36734.

Zetter, Roger, and Heloise Ruaudel. 2016. *Refugees' Right to Work and Access to Labor Markets—An Assessment—Country Case Studies (Part 2).* KNOMAD. Washington, DC: KNOMAD Secretariat. https://www.knomad.org/publication/refugees-right-work-and-access-labor-markets -assessment-country-case-studies-part-2.

3. A Comparative Analysis of Labor Market Impacts among Hosts

Introduction

This chapter provides a comparative analysis of forced displacement's impacts on labor markets for hosts in four economies. Using consistent methods and indicator definitions, it assesses the impact of displacement on labor market outcomes for hosts in two low-income countries (LICs), Ethiopia and Uganda, and two middle-income countries (MICs), Colombia[1] and Jordan.

Labor markets are complex, and no single outcome measure provides an understanding of all impacts that are important to policy. Thus, this report considers a range of outcome measures. First, the chapter analyzes direct proxy welfare measures, namely household consumption in the two LICs and earnings in the two MICs (all earnings in Colombia; wage earnings only in Jordan). Second, the analysis considers hourly wages, a rough proxy of productivity. Next, it studies measures of activity in the labor market: the employment rate, the unemployment rate, and time worked per week. Finally, the chapter looks at measures of

Chapter 3 online annexes available at https://openknowledge.worldbank.org/handle/10986/40701: annex 3C, "Table of Main Results"; annex 3D, "More Results of the Specification Using an Instrumental Variable"; annex 3E, "Robustness to Changes in Specification"; and annex 3F, "Local Effect."

the economy's structure, specifically the economic sectors in which workers are active and the type of activity (wage work, self-employment, and more temporary employment).

The chapter seeks to describe both aggregate effects and impacts on important groups of workers. In assessing the impact of displacement on labor markets in host communities, it is important to understand aggregate effects, but it is also critical to assess whether there are groups within the labor market that are particularly affected, and whether they win or lose from the changes in the labor market. Aggregate effects are important because they circumscribe the space for policy: if, on balance, labor market effects are favorable, it is far easier to imagine policies that compensate those who lose out than if there are adverse effects overall. However, even when there are no or favorable effects in the aggregate, impacts on particular groups of workers matter, not only from a welfare and a fairness perspective but also because those impacts can determine political support for the integration of refugees into the labor market. To provide a balanced picture, this chapter therefore considers the aggregate effects as well as impacts on groups in the labor market defined by, for instance, gender, age, location (urban versus rural), skill level, and wealth.

The intention of the analysis is to facilitate qualitative comparisons of the impact of forced displacement in economies with different characteristics. In the absence of harmonizing methods and definitions, comparisons across country contexts are difficult because it is unclear whether any observed differences are due to context or to different approaches taken in the analysis. Though every aspect of the analysis cannot be fully harmonized, it is possible to greatly reduce the differences in approaches between countries, hopefully to the extent that their potential impact on results can be clearly discussed. With that goal in mind, this chapter aims to draw qualitative comparisons between four dissimilar economies—LICs and MICs, and those with open and those with restrictive labor market access for the displaced.

Although considering patterns across countries is useful, the evidence shown here for this purpose consists of comparative case studies and is of a different nature than causally identified effects found within a given country. For background on the displacement situation and on labor markets in each country included in the analysis, refer to chapter 2.

The remainder of this chapter is organized as follows. It first provides a brief summary of methods and results. It then offers a detailed description of data and methods, analyzes results in detail, assesses robustness of results to different modeling choices, and, finally, discusses policy relevance.

Overview of methods used

Although this analysis endeavors to use consistent methods across all four settings, data idiosyncrasies ensure that some differences across assessments remain. The common approach and remaining differences are discussed in detail in this chapter. Some differences are perhaps less pivotal, such as variations in recall periods for economic activities. Others clearly matter for the interpretation of results, such as differences in the time between survey rounds and, thus, in whether shorter- or longer-term effects are estimated. However, the attention paid to harmonization has arguably reduced the number of such differences to the point at which they are tractable and their bearing upon results can be clearly assessed, thereby facilitating clear comparisons.

The analysis considers aggregate effects across the labor market, as well as effects on a number of important groups within the labor force. Aggregate numbers are important to consider but can mask opposing effects on specific groups within the labor market. To assess such effects, the study always separately considers rural and urban settings, female and male workers, young workers of no more than 25 years of age and their older peers, and those with higher and lower levels of education. Further, the inquiry probes for effects within each of the main sectors of the economy and among workers who hold different types of jobs.

The analysis compares a range of indicators and econometric models to provide a well-rounded assessment of the credibility of findings. The examination of the labor market impact of displacement raises difficult challenges of causal attribution. In addition, the available data sets impose limitations: with a limited sample size in all countries but Colombia, assessments of effects on subgroups within the labor market have to contend with noise, and the absence of an individual panel dimension in Colombia poses obstacles to causal attribution. Given these challenges, the analysis uses several techniques to provide an assessment of the credibility of apparent patterns.

As described later in detail, this chapter uses various ordinary least squares (OLS) fixed effects (FE) and instrumental variables (IV) models. The discussion emphasizes OLS FE results because the method is more transparent; IV results are used as a robustness check (refer to the section on instrumental variables under "Methods"). In particular, to limit complexity, the analysis considers only OLS FE models when results are disaggregated by labor market subgroups. It also primarily relies on them in discussing the magnitude of the effects. Given small sample sizes, results that are not statistically significant are sometimes discussed. These instances are flagged for the reader by referring to the findings as "weak," as is conventional. Instances in which estimates rely on small samples (roughly, fewer than 100 observations per survey round) are also flagged.

Next, to check for potential measurement error in labor market outcome variables, versions of core indicators computed with different data are compared. Measurement error can have a substantial effect on labor market analyses. When possible, the study guards against the impact of such error by considering indicators that measure the same phenomenon but are derived independently from different information within each survey. For instance, the analysis uses information on the sector of activity derived from both household and individual worker data. As another example, in some cases, activity data are available for both a 7-day and a 12-month reference period. The analysis checks for consistency and reports major divergences.

Finally, the chapter discusses at length whether findings can be cross-validated. Because various indicators of labor market impacts are studied, it is sometimes possible to ask whether various findings are consistent with each other. For instance, in ascertaining whether an observed welfare gain for those in commercial agriculture is credible, it is interesting to ask whether there is a move toward such activity, and whether workers who might be employed by commercial farmers also see gains.

Summary of findings

In each of the four economies analyzed in this report, displacement either causes no change in aggregate welfare (proxied by consumption or earnings) in host communities or is associated with gains. However, in some cases, there are estimated adverse effects for some groups in the labor market even when the aggregate effect is positive. That is, there sometimes are winners and losers in refugee-hosting communities. Further, however, there are no estimates of adverse effects for subgroups in Ethiopia and Jordan, where medium- and long-term effects are studied, respectively. It is only in the two economies for which results reflect short-term effects that the analysis shows winners and losers, with aggregate gains.

Host workers in agriculture appear well positioned to gain, highlighting the potential role of consumer demand for food in transmitting the effect of displacement into the labor market. In the four economies analyzed, those active in agriculture often benefit. Significant gains are found in Ethiopia and Uganda, with an additional pattern of greater activity in market-oriented agriculture in Uganda. In Colombia and Jordan, there are weak gains. The preponderance of positive effects in agriculture—more clearly observed in LIC economies where markets are less integrated—points toward the importance of product market demand as a conduit through which displacement affects labor markets in lower-income countries.

Results from the four economies suggest that gains in income do not simply arise because of longer work hours. Significance patterns in hourly wages are sparse, partly because the sample of wage workers in the two LICs is small. However, groups that experience gains in consumption or total earnings generally show at least a weak rise in hourly wages (regardless of whether there is also a change in time worked per week). This finding can be interpreted in several ways. With significant assumptions, it can be viewed as suggesting an increase in labor productivity. Another possibility is that workers benefit from a change in local output prices that is not fully captured by inflation adjustment (Eberhard-Ruiz, forthcoming). Most simply put, the evidence suggests, on balance, that some contribution to income or consumption gains in host communities comes from higher returns to work, and that it is not the case that host workers simply work more.

There is little evidence of adverse impacts on employment and unemployment rates in host communities, with the notable exception of some models and some groups of workers in Colombia. Potential impacts on the availability of jobs for hosts play a prominent role in policy makers' concerns about hosting refugees. However, across the four economies analyzed here, there is little evidence of an adverse impact, and no evidence of an adverse impact over the medium or longer term. Significant short-term adverse effects on the unemployment or employment rate are, however, observed for some groups of workers in Colombia, specifically men, youth, and less-educated workers. Elsewhere, there are no impacts or weak positive impacts. In the two economies in which medium-term (Ethiopia) and longer-term (Jordan) outcomes are measured, there are no significant effects, whereas there are weak indications of short-term gains in Uganda.

Changes in sector and type of activity largely mirror shifts in welfare and suggest a tendency toward adaptation to the opportunities and challenges that result from refugee arrival. This finding can be read as indicative of adaptations to the opportunities and challenges arising from hosting displaced groups as, for instance, with sectoral shifts into agriculture alongside benefits to those active in agriculture.

Data and variable descriptions

This analysis seeks to extract comparable information from the best available labor market data in each country, despite disparate survey formats. In each of the four countries, the analysis uses geolocated information on the presence of refugees (and on work permits) alongside information on welfare and labor market outcomes from household or labor force surveys. Middle-income labor markets are more clearly characterized by the interplay of firms and workers typical of high-income economies and tend to have higher shares of wage employment. Labor market outcomes are captured well in labor force surveys. By contrast, lower-income labor markets see much self-employment and household work, not all of which is oriented toward the market. Labor force surveys do not always satisfactorily capture information on these types of work. Thus, labor force surveys are used to measure outcomes in the two MICs, and household surveys in the two LICs. As a consequence, however, because household surveys usually contain more modest labor market modules, the analysis, in some instances, had to be inventive in creating comparable outcome variables. Refer to annex 3A for a detailed description of data sources.

In Ethiopia and Uganda, geolocated data are used to define the number of refugees hosted by a community; in Colombia and Jordan, the analysis is carried out at the level of administrative districts, as discussed further in annex 3A. With the exception of Colombia, panel data in which households and individual respondents participate in several rounds of the survey are used. Table 3.1 summarizes which surveys are used.

TABLE 3.1   Data sources, case study countries

	Ethiopia	Uganda	Colombia	Jordan
Household				
Data source	ERSS/ESS	LSMS-ISA	GEIH	JLMPS
Years	2011–12, 2013–14, 2015–16	2009–10, 2011, 2012	2015, 2016, 2017, 2018, 2019	2010, 2016
Sample size, working-age individuals (yearly)	9,233 in 2012 13,814 in 2014 12,910 in 2016	6,773 in 2010 6,647 in 2011 6,808 in 2012	510,557 in 2015 507,599 in 2016 502,399 in 2017 500,829 in 2018 496,472 in 2019	15,115 in 2010 19,964 in 2016
Survey type	Panel	Panel	Repeated cross section	Panel
Refugee				
Data source	UNHCR data on camp-based refugees and additional data sources	UNHCR data on refugees living in camps and settlements, and data on self-settled refugees in Kampala	Number of Venezuelan migrants from GEIH and the 2005 and 2018 censuses	Number of Syrian refugees by district from the 2015 census

Source: Original table for this report.
Note: ERSS/ESS = Ethiopian Socio-Economic Survey; GEIH = Gran Encuesta Integrada de Hogares (Large Integrated Household Survey); JLMPS = Jordan Labor Market Panel Surveys; LSMS-ISA = Living-Standards Measurement Study–Integrated Studies on Agriculture; UNHCR = United Nations High Commissioner for Refugees.

Data on refugees in Ethiopia and Uganda were obtained from the United Nations High Commissioner for Refugees, and for Colombia and Jordan from national statistics offices. Chapter 2 provides a full discussion of the displacement situation in each of the four countries included in the study. The data sources used in this chapter are as follows: In Ethiopia and Uganda, the United Nations data cover refugees living in (geolocated) camps and settlements. Maps 3.1 and 3.2 provide an overview of these settlement patterns. Additional data sources supply the number of refugees living in Kampala. There are no disaggregated data available on self-settled refugees; annex 3A discusses the relevance of this issue at survey time. Data for Colombia and Jordan, collected by the national statistics offices, cover, respectively, Venezuelan and Syrian refugees residing in any kind of locality. In these two countries, data are aggregated at the district level.

Although the study largely harmonizes data on labor market outcomes, some differences across countries remain, both because of context and because of survey structure. The analysis seeks to compare across contexts and across distinct data sets. As a consequence, not all indicators are fully consistent across the four countries. Table 3A.1 in annex 3A provides an overview. Notably, as discussed later in the chapter, consumption is used as a welfare proxy in the LICs and earnings in the MICs, reflecting both context and data availability. Second, the recall period differs for some variables between one year in the LICs and seven days in the MICs, reflecting differences in the seasonality of work.

MAP 3.1 Ethiopia: Refugee camps, 2000–16, and ERSS clusters, 2011–16

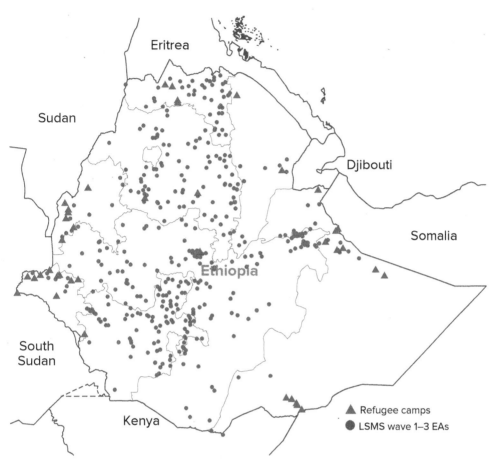

Source: World Bank based on data from ERSS/ESS 2011–12, 2013–14, 2015–16. See table 3.1 for additional details.
Note: EA = enumeration area; ERSS = Ethiopian Socio-Economic Survey.

Third, no data on formality and unemployment are available in Ethiopia (though there are data on the employment rate).

For the analysis, a broad set of labor market outcomes is constructed, relying on standard indicator definitions. Annex 3A provides a detailed description of the outcome variables and of covariates. The outcome variables used include the following:

- *Proxy measures of welfare*, namely overall earnings in Colombia, wage earnings in Jordan, and consumption per adult equivalent in Ethiopia and Uganda
- *Measures of labor market activity and job quality*, including the employment rate and unemployment rate (which, together, also imply the rate of labor force participation), work hours per week, formality of employment, and hourly wages

MAP 3.2   Refugee settlements and LSMS clusters in Uganda, 2009–12

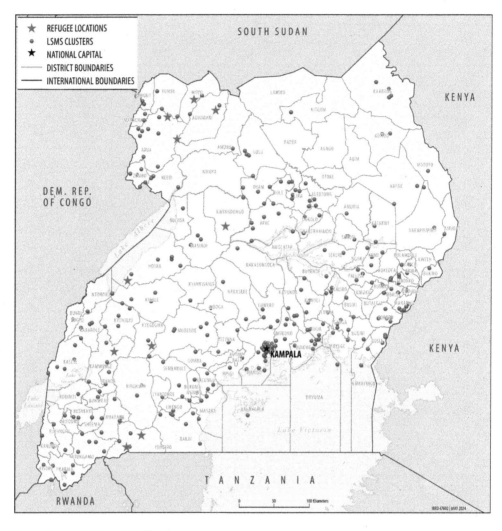

Source: Kadigo and Maystadt 2023.
Note: LSMS = Living Standards Measurement Study.

- *Measures of the structure of employment,* such as the type of work (wage worker, temporary worker, and self-employment in or outside of agriculture) and the sector of activity (agriculture, manufacturing, commerce, and other services).

Summary statistics reflect the structural differences between the low- and middle-income labor markets studied here. Table 3.2 presents summary statistics for the variables used in the analysis, showing average values over the included survey rounds. In addition to the outcome variables described in the previous

TABLE 3.2 Summary statistics, case study countries

Variable	Ethiopia			Uganda			Colombia			Jordan		
	Mean	Standard deviation	Observations	Mean	Standard deviation	Observations	Mean	Standard deviation	Observations	Mean	Standard deviation	Observations
Treatment variable (ln)	0.46	1.71	26,724	2.48	3.50	16,922	9.29	1.73	2,476,744	5.09	4.46	18,557
Employed	0.81	0.39	26,724	0.87	0.34	20,222	0.68	0.47	2,476,744	0.36	0.48	18,424
Unemployed	—	—	—	0.02	0.12	17,674	0.10	0.30	1,822,448	0.16	0.37	7,720
Wage employee	0.10	0.31	21,071	0.11	0.31	15,231	0.45	0.50	1,620,616	0.72	0.45	6,544
Temporary worker	0.15	0.36	21,071	0.01	0.11	15,533	0.12	0.32	1,620,529	0.05	0.23	6,544
Self-employment, not in agriculture	0.56	0.50	21,071	0.17	0.38	15,761	0.36	0.48	1,620,616	0.13	0.34	6,544
Self-employment in agriculture	0.62	0.49	21,071	0.64	0.48	15,507	0.09	0.29	1,620,616	—	—	—
Agriculture	0.04	0.20	2,974	0.72	0.45	15,539	0.15	0.36	1,620,616	0.04	0.21	6,483
Manufacturing	0.25	0.44	2,974	0.05	0.22	15,539	0.20	0.40	1,620,616	0.18	0.38	6,483
Commerce	0.09	0.28	2,974	0.09	0.29	15,539	0.19	0.39	1,620,616	0.17	0.37	6,483
Services	0.48	0.50	2,974	0.13	0.34	15,539	0.46	0.50	1,620,616	0.61	0.49	6,483
Monthly wage (ln)	8.86	1.60	2,964	10.99	3.18	2,473	13.38	0.87	1,324,077	5.82	0.73	5,499
Hourly wage (ln)	1.85	1.04	2,954	4.33	1.57	2,285	8.17	0.76	1,324,077	1.22	0.74	5,399
Hours worked per week (ln)	3.65	0.61	2,975	2.82	1.15	14,677	3.73	0.49	1,513,746	3.78	0.40	5,874
Formal	—	—	—	0.18	0.38	4,799	0.41	0.49	1,620,616	0.59	0.49	5,978
Consumption p.a.e. (ln)	7.86	0.64	9,781	10.73	0.79	7,195	—	—	—	—	—	—
Household earnings: Commercial farming	0.09	0.28	10,207	0.02	0.13	6,731	—	—	—	—	—	—
Household earnings: Subsistence farming	0.10	0.30	10,207	0.51	0.50	6,731	—	—	—	—	—	—
Daily worker	—	—	—	—	—	—	0.03	0.18	1,620,616	—	—	—
Monthly wage, self-employment (ln)	—	—	—	—	—	—	13.01	1.00	654,136	—	—	—

Source: Original table for this report based on data from ERSS/ESS 2011–12, 2013–14, 2015–16, LSMS-ISA 2009–10, 2011, 2012, JLMPS 2010, 2016, and GEIH 2015, 2016, 2017, 2018, 2019. See table 3.1 for additional details.

Note: Activity categories (for example, wage employment, temporary work, etc.) are mutually exclusive in all countries except Ethiopia. In Ethiopia and Uganda, most outcome variables are based on a 12-month recall period; in Colombia and Jordan, most outcome variables are based on a 7-day recall period. p.a.e. = per adult equivalent. — = not available.

paragraph, summary statistics are also shown for the "treatment variable," that is, the log of the total number of refugees in each country. The data vividly reflect the profound differences between LIC and MIC labor markets. Thus, the labor markets in Ethiopia and Uganda show high participation rates, a predominance of self-employment over wage work, and a high employment share in agriculture. The MIC labor markets in Colombia and Jordan exhibit a higher wage share, greater engagement in commerce and manufacturing, and higher formality.

Methods

This analysis relies on an OLS FE panel model as its preferred specification but uses an IV FE model as a robustness check. This section provides a technical description of the econometric methods used in this chapter; box 3.1 provides a nontechnical summary. Locality fixed effects are allowed for in all countries (at the level of enumeration areas in Ethiopia and Uganda, districts in Jordan, and departments in Colombia). In the LICs and in Jordan, individual-level panel data are available, so the study also applies as an alternative specification individual fixed effects. All models include year fixed effects. In addition, an IV strategy is used as a robustness check to guard against potential endogeneity issues that could arise, most obviously when refugees sort geographically into areas with particular labor market trends, for instance, if they prefer to move to cities with growing incomes and opportunities, or if they are constrained to living in remote rural areas with stagnant growth. This section describes the OLS specification and the IV specification.

This report analyzes the effect of refugee inflows on the host population's labor market outcomes. As the preferred baseline specification, the investigation uses a standard two-way fixed effect estimating the following model:

$$Y_{ilt} = \beta_1 \, Ref_{lt-1} + \tau X'_{ilt} + \alpha_l + \alpha_t + \gamma \, Dist \, Border_l \times \alpha_t + \in_{ilt}, \qquad (3.1)$$

where i stands for individual, l for locality, and t for year. The model is estimated with OLS. Standard errors are clustered at the locality level to deal with within-location correlation in the error terms. Y_{ilt} represents labor market outcomes among the hosting population. The treatment variable of interest differs depending on the context: in the MICs, it is the number of refugees in location l at lag year $t-1$, denoted Ref_{lt-1}; in the LICs, it is a refugee index weighting camp-level refugee population by the distance of the enumeration area to the camps and settlements in the data. The treatment variables and instruments are described in the "Treatment variables" section. In the preferred model, the interaction of the distance of each locality to the nearest international border is controlled for with the year fixed effects $Dist \, Border_l \times \alpha_t$. The intention in adding this control is to avoid any confounding effect that events in neighboring refugee-sending countries could have on labor market outcomes for hosts through channels other than displacement, for instance, through the disruption of trade links or other deleterious effects of insecurity. The model further uses a sparse set of individual-level controls X'_{ilt}, including a quadratic in age and gender. Online annex 3E discusses robustness to various changes to this specification.

Treatment variables

Treatment definitions vary across the four countries but are designed to best capture the presence of displaced workers in each context with the information available. In Colombia and Jordan, the treatment variable is the number of refugees at time t–1 at the lowest geographic level for which information was available, namely the first subnational administrative level. In Ethiopia and Uganda, geolocated information is available on refugees living in camps or settlements, and the treatment variable is a distance-weighted refugee index at t–1 that weights the number of refugees within a buffer zone around each sampling cluster by distance from the camp, as in equation (3.2).

$$Ref_{v,t-1} = \sum_{c} \frac{Refugee_{c,t-1}}{Distance_{v,c}} \qquad (3.2)$$

where $Ref_{v,t-1}$ is an index of refugee exposure of survey cluster v at time t–1 in Ethiopia, and at t in Uganda; $Refugee_{c,t-1}$ denotes the total number of refugees living in camp c at time t–1, and $Distance_{v,c}$ refers to the distance between cluster v and camp c, measured in kilometers. The analysis considers refugees within a 50-kilometer buffer from each Living Standards Measurement Study cluster. In all countries except Uganda, the analysis takes the lag value of the refugee inflow before the survey was collected to better capture how the number of refugees affected the current labor market at t. In Uganda, the study does not use lagged values because camp closures in the year before the first survey round introduce discontinuities that make it impossible to construct a viable instrumental variable. Results in the preferred model using lagged values in Uganda are consistent with results obtained with contemporaneous values.[2] The study always works with the natural logarithm of treatment variables to facilitate the comparison of results across the four countries.

With a slight modification, the preferred model is also used to assess whether there are differential impacts on subgroups in the labor market. As discussed earlier, there are good reasons to suspect that certain groups of workers may be more likely to be affected in their job outcomes when refugee workers join the labor market. Such differential outcomes are assessed with a straightforward modification of the preferred model, that is, by interacting the treatment variable with a binary variable capturing characteristics such as gender, age group, skill level, or wealth.[3] This specification allows different effects of hosting refugees to be estimated for each subgroup. A particular variant of this approach is used to further ask whether hosting more refugees has a different impact in communities that host a more modest number of refugees and those that host a more elevated number. In technical terms, this measures whether there is a nonlinear effect of hosting refugees on labor market outcomes. For this purpose, the treatment is interacted with a binary variable that indicates whether the locality in which the worker resides hosts a number of refugees that is higher or lower than the median among all communities.[4]

BOX 3.1   A nontechnical perspective on the methods used in this chapter

The statistical approach used in this chapter studies the overall impact of forced displacement on jobs, regardless of the conduits through which such effects come about. It is sometimes referred to as a "reduced-form" approach. For instance, the effect measured can occur through changes in market demand for certain goods as much as through the change in the number of workers looking for jobs. It also includes adaptations, for instance, the effect of aid provided to host communities, or the effect of host workers moving out of localities in which they experience labor market competition, or into localities where there is high market demand. This is a common empirical strategy given that isolating the ways through which effects come about can be hard to do. Still, it is of interest to understand these conduits. Therefore, this study compares the effects on different subgroups of workers and on different labor market features to suggest what the more likely conduits may be. Chapter 4 also sheds light on this issue using primary data.

This chapter relies on fixed effects models, a statistical method that focuses analysis on deviations from what is usual. It is useful to contrast such models with more traditional "pooled" regression models.[a] Pooled models estimate the effect of displacement on labor markets based on the way workers' outcomes differ when communities host more or fewer refugees, comparing without distinction any community and time period. By way of contrast, by including locality fixed effects, the baseline model estimates these effects based on *deviations from what is normal* for

each locality, for instance, whether the locality hosts more or fewer refugees than it does on average over the study's time horizon, and whether labor market outcomes were more or less favorable than usual. By adding time fixed effects, the analysis further removes any deviation that all localities have in common during a certain year. For instance, the study considers not just whether a locality hosted more or fewer refugees than it usually does, but also whether this deviation from what is normal for the locality differs much from the way most localities deviated from their mean in a given year.

Fixed effects models are used because they help differentiate the effect of displacement on labor markets from the effect of other characteristics of localities and common shifts in a given year. There are several good reasons to prefer fixed effects models over pooled regression models. A particularly important one is that they ensure that the investigation does not conflate the impact of displacement with the effect of any other locality characteristic that does not change over time. For instance, refugees may be hosted only in certain parts of a country—perhaps border areas—and these areas may be typically better (or worse) off than other parts of the country. If the study were to use pooled analysis, it might conclude that hosting refugees is good (or bad) for workers, not because of a true association but because of the underlying difference between the localities. Similarly, without year fixed effects, the effect of displacement might be conflated with other events that affect aggregate labor market outcomes in years when many refugees

(continued)

BOX 3.1 A nontechnical perspective on the methods used in this chapter (*continued*)

arrive, such as droughts or particularly good rains, or price shocks that are good for or detrimental to the host country's terms of trade.

Fixed effects models are similar to before-and-after comparisons. When there are just two survey periods, it can be shown mathematically that a fixed effects model gives the same result as a model that asks how the *change over time* in how many refugees a locality hosts relates to the change in workers' outcomes. When there are more than two periods, the models are not identical. However, they are conceptually similar—both try to remove from the analysis differences across localities (or workers) that persist. It can be argued that fixed effects estimators use the available data more efficiently. However, the practical reason fixed effects models are more commonly used in the displacement literature (and more broadly with the kind of data available for this study) is that it is often easier to add some other important features to the model.

Despite their strengths, fixed effects models cannot account for all potential confounding effects, and they may make a difference for how the effects are interpreted. The advantages of fixed effects models described here and the fact that they often work well in small samples make them one of the most useful econometric tools. However, they do have their limitations. First, because time fixed effects abstract from any change that affects all localities in a given year, they also remove any effect of displacement shared by all localities. This often does not matter: the analysis still accurately measures any effects of displacement that do not *only* play out in a way that affects all equally. However, there are examples of what are often called "general equilibrium" effects that the model cannot capture, for instance, increases in budget support for refugee-hosting nations. Second, fixed effects cannot help differentiate the effect of displacement from other factors that change over time in ways that are different across localities. For this study, the most obvious concern is that refugees might systematically choose to settle in parts of the country that have more dynamic labor markets than others (perhaps because refugees seek opportunity) or in those that are less dynamic than others

(perhaps because they prefer to live close to borders or are not allowed to move and settle freely). This phenomenon is sometimes called "residential sorting." If this were the case, then accounting for locality effects does not help distinguish the effect of displacement from economic dynamics that were already under way. (By way of contrast, they do help when refugees settle in areas that are always poorer or less poor than others during the study's time horizon and the gap between the two stays the same.) Sometimes, these challenges can be addressed by using an instrumental variables strategy.

Whereas fixed effects do not help distinguish the impact of displacement from that of other factors that change over time in ways that are systematically different in refugee-hosting communities, the instrumental variables method can sometimes help solve this issue. The basic insight of instrumental variables is that forced displacement could be closely related to other phenomena that are in turn related *only* to the outcomes we want to measure through displacement. Such a phenomenon is referred to as an instrumental variable and can help separate the effect of displacement from any other time-varying factor that could affect labor market outcomes. In the literature on migration and displacement, common instrumental variables include the distance of a host community from the border, the share of refugees that lived in the locality before the recent wave of arrivals that is being studied, or combinations and variations of the two. It can usually be shown that these instrumental variables are closely related to where refugees settle. And it is sometimes, but not always, plausible to argue that they do not relate to labor market outcomes other than through the impact of displacement.

Fixed effects and instrumental variables have complementary strengths and weaknesses; this chapter considers both but relies mostly on the fixed effects results. Instrumental variables estimates can provide reassurance that the effect of displacement is not being conflated with other economic trends that affect host communities. However, fixed effects estimates are more suitable when there is reason to question the assumptions that need to hold for

(continued)

An instrumental variables approach

To provide further reassurance against endogeneity, the investigation includes an IV approach common in the literature. The instrument is based on a standard approach referred to as Bartik shocks or shift-share instruments. The instrument aims to predict the number of refugees in a particular location on the basis of characteristics before displacement that are arguably unrelated to labor market outcomes (or exogenous), and changes over time that are common and exogenous to local labor market dynamics. The IV models are estimated in the following equations. The first stage, explained on a country-case basis below, is defined by equation (3.3):

$$Refugees_{lt-1} = \gamma IV_{lt-1} + \alpha_l + \alpha_{t-1} + \in_{ilt-1} \qquad (3.3)$$

The second stage is described as in equation (3.4):

$$Y_{lit} = \beta_1 \widehat{Refugees}_{lt-1} + \alpha_l + \alpha_t + \tau X'_{ilt} + \varepsilon_{ilt} \qquad (3.4)$$

where IV_{lt} is instrumenting for $Refugees_{lt}$, the number of refugees per location. As in equations (3.1) and (3.2), l and t index location and year, α_l and α_t are the location and time fixed effects, and X'_{ilt} are control variables. In the main specification, year and location or individual fixed effects are applied. Alternate specifications also include month fixed effects to control for seasonal effects.

Shift-share instruments are a standard tool in the literature but have some well-established weaknesses. To measure the effect of the common shock on individual units of observation, shift-share instruments use variation in an initial "share" associated with the expected exposure of different units. It can thus be interpreted as a difference-in-differences setup using an exogenous shock and its distribution across units of observation. The method was first proposed by Perloff (1957) and Freeman (1980) and later popularized by Bartik (1991), Blanchard et al. (1992), and Card (2009). It has a broad range of applications in trade economics, migration economics, and public economics. Migration studies using shift-share instruments are ubiquitous (Card 2009; Jaeger, Ruist, and Stuhler 2018). At the same time, however, recent literature has shown that the assumptions required for shift-share instruments to be valid are more demanding than is sometimes believed. In particular, Goldsmith-Pinkham, Sorkin, and Swift (2020) show that validity requires that the initial shares be exogenous. In the current context, this would require that the original shares of refugees hosted in different localities be independent, for example, of diverging labor market trends associated with distance to a conflict-affected neighbor. Because this concern coexists with some questions as to the strength of the instruments in these relatively small data sets, as well as their robustness to changes in definitions, the OLS FE estimates are preferred as a baseline specification whose strengths and weaknesses are readily understood; the IV results are used as a robustness check.

The information used in instruments varies by country, but in each case aims to predict refugee inflows in a consistent way. Because the variable the analysis instruments for is the same across contexts, IV regression results are comparable. At the same time, by applying the instrument that is most appropriate in each context, the study ensures that the instruments are as strong and as relevant as they can be. A detailed description of the instrument used in each country is provided in online annex 3D. Briefly, the shift-share IV combines in each case the number of refugees arriving in the host country each year with predictors of the probability that refugees will settle in a certain location. These predictors are, in Colombia, the settlement pattern of Venezuelan migrants about a decade before the onset of the crisis; in Ethiopia, a combination of distance to the nearest refugee camp and the nationalities represented in each refugee camp; in Jordan, distance to the country's largest refugee camp; and, in Uganda, distance to the closest border crossing.

Results

This section discusses empirical findings on the impact of the arrival of displaced workers on jobs for hosts in terms of proxy measures of welfare, returns to labor, activity level, and sector of employment.

Proxy measures of welfare: Consumption and wage earnings

Although a range of labor market outcomes are relevant, proxy measures of welfare are pivotal in evaluating the labor market impact of forced migration. This chapter considers a variety of core labor market measures in studying the impact of forced displacement on the working lives of hosts. Such a diverse perspective helps provide an understanding of the economic impacts host communities experience. However, assessing impacts on welfare is especially important, given that welfare captures the combined effect of all changes in the labor market on standards of living—what ultimately matters to policy makers. Although measuring welfare in a technically clean way is difficult, two proxy measures available in the data are of great practical use: consumption in the LICs, and earnings in the MICs.

In line with the available data, this study uses household consumption (per adult equivalent, and appropriately deflated) as its proxy measure of welfare in Ethiopia and Uganda (where the analysis works with household surveys), earnings from any gainful activity in Colombia, and wage earnings in Jordan (where labor force surveys are used). These choices also make sense from the perspective of the different labor market structures in the low- and middle-income countries studied here. In the two LICs, self-employment is the norm, and it often includes production for own consumption; what is more, forced displacement is likely to influence the degree to which households engage in subsistence activities. Thus, consumption is a meaningful welfare measure. In the two MICs, wage employment is far more common, and self-employment is rarely subsistence oriented. Although it would be preferable to have information on earnings from self-employment as well as wage work to measure welfare in Jordan, in the absence of such data, wage earnings provide a meaningful picture of labor market impacts. For completeness, results on wage earnings in the two LICs are also shown where data are available (table 3C.1 in online annex 3C). However, given the limited role of wage work among job strategies, these results cannot be used as a broadly valid proxy welfare measure like they can in MICs.

In each of the four economies analyzed in this report, either there is no change in aggregate welfare in host communities due to displacement or there are gains (table 3.3). However, in some cases, there are estimated adverse effects for some groups in the labor market even where the aggregate effect is positive. That is, there sometimes are winners and losers in refugee-hosting communities. Further, although the analysis can compare only four case studies, it is worth noting a pattern among them. Thus, there are no estimates of adverse effects for subgroups in the two economies where medium-term effects are studied, Ethiopia and Jordan. The analysis shows winners and losers (with aggregate gains) in the two economies in which it reflects short-term effects.

TABLE 3.3 Effects on consumption per adult equivalent (ln) and monthly wages (ln), case study countries

	Consumption p.a.e. (ln) 12 months		Monthly wage (ln) 7 days	
	(1) Ethiopia	(2) Uganda	(3) Colombia	(4) Jordan
Location and year fixed effects OLS				
Number of refugees (ln)	0.030* (0.015)	0.026** (0.012)	0.006 (0.013)	−0.009 (0.024)
Observations	9,758	5,990	1,324,077	5,499
Mean	7.91	10.79	13.43	5.81
Individual and year fixed effects OLS				
Number of refugees (ln)	0.029* (0.015)	0.018 (0.014)		0.016 (0.027)
Observations	8,968	5,981		3,268
Mean	7.90	10.79		5.86
Subgroup results, location and year fixed effects OLS				
Location				
Number of refugees (ln)				
Rural	0.009 (0.011)	0.031** (0.012)	0.017 (0.018)	−0.028 (0.023)
Urban	0.067*** (0.025)	−0.036 (0.023)	−0.001 (0.013)	−0.016 (0.023)
HH earnings: Commercial farming				
Commercial	0.020 (0.024)	0.073** (0.032)		
Other households	0.030* (0.016)	0.023* (0.013)		
HH earnings: Subsistence farming				
Subsistence	0.037** (0.019)	0.026* (0.014)		
Other households	0.029* (0.016)	0.029** (0.014)		
HH earnings: Wage workers				
Wage workers	0.066*** (0.023)	0.033** (0.015)	−0.001 (0.016)	−0.007 (0.022)
Other workers	0.027* (0.015)	0.020 (0.014)	0.030 (0.018)	0.034 (0.040)
Temporary workers				
Temporary workers			−0.049** (0.019)	0.004 (0.025)
Other workers			0.013 (0.013)	−0.007 (0.025)
Agriculture				
Agriculture workers			0.033 (0.020)	0.031 (0.030)
Other workers			0.000 (0.012)	−0.005 (0.025)

Source: Original table for this report based on data from ERSS/ESS 2011–12, 2013–14, 2015–16, LSMS-ISA 2009–10, 2011, 2012, JLMPS 2010, 2016, and GEIH 2015, 2016, 2017, 2018, 2019. See table 3.1 for additional details.
Note: Standard errors clustered at the administrative level (enumeration areas in Ethiopia and Uganda; departments in Colombia; and districts in Jordan). Weighted regressions. Sub-group results test for significance of each group estimate, rather than significance of the difference between the estimates. Controls include age, age squared, and gender.
FE = fixed effects; HH = household; OLS = ordinary least squares; p.a.e. = per adult equivalent.
* $p < .10$, ** $p < .05$, *** $p < .01$.

Workers in agriculture appear well positioned to gain in host communities in the four economies analyzed, highlighting the potential role of consumer demand for food in transmitting the effect of displacement into the labor market. In Ethiopia and Uganda, there are significant gains, with an additional pattern of greater activity in market-oriented agriculture in Uganda. In Colombia and Jordan, there are weak positive effects; and, in Colombia, those active in agriculture do significantly better in host communities than those who pursue other activities. The preponderance of positive effects in agriculture—more clearly observed in the lower-income economies in which markets are less integrated—points to the importance of product market demand as a conduit through which displacement affects labor markets in lower-income countries.

Low-income countries

In the two LICs, there is a clear impression of an increase in consumption in the aggregate (panels a and b of table 3.3). But the story behind this aggregate impact is quite different between the two countries (panel c of table 3.3). In Ethiopia, gains are concentrated among urban workers and households that rely on wage work (and perhaps among women and the better-educated). There are no changes in rural areas. These results may suggest a process related to job upgrading, or—perhaps more likely, given the very limited labor force participation among refugees—gains from additional demand or investment in urban areas that host refugees. In Uganda, in contrast, gains are clearly observed only in rural areas, with null or negative point estimates in urban areas. Agriculture wage workers and commercial farmers see large gains, as do those in the poorest quintile. This pattern points to gains from increases in aggregate demand in rural areas, but also potentially to losses from a labor supply shock in urban areas. (With respect to both patterns, please refer to chapter 4 for an in-depth exploration of rural and urban labor market interactions.)

Ethiopia

At the aggregate level, the data show a moderate increase in consumption in Ethiopia, of about 3 percent per log unit. This result is observed with both location FE and individual FE (though not in the IV models in table 3.10 later in this chapter). The aggregate welfare effect is strongly driven by changes in urban areas, where there is an estimated increase in consumption of about 7 percent for a doubling of the number of refugees hosted. This effect contrasts with a noisy and small positive coefficient of slightly less than 1 percent in rural areas. The difference between the effects in the two geographic areas is statistically significant. (Although there is some indication that gains may have been larger for women and among the better-educated, the two FE models do not agree.) The absence of an effect in rural areas is intuitive: tight restrictions on place of residence, movement, and employment as in Ethiopia make it hard for displaced workers to integrate into rural labor markets. Urban areas may offer more opportunities for participation that circumvent the restrictive rules and, thus, for labor market effects. Perhaps more important, urban areas are where some better-off refugees settle without participating in the labor market, with potential effects on demand for goods and services. It is worth noting that the magnitude of the effect is modest though meaningful: at the median, the number of refugees changed by 0.6 log unit between survey rounds, suggesting a rise in consumption of 4 percent for the median urban household over two years (table 3C.3 in online annex 3C).

Although there are few other sectoral correlates of consumption gains, increases are concentrated among households with wage workers. Among such households, the mean gain is about 7 percent for a doubling of the number of refugees, and the estimate is highly significant (it is estimated using a reasonable sample size of 600–700 wage workers per survey round). Among other households, the increase is about 3 percent, and is statistically significant, but is considerably lower than for those with some wage income. However, there is little indication of any change in total wage earnings, and it is worth recalling that wage work is the rare exception for Ethiopian workers (10 percent in both the 7-day and 12-month recall, across survey rounds).

Uganda

Consumption is at least weakly increased across host communities, reflecting the balance of significant increases in rural areas and potential losses in urban areas. Across the country, there is an estimated increase in consumption of about 2–3 percent associated with a doubling of the number of refugees hosted. With a limited sample size, the estimate is not always significant, but it is consistent in sign and approximate magnitude across models, including the IV model. This aggregate increase is clearly due to significant gains in rural areas, whereas the models estimate either no change or a marginally insignificant loss of 4 percent for urban areas. With median changes in the number of refugees of 0.1 log unit in rural areas, these gains are typically small, though some communities see more pronounced gains (table 3B.1 in annex 3B and table 3C.2 in online annex 3C). The pattern of gains arising in rural areas is highly consistent with other dimensions of positive labor market impacts in rural areas, as discussed further below.

Gains are widespread in rural areas, including for subsistence farmers and the poorest households. Workers across many different activities benefit from living in refugee-hosting areas. Thus, those active in subsistence farming are estimated to see their consumption rise by 3 percent, and the most consumption-poor households realize gains of 4 percent, weakly larger gains than others. As is intuitive, both characteristics correlate with rural residence, so gains among these groups partially account for the pronounced rural gains. It is notable that the point estimate of gains among the self-employed outside of agriculture is close to significantly lower than for other groups ($t = 1.5$) (table 3C.2 in online annex 3C). Without overinterpreting this weak pattern, it is worth considering whether added competition in nonagricultural activities may pose some challenges.

Commercial farmers and those they employ may benefit the most from hosting refugees. The data clearly suggest that rural welfare gains come in the context of greater commercial opportunities in agriculture, plausibly linked to increased product market demand. Although the gains for host communities are widespread, commercial farmers see particularly large gains, of 7 percent, with a doubling of the number of refugees, about twice the average among all rural households. The finding is corroborated by other patterns: among the few wage workers in agriculture, there are very large estimated wage income gains of about 17 percent for a doubling of the number of refugees, and there is a shift into agriculture among wage workers (as discussed later in the chapter). Further, another investigation by Kadigo and Maystadt (2023) using the same data source but somewhat different specifications identifies that workers who switched from subsistence farming to commercial farming saw benefits. This outcome is consistent with some strategic job mobility and job upgrading among hosts, in which workers seize the opportunity arising from product market demand on the part of the displaced as a new source of income that was not previously available. In the same study, the change in the type of farming activity is also reflected in higher total agricultural production, further supporting the idea that agriculture is a welfare-improving channel, especially in rural areas.

Gains among those active in commercial farming are consistent with higher product market demand due to the arrival of refugees and, in consequence, additional demand for workers in agriculture, outpacing the potential increase in labor supply in rural host communities. The gains are less consistent with a rise in profits for commercial farmers with the availability of additional labor given that such a mechanism would suggest lower sector wages and, thus, lower incomes for wage workers in agriculture. Although the estimated gains in commercial farming are quite large, they benefit only small segments of the labor force: at baseline, only 2 percent of households relied primarily on commercial farming, and merely 5 percent of the 11 percent of all workers who were wage workers were employed in agriculture activities. For the same reason, it is prudent to caution that the effect is estimated on a small sample of only a few dozen households per survey round.

Middle-income countries

There is no indication of aggregate losses in wage earnings in either Colombia or Jordan. With yearly data, the estimates for Colombia measure the short-run effect of hosting the displaced. The canonical model of migration predicts short-run losses in wages that dissipate over the longer run. It is therefore particularly noteworthy that the data show no indication of losses and a weak indication of gains in total earnings—the coefficient never has a negative sign and is significant in some models. Effects are small: the median change in the number of migrants is about 0.6 log unit, suggesting changes in earnings of less than 1 percent per year at the median (table 3B.1 in annex 3B). In Jordan, the estimates pertain to the medium to long term, with six years between survey rounds. There is no indication of an aggregate effect on wage earnings, with a limited indication of higher earnings among women in host communities in the individual effects model only. Although wage earnings necessarily provide only a partial picture of welfare impacts, wage employment is the norm in Jordan and the data do reflect welfare impacts among a large majority of workers.

In Colombia, workers in temporary employment lose out, perhaps because of higher labor supply, and those in agriculture do better than others, perhaps consistent with higher food sector demand. Although there are weakly positive effects on aggregate income, there is an observed 5 percent decline in wages among temporary workers. As discussed later in the chapter, this decline comes with a decrease in hourly wage rates for the same group. Note also that a point estimate of a 3 percent increase per log unit among workers in agriculture is just below significant ($t = 1.65$). The difference with other sectors, where estimates are centered on zero, is statistically significant. Prima facie, one could speculate whether this pattern may have been due, respectively, to higher labor supply for temporary work outside of agriculture and increased demand for agricultural products.

The data from Jordan show no significant effects in the aggregate, nor are there significant or even near-significant effects for any of the main subgroups analyzed (although the difference in impacts between temporary and wage workers is significant). Without interpreting any of the nonsignificant changes in subgroups, some are consistent in direction with statistically significant shifts in employment patterns reported later in the chapter. Thus, there is a decline in aggregate wage employment and an increase in temporary work for some groups, suggesting a transfer to less stable types of employment without clear changes in wages. Finally, sectoral patterns weakly suggest gains in agriculture; given the lack of significance, the finding is not noteworthy in isolation but perhaps worth pointing out in light of gains in the sector observed more clearly in Ethiopia and Uganda and the increase in agricultural work in Jordanian host communities reported later in the chapter.

Returns to labor: Wage per hour

Estimates suggest that gains in income are likely to reflect higher returns to labor, not simply "more work." Conceptually, hourly wages are a direct measure of productivity in an ideal labor market that is fully competitive and free of friction, if price differences have been properly accounted for. These assumptions do not hold in any of the labor markets studied here. Still, the contrast between hourly wages and hours worked provides a limited perspective on whether changes in earnings are likely to be related to changes in returns to labor or likely to reflect a change in time spent at work. In this context, the analysis notes that, as is evident in figure 3.1, the labor market groups considered here are more likely to experience a weak gain in hourly wages than a decline. Groups that experience gains in aggregate consumption or earnings generally show at least a weak rise in hourly wages (figure 3.2). At the same time, there is most often either a decrease or no change in time worked per week (refer to figure 3.5 later in the chapter) and in labor market participation. Together, both

FIGURE 3.1 Hourly wage (ln), main results, 7-day reference period, case study countries

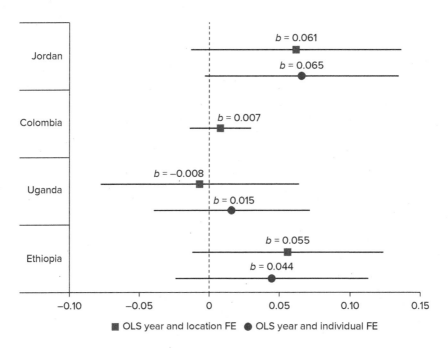

Source: Original figure for this report based on data from ERSS/ESS 2011–12, 2013–14, 2015–16, LSMS-ISA 2009–10, 2011, 2012, JLMPS 2010, 2016, and GEIH 2015, 2016, 2017, 2018, 2019. See table 3.1 for additional details.
Note: Coefficient estimates (*b*) and 95 percent confidence intervals shown. FE = fixed effects; OLS = ordinary least squares.

FIGURE 3.2 Hourly wage (ln), by gender, location, education, and age, 7-day reference period, case study countries

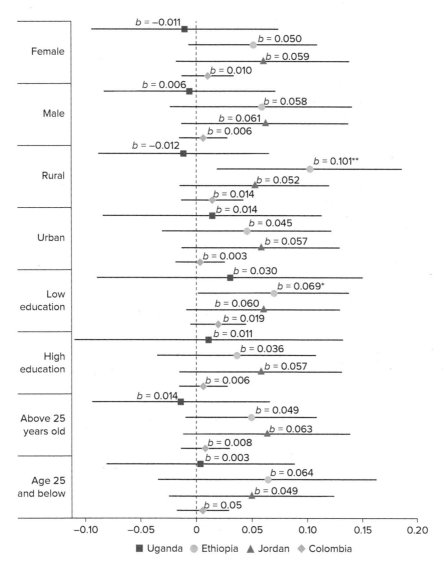

Source: Original figure for this report based on data from ERSS/ESS 2011–12, 2013–14, 2015–16, LSMS-ISA 2009–10, 2011, 2012, JLMPS 2010, 2016, and GEIH 2015, 2016, 2017, 2018, 2019. See table 3.1 for additional details.
Note: Coefficient estimates (b) are shown for each subgroup indicated on the category axis. Location and year fixed effects.
* $p < .10$, ** $p < .05$, *** $p < .01$.

findings point to higher returns to labor as a driver of welfare gains in communities that host refugees. For instance, in Ethiopia, consumption gains among households that rely on wage labor for most of their income come alongside a weak rise in hourly wages and a weak decline in time at work. In turn, such gains could be due to productivity increases, or to changes in output prices that are not fully captured in the data.

Context determines whether changes in hourly wages should best be thought of as being due to shifts in labor supply or to consumer demand. As noted, hosting displaced groups is chiefly expected to affect labor market outcomes through two channels: changes in labor supply and changes in product market demand. These two channels can also have some bearing on changes in hourly wages. Wage changes can reflect a shift in the balance of bargaining power toward employers, which would be expected to exert downward pressure on wages in host communities. The change could, however, also reflect productivity gains from increased demand in product markets, which would exert upward pressure.

Wage changes are inherently difficult to observe in the two LICs, with small wage employment sectors and, thus, small samples of wage data. The overall employment share of wage work (including the public sector) is 10 percent in Ethiopia and 11 percent in Uganda; wage data are available for 200–500 respondents per survey round in Ethiopia and 200–500 in Uganda.

In Colombia, much as is the case for total wage earnings, there is little indication of clear aggregate changes in hourly wages, with quite tightly estimated point estimates near zero (figure 3.1). Sectoral patterns at least weakly mirror those for total wage earnings: temporary workers experience a significant decrease in hourly wages of 4 percent per log unit, along with the decrease in total wage reported above, suggesting competitive pressure. Hourly wages in the agriculture sector are weakly higher in refugee-hosting communities, in line with total wage earnings (figure 3.3). On a technical note, data in Colombia could not be spatially deflated in the absence of a price index that covers all localities. It is therefore possible that host communities experience price changes that erode the observed wage gains. However, Delgado-Prieto (2022) shows that, within the available data, price levels do not correlate with whether communities host refugees, and thus provides prima facie evidence against such a possibility.

In Ethiopia, there is an overall impression of a rise in wages among hosts; however, with conservative standard errors, the effect is not statistically significant (figure 3.1). Such an increase would be consistent with welfare gains observed among wage workers. Though there are no statistically significant results in the preferred model in the aggregate, stable coefficients with moderate noise give a weak impression of an increase in hourly wages of about 5–6 percent for a doubling of the number of displaced persons hosted. There are significant increases among rural wage workers (10 percent), and less-educated workers (7 percent). Together

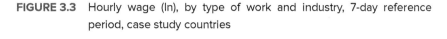

FIGURE 3.3 Hourly wage (ln), by type of work and industry, 7-day reference period, case study countries

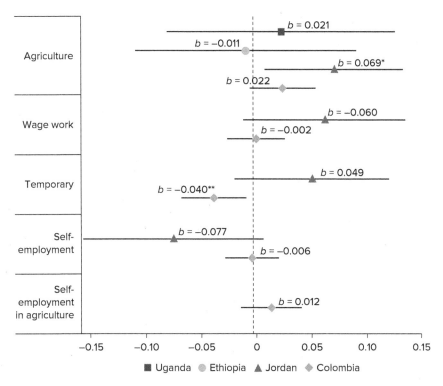

Source: Original figure for this report based on data from ERSS/ESS 2011–12, 2013–14, 2015–16, LSMS-ISA 2009–10, 2011, 2012, JLMPS 2010, 2016, and GEIH 2015, 2016, 2017, 2018, 2019. See table 3.1 for additional details.
Note: Coefficient estimates (*b*) are shown for each subgroup indicated on the category axis. Location and year fixed effects. Standard errors clustered at the administrative level (enumeration areas in Ethiopia and Uganda; departments in Colombia; and districts in Jordan). Weighted regressions. Controls include age, age squared, and gender. These results are also available in tables 3C.3 and 3C.4 in online annex 3C.
$* p < .10, ** p < .05, *** p < .01.$

with a weak indication of a reduction of hours worked among wage workers, the weak increase in hourly wages suggests that gains in consumption among families that rely on wage work are likely to have resulted from higher returns to labor. Recalling the welfare proxy results discussed earlier, it is a testament to the limited role of wage work that the productivity gains for rural wage workers do not translate into mean welfare gains in rural areas, whereas the absence of productivity gains for wage workers in urban areas does not preclude welfare gains.

There is a weak indication of an increase in overall wage levels in Jordan, along with clearer gains in agriculture. In both the OLS and the IV models, there is a weak indication of an aggregate increase in productivity (table 3D.1 in online annex 3D and figure 3.1). Those coefficients that are near significant are on the order of a 6 percent gain with a doubling of the number of refugees. Perhaps surprisingly, there are no clear correlates in terms of location, gender, and education (figure 3.2). There is, however, a significant increase in hourly wages among those active in agriculture of 7 percent per log unit. This effect corresponds to the weak pattern of gains in total wages in agriculture reported earlier, as well as to a shift of employment into the agriculture sector, as further discussed later.

There is no indication of changes in hourly wages in Uganda's small wage work sector. The data largely suggest that hourly wages in Uganda were unaffected by displacement, with no effect in the aggregate, and little indication of changes among the main subgroups. The sign of the estimated effect on hourly wages in agriculture is positive, consistent with gains in total wages in the sector as reported in figure 3.3, but the estimate is nowhere near significant. It is important to recall that wage work accounts for a small share of all jobs, and perhaps an even lower share of jobs that are susceptible to either increased competition in the labor market or higher consumer demand due to displacement.

Activity level: Employment, unemployment, and hours worked

This section assesses the impact of displacement on labor market activity among hosts. First, it considers whether there is any change in the share of the working-age population that is employed ("employment rate") or the share of the labor force that is unemployed ("unemployment rate"). These rates is sometimes referred to as the "extensive margin" of labor market participation. It is useful to note that the employment and unemployment rates, taken together, imply a third important measure of labor market engagement, namely the labor market participation rate (ratio of those employed and unemployed to the working-age population).[5] Second, the section also asks whether there is (among wage workers) a change in the number of hours worked, sometimes called the "intensive margin" of labor market participation. Higher participation in the labor market is most commonly viewed as desirable and indicative of the availability of work opportunities; however, depending on the context, it can also be interpreted as an indication of economic hardship forcing participation among workers who might have preferred domestic work, schooling, or retirement.

Whereas an influx of displaced workers might be expected to affect employment rates in an MIC context, there is little expectation of change in LICs. Arguably, labor markets in MICs can usefully be modeled with the canonical labor market model. It is therefore reasonable to suspect that a labor supply shock due to displacement might affect employment through low elasticity in labor demand and a resulting wage effect, in the context of meaningful reservation wages. By contrast, in LICs, much work is in self-employment and takes place in a context of very low (shadow) reservation wages. It is thus not clear that employment rates should be expected to react to a labor supply shock.

Potential impacts on the availability of work for hosts play a prominent role in policy makers' concerns about hosting refugees. However, across the four economies analyzed here, there is little evidence of an adverse impact, and none over the medium or longer term. Significant negative effects are observed only under some specifications in Colombia, where the measured effects should be interpreted as pertaining to the short run. In the economies in which medium-term outcomes (Ethiopia) and long-term outcomes (Jordan) are measured, there are no significant effects, whereas there are weak indications of short-term gains in Uganda.

Colombia

Host communities in Colombia experience a small increase in unemployment among men, youth, and less-educated workers. In the aggregate, there is limited evidence of changes in employment. One model indicates a small (0.4 percentage point) increase in unemployment (table 3.4) and a concomitant weak reduction in the employment rate (table 3.5). By way of contrast, as discussed in the section titled "Robustness," some other model specifications suggest a potential positive effect on employment This pattern is in line with the literature, which has found estimates of employment and unemployment effects to be sensitive to specification (Lebow, 2024; please see Chapter 1 for a full discussion). Despite the absence of an unambiguous aggregate effect, men and younger workers do experience a small and significant increase in unemployment of 0.6 percentage point and 0.9 percentage point, respectively, with a doubling of the number of refugees. A slightly larger decline in the employment rate (1.2 percentage points and 1.4 percentage points, respectively) suggests that there is also likely to be a small reduction in labor market participation among the same groups of workers. Among less-educated workers, there is a small (0.6 percentage point) increase in unemployment only. These effects are very small, given that the median change in the number of migrants is about 0.6 log unit. Thus, for the median male worker, the probability of being unemployed has increased by about 0.4 percentage point (although the impact may be larger in some communities that host many refugees) (refer to table 3B.1 in annex 3B).

In a further reflection of the limited impact of displacement on participation, there is no indication of a change in average work hours (figure 3.4). The data do show that those active in commerce and manufacturing see a significantly larger drop in time worked than other professional groups, and those in agriculture see larger gains (in the case of commerce, the effect is also individually significant) (figure 3.5). This sector pattern is consistent with patterns in earnings. However, the effect sizes are very small, with a change in hours of 1 percent or less per log unit. Similarly, temporary and self-employed workers

TABLE 3.4 Unemployment rate over correlates of gender, location, education, and age, Uganda, Columbia, and Jordan

	12 months		7 days			
	(1) Uganda		(2) Colombia		(3) Jordan	
Location and year fixed effects OLS						
Number of refugees (ln)	−0.003	(0.002)	0.004*	(0.002)	0.003	(0.005)
Observations	14,649	7,720	1,822,448			
Mean	0.02	0.17	0.11			
Individual and year fixed effects OLS						
Number of refugees (ln)	−0.004*	(0.002)			0.009	(0.008)
Observations	12,732		.		4,996	
Mean	0.01				0.11	
Margins of correlates, location and year fixed effects OLS						
Gender						
Number of refugees (ln)						
Female	−0.001	(0.002)	0.001	(0.003)	0.005	(0.007)
Male	−0.004**	(0.002)	0.006***	(0.002)	−0.004	(0.005)
Location						
Rural	−0.003	(0.002)	0.004	(0.002)	0.000	(0.006)
Urban	−0.000	(0.003)	0.004	(0.002)	−0.002	(0.005)
Education						
Low education	−0.004	(0.003)	0.006**	(0.002)	−0.003	(0.005)
High education	−0.003	(0.003)	0.003	(0.002)	−0.004	(0.006)
Age						
Above 25 years old	−0.003	(0.002)	0.003	(0.002)	−0.004	(0.005)
25 years old and below	−0.002	(0.002)	0.009***	(0.002)	0.001	(0.008)

Source: Original table for this report based on data from ERSS/ESS 2011–12, 2013–14, 2015–16, LSMS-ISA 2009–10, 2011, 2012, JLMPS 2010, 2016, and GEIH 2015, 2016, 2017, 2018, 2019. See table 3.1 for additional details.
Note: Standard errors clustered at the administrative level (enumeration areas in Ethiopia and Uganda; departments in Colombia; and districts in Jordan). Weighted regressions. Controls include age, age squared, and gender. OLS = ordinary least squares.
* $p < .10$, ** $p < .05$, *** $p < .01$.

both experience a significantly greater decrease in time at work than other groups, with differences of about 1 percent, although neither effect is individually significant. This finding could be viewed in light of welfare losses among temporary workers reported earlier and may suggest that more precarious types of work may have become less available as a result of the migrant inflow, perhaps because of increased competition.

TABLE 3.5 Employment rate over correlates of gender, location, education, and age, case study countries

	12 months				7 days			
	(1) Ethiopia		(2) Uganda		(3) Colombia		(4) Jordan	
Location and year fixed effects OLS								
Number of refugees (ln)	0.007	(0.008)	0.008	(0.006)	−0.004	(0.004)	0.002	(0.006)
Observations			16,908	26,491	2,476,744		18,424	
Mean			0.85	0.79	0.65		0.36	
Individual and year fixed effects OLS								
Number of refugees (ln)	0.006	(0.006)	0.000	(0.007)			0.004	(0.010)
Observations			15,124	20,828	.		15,172	
Mean			0.86	0.83			0.40	
Margins of correlates, location and year fixed effects OLS								
Gender								
Number of refugees (ln)								
Female	0.004	(0.009)	0.004	(0.006)	0.003	(0.007)	0.006	(0.006)
Male	0.010	(0.008)	0.013*	(0.007)	−0.012**	(0.005)	0.001	(0.006)
Location								
Rural	0.005	(0.004)	0.008	(0.006)	−0.006	(0.006)	−0.004	(0.007)
Urban	0.013	(0.020)	0.010	(0.010)	−0.003	(0.004)	0.000	(0.006)
Education								
Low education	0.008	(0.007)	−0.004	(0.008)	−0.005	(0.005)	0.003	(0.006)
High education	0.006	(0.012)	−0.010	(0.008)	−0.003	(0.005)	0.002	(0.006)
Age								
Above 25 years old	0.007	(0.008)	0.013**	(0.007)	−0.001	(0.004)	0.003	(0.006)
25 years old and below	0.007	(0.009)	0.002	(0.007)	−0.014**	(0.005)	0.002	(0.007)

Source: Original table for this report based on data from ERŚS/ESS 2011–12, 2013–14, 2015–16, LSMS-ISA 2009–10, 2011, 2012, JLMPS 2010, 2016, and GEIH 2015, 2016, 2017, 2018, 2019. See table 3.1 for additional details.
Note: Standard errors clustered at the administrative level (enumeration areas in Ethiopia and Uganda; departments in Colombia; and districts in Jordan). Weighted regressions. Controls include age, age squared, and gender. OLS = ordinary least squares.
* $p < .10$, ** $p < .05$, *** $p < .01$.

FIGURE 3.4   Work hours per week (ln), main results, 7-day reference period, case study countries

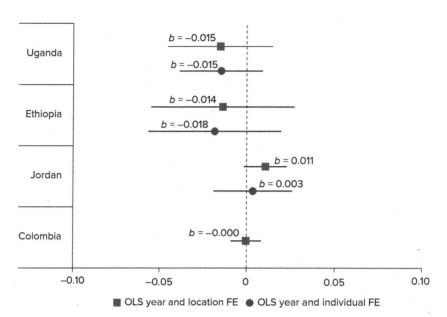

Source: Original figure for this report based on data from ERSS/ESS 2011–12, 2013–14, 2015–16, LSMS-ISA 2009–10, 2011, 2012, JLMPS 2010, 2016, and GEIH 2015, 2016, 2017, 2018, 2019. See table 3.1 for additional details.
Note: Coefficient estimates (b) are shown for each subgroup indicated on the category axis. Location and year fixed effects. FE = fixed effects; OLS = ordinary least squares.

Ethiopia

As is to be expected, there is no indication of a change in the aggregate employment rate in Ethiopia; coefficients show noisy estimates near zero, with a changing sign. Nor is there much indication of a change when standard disaggregations are made (table 3.5). Because of the structure of the Ethiopia data, unemployment cannot be observed, although unemployment is generally rare in countries of Ethiopia's income level (2.3 percent in 2012 according to the International Labour Organization's estimates); however, because the overall labor market impacts suggest that effects are concentrated among wealthier urban workers, it is not impossible that there might be an effect. Given the absence of a change in the employment rate, however, any increase in unemployment would be driven by an increase in labor force participation.

There is no significant change in time at work among wage workers, with the exception of the few rural wage workers, among whom there is a decrease. Data on time at work are available only for wage workers. Among this limited group, the estimated effect consistently has a negative sign but is almost never significant across subgroups. The exceptions are an estimated 11 percent decrease among the few wage workers in rural areas, among whom, as noted earlier, there are estimated productivity gains (figure 3.5).

FIGURE 3.5   Work hours per week (ln), by type of work and industry, 7-day reference period, case study countries

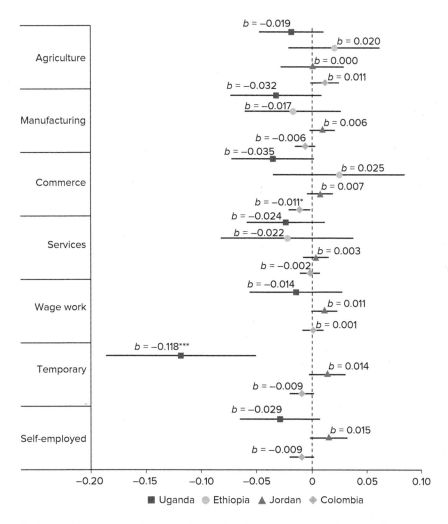

Source: Original figure for this report based on data from ERSS/ESS 2011–12, 2013–14, 2015–16, LSMS-ISA 2009–10, 2011, 2012, JLMPS 2010, 2016, and GEIH 2015, 2016, 2017, 2018, 2019. See table 3.1 for additional details.
Note: Coefficient estimates (**b**) are shown for each subgroup indicated on the category axis. Location and year fixed effects. Standard errors clustered at the administrative level (enumeration areas in Ethiopia and Uganda; departments in Colombia; and districts in Jordan). Weighted regressions. Controls include age, age squared, and gender. These results are also available in tables 3C.5 and 3C.6 in online annex 3C. * $p < .10$, ** $p < .05$, *** $p < .01$.

Jordan

There is no suggestion of an increase in unemployment in Jordan, and only a limited indication of a reduction in time worked for those outside of wage employment. The estimates of longer-term effects in Jordan suggest no impact of hosting refugees on employment or unemployment rates, either in the aggregate or in subgroups. In both the 7-day and 3-month recall data, the sign of point estimates varies, and the estimates are never close to significant. Nor are there subgroup effects that appear consistently across models. The data suggest no aggregate change in time worked per week and offer evidence of increases among women and, arguably, a pattern of weak increases among most subgroups analyzed (figures 3.4 and 3.6).

Uganda

There is little indication that employment rates have shifted in Uganda, with some weak suggestions of a gain. In the 7-day recall data, there is no indication of any change in the employment or unemployment rates.[6] The 12-month data occasionally suggest an increase in employment (table 3.5) and decrease in unemployment (table 3.4); the estimates are consistent in sign and occasionally significant. There is more indication of gains among men than among women over both recall periods. With the sparse significance patterns, not much can be said about the magnitude of estimated effects; however, the coefficients do roughly suggest that effects are not large: an increase in the employment rate of not more than 1 percentage point with a doubling of the number of refugees, and a decline in unemployment of not more than half a percentage point.

Time worked per week has declined in urban areas and among temporary workers. There is a consistent but weak indication in the aggregate of a small decrease in time worked (1 percent or less), driven by a larger and significant decline of work time in urban areas of 9 percent (data are available for all types of work, not only wage work) (figure 3.6). As shown earlier, this decline comes in the context of some welfare losses in urban areas, further reinforcing the impression of heightened labor market competition. Perhaps tellingly, it can also be decomposed into a marked decrease in work time among temporary workers (12 percent), again plausibly resulting from an increase in labor supply (figure 3.4). This estimate rests, however, on a relatively small subsample of about a few dozen per survey round.

Sector and type of employment

Shifts in the sectors in which workers are active and in the type of employment they have are indications of changes in the structure of the local economy caused by displacement. The shares of workers active in different economic sectors are indicative of changes in the relative importance of different economic activities. Such shifts could arise from changes in consumer demand as well as through changes in the price of labor that affect sectors differently. Type of work—wage employment or self-employment—similarly reflects changes in the structure of

FIGURE 3.6 Work hours per week (ln), by gender, location, education, and consumption quintiles, 7-day reference period, case study countries

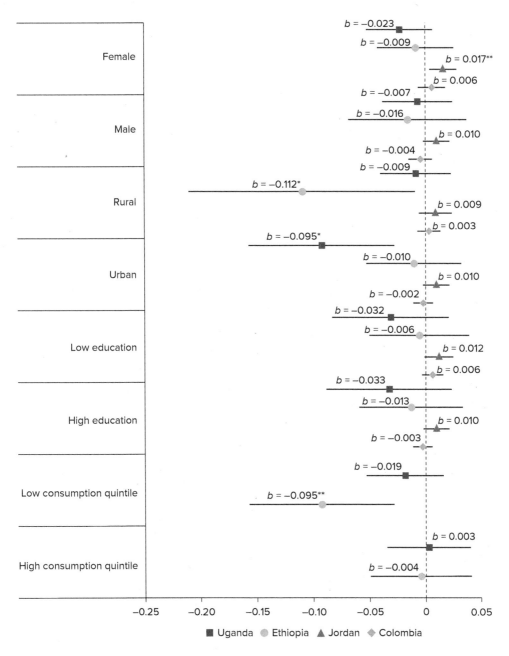

Source: Original figure for this report based on data from ERSS/ESS 2011–12, 2013–14, 2015–16, LSMS-ISA 2009–10, 2011, 2012, JLMPS 2010, 2016, and GEIH 2015, 2016, 2017, 2018, 2019. See table 3.1 for additional details.
Note: Coefficient estimates (*b*) are shown for each subgroup indicated on the category axis. Location and year fixed effects.

the economy, namely the prevalence of different types of economic actors. Note that the delineation between sector and type of employment is less than crisp in LICs; specifically, there is typically little wage employment in agriculture. The prevalence of work in the formal sector, which the study also considers, is of limited practical importance in LICs, where formal employment is typically limited to the most well-off workers (no data are available in Ethiopia), but it is a meaningful dimension of the type of work available in MICs.

Shifts in sector and type of activity across the four economies largely mirror welfare gains and suggest a tendency toward adaptation to the opportunities and challenges that result from refugee arrival. For instance, the gains observed among those in host communities who are active in agriculture go hand in hand with sectoral shifts into agriculture—potentially a move toward opportunity. In Jordan, weak welfare losses for wage workers come alongside a shift out of wage employment, potentially a move away from competition.

In addition to assessing shifts in individual workers' activities, the investigation also considers changes in the activity baskets of households. This analysis first captures an element of the qualitative importance of changes. Thus, where households begin to change the sector they rely on for their main income source, the shift may be "deeper" than where individual workers change what they do. Conversely, worker-level sector changes may overstate shifts in the economic structure. Second, there is a pragmatic reason for adding this dimension of analysis that arises from the limitations of the data: in Ethiopia, the traditional sector breakdown of the activities of individual workers is available only for wage workers, so the results from these data pertain only to a thin and possibly quite privileged stratum of the labor market. The household-level analysis allows for a broader picture of the importance of different sectors.

This study tries to distinguish between regular salaried work and more casual work as a paid employee, but the distinction is not easy to make in the data. The concept of "wage employment" commonly evokes notions of full-time paid work for established businesses. However, surveys tend to conceive of the employment category more broadly, and define it simply as "paid work for someone outside of the worker's household." This broad definition encompasses regular salaried work of the kind the term wage employment brings to mind, but it also includes temporary employment in casual business activities, as well as work as a day laborer. That is, it spans the range from some of the most desirable jobs—regular salaried work for formal businesses or the government—to daily labor, perhaps the most precarious work. This analysis tries to distinguish to the degree possible between more regular wage work and temporary work or daily labor. However, the data are not designed to capture this distinction, and it must be kept in mind that different types of work may be subsumed under wage employment.

With the limited data available, this study attempts to differentiate between work in agriculture that is more geared toward producing for the market and work that is less so. Work in agriculture in lower-income countries spans a wide range, from pure subsistence farming to fully commercial farming. Because activities differ meaningfully in their degree of market orientation, the analysis tries to provide some perspective. Although the available data distinguish subsistence farmers from other farming households, analysis suggests that the term should not be taken literally because many households considered "subsistence" farmers likely sell at least some products in the market. Rather, the two categories are interpreted as reflecting degrees of market orientation so that, for those considered subsistence farmers, market activities play a lesser role than for other farming households.

Colombia

There is some indication of small shifts in aggregate employment from manufacturing to services in Colombia, but effects are small and estimates not very robust. Although the preferred specification shows no significant change in manufacturing employment, some other models suggest a small decline. There is mixed evidence on whether this decline was accompanied by an increase in employment in commerce (table 3C.11 in online annex 3C) or employment in other services (table 3C.12 in online annex 3C). However, in line with the short-run nature of the impact estimate, these are very small shifts, between 0.05 and 0.10 percentage point per 10,000 migrants hosted, with a median change in the number of migrants of 8,200 (tables 3B.1 and 3B.2) in annex 3B. Meaningful impacts are therefore likely to have occurred only in the communities with the largest inflows of migrants.

Disaggregation consistently suggests that, for certain segments of the labor force, there have been small shifts in the relative importance of agriculture on the one hand and commerce and other services on the other. The increase in commerce and other services is concentrated in rural areas and among men, less-educated workers, and those who are not self-employed. By way of contrast, in urban centers, among women, and among more-educated workers and self-employed workers, there is an increase in work in agriculture (table 3.6). There are also shifts in the types of jobs that mirror these sector changes and their correlates; for instance, self-employment in agriculture is up among more-educated workers but down among the less-educated (table 3C.9 in online annex 3C). These shifts are again mostly small—no more than 1 percentage point per log unit—though some shifts among the self-employed are larger (table 3.7), with a 4 percentage point increase in the agriculture share and an equivalent shift out of other activities per log unit.

Workers in host communities experience a modest increase in formality, again favoring those with regular salaried jobs over those in temporary employment. In the aggregate, there is a small increase in the share of formal jobs, by 0.4 percentage point per log unit from a base of about 40 percent (table 3C.7 in online annex 3C). This increase is concentrated among wage workers

TABLE 3.6 Share of agricultural workers, by gender, location, education, and type of work, case study countries

	12 months				7 days			
	(1) Ethiopia		(2) Uganda		(3) Colombia		(4) Jordan	
Location and year fixed effects OLS								
Number of refugees (ln)	0.012	(0.007)	0.007*	(0.004)	−0.001	(0.002)	0.011**	(0.005)
Observations	2,905		12,956		1,620,616		6,483	
Mean	0.04		0.71		0.07		0.05	
Individual and year fixed effects OLS								
Number of refugees (ln)	0.017	(0.016)	0.008	(0.006)			0.002	(0.004)
Observations	1,616		10,874				4,074	
Mean	0.05		0.71				0.03	
Margins of correlates, location and year fixed effects OLS								
Gender								
Number of refugees (ln)								
Female	0.012	(0.009)	0.007	(0.004)	0.016**	(0.006)	0.004	(0.005)
Male	0.011	(0.008)	0.008	(0.005)	−0.012***	(0.004)	0.011**	(0.005)
Location								
Rural	0.001	(0.003)	0.003	(0.005)	−0.010	(0.007)	0.022***	(0.008)
Urban	0.013	(0.008)	0.055***	(0.016)	0.007**	(0.003)	0.014***	(0.004)
Education								
Low education	0.011	(0.012)	0.005	(0.008)	−0.028***	(0.008)	0.010**	(0.004)
High education	0.011	(0.007)	0.010	(0.008)	0.009**	(0.004)	0.011**	(0.005)
Wage workers								
Wage workers			0.027***	(0.006)	0.020***	(0.007)	0.012**	(0.005)
Other than wage workers			0.000	(0.003)	−0.025***	(0.006)	0.004	(0.004)
Self-employed								
Self-employed			0.025***	(0.006)	0.043***	(0.009)	0.007	(0.005)
Other than self-employed			0.006*	(0.004)	−0.013***	(0.004)	0.011**	(0.005)

Source: Original table for this report based on data from ERSS/ESS 2011–12, 2013–14, 2015–16, LSMS-ISA 2009–10, 2011, 2012, JLMPS 2010, 2016, and GEIH 2015, 2016, 2017, 2018, 2019. See table 3.1 for additional details.
Note: Standard errors clustered at the administrative level (enumeration areas in Ethiopia and Uganda; departments in Colombia; and districts in Jordan). Weighted regressions. Controls include age, age squared, and gender. OLS = ordinary least squares.
* $p < .10$, ** $p < .05$, *** $p < .01$.

TABLE 3.7 Share of self-employed workers, by gender, location, education, age, and employment in agriculture and services, case study countries

	12 months				7 days			
	(1) Ethiopia		(2) Uganda		(3) Colombia		(4) Jordan	
Location and year fixed effects OLS								
Number of refugees (ln)	−0.006	(0.011)	0.002	(0.004)	0.008**	(0.003)	0.005	(0.010)
Observations	20,972		13,149		1,620,616		6,544	
Mean	0.58		0.18		0.43		0.12	
Individual and year fixed effects OLS								
Number of refugees (ln)	−0.004	(0.010)	0.004	(0.005)			0.009	(0.009)
Observations	15,596		11,087				4,148	
Mean	0.58		0.19				0.10	
Margins of correlates, location and year fixed effects OLS								
Gender								
Number of refugees (ln)								
Female	−0.003	(0.011)	0.009*	(0.005)	−0.004	(0.005)	−0.005	(0.009)
Male	−0.009	(0.012)	−0.005	(0.005)	0.016***	(0.004)	0.005	(0.010)
Location								
Rural	0.004	(0.009)	0.003	(0.004)	0.015**	(0.007)	−0.003	(0.010)
Urban	0.012	(0.011)	−0.017**	(0.008)	0.003	(0.004)	0.001	(0.009)
Education								
Low education	−0.007	(0.011)	0.001	(0.007)	0.025***	(0.006)	0.008	(0.010)
High education	−0.003	(0.011)	0.004	(0.008)	0.000	(0.004)	0.004	(0.009)
Age								
Above 25 years old	−0.009	(0.011)	0.003	(0.004)	0.008**	(0.003)	0.005	(0.010)
25 years old and below	0.001	(0.011)	0.001	(0.005)	0.006	(0.006)	0.003	(0.011)
Agriculture								
Agriculture			0.005	(0.004)	0.007	(0.008)	0.003	(0.013)
Other than agriculture			0.001	(0.006)	0.007*	(0.004)	0.002	(0.009)
Services								
Services			−0.020***	(0.008)	−0.009	(0.006)	0.005	(0.010)
Other than services			0.003	(0.004)	0.019***	(0.005)	0.004	(0.010)

Source: Original table for this report based on data from ERSS/ESS 2011–12, 2013–14, 2015–16, LSMS-ISA 2009–10, 2011, 2012, JLMPS 2010, 2016, and GEIH 2015, 2016, 2017, 2018, 2019. See table 3.1 for additional details.
Note: Standard errors clustered at the administrative level (enumeration areas in Ethiopia and Uganda; departments in Colombia; and districts in Jordan). Weighted regressions. Controls include age, age squared, and gender. OLS = ordinary least squares.
* $p < .10$, ** $p < .05$, *** $p < .01$.

(1.3 percentage points), whereas there is a decline in formality among temporary workers (3.4 percentage points) and the self-employed (2.8 percentage points). It thus adds a qualitative dimension to the pattern of wage gains and losses among regular and temporary paid employees. It further adds to the puzzle of why, in a relatively open labor market, losses are highly concentrated in more tenuous jobs. Given the slight decline in both labor force participation and wage work among men, it is possible that the increase in formality is at least partially due to the exit of workers from the informal economy and informal wage jobs. Because the data do not have a panel structure, this hypothesis cannot be directly tested.

Ethiopia

There are few indications of structural changes caused by displacement in Ethiopia, in line with a high degree of labor market insulation. Perhaps the clearest indication of a change is a 1 percentage point increase in the share of host households that rely on subsistence farming (with weak results with the same sign in the IV models) (table 3.8 and table 3D.5 in online annex 3D). There is also a suggestion of a small (1 percentage point per log unit) increase in the share of agriculture work in wage employment (table 3.6) and a decrease in agriculture self-employment in urban areas (table 3C.9 in online annex 3C).

TABLE 3.8   Households' main earnings source, Ethiopia and Uganda

	Commercial farming		Subsistence Farming		Wage Workers	
	(1) Ethiopia	(2) Uganda	(3) Ethiopia	(4) Uganda	(5) Ethiopia	(6) Uganda
Location and year fixed effects OLS						
Number of refugees (ln)	0.001	0.003***	0.012**	0.032***	−0.003	−0.025***
	(0.008)	(0.001)	(0.006)	(0.007)	(0.004)	(0.007)
Observations	10,182	5,665	10,182	5,665	10,182	5,665
Mean	0.07	0.02	0.09	0.50	0.14	0.17
Individual and year fixed effects OLS						
Number of refugees (ln)	0.001	0.002**	0.011*	0.026***	−0.003	−0.020***
	(0.008)	(0.001)	(0.006)	(0.006)	(0.004)	(0.006)
Observations	9,718	5,597	9,718	5,597	9,718	5,597
Mean	0.07	0.02	0.09	0.51	0.13	0.16

Source: Original table for this report based on data from ERSS/ESS 2011–12, 2013–14, 2015–16, LSMS-ISA 2009–10, 2011, 2012, JLMPS 2010, 2016, and GEIH 2015, 2016, 2017, 2018, 2019. See table 3.1 for additional details.
Note: Standard errors clustered at the administrative level (enumeration areas in Ethiopia and Uganda). Weighted regressions. Controls include age, age squared, and gender. OLS = ordinary least squares.
* $p < .10$, ** $p < .05$, *** $p < .01$.

Taken at face value, these changes might suggest heightened engagement in farming activities that are either highly market linked (and employ wage labor) or mostly subsistence oriented, with less engagement in activities that fall between the two extremes in terms of their market orientation. However, the shifts are quite small and are not reflected in welfare patterns. In addition, unlike in the case of Uganda, there are few corroborating pieces of evidence that would help solidify the impression of changes in the sector.

Whereas the 7-day recall data may indicate a decline in the share of wage work, the 12-month data do not confirm it. Among the activities of wage employees, the data suggest a decline in the share of manufacturing among rural wage workers by 9 percentage points for a doubling of the number of refugees (table 3C.10 in online annex C), with a weak indication of a compensating increase in services (table 3C.12 in online annex 3C).

Jordan

Work in host communities in Jordan has shifted out of wage employment. Aggregate effects indicate a shift out of wage employment of roughly 2 percentage points for a doubling of the number of refugees hosted (table 3.9). The pattern is broadly observed across groups, but the effect is weakly larger among men and among younger and less-educated workers. Among younger workers, there is also an indication that the shift out of wage employment goes hand in hand with an increase in temporary employment (table 3C.8 in online annex 3C).

In the aggregate, there is some evidence that displacement has caused a modest sectoral shift into agriculture (table 3.6), and (weakly) out of services (table 3C.12 in online annex 3C), especially among men (the shift out of services is also concentrated among wage workers). In agriculture, the analysis finds an increase in formal labor, contrasting with a weak decline in formal labor in services, a pattern that may suggest a services market more pressured by the refugee inflow (table 3C.7 in online annex 3C).

Uganda

Consistent with welfare and productivity gains in the food sector, household-level data in Uganda show a shift of job strategies from wage employment into agriculture. In a finding consistent with the apparent benefits to agriculture in host communities, there is clear evidence of a 2–3 percentage point shift of household job strategies to reliance on subsistence farming (significant in the fixed effects, consistent in sign and magnitude in the IV models and occasionally significant) (table 3.8 and table 3D.5 in online annex 3D). As noted, the notion of subsistence farming is best interpreted as "farming with limited market orientation" rather than "farming with no market orientation." It is offset by a 2 percentage point decline in reliance on wage employment.

TABLE 3.9 Share of wage workers, by gender, location, education, age, and employment in agriculture and services, case study countries

	12 months				7 days			
	(1) Ethiopia		(2) Uganda		(3) Colombia		(4) Jordan	
Location and year fixed effects OLS								
Number of refugees (ln)	−0.001	(0.001)	−0.004	(0.004)	−0.007	(0.004)	−0.023*	(0.011)
Observations	20,972		12,703		1,620,616		6,544	
Mean	0.14		0.11		0.44		0.75	
Individual and year fixed effects OLS								
Number of refugees (ln)	0.003	(0.002)	−0.002	(0.003)			−0.018	(0.015)
Observations	15,596		10,619				4,148	
Mean	0.14		0.09				0.78	
Number of refugees (ln)								
Margins of correlates, location and year fixed effects OLS								
Gender								
Female	−0.004*	(0.002)	−0.009*	(0.005)	−0.010*	(0.005)	−0.011	(0.013)
Male	0.003	(0.002)	0.000	(0.005)	−0.005	(0.004)	−0.023*	(0.012)
Location								
Rural	−0.000	(0.002)	−0.004	(0.004)	−0.005	(0.009)	−0.006	(0.011)
Urban	−0.002	(0.002)	0.000	(0.010)	−0.009**	(0.004)	−0.017	(0.011)
Education								
Low education	−0.001	(0.002)	−0.006	(0.006)	−0.004	(0.005)	−0.030**	(0.011)
High education	0.002	(0.006)	−0.012*	(0.006)	−0.007	(0.004)	−0.020*	(0.010)
Age								
Above 25 years old	0.001	(0.002)	−0.006	(0.004)	−0.008*	(0.004)	0.021*	(0.011)
25 years old and below	−0.003	(0.004)	0.000	(0.005)	0.001	(0.008)	0.032**	(0.012)
Agriculture								
Agriculture			−0.004	(0.004)	0.003	(0.012)	−0.003	(0.018)
Other than agriculture			0.000	(0.007)	−0.009**	(0.004)	−0.016	(0.011)
Services								
Services			−0.002	(0.007)	−0.022***	(0.005)	−0.021*	(0.012)
Other than services			−0.005	(0.004)	0.004	(0.005)	−0.022*	(0.013)

Source: Original table for this report based on data from ERSS/ESS 2011–12, 2013–14, 2015–16, LSMS-ISA 2009–10, 2011, 2012, JLMPS 2010, 2016, and GEIH 2015, 2016, 2017, 2018, 2019. See table 3.1 for additional details.
Note: Standard errors clustered at the administrative level (enumeration areas in Ethiopia and Uganda; departments in Colombia; and districts in Jordan). Weighted regressions. Controls include age, age squared, and gender. OLS = ordinary least squares.
* $p < .10$, ** $p < .05$, *** $p < .01$.

Models disagree on whether it is concentrated in rural areas only or observed in both urban and rural settings.

Although models do not always agree, worker-level data further suggest a move from services into agriculture, particularly in urban areas. In addition to the increase in wage employment in agriculture reported in the discussion of welfare effects, worker-level data also suggest that, in host communities, there is a small overall increase in the prevalence of any work in agriculture, by about 1 percentage point (table 3.6). The effect is concentrated in urban areas (6 percentage points) and matched by a decrease in services (5 percentage points) (table 3C.12 in online annex 3C). This pattern is also reflected in an increase in urban self-employed work in agriculture of 2 percentage points (table 3C.9 in online annex 3C) offset by a 2 percentage point decline in other self-employment (table 3.7). Given the welfare losses in urban areas, this shift may reflect adaptation to heightened labor market competition in services.

Robustness

To further bolster the reliability of the empirical results shown above, this section shows robustness to using different estimation strategies and model specifications, and to allowing for local effects in communities with a high number of refugees.

Comparing OLS FE and IV results

The analysis in this chapter uses a range of statistical methods to provide complementary perspectives on the labor market impacts of displacement. As explained in the technical discussion in the section titled "Methods," two statistical methods are used to estimate results for this chapter, namely an IV model and an OLS FE approach. Estimates from the two approaches have complementary strengths and weaknesses in this investigation. IV estimates can provide reassurance that apparent impacts are not due to refugees settling preferentially in localities that experience different economic trends than other localities. Such bias would arise, for instance, if refugees systematically prefer to settle in localities with particularly strong economic growth. Conversely, OLS FE estimates are more suitable when there is reason to believe that job outcomes in localities close to borders with refugee-sending countries are different from other localities in ways that do not relate to forced displacement, for instance, because of trade disruptions or because investment in these localities is perceived as being risky. OLS FE estimates are also less sensitive to the way the empirical model is specified.

In describing results, this chapter always considers whether different methods conform; this section provides a direct comparison between OLS FE and IV results. Measuring the labor market impacts of forced displacement is difficult because no single econometric method accounts fully for all alternative explanations of the observed patterns. Therefore, the analysis in this chapter is based on looking side by side at estimates derived from different approaches—those that come from an IV and an OLS FE approach, and those that are obtained by using more- and less-restrictive fixed effects. For tractability, the chapter does not show all results; however, the results sections flag instances in which estimates disagree to a meaningful extent. For ease of reference, tables 3.10 and 3.11 provide examples of how results obtained from the different approaches

TABLE 3.10 Welfare: Consumption per adult equivalent (ln) and monthly wages (ln), case study countries

	Consumption p.a.e. (ln), 12 months				Monthly wage (ln), 7 days					
	Number of refugees (ln)				Number of migrants (ln)				Number of migrants (10,000)	
	(1) Ethiopia		(2) Uganda		(3) Jordan		(4) Colombia		(5) Colombia	
Location and year fixed effects OLS										
	0.030*	(0.015)	0.026**	(0.012)	−0.009	(0.024)	0.006	(0.013)	0.002**	(0.001)
Observations	9,758		5,990		5,499		1,324,077		1,324,077	
Mean	7.91		10.79		5.81		13.43		13.43	
Location and year fixed effects IV										
	−0.003	(0.075)	0.022	(0.043)	−0.050	(0.030)			0.003**	(0.001)
Observations	9,758		5,990		5,499				1,324,077	
KP statistic	4		24		10				12	
Individual and year fixed effects OLS										
	0.029*	(0.015)	0.018	(0.014)	0.016	(0.027)				
Observations	8,968		5,981		3,268					
Mean	7.90		10.79		5.86					
Individual and year fixed effects IV										
	−0.003	(0.076)	0.054*	(0.032)	−0.001	(0.035)				
Observations	8,968		5,981		3,268					
KP statistic	4		23		5					

Source: Original table for this report based on data from ERSS/ESS 2011–12, 2013–14, 2015–16, LSMS-ISA 2009–10, 2011, 2012, JLMPS 2010, 2016, and GEIH 2015, 2016, 2017, 2018, 2019. See table 3.1 for additional details.
Note: Note that, in Colombia, the IV model cannot be estimated in log-log form because of the definition of the instrument. To facilitate comparison, results are shown in log-log as well as in log-level form as possible. Fixed effects as indicated. IV = instrumental variables; OLS = ordinary least squares; p.a.e. = per adult equivalent.
* $p < .10$, ** $p < .05$, *** $p < .01$.

TABLE 3.11 Employment, case study countries

	Number of refugees (ln) 12 months				Number of migrants (ln) 7 days				Number of migrants (10,000) 7 days	
	(1) Ethiopia		(2) Uganda		(3) Jordan		(4) Colombia		(5) Colombia	
Location and year fixed effects OLS										
	0.007	(0.008)	0.008	(0.006)	0.002	(0.006)	0.004	(0.004)	0.000	(0.001)
Observations	26,491		16,908		18,424	2,476,744			2,476,744	
Mean	0.79		0.85		0.36	0.65			0.65	
Location and year fixed effects IV										
	0.003	(0.030)	0.039**	(0.018)	−0.005	(0.010)			0.000	(0.001)
Observations	26,491		16,908		18,424				2,476,744	
KP statistic	3		24		10				11	
Individual and year fixed effects OLS										
	0.006	(0.006)	0.000	(0.007)	0.004	(0.010)				
Observations	20,828		15,124		15,172					
Mean	0.83		0.86		0.40					
Individual and year fixed effects IV										
	−0.003	(0.033)	0.029*	(0.017)	−0.010	(0.017)				
Observations	26,266		16,895		15,172					
KP statistic	4		24		5					

Source: Original table for this report based on data from ERSS/ESS 2011–12, 2013–14, 2015–16, LSMS-ISA 2009–10, 2011, 2012, JLMPS 2010, 2016, and GEIH 2015, 2016, 2017, 2018, 2019. See table 3.1 for additional details.
Note: Note that, in Colombia, the IV model cannot be estimated in log-log form due to the definition of the instrument. To facilitate comparison, results are shown in log-log as well as in log-level form as possible. IV = instrumental variables; OLS = ordinary least squares.

compare, both for the two proxy measures of welfare and for employment. The supporting tables for this section are tables 3D.1 through 3D.13 in online annex 3D.

The key observation from the comparison of results based on the two methods is that, although they sometimes do not agree on whether there is an effect, they never disagree on the direction of effects (technically, the two methods never yield results with a different sign that are both statistically significant). Most of the time, there is little qualitative difference between the estimates, even when patterns of statistical significance vary. For instance, in table 3.10, both methods agree on the direction and magnitude of the effect on earnings in Colombia, and, although significance patterns vary, the estimates of effects on consumption in Uganda are similar in magnitude and direction. However, there are some meaningful differences. For instance, the OLS FE approach suggests that host communities enjoyed consumption gains in Ethiopia, whereas the IV approach suggests that there was no change. Conversely, for instance, the IV approach suggests that employment rose in host communities in Uganda, whereas the OLS FE model shows no change. (In the other countries, neither approach shows an effect, with estimates centered near zero in both.)

Checks for robustness to changes in the empirical approach

Studying the ways that displacement affects job outcomes for hosts requires making a number of choices in the way the data are analyzed, which could have a bearing upon the results. This section explores whether results are robust when the definition of the treatment is changed, when controls for distance to the nearest border are included or excluded, and when the investigation works with a sparse or a broader set of individual-level controls. The supporting tables for this section are tables 3E.1 to 3E.5 in online annex 3E.

- *Proportion of refugees in the labor force as the treatment.* In the literature on the labor market impact of displacement and migration, it is common to work with the proportion of displaced or migrant workers in the local labor force as the treatment variable. By way of contrast, this study works with the (log) number of displaced workers. This choice was made because it is difficult to determine the size of the labor force in the spatially explicit data used in Ethiopia and Uganda without aggregating the data to the level of administrative units and thereby discarding much information—and because the fixed effects included in the model account for static differences in the size of the labor force. However, it can still be argued that the preferred model does not account for differences in the growth of the host labor force between localities. The study therefore assesses robustness to using the proportion of refugees among the labor force as the treatment.

- *Omitting controls for distance to the nearest border.* The preferred model controls for distance between each locality and the nearest border and allows the effect of distance to vary for each year of data. As noted, proximity to a border and to refugee-sending areas could affect job outcomes not only through the arrival of displaced workers but also through other phenomena, such as disruptions in trade or changes in risk perceptions. Without controlling for distance to the border, such effects may erroneously be attributed to the impact of hosting refugees. Conversely, however, it can also be argued that controlling for distance risks removing from the study of the impact of displacement some variation in the locality choice of refugees that is not driven by different economic trends: refugees may stay in border areas because they are close to home, whereas they may move to other localities because the economy is thriving there. If this were the case, including a control for distance would weaken the causal interpretation of results. (This trade-off mirrors the challenges in both the OLS FE and IV approaches pointed out above.) Because of these dueling issues, the analysis explores robustness to omitting controls.

- *Control for additional individual characteristics.* The preferred specification is parsimonious in controls because many worker characteristics that could influence outcomes (such as education or family structure) may also be influenced by hosting refugees; in technical terms, they are potentially endogenous. As is well-known, including such variables causes a "bad control" problem and biases results. Rather than specifying a broad set of regressors, this analysis therefore relies on fixed effects to account for unobserved characteristics of workers, including the aggressive individual-level fixed effects. However, fixed effects do not capture characteristics that vary in time. In addition, the use of fixed effects is less convincing in Colombia, where the study cannot account for individual-level effects. Therefore, the analysis shows robustness to including a broader set of controls, namely household size and parents' education.

Results from all robustness checks on all aggregate checks are shown in tables 3E.1 through 3E.5 in online annex 3E. Encouragingly, findings are largely robust to changes in specification. Most important, although patterns of statistical significance differ, there are no instances in which different modeling choices yield statistically significant results with different signs. Further, although the coefficients obtained by working with the proportion of refugees as a treatment are much larger than those obtained by working with the (log) number, this occurs because the scale of the two treatment variables differs. When interpreting results at the median change in the respective treatment (shown in table tables 3B.1 and 3B.2 in annex 3B), effects are of the same order of magnitude, and often qualitatively similar.

Working with the proportion of refugees yields more results that suggest significant increases in employment rather than findings that suggest no results. Within the general pattern of robustness, the results sections have discussed the few notable instances in which there is some sensitivity in the estimates. Thus, it is worth highlighting that working with the proportion rather than the number of refugees yields estimates of a significant increase in the employment rate in the Ugandan data and, in some specifications, also for Colombia and Jordan. This outcome contrasts with an estimate of no change in each case with the preferred specification.

Local effects in communities that host a high number of refugees

Whereas predicted impacts are modest in the typical host community, those impacts can be sizable in communities that host many refugees. Throughout this report, the investigation interprets effect sizes at the median (absolute) change in the number of refugees. More often than not, such "typical" changes in host communities are modest. However, it is worth considering what the effect size might be in communities that experience particularly large changes in the number of refugees they host. For instance, at the median, the predicted consumption increase for rural hosts in Uganda is small, at less than 0.5 percent. However, for 1 in 4 host communities (at the 75th percentile), it is about 1 percent, and for 1 in 10 (at the 90th percentile), nearly 4 percent. These are more sizable short-run effects, particularly in an economic environment in which there was no growth in mean consumption over the period covered by the data. In Colombia, the differences between areas with more and with fewer refugees are less pronounced but still worth noting. For instance, in the median community, youth employment is predicted to have declined by just less than 1.0 percentage point, compared with 1.4 percentage points at the 75th percentile and 1.7 percentage points at the 90th (for details, refer to tables 3F.1 through 3F.6 in online annex 3F).

When the data permit, the analysis investigates whether impacts are systematically different in communities that host particularly high numbers of refugees. The main model used in the chapter is (log) linear; that is, it estimates impacts based on the assumption that an increase in the number of displaced workers hosted by, say, 20 percent has the same effect on labor market outcomes in a locality that hosts few refugees as in a community that hosts many refugees. This discussion considers a variation of this model that asks whether effects are systematically different in localities that host a particularly high number of the displaced. To this end, the treatment variable is interacted with an indicator variable for whether a locality hosts a larger or a smaller number of refugees than the median locality, sometimes called a "piecewise linear" model. Although technically distinct, this approach is conceptually similar to the one that underlies the earlier discussion of whether specific groups in the labor market—for instance, the young, or less-skilled workers—experience different effects. The chapter checks robustness to this variation of the model for the effect on consumption in Ethiopia and Uganda. In these two countries, the treatment varies at the level of enumeration areas, so more data are available with which to explore nonlinear patterns than in Colombia and Jordan, where the treatment varies at the level of larger administrative units.

In Ethiopia and Uganda, the direction of the effect on consumption is the same in localities that host many refugees as in the main model, but it is smaller in Ethiopia and larger in rural Uganda. When the piecewise linear model is estimated, any localities that never host any refugees are omitted from the data, so the indicator for communities with more or fewer refugees than the median has a more appealing interpretation.[7] Therefore, for reference, column (2) in table 3F.1 in online annex 3F shows results obtained from the baseline model when these localities have been removed. Column (3) of that table shows the results of the piecewise linear specification. For Ethiopia, results suggest that hosting refugees is associated with higher consumption both in localities that host smaller and in localities that host greater numbers of the displaced than is typical, but that the effect is smaller in localities with greater numbers of refugees. In Uganda, when rural and urban observations are pooled, the point estimate of the consumption effect in localities with a higher number of refugees is negative and nonsignificant. Closer examination of the data shows that this result is due to the countervailing effects in urban and rural areas reported earlier. In rural areas, the beneficial effects on consumption are concentrated only in localities that host many refugees; in urban areas the effect is larger in such localities but is not significant.

Conclusion

This chapter presents results from a harmonized analysis that uses consistent methods to study the impacts of forced displacement on host job outcomes in four countries. As noted, the four economies studied include two low-income and two middle-income countries and, within each income group, one country with more liberal policies toward labor market participation of refugees and one with more restrictive policies. The commonalities and differences that emerge between the settings allow for some conclusions to be drawn for policy.

Losses incurred by groups of host workers demand policy attention; however, in aggregate employment outcomes, even the arrival of large numbers of refugees may make little difference. Although all four countries studied here experienced very large refugee inflows, there are surprisingly few changes in aggregate labor market participation and unemployment. Notable exceptions include some groups of workers in Colombia. However, much as there are pronounced welfare gains for some parts of the population, there are adverse effects on some groups in the labor market, for instance, temporary workers in Colombia and urban workers in Uganda. Although the analysis suggests that these effects are more readily apparent in the short run and may abate over time, policy makers should direct their attention to assistance for workers who encounter disruption, even if it may be temporary.

The arrival of displaced workers presents opportunities that deserve as much policy attention as is given to concerns about labor market competition. In the public discourse on the potential impact of displacement on jobs for hosts, fears over greater competition and depressed wages tend to dominate. Far less attention goes to opportunities arising from the arrival of additional consumers and aid and investment that often accompany refugee flows. However, the analysis presented here shows that there is the potential for large gains in host communities. Policies should consider how best to help workers and businesses seize these opportunities.

The analysis of the types of work and sectors of activities in host communities shows that host workers make significant efforts to adapt to the arrival of refugee workers. Overall, there is an impression of a "move toward opportunity," toward sectors and activity types in which there is likely to be additional demand and less competition. Policies can seek to facilitate such shifts. In LICs, such policies will often mean supporting self-employed workers in making small investments to change their activities; in higher-income economies, policies are likely to involve capital support and training opportunities.

Across the four countries analyzed, there are multiple indications that workers in agriculture do well in host communities and that the sector provides opportunities for additional workers. To the degree that local food markets are not necessarily fully integrated, it is intuitive that a rise in demand due to the arrival of refugees opens up such opportunities. Policies should consider investment needs to help local communities benefit from such openings.

Notes

1 | For historical or political reasons, terms other than "refugee" are used in some settings to describe those who have been forcibly displaced across borders. Thus, in Colombia, Venezuelans who leave their country to live in Colombia are generally referred to as "migrants." This report uses this term to refer specifically to Colombia but speaks of "refugees" when referring to Colombia alongside other countries.

2 | Results omitted for conciseness.

3 | $Y_{ilt} = \beta_1 Ref_{lt-1} \times Inter_{it} + \tau X'_{ilt} + \alpha_l + \alpha_t + \gamma Dis Border_l \times \alpha_t + \epsilon_{ilt}$; where $Inter_{it}$ characterizes the interaction between one of the variables cited with the treatment variable.

4 | $Y_{ilt} = \beta_1 Ref_{lt-1} \times High_{lt} + \tau X'_{ilt} + \alpha_l + \alpha_t + \gamma Dis Border_l \times \alpha_t + \epsilon_{ilt}$; where $High_{lt}$ characterizes the interaction between locality with a high number of refugees and the treatment variable.

5 | Specifically, *Labor force participation = Employment Rate / (1 – Unemployment Rate).*

6 | Results ommitted for conciseness.

7 | Note that, because all models used in this chapter rely on fixed effects, including observations where no refugees are ever hosted affects estimates only through the way control variables are fitted. The baseline model thus includes such localities by way of using all available information to fit variables other than the measure of displacement.

References

Bartik, Timothy J. 1991. Who Benefits from State and Local Economic Development Policies? Kalamazoo, MI: WE Upjohn Institute for Employment Research.

Blanchard, Olivier Jean, Lawrence F. Katz, Robert E. Hall, and Barry Eichengreen. 1992. "Regional Evolutions." Brookings Papers on Economic Activity, (1):1–75.

Card, David. 2009. "Immigration and Inequality." American Economic Review 99 (2):1–21.

Delgado-Prieto, Lukas A. 2022. "Immigration, Wages, and Employment under Informal Labor Markets." Unpublished technical report.

Eberhard-Ruiz, A. 2024. "The Impact of Armed Conflict Shocks on Local Cross-Border Trade: Evidence from the Border between Uganda and the Democratic Republic of Congo." *Economic Development and Cultural Change* 72, (3): 1151-1187.

Freeman, R. B. 1980. "An Empirical Analysis of the Fixed Coefficient 'Manpower Requirements' Model, 1960–1970." *Journal of Human Resources* 15, (2): 176–99.

Goldsmith-Pinkham, Paul, Isaac Sorkin, and Henry Swift. 2020. "Bartik Instruments: What, When, Why, and How." *American Economic Review* 110, (8):2586–624.

Jaeger, David A., Joakim Ruist, and Jan Stuhler. 2018. "Shift-Share Instruments and the Impact of Immigration." NBER Working Paper 24285, National Bureau of Economic Research, Cambridge, MA.

Kadigo, Mark Marvin, and Jean-Francois Maystadt. 2023. "How to Cope with a Refugee Population? Evidence from Uganda." *World Development* 169:106293. doi: https://doi.org/10.1016/j.worlddev.2023.106293. https://www.sciencedirect.com/science/article/pii/S0305750X23001110.

Perloff, Harvey S. 1957. "Interrelations of State Income and Industrial Structure." *The Review of Economics and Statistics* 39, (2): 162–71.

Annex 3A

Detailed Information on Variables and Data Sources

Ethiopia

Household data. The study uses the Ethiopian Socio-Economic Survey (ERSS/ ESS) collected as part of the Living Standards Measurement Study (LSMS). The ERSS/ESS is a panel survey with three waves over the period 2011 to 2016. The survey initially sampled only households from rural and semiurban localities (3,969 households from 290 rural and 43 small town enumeration areas in the first wave, collected in 2011 and 2012); it was expanded to cover individuals from urban areas in subsequent waves. The second wave was collected in 2013–14 and comprises 5,262 households from the initial 333 enumeration areas, as well as an additional 100 urban enumeration areas. The response rate for the initially interviewed households from the first wave and the newly sampled households was 96 percent. The third wave, collected in 2015–16, covers 4,954 households. The response rate was still relatively high at 94 percent. The ERSS/ESS data set covers socioeconomic characteristics, labor market participation, educational and health indicators of the households, and an extensive module on shocks and coping mechanisms. Because the first wave (2012) of the LSMS did not cover urban areas, only waves two and three (2013–14 and 2015–16) were used in the main analysis, but the first wave was included in models that disaggregate between urban and rural treatment effects.

Refugee data. The study uses camp-based refugee data provided by the United Nations High Commissioner for Refugees (UNHCR) and additional data from

UNHCR camp fact sheets, newspapers, and social media on the exact location of camps and opening and closure dates, as well as yearly refugee numbers. The data capture the number of refugees in formal camps and semiformal settlements, such as transit centers or entry points. The data exclude, however, self-settled refugees and refugees who live dispersed in urban areas. In the Ethiopian context, qualitative information indicates that most refugees lived in camps during the period studied in this analysis. Refugees were granted the right to live and work outside of camps in 2019, after the time frame covered in this analysis. Over the period 2000–16, Ethiopia hosted a rapidly rising number of refugees. There were, on average, 120,000 refugees living in camps from 2000 to 2010, with the number steeply increasing in the following years, reaching almost 680,000 by 2016 as a result of numerous conflicts in neighboring countries. As of 2020, Ethiopia had become the second-largest refugee-hosting economy in Africa, with almost 800,000 refugees. The empirical analysis exploits the location of refugee camps across space to explore how Ethiopian households have been differentially affected by subsequent refugee inflows. After complementing the official UNHCR camp data with additional publicly available information on the precise location of refugee camps, 96 percent of the refugees living in formal camps and semiformal transit points can be geographically located (on average across survey rounds).

Uganda

Household data. The study uses the Living Standards Measurement Study–Integrated Studies on Agriculture (LSMS-ISA) data set for Uganda. These LSMS-ISA data sets are derived from the Uganda National Panel Survey (UNPS), which comprises five waves of interviews (2009–10, 2010–11, 2011–12, 2013–14, and 2015–16). The UNPS collects information from a sample of households that is representative at the national level, at the level of urban and rural areas, and at the main regional levels (North, East, West, and Central regions). The LSMS-ISA data set provides household and individual-level information, including household welfare measured using a per adult equivalent consumption aggregate, and indicators of participation and performance in the workforce within the agricultural and nonagricultural sectors. The study retains only the first three waves of the UNPS because they minimize attrition and have a similar structure. The household data provide a strongly balanced panel data set comprising 2,458 households distributed across 320 enumeration areas and surveyed in the first three rounds of the UNPS. The data cover 106 districts out of the 111 where a listing of households for the survey was conducted in 2010.

Refugee data. The study uses georeferenced data on the number of refugees received per year from 2000 to 2016 in camps or settlements within 14 districts in Uganda. The disaggregated data cover refugees in camps and settlements but do not generally include self-settled refugees. However, the study includes within its refugee data set the total number of refugees reported to have settled in Kampala every year. Because of the promotion of the Self-Reliance Strategy, many of the refugees moved out of the settlements and self-settled in major cities including Kampala. Moreover, according to Omata and Kaplan (2013), there was an unprecedented increase in the number of refugees residing in Kampala in 2012, making the capital the second-largest refugee-hosting site in the country at the time. This analysis focuses on the period from 2009 to 2012, making the latter issue secondary.

Colombia

Household data. The study uses the Gran Encuesta Integrada de Hogares (Large Integrated Household Survey, or GEIH) collected by the National Statistics Office of Colombia (DANE) (DANE 2018). GEIH is a monthly repeated cross-section survey that collects information about the labor market, income, housing, migration, education, and other sociodemographic features. Note that the data available in Colombia do not comprise an individual-level panel, so they require different empirical methods than the other three countries and call for a different interpretation of results. The GEIH survey has been undertaken since 2010 and includes information for about 790,000 people each year for 24 departments, including urban and rural areas. This study uses the information on the working-age population from 2015 to 2019 to cover periods before and after the mass influx of Venezuelan migrants that occurred from 2017. The sample is representative of about 31 million Colombians and 32,000 migrants in 2015, and 31 million Colombians and 1.9 million migrants in 2020.

Data on migrants and work permits.[1] In addition to the GEIH information on migrants, the study uses DANE's 2005 and 2018 national censuses to construct the instrumental variable. The census presents information about the location and sociodemographic characteristics of the population, households, and dwellings. Preliminary descriptive analysis shows a correlation of 0.87 between the location of previous migrants in 2005 and the location of the new migrants in 2018. The total number of migrants from República Bolivariana de Venezuela remained relatively stable until 2015 when there were about 45,000 migrants in total. From that year onward, the number of migrants rose markedly, and as of 2020, Colombia had welcomed approximately 1.9 million Venezuelans. The analysis also uses the number of work permits granted in each of Colombia's 32 departments, reported since 2017 by the National Office of Migration (Migración Colombia), and available on its web page.[2] Work permits allow migrants to work legally in the formal sector and to access public health and education services. In 2017, the Colombian government granted about 69,000 work permits. This number increased sevenfold in 2018, when about 481,000 work permits were granted as a result of an increase in registration stations across the country and more flexible requirements. In 2019, about 48,000 work permits were granted.

Jordan

Household data. The study uses Jordan Labor Market Panel Surveys (JLMPS) collected in 2010 and 2016.[3] The JLMPS are broad surveys that collect information on individual socioeconomic characteristics, including health and education, migration background, information technology, saving and borrowing, and gender attitude, and contain an extensive labor market module. The data consist of an individual-level panel. In total, the sample consists of 59,403 individuals, including a refresher sample of 3,000 Jordanians in the 2016 round to account for attrition and demographic change. The 2016 survey further includes a sample of 1,292 refugees, 96 percent of whom are Syrians; however, these refugee respondents are not part of this analytical sample.

Refugee data and work permit data. To measure the refugee inflow into Jordan, the study uses the total number of Syrian refugees per district recorded in the 2015 Census, following Krafft et al. (2019). In addition, it uses Jordan's Department of Statistics' "Syrian Refugee Unit WP Progress" to obtain the total number of work permits granted. To create instrumental variables that predict the refugee inflow and the number of work permits, the study uses Google Maps to identify centroids of each geographic unit in the sample and calculate the distance between each Syrian governorate and each Jordanian district.

Outcome variables

Someone is considered to be *Employed* if they undertake any legal activity for own or family gain, with revenues in cash or in-kind, following the 2013 World Development Report's broad definition of "jobs" (World Bank 2012). More specifically, employed persons are defined as those persons of working age (15–64 years of age) who were working for pay as employees or for gain in a self-employed capacity, or who were working in a household business or farm for at least one hour during the reference period, as well as those who did not work during the reference period but held a job from which they were temporarily absent. This variable is comparable for the 7-day reference period across the four countries (table 3A.1). In addition, it is also available for a 12-month recall period in the low-income countries and for three months in Jordan. The employment rate is defined as the share of the working-age population who are employed.

Unemployed persons are classified as individuals who did not work at all during the reference period and who were not temporarily absent from a job, but who actively looked for work during the past four weeks and were available to work in the reference period. Persons who were on layoff from a job to which they expected to return and were available to work during the reference week are also classified as unemployed, even if they did not actively look for work. The sum of the employed and the unemployed constitutes the labor force (or "active" population). Individuals not in the labor force (or "inactive") are those who are of working age, but neither employed nor unemployed. The unemployment rate is defined as the share of the labor force that is unemployed.

The study characterizes the *Type of Work* a person engages in as consisting of wage employment, temporary labor, self-employment in nonagricultural activities (including family labor), self-employment in agricultural activities (also including family workers), daily labor, or being an employer. These variables are comparable for the 7-day reference period in the four countries. However, the study also has these variables for 12 months in the low-income countries and for 3 months in Jordan. The analysis considers the share of each type of work among all employment, omitting unemployment and the inactive. Each category is treated as a binary, meaning that in the analysis one can assume that the opposite of being wage employed is being employed in any of the other categories. In both the "daily labor" and "temporary labor" categories, the intention is to distinguish regular salaried work from more tenuous types of employment. However, because the available data vary by country, definitions also vary. In Colombia, the daily labor category includes work as a daily worker

TABLE 3A.1   Set of outcome variables and comparability, case study countries

Outcome variable	Ethiopia	Uganda	Colombia	Jordan
Employment (7 day)	Comparable	Comparable	Comparable	Comparable
Type of work (7 day)	Comparable	Comparable	Comparable	Comparable
Sector of activity	Comparable over 12 months	Comparable over 12 months	Comparable over 7 days	Comparable over 7 days
Hourly wages or earnings	Comparable over 12 months	Comparable over 12 months	Comparable over 7 days	Comparable over 7 days
Hours worked per week	Comparable over 12 months	Comparable over 12 months	Comparable over 7 days	Comparable over 7 days
Welfare	Comparable, Consumption	Comparable, Consumption	Comparable, Monthly earnings	Comparable, Monthly earnings
Unemployment	Comparable	Comparable	Comparable	Comparable
Formality	Comparable	Comparable	Comparable	Comparable

Source: Original table for this preport.

or daily farm worker (*jornalero*), whereas a temporary worker is an individual with a contract that does not guarantee a minimum employment period. In Uganda, those who report having a contract of no more than one year are defined as "temporary." In Ethiopia, there are no data on contract length, but there is a question that directly asks whether wage workers were engaged in temporary labor; the analysis uses this definition. In Jordan, temporary workers are defined as either holding a temporary contract or holding a seasonal contract. These variables of *Type of Work* are conditional on being employed and in Ethiopia, conditional on being a wage worker.

To explore the *Sector of Activity*, four large categories are created that encompass the traditional three one-digit-level industries of agriculture, manufacturing, and services. Agricultural activities (including forestry and fishing) and manufacturing activities (including construction, mining and quarrying, manufacturing, and others) use the standard definitions. However, because commerce is a very large employer in developing economies and has characteristics distinct from other activities in services, the study distinguishes between commerce (wholesale and retail trade) and activities in other services. In terms of the recall period, the study uses 12 months in Ethiopia and Uganda, and 7 days in Colombia and Jordan. Binary variables are created in the same way as described for types of work. These variables are conditional on being employed and, in Ethiopia, conditional on being a wage worker.

For earnings information, the study looks at *Hourly Wages or Earnings* and *Monthly Wages or Earnings* from the respondent's primary job, expressed as the log of local currency values. In Ethiopia, Uganda, and Jordan, only data on the wage employed are available. The study corrects for inflation in all countries, and for spatial price differences in each year in all countries with the exception of Colombia, where no spatial index is available for all localities. (Refer to Delgado-Prieto [2022] for evidence that spatial price differences do not correlate with whether communities host more or fewer refugees.) In Ethiopia and Uganda, wages include cash payments, in-kind payments, additional allowances, and gratuities. In Colombia and Jordan, wages include overtime, subsidies (housing, transportation, food), bonuses and incentives, other wages, profit sharing, vacation payments, and in-kind payments. In Colombia, information is also available on the net earnings of the self-employed from any job activity including businesses, professional work, or farming. The recall period, as before, is 12 months for the low-income countries and 7 days for the middle-income countries.

Consumption, a direct measure of welfare, is measured using consumption aggregates provided in the two low-income country data sets. No consumption data are available for the two middle-income countries. The aggregate is adjusted for household demographic composition in terms of sex and age and corrected for inflation and spatial price differences as noted earlier. Thus, the analysis uses the *Consumption Aggregate per Adult Equivalent* scales for Ethiopian and Ugandan households as the proxy for household welfare. This variable is defined at the household level, so the analyses are also run at this level.

Work Hours per Week refers to the number of hours spent at work for wage employees and temporary workers, except in Ethiopia, where work hours are not reported for temporary workers.

Finally, the variable of *Formal* employment is defined as being entitled to social security payments or holding a formal contract. Because the Ethiopian data set does not ask about contracts, this variable is available only in Uganda, Colombia, and Jordan.

Annex 3B

Median Change in Number of Refugees

To interpret the magnitude of the results reported in chapter 3, tables 3B.1 and 3B.2 show the median changes in the number of refugees or migrants for each of the outcome variables studied in chapter 3.

TABLE 3B.1 Median change in number of refugees (ln), with regard to proxy measures of welfare, case study countries

	Ethiopia	Uganda	Colombia	Jordan
Consumption				
Rural	0.20	0.07	—	—
Urban	5.54	0.34	—	—
Earnings, commercial farmers	0.63	0.12	—	—
Earnings, other than commercial farmers	0.30	0.12	—	—
Earnings, subsistence farmers	0.38	0.02	—	—
Earnings, other than subsistence farmers	0.30	0.12	—	—
Earnings, wage workers	0.20	0.12	—	—
Earnings, other than wage workers	0.30	0.12	—	—
Monthly wage				
Rural	—	—	0.61	7.37
Urban	—	—	0.65	9.37
Wage workers	—	—	0.66	9.10

(continued)

TABLE 3B.1 Median change in number of refugees (ln), with regard to proxy measures of welfare *(continued)*

	Ethiopia	Uganda	Colombia	Jordan
Other than wage workers	—	—	0.61	9.14
Temporary workers	—	—	0.65	9.14
Other than temporary workers	—	—	0.65	9.14
Agricultural workers	—	—	0.59	7.37
Other than agricultural workers	—	—	0.65	9.14

Source: Original table for this report based on data from ERSS/ESS 2011–12, 2013–14, 2015–16, LSMS-ISA 2009–10, 2011, 2012, JLMPS 2010, 2016, and GEIH 2015, 2016, 2017, 2018, 2019. See table 3.1 for additional details.
Note: — = not available.

TABLE 3B.2 Median change in number of refugees (ln), with regard to proxy measures of productivity

	Ethiopia	Uganda	Colombia	Jordan
Hourly wage (ln)				
Female	0.43	0.12	0.65	9.14
Male	0.39	0.12	0.65	9.14
Rural	0.36	0.10	0.61	7.37
Urban	0.64	0.34	0.65	9.37
Low education	0.38	0.12	0.61	9.14
High education	2.25	0.12	0.65	9.14
Above 25 years old	0.39	0.12	0.65	9.14
25 years old and below	0.48	0.12	0.65	9.14
Agricultural workers	6.15	0.07	0.59	7.37
Other than agricultural workers	0.43	0.12	0.65	9.14
Wage workers	—	—	0.66	9.10
Other than wage workers	—	—	0.61	9.14
Temporary workers	—	—	0.65	9.14
Other than temporary workers	—	—	0.65	9.14
Self-employed workers	—	—	0.61	9.14
Other than self-employed workers	—	—	0.65	9.14
Self-employed workers in agriculture	—	—	0.57	—
Other than self-employed workers in agriculture	—	—	0.65	—

Source: Original table for this report based on data from ERSS/ESS 2011–12, 2013–14, 2015–16, LSMS-ISA 2009–10, 2011, 2012, JLMPS 2010, 2016, and GEIH 2015, 2016, 2017, 2018, 2019. See table 3.1 for additional details.
Note: — = not available.

Notes

1 | For historical or political reasons, terms other than "refugee" are used in some settings to describe those who have been forcibly displaced across borders. Thus, in Colombia, Venezuelans who leave their country to live in Colombia are generally referred to as "migrants." This report uses this term to refer specifically to Colombia but speaks of "refugees" when referring to Colombia alongside other countries.

2 | "For the latest available report (through 2021) see Migración Colombia, https://public.tableau.com /app/profile/migraci.n.colombia/viz/PermisoEspecialdePermanencia-PEP/Inicio.

3 | Economic Research Forum, Labor Market Panel Survey, JLMPS 2016, https://www.erfdataportal .com/index.php/catalog/139.

References

DANE (Departamento Administrativo Nacional de Estadística.) 2018. Gran Encuesta Integrada de Hogares (GEIH). https://www.datos.gov.co/Estad-sticas-Nacionales/Gran-Encuesta -Integrada-de-Hogares-GEIH/mcpt-3dws.

Delgado-Prieto, Lukas. 2022. "Immigration, Wages, and Employment under Informal Labor Markets." Center for Open Science, Charlottesville, VA. https://www.dropbox.com/s/udld8y6oh58fq8r /Col_Immigration_LADP_2022.pdf?dl=0&unfurl=1.

Krafft, Caroline, Maia Sieverding, Colette Salemi, and Caitlyn Keo. 2019. "Syrian Refugees in Jordan: Demographics, Livelihoods, Education, and Health." In *The Jordanian Labor Market: Between Fragility and Resilience.* Edited by Caroline Krafft and Ragui Assaad. Oxford, UK: Oxford University Press. doi:10.1093/oso/9780198846079.003.0006.

Omata, Naohiko, and Josiah Kaplan. 2012. "Refugee Livelihoods in Kampala, Nakivale and Kyangwali Refugee Settlements: Patterns of Engagement with the Private Sector." Refugee Studies Centre, Oxford Department of International Development, University of Oxford, Oxford, UK.

World Bank. 2013. *World Development Report 2103: Jobs.* Washington, DC: World Bank.

Special Topic 1. The Impact of Work Permits on Job Outcomes for Hosts and Refugees

Issue

Work permits are one important factor in how refugees can engage in labor markets, particularly in economies with a substantial share of formal sector employment. Many legal, social, and economic factors determine the degree to which refugees are able to be active in the labor market. These factors include, for instance, freedom of movement, the degree of welcome or ostracism refugees are met with, and asset ownership among refugees. Another important dimension

Special Topic 1 online annex available at https://openknowledge.worldbank.org/handle/10986/40701: annex ST.1, "Table of Main Results."

that attracts particular policy attention is the right to work, often granted through formal work permits. In developing countries, access to work permits is likely neither sufficient nor necessary for the ability to work. For instance, where there is scant wage work and most jobs are self-employed, the right to work may not be effective without access to capital. Conversely, where most economic activity is informal, finding paid work without work permits is possible. However, at least in middle-income countries, work permits will affect the degree to which refugees can access jobs, particularly good jobs in the formal sector. Because they somewhat determine entry for refugees to sought-after employment, the availability of work permits is an important political issue. Also, even if refugees continue to work in the informal sector in lower-income economies where there is little formal work, they will do so on an equal footing with hosts if they have the right to work, regardless of whether they actually apply for a work permit. Their bargaining power and ability to defend their rights will increase.

This special topic provides an analysis of the jobs impact of three well-known work permit programs, including novel results on the impact of a large and generous program in Colombia. These programs include the Jordan Compact (2015), which created access for some Syrian refugees to formal sector jobs in selected industries, as well as two successive large permit schemes in Colombia, intended to regularize Venezuelan migrants, namely the Special Permanence Permit (2017; henceforth, "PEP" after the official Spanish title of the program—Permiso Especial de Permanencia) and the Temporary Protection Permit (2021; henceforth, "PPT" for Permiso por Protección Temporal). These programs are described in detail in chapter 2. For each of these programs, this section summarizes the impacts of the work permits on job outcomes for hosts and, in Colombia, for migrants. Unless otherwise indicated, results pertaining to the Jordan compact and the PEP come from background studies prepared for this report (for the Jordan Compact, Bousquet and Maystadt (2023); for the PEP, Garcia-Suaza et al. (2023)). Of the three schemes, the PEP program has been studied in the literature (Bahar, Ibanez, and Rozo 2021; Ibanez et al. 2021); there seem to be no prior studies that establish the causal effect of the Jordan Compact on jobs outcomes for hosts,[1] and, because of its recency, no studies seem to be available that investigate the impact of the PPT program on hosts or migrants.

Assessing the impact of work permit schemes highlights the role of one particular policy decision in shaping the overall impact of displacement on job outcomes analyzed in chapter 3. Chapter 3 provides a harmonized analysis of the impact the presence of refugees has on host labor market outcomes. Its approach is "reduced form"; that is, it takes all of the conditions under which refugees engage in the labor market as a given and does not seek to identify whether the impact arises through any particular rules or circumstances. The following analysis moves beyond this analytical framework and seeks to isolate the role of work permits as a particular phenomenon associated with the presence of refugees in the labor market.

Permit programs analyzed

Although significantly limited in scope, the Jordan Compact, initiated in 2015, promised to open parts of Jordan's very tight labor market to Syrian refugees for the first time. Refugees at this time already participated to a significant degree in the labor market—a 2014 survey found that 49 percent of working-age refugees were active (Ajluni and Kawar 2014). However, this engagement in the labor market was nearly fully informal; in 2014, fewer than 2 percent of all migrants had a work permit (ILO 2015). The compact restricted work permits to certain sectors of the economy, specifically construction, care work, agriculture, manufacturing, and the food industry. It also issued only between 40,000 and 90,000 work permits in total in its first two years of operation, roughly 10 percent of the working-age Syrian refugee population in Jordan (Ajluni and Lockhart 2019), and well below the goal of providing 200,000 permits. However, it was a notable first step toward permitting access to highly sought-after formal employment in an economy characterized by low participation and very high youth unemployment. The analysis shown here uses data collected in 2016, and thus measures the effect of the first year of operation; results should be interpreted as showing the short-term impact of a work permit scheme that somewhat eases restrictions on access to formal employment in a very tight labor market.[2]

In 2017, Colombia initiated the PEP, a very generous program to provide work permits to Venezuelan migrants, allowing access to the labor market for two years with no restrictions on the sector or type of work refugees could engage in. Although the program was initially restricted to those who had arrived legally, it was eventually extended to irregular migrants who had arrived before the program was announced. Uptake was extensive, and by 2021, some 700,000 Venezuelan workers had obtained a PEP, equivalent to about 2 percent of the entire labor force in Colombia. The analysis shown here assesses the impact of the program using yearly data from 2018 to 2021. It should be thought of as showing the short-term impact of a broadly available work permit scheme in a labor market with relatively easy prior access to informal employment.

Colombia's PPT program further expanded access to work permits and offered longer-term permits. The program offered the opportunity to obtain a permit to migrants who had arrived irregularly, and it provided applicants with a 10-year permit, in contrast to the 2 years offered by the PEP. It has expanded rapidly, and Migracíon Colombia data show that, about a year after its inception, it covered about 570,000 Venezuelan workers (or 26 percent of working-age migrants) in May 2022, and about 1.5 million workers by October 2022. Data analyzed here measure the impact of the program about one year after it began. Estimates are best thought of as showing the short-term effect of an expansion of a generous permit program, offering long-term work permits.

Data and methods

The analysis of the Jordan Compact and the PEP program relies on secondary data, whereas the study of the PPT program's impact uses primary data, including labor market data collected for this report. To analyze the Jordan Compact, this report uses two rounds of the Jordan Labor Market Panel Surveys, collected in 2010 and 2016. These data and the other data sets used are further described in chapter 4. Data on work permits come from the 2016 survey round, in which refugees were asked whether they held a work permit. No work permit scheme was in place in 2010. The PEP program in Colombia is studied using Colombia's Gran Encuesta Integrada de Hogares, or GEIH (Large Integrated Household Survey) rolling household survey, collected between 2018 and 2021. The data contain information on PEP work permits held by migrants. To analyze the PPT work permit scheme, the study uses data from the GEIH as well as four rounds of the Pulso de las Migraciones collected in 2021 and 2022, including a round dedicated to labor market outcomes collected for this report.

Estimates of the impact of the three work permit schemes on hosts use largely comparable methods. In Jordan, the number of work permits is measured at the district level; in Colombia, it is measured at the department level.[3] It is expressed as a share of work permit holders among the working-age population (hosts and refugees combined). In the case of Colombia, it is explicitly defined as the current level of work permits in a given year (as opposed to the change in the number of work permits in the same year); in Jordan, there is only one period in which there are any work permits so there is no distinction. In Colombia, the models further control for distance to the border in each locality, as discussed in chapter 3. The Jordan analysis explicitly controls for the share of refugees in each district whereas the Colombia analyses do not.

Results rely on the difference-in-differences and instrumental variables (IV) approaches. For the Jordan Compact and the PEP, results are obtained from district-level fixed effects regressions and, in the case of Jordan, also from individual-level fixed effects regressions (the preferred estimate). For the PPT's impact on hosts, the model is cross-sectional. In each case, an IV approach is used to further ascertain robustness. Each analysis applies shift-share instruments, using in each case the number of work permits issued nationally as the "shift," and as the "share," for Jordan, each district's distance to the Za'atari refugee camp; for the PEP, the share of migrants in the working-age population in each department; and for the PPT, the share of PEP permit holders in each department. The IV estimates provide some reassurance against the concern that department-level uptake of work permits may relate to other economic dynamics that matter for hosts' job outcomes. At the same time, however, IV estimates require a strong assumption that, with controls, the presence of refugees affects outcomes only through work permits. This analysis, therefore, shows both estimates with the understanding that they have complementary strengths and weaknesses.

Data collected for this report allow particularly credible estimates of the impact of the PPT program on Venezuelan migrants to be made. Because the Pulso de las Migraciones partially follows respondents over several rounds, with the GEIH 2021 serving as a baseline, job outcomes for migrants who did and did not obtain the PPT permit can be compared, allowing for individual-level fixed effects. What is more, it allows for a potent placebo check on the measured effect; that is, the study can ascertain whether those who applied for the PPT but had not yet received it experienced different changes in job outcomes than those who had not applied. This is akin to a pretrend analysis, such that the study can establish that those interested in the PPT did not experience different trends in their labor market performance, as might, for instance, be the case if particularly motivated or well-connected workers were more likely than others to apply for the PPT.

Results

In the aggregate, the Jordan Compact is associated with a positive effect on wage earnings and a small adverse effect on employment in formal sector jobs among hosts.[4] There is no evidence of adverse aggregate effects on employment or unemployment rates. Estimates suggest an increase in wage earnings among host workers in the formal sector, with an indication that the increase may have been the result of an increase in hours worked (table ST1.1). The share of formal employment is also estimated to have fallen. Both of these shifts are consistent with the fact that the Jordan Compact was the first limited opening of formal jobs for competition. Given the modest number of work permits issued, the shift in wages is quite small: at the median of the change in the number of work permits, wage earnings are estimated to have increased by 4 percent (column (7) in table ST1.1); the drop in the formal employment share is somewhat more sizable, with a change of 1 percentage point relative to a baseline of 59 percent (column (6)).

In addition to a shift out of formality, there is some indication that hosts adapted by moving toward more highly skilled agriculture jobs and some jobs closed to refugee permit holders. The work permit program first allowed refugees access to work in the formal sector, such that the estimated shift out of formal employment can be read as host workers' adaptation to greater competition for these jobs. Beyond this shift, there is an effect on the likelihood of formal workers entering public sector employment (which remained unattainable to refugees) (column (11) in table ST1.1) and toward more highly skilled jobs (column (10)). Furthermore, there are other indications of plausible adaptations in parts of the labor market. For instance, within the agriculture sector, workers in areas where more refugees obtained permits worked longer hours and moved toward skilled tasks within the sector. In addition, workers in the service sector shifted

TABLE ST1.1 Effect of work permits on hosts' labor market outcomes in Jordan

	(1) Employed	(2) Unemployed	(3) Wage earnings	(4) Hourly wage (ln)	(5) Work hours per week (ln)	(6) Formal sector	(7) Formal wage earnings	(8) Hourly formal wage	(9) Formal work hours	(10) Formal job requires skills	(11) Job in formal private sector	(12) Formal industry open to refugees
District and year fixed effects												
OLS												
Work permits per 100 workers	-0.16 (0.23)	-0.17 (0.17)	1.84 (1.42)	0.20 (1.49)	1.63*** (0.59)	-0.37* (0.20)	2.16 (1.46)	1.07 (1.51)	0.84* (0.42)	1.45* (0.83)	-0.57* (0.33)	-0.45 (0.32)
Observations	17,986	7,545	5,385	5,288	6,225	6,374	4,343	4,270	4,369	4,438	4,435	4,425
Adjusted R^2	0.38	0.14	0.07	0.04	0.07	0.10	0.09	0.03	0.05	0.11	0.30	0.20
IV												
Work permits per 100 workers	-0.41 (0.38)	-0.15 (0.25)	0.57 (0.75)	-0.49 (0.54)	1.03** (0.48)	-0.23 (0.18)	2.08* (1.26)	0.89 (1.21)	0.77** (0.37)	1.93 (1.19)	-0.51 (0.32)	-0.27 (0.22)
Observations	17,986	7,545	5,385	5,288	6,225	6,374	4,343	4,270	4,369	4,438	4,435	4,425
Adjusted R^2	0.37	0.12	0.01	-0.00	0.03	0.02	0.01	-0.01	0.02	0.08	0.00	0.02
KP statistic	20	20	21	20	20	20	20	20	20	20	20	20

Source: Original table for this report based on data from JLMPS 2010, 2016.
Note: Standard errors clustered at the district level. Weighted regressions. Controls include age, age squared, and gender. IV = instrumental variables; OLS = ordinary least squares.
* $p < .10$, ** $p < .05$, *** $p < .01$.

into public sector and closed sector jobs.[5] It is possible that the limited degree of adaptation could be due to either the short-term nature of the estimates or the moderate degree of participation in the work permit scheme. (More detailed results are available in Bousquet and Maystadt (2023).)

The available data suggest that the PEP program had no noticeable impacts on the average job outcomes in the Colombian labor market across a range of indicators of activity, earnings, and formality (table ST1.2). Although there are near-significant estimates of a small increase in unemployment but also in participation, the sample size is very large, so there is little reason to interpret near-significant results. This finding is in line with prior analyses that showed "negligible effects" on formal employment, primarily among highly educated workers and female workers (Bahar, Ibanez, and Rozo 2021). Note that, although it is less aligned with the reduction of potential negative impacts of displacement on Colombians in lower-paid jobs reported in Lombardo et al. (2021), the analysis in chapter 3 finds no such impacts for the pre-PEP period.

Cross-sectional estimates suggest that the PPT scheme in its first year had no effects on host participation and employment and small beneficial effects on hourly earnings and formality.[6] Analysis of GEIH data collected after the PPT was first offered suggests that further liberalization of access to work permits came without any adverse impacts on employment or labor force participation among hosts (table ST1.3). IV estimates even suggest that, on average, host

---

TABLE ST1.2 Estimates of the impact of the PEP on the labor market outcomes of hosts in Colombia

	(1) Employment rate	(2) Hourly wage (ln)	(3) Unemployment	(4) Work hours per week (ln)	(5) Labor force participation	(6) Informality rate
OLS						
PEP rate per 100 workers	0.0032 (0.0213)	−0.0081 (0.0312)	0.0175 (0.0107)	0.0117 (0.0127)	0.0239 (0.0169)	−0.0107** (0.0051)
Observations						
IV						
PEP rate per 100 workers	0.0740 (0.0593)	0.0195 (0.1169)	−0.0083 (0.0271)	−0.0896 (0.0599)	0.0763 (0.0583)	0.0108 (0.0433)
KP statistic	10.64	8.064	8.280	7.871	10.64	7.732
F statistic	1,282	4,899	6,201	11,563	1,792	19,799
Observations	1,876,049	956,228	1,326,454	1,068,992	1,876,049	1,136,266

Source: Original table for this report based on data GEIH and PM 2018, 2019, 2020, and 2021.
Note: The table reports estimates of the labor market outcomes of Colombians. All specifications include individual controls (age, age squared, and gender), department, and year fixed effects. Standard errors at the department level are in parentheses. IV = instrumental variables; OLS = ordinary least squares; PEP = Permiso Especial de Permanencia (Special Permanence Permit).
* $p < .10$, ** $p < .05$, *** $p < .01$.

TABLE ST1.3 Estimates of the impact of the PPT on the labor market outcomes of hosts in Colombia using a panel specification

	(1)	(2)	(3)	(4)	(5)	(6)
	Total wage (ln)	Employed	Unemployed	Hourly wage (ln)	Work hours per week (ln)	Employment in formal private sector businesses
OLS						
PPT work permits per 100 workers	0.000 (0.003)	−0.002 (0.001)	−0.008 0.010)	0.000 (0.003)	−0.002 (0.003)	0.016 (0.011)
Observations	909,129	624,731	468,805	236,989	524,067	524,069
Adjusted R^2	0.20	0.04	0.13	0.07	0.10	0.08
IV						
PPT work permits per 100 workers	−0.009 (0.005)	0.003 (0.003)	−0.043** (0.018)	−0.000 (0.005)	−0.001 (0.003)	0.088*** (0.025)
Observations	909,129	624,731	468,805	236,989	524,067	524,069
Adjusted R^2	0.19	0.03	0.05	0.05	0.08	0.01
KP statistic	10.6	11.8	11.8	13.6	12.3	12.3

Source: Original table for this report based on data from GEIH 2020 and 2021, and PM 2021 and 2022.
Note: The table reports estimates of the labor market outcomes of Colombians. All specifications include individual controls (age, age squared, and gender), department, and year fixed effects. Standard errors at the department level are in parentheses. IV = instrumental variables; OLS = ordinary least squares; PPT = Permiso de Permanencia Temporal (Temporary Protection Permit).
* $p < .10$, ** $p < .05$, *** $p < .01$.

workers enjoyed a decrease in unemployment rates and an increase in the share of formal employment. When results were measured, the number of migrants with work permits accounted for about 2 percent of the total working-age population. Thus, the estimated average effects are small.

Migrants who participated in the PPT enjoyed a large increase—about a one-third gain—in wages (table ST1.4). Participation in the PPT is estimated to have left a number of job outcomes among migrants unaffected. Notably, there is no estimated effect on participation or employment, which is consistent with an economy in which (as reported in chapter 4) migrants were more likely than their hosts to participate in the economy even before the introduction of the program. However, wage workers among PPT participants report large increases in earnings compared with nonparticipants, by about 33 percent. These increases obtain among a group of workers who, when they had only applied for the PPT but had not yet received it, reported lower gains in wage earnings relative to migrants who had not applied. Similarly, those who had obtained the permit by the time the final Pulso de las Migraciones round was collected reported higher earnings than others who had applied for but not yet received the permit. Both findings

TABLE ST1.4 Impact of the PPT on the labor market outcomes of migrants in Colombia—all migrants

	(1) Employed	(2) Unemployed	(3) Total wage (ln)	(4) Hourly wage	(5) Total wage, wage work	(6) Hourly wage, wage work	(7) Total wage, self-employed	(8) Work hours per week (ln)	(9) Employment in formal private sector businesses	(10) Wage worker	(11) Self-employed	(12) Temporary	(13) Daily	(14) Agriculture	(15) Manufacturing	(16) Commerce	(17) Services
Fixed effects: Individual and year and all controls																	
Has PPT	-0.022 (0.028)	0.016 (0.041)	0.105 (0.106)	0.031 (0.045)	0.328*** (0.053)	0.008 (0.078)	0.098 (0.171)	0.012 (0.046)	0.001 (0.023)	0.057 (0.057)	-0.077 (0.045)	-0.003 (0.020)	0.024 (0.015)	0.024** (0.011)	0.045 (0.034)	0.013 (0.035)	-0.081* (0.045)
Observations	6,330	4,168	2,098	2,098	644	350	792	2,982	2,984	1,792	1,792	1,792	1,792	2,788	2,788	2,788	2,788
Adjusted R²	0.85	0.80	0.83	0.87	0.83	0.85	0.78	0.83	0.85	0.83	0.84	-0.06	0.84	0.94	0.84	0.85	0.84
Fixed effects: Department and year and all controls																	
Has PPT	0.026 (0.024)	0.007 (0.025)	-0.012 (0.026)	0.019 (0.048)	0.013 (0.036)	0.095** (0.040)	0.074 (0.047)	0.086 (0.050)	0.014 (0.027)	0.054 (0.049)	-0.077 (0.045)	-0.005 (0.010)	-0.003 (0.013)	0.001 (0.015)	0.003 (0.027)	0.017 (0.043)	-0.021 (0.035)
Observations	7,191	5,408	4,478	3,568	3,568	1,527	1,169	2,007	4,482	3,499	1,792	3,499	3,499	4,330	4,330	4,330	4,330
Adjusted R²	0.18	0.05	0.10	0.29	0.21	0.25	0.19	0.26	0.09	0.10	0.84	0.01	0.08	0.16	0.07	0.03	0.13

Source: Original table for this report based on data from GEIH and PM 2020 and 2021.

Note: Models (1) and (2) include the yearly number of migrants by department (ln); the yearly number of Colombians by department to the Venezuelan border (ln) interacted with the year fixed effects; a control for having the PEP; and controls for having applied for the PPT early, at the time the first and second rounds of the PM survey were collected. OLS = ordinary least squares; PEP = Permiso Especial de Permanencia (Special Permanence Permit); PPT = Permiso de Permanencia Temporal (Temporary Protection Permit).

* $p < .10,$ ** $p < .05,$ *** $p < .01.$

strengthen the case for arguing that the observed gains are causally due to receiving the PPT permit. The magnitude of the income gains is similar to those measured previously for the PEP (Ibanez et al. 2021).

Migrants for whom the PPT was their first work permit shifted out of self-employment, and earnings rose by nearly one-quarter for those who remained self-employed. Among all migrants who received a PPT, earnings among self-employed workers increased weakly when allowing for individual fixed effects; the estimated increase of about 16 percent is just below significant when allowing instead for department-level fixed effects. The differences in estimated impacts between the two models may suggest that there is no true effect and that the results obtained with less-demanding fixed effects are due to the unobserved characteristics of participating workers. However, they could also be due to a change in the composition of workers who switch from other activities to self-employment between survey rounds. Results among migrants who had not held a PEP before receiving the PPT suggest that the latter is the case. Thus, among this group, the share of self-employment decreases by 12 percentage points—a large change in the type of work over one year. Although those who are wage-employed see large gains (39 percent), there are also gains on the order of nearly one-quarter among those in self-employment (23 percent) (table ST1.5).

Implications

Comparative analysis of the three work permit schemes suggests that large adverse effects on hosts' jobs in the aggregate may be unlikely. In each of the three programs studied here, any effects on hosts' level of participation, access to employment, or overall earnings (positive in Jordan) appear to be limited. In two cases, there are small beneficial impacts on hourly earnings. One possible explanation for this finding is that, even in the three rather large schemes studied here, the number of workers who received permits is small relative to the overall labor force.

The absence of large adverse economywide effects does not imply that there are not host workers who are affected by work permit schemes, particularly where the formal labor market is small. The origin of refugees and their characteristics as workers often mean that refugee workers are concentrated in certain parts of the labor market, whether in particular sectors, occupations, or localities (as discussed in chapter 3). Therefore, even in the absence of economywide effects, host workers in parts of the economy may be more affected by greater competition from refugee workers; in the case of work permit programs, impacts are particularly likely for those in the more formal, productive, and better-protected parts of the economy. In this respect, note that no adverse impacts were reported from Jordan's less-dynamic labor market, nor from either of the programs implemented in Colombia. It is plausible that hourly

TABLE ST1.5 Impact of the PPT on the labor market outcomes of migrants in Colombia who did not previously have a PEP

	(1) Employed	(2) Unemployed	(3) Total wage (ln)	(4) Hourly wage	(5) Total wage, wage work	(6) Hourly wage, wage work	(7) Total wage, self-employed	(8) Work hours per week (ln)	(9) Employment in formal private sector businesses	(10) Wage worker	(11) Self-employed	(12) Temporary	(13) Daily	(14) Agriculture	(15) Manufacturing	(16) Commerce	(17) Services
FEs Individual and Year and All Controls																	
Has PPT	-0.044 (0.035)	0.061 (0.052)	0.205 (0.125)	0.093 (0.060)	0.388*** (0.113)	0.027 (0.078)	0.230* (0.133)	0.029 (0.049)	-0.002 (0.030)	0.101 (0.073)	-0.119** (0.053)	-0.008 (0.012)	0.030 (0.019)	0.030* (0.015)	0.048** (0.022)	0.031 (0.032)	-0.109*** (0.030)
Observations	4,944	3,168	1,544	1,544	412	212	626	2,200	2,202	1,310	1,310	1,310	1,310	2,080	2,080	2,080	2,080
Adjusted R²	0.84	0.79	0.83	0.88	0.83	0.86	0.79	0.84	0.79	0.83	0.84	0.53	0.83	0.94	0.84	0.85	0.83
FEs Individual and Year and All Controls																	
Has PPT	0.035 (0.026)	0.007 (0.031)	-0.002 (0.032)	0.006 (0.055)	0.010 (0.040)	0.080* (0.046)	0.060 (0.050)	0.059 (0.070)	0.009 (0.027)	0.050 (0.049)	-0.119** (0.053)	-0.007 (0.014)	-0.003 (0.018)	-0.003 (0.021)	-0.001 (0.038)	0.018 (0.049)	-0.014 (0.047)
Observations	5,718	4,239	3,448	2,745	2,745	1,119	861	1,594	3,451	2,691	1,310	2,691	2,691	3,351	3,351	3,351	3,351
Adjusted R²	0.18	0.05	0.10	0.28	0.21	0.28	0.23	0.24	0.09	0.12	0.84	0.02	0.09	0.18	0.07	0.03	0.12

Source: Original table for this report based on data from GEIH and PM 2020 and 2021.

Note: Models (1) and (2) include the yearly number of migrants by department (ln); the yearly number of Colombians by department to the Venezuelan border (ln) interacted with the year fixed effects; a control for having the PEP; and controls for having applied to the PPT early, at the time the first and second rounds of the PM survey were collected; 83 percent of migrants did not have a PEP permit when the PPT became available. OLS = ordinary least squares; PEP = Permiso Especial de Permanencia (Special Permanence Permit); PPT = Permiso de Permanencia Temporal (Temporary Protection Permit).
* $p < .10$, ** $p < .05$, *** $p < .01$.

wages, in particular, would be more affected by allowing refugees access to formal employment in an economy where the formal labor market is small relative to the number of potentially competitive refugees.

However, without substantial economywide effects, host workers who experience worse job outcomes can likely be compensated—and policy should consider that there are other hosts who might benefit. The absence or small magnitude of economywide effects from work permits should not blind policy makers to impacts on groups of workers who are more exposed to competition. However, it does suggest that the effects are limited enough for resources to be available for policies to be implemented to help workers adapt, compensate those affected, or boost overall demand for labor where competition has increased. Further, where work permits ease access to higher-quality jobs, they likely reduce the labor market competition that less-qualified workers may have experienced from refugees before the work permit scheme, as long as hosts who no longer find higher-quality jobs do not overwhelmingly begin competing for the jobs these less-qualified workers rely on. Thus, policy should consider that, where work permit schemes may be detrimental to some better-off workers, there is the potential for some of the more vulnerable workers to benefit. However, some action may still be needed to promote good outcomes for both groups of host workers.

Regardless of whether they increase access to formal jobs in practice, work permits can greatly benefit refugees, but complementary policies may be needed. Although policy attention on the impacts of work permits on hosts is warranted, one—relatively small—group of workers stands to benefit substantially from the introduction of work permit programs, and that is refugees. This is obviously true where those who can obtain a permit have good chances of finding the kind of relatively higher-earning formal jobs with better working conditions that permits are meant to provide access to. Even in labor markets where there is little demand for workers in such jobs, work permits can be an effective tool in empowering refugee workers because they are a potent and visible signal that some refugees have a right to work and, thus, can bolster the bargaining power and reduce the vulnerability of refugee workers. In economies where informality and self-employment are the norm, policy should note that this signaling effect may be the most important function of a work permit scheme, and consider additional ways of sending the same message, for instance, through permit programs that are easy to obtain and not tied to formal work, or even through government communications. In addition, in such labor markets, policy attention also needs to be directed toward obstacles that are similarly stark for refugees, such as access to land and access to capital for self-employed activities.

Notes

1 | Some papers have sought to assess the effect of the compact policy without seeking to establish causality, for instance, Gray Meral (2020); Stave, Kebede, and Kattaa (2021); and Temprano-Arroyo (2018).

2 | The work permits are valid for a duration of one year and are renewable.

3 | Districts are Admin-2 level units in Jordan and department, Admin-1 level units in Colombia. However, both are relatively similar regarding the number of units per country, with 31 departments in Colombia and 48 districts in Jordan.

4 | Results of the individual fixed effects can be found in table ST1A.1 in online annex ST1A.

5 | Results omitted for conciseness.

6 | Results ommited for conciseness.

References

Ajluni, Salem, and Mary Kawar. 2014. *The Impact of the Syrian Refugee Crisis on the Labour Market in Jordan: A Preliminary Analysis*. Beirut: International Labour Organization, Regional Office for Arab States.

Ajluni, Salem, and Dorsey Lockhart. 2019. *The Syrian Refugee Crisis and Its Impact on the Jordanian Labour Market*. Amman: West Asia-North Africa Institute.

Bahar, Dany, Ana María Ibanez, and Sandra V. Rozo. 2021. "Give Me Your Tired and Your Poor: Impact of a Large-Scale Amnesty Program for Undocumented Refugees." *Journal of Development Economics* 151: 102652.

Bousquet, Julie and Jean-Francois Maystadt. 2023. "Is Giving Working Rights to Refugees Hurting Their Hosts? Evidence fro Jordan." In Bousquet, Julie. 2023 "Labor Market Dynamics, Refugee Integrations, and Social Cohesion in Conflict and Displacement Contexts." PhD Dissertation, University of Leuven.

Garcia-Suaza, Andres, Juan Miguel Gallego, Juan Diego Mayorga, Angie Mondragon-Mayo, Carlos Sepulveda, and Alexander Sarago Iturralde. 2023. "Impacts of Venezuelan Migration on the Colombian Labor Market." Background paper written for this report. World Bank, Washington, DC.

Gray Meral, Amanda. 2020. "Assessing the Jordan Compact One Year On: An Opportunity or a Barrier to Better Achieving Refugees' Right to Work." *Journal of Refugee Studies* 33 (1): 42–61.

Ibanez, Ana María, Andres Moya, María Adelaida Ortega, Marisol Rodríguez Chatruc, and Sandra V. Rozo. 2021. "Life Out of the Shadows: Impacts of Amnesty Programs on Migrant's Lives." Discussion Paper 15049, Institute of Labor Economics, Bonn.

ILO (International Labour Organization). 2015. "Work Permits for Syrian Refugees in Jordan." International Labour Organization, Regional Office for Arab States, Beirut.

Lombardo, Carlo, Julian Martínez Correa, Leonardo Jose Peñaloza Pacheco, and Leonardo Carlos Gasparini. 2021. "The Distributional Effect of a Massive Exodus in Latin America and the Role of Downgrading and Regularization." Documento de Trabajo, No. 290, Universidad Nacional de La Plata, Centro de Estudios Distributivos, Laborales y Sociales (CEDLAS), La Plata.

Stave, Svein Erik, Tewodros Aragie Kebede, and Maha Kattaa. 2021. *Impact of Work Permits on Decent Work for Syrians in Jordan*. Beirut: International Labour Organization, Regional Office for Arab States. https://www.ilo.org/wcmsp5/groups/public/—arabstates/—robeirut/documents/publication /wcms820822.pdf.

Temprano-Arroyo, Heliodoro. 2018. "Promoting Labour Market Integration of Refugees with Trade Preferences: Beyond the EU Jordan Compact." Kiel Working Papers 2108, Kiel Institute for the World Economy (IfW Kiel).

4. Comparative Job Outcomes and Labor Market Interactions of Hosts and Refugees

Introduction

This chapter discusses in detail the labor market outcomes and interactions of hosts and refugees in four labor markets in two low-income countries, Ethiopia and Uganda, with additional perspectives on two middle-income countries, Colombia and Jordan. As this study argues, labor markets are diverse, and refugees and their hosts engage with the market and with each other in complex ways. Standard nationally representative data provide an indispensable

---

Chapter 4 online annex available at https://openknowledge.worldbank.org/handle/10986/40701: annex 4A "Additional Descriptive Statistics."

overview of the issues arising from refugees' labor market participation. However, these data are not designed to capture the specificities of labor market interactions in detail, nor to provide sufficient sample size within a given labor market to reliably observe host and refugee activities, outcomes, and interactions side by side. This chapter presents such an analysis based on data collected for this report in two labor markets in Ethiopia and two labor markets in Uganda. Further, it provides a perspective of whether patterns in Colombia and Jordan correspond with or diverge from findings in Ethiopia and Uganda. The analysis draws upon new labor market data on refugees collected for this report in Colombia that deepen nationally representative information, and the chapter reanalyzes rich data available in Jordan.

The investigation in this chapter seeks to clarify mechanisms through which displacement affects job outcomes for hosts, and to identify policies to improve job outcomes for both hosts and refugees. As seen in previous chapters, effects of displacement on host job outcomes that are observed at the aggregate level can mask a multitude of effects on distinct groups of workers. In addition, where analysis considers only the "reduced-form" effects of displacement on job outcomes and does not describe mechanisms through which such effects arise, useful policy levers with which to enhance outcomes for each or both groups may not be identified. The analysis in this chapter seeks to shed further light on results presented in chapter 3 by providing a far greater level of granularity about different groups in the labor market and by discussing in detail mechanisms through which different groups of workers may affect one another. Based on this assessment, it then seeks to inform policy recommendations for better job outcomes for hosts and refugees.

The analysis in this chapter explores the following issues: It begins with a description of the comparative demographics of refugee and host households as well as of displacement history. It then discusses the labor market engagement of refugees and hosts and assesses the role that unearned income plays among both groups, and then compares the types of activities each group relies on for earnings. Further, it explores how assets and savings provide different conditions for hosts and refugees in potential labor market endeavors and assesses comparative skill levels and the question of skill mismatches. Finally, it delves into the three main employment types in the labor markets considered here—paid work for others (whether wage work or more casual labor), self-employment outside of agriculture, and self-employment in agriculture—and explores facets such as types of activities, determinants of earnings, and barriers to better outcomes in each type of job.

To characterize outcomes and interactions in detail, this chapter draws on new purpose-built data sets from Colombia, Ethiopia, and Uganda. In Ethiopia and Uganda, this analysis relies on data sets with information on refugees and hosts in four labor markets collected for this report and purpose-designed to capture labor market interactions and outcomes. To provide a perspective on labor markets in Colombia, it uses available secondary data as well as data collected for this report that added greater detail about labor market activity and outcomes to a series of nationally representative surveys of refugees. Finally, to explore patterns in Jordan, the chapter relies on two complementary existing data sets. All data are described in more detail in the following sections.

In low-income countries, urban and rural labor markets are starkly different, and there is a pronounced gap between central localities and those that are more remote. In both Ethiopia and Uganda, data were collected to describe the most urban and central labor market—that in each country's capital city—and one labor market in a largely rural and less-connected area, specifically the city of Jijiga and Kebribeyah refugee camp in Ethiopia's Somali Region, and the Nakivale refugee settlement and the towns and villages in the surrounding Isingiro district in Uganda.

The labor market analyses shown here for Ethiopia and Uganda should be considered case studies that aim to provide a perspective on and explain patterns observed at the national level. The localities in Ethiopia and Uganda were selected with the goal of representing in a meaningful way two important types of labor markets (and they were chosen based on expert consultations). Still, the analysis of these localities must be put in context to distill lessons with wider relevance. Therefore, this chapter aims to situate results and to explain how they are relevant to patterns observed at the national level, such as those discussed in chapter 3.

Data and methods

This section describes the data used in the chapter as well as the methods used in analyzing data.

Overall approach

Data collection for this report sought to complement other survey efforts and to obtain detailed information on how hosts and refugees engage in a labor market they share. A global effort has been undertaken recently to collect data on refugees and their host communities, including through substantial investments made by the World Bank (refer to chapter 1). Many recent data collection efforts have been made in Jordan, and no additional data were collected under this project. In the other three countries, data collection for this initiative was designed to complement available information, with the goal of (1) having sufficiently granular labor market information to observe outcomes and mechanisms of interest, and (2) having an adequate sample size of both hosts and refugees within a certain labor market to reliably measure outcomes while disaggregating between subgroups of workers.

Data were collected in Colombia, Ethiopia, and Uganda with the goal of describing comparative labor market performance and interactions in detail. In Ethiopia and Uganda, data collection focused on two labor markets in each country, and aimed to produce data that would achieve sufficient sample sizes among both hosts and refugees, in an urban and a rural labor market in each country, to allow for a detailed exploration of comparative labor market outcomes and interactions between the two groups. The two resulting surveys are the Harmonized Host and Refugee Labor Market Surveys (HHR-LFS) for Ethiopia and Uganda.[1] In Colombia, data collection for this project was designed to complement an ongoing large and representative rolling survey of displaced Venezuelans based on the national household sample survey by conducting a survey wave timed to measure the impact of a new residence and work permit scheme, and by including an additional module of labor market questions in the questionnaire.

Data description

Survey work for the HHR-LMS in Uganda yielded a representative sample of hosts and refugees in Kampala and the district that hosts the Nakivale refugee settlement. In both Ethiopia and Uganda, the World Bank contracted with the Norwegian think tank Fafo to collect data in concert with local academic institutions. The survey covers two locations in Uganda: the capital, Kampala, and Isingiro district, including the Nakivale refugee settlement (this report uses "Isingiro" as shorthand for all localities in Isingiro district, including Nakivale). The sampling design included 265 initial enumeration areas (EAs) selected from census maps, using probability proportionate to size (PPS), with the number of households used as a measure of size. The EAs were selected using the sample frame constructed during the 2014 Ugandan population census. The Uganda Bureau of Statistics selected the EAs and provided detailed maps of the areas. Using these maps, the study team conducted a listing of all households in the selected EAs with door-to-door visits.[2] The listing exercise was carried out from November 2021 through January 2022 by a team of local field workers recruited and trained for this purpose.

Data were collected from a sizable sample of both hosts and refugees within the two target labor markets to allow for detailed disaggregation in the analysis. The overall sample design is a two-stage sample in which first EAs and then households were sampled. Individuals from among eligible respondents within a household were randomly selected in a third stage. Persons between ages 18 and 65 in a host household, and refugees between ages 18 and 65 in a refugee household, were eligible to be interviewed. The questionnaires were administered in local languages during February through April 2022 by a team of local interviewers recruited and trained for the purpose. The survey resulted in a completed sample size of 4,102 households, of which 2,367 are host and 1,735 are refugee households. Furthermore, the survey resulted in a completed sample size of 3,357 individual respondents, of whom 1,841 are hosts and 1,516 are refugees. (Map 4.1 shows the location of respondent households in Uganda.)

Survey work for the HHR-LMS in Ethiopia focused on two labor markets—the capital, Addis Ababa, as well as the localities of Jijiga city and the linked labor markets of Kebribeyah town and Kebribeyah refugee camp in Somali Region. The sample design included 150 initial EAs in Addis Ababa and 79 in Somali Region. These EAs were selected using PPS sampling. EAs were selected using a sample frame prepared for the population census of Ethiopia that had been planned for 2020 but not implemented because of the COVID-19

MAP 4.1 Location of HHR-LMS respondent households, Uganda

a. Uganda

(continued)

MAP 4.1   Location of HHR-LMS respondent households in Uganda *(continued)*

b. Kampala

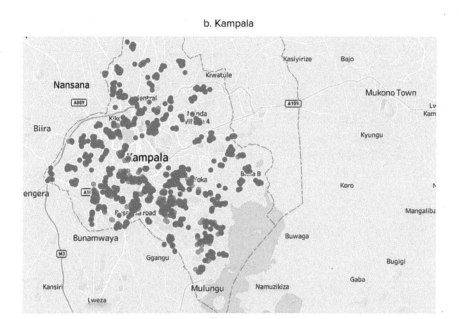

c. Isingiro district, Nakivale

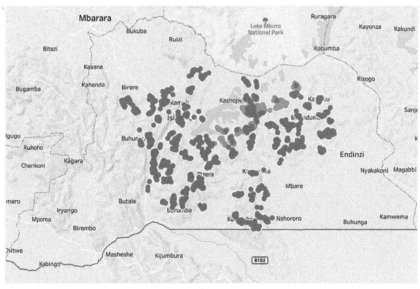

● Host household   ● Refugee household

Source: Original maps for this report.

(coronavirus) pandemic and security challenges. The Ethiopian Central Statistical Service selected the EAs and provided the list along with detailed maps. Using these maps, the study team conducted a listing of all households in the selected EAs with door-to-door visits. The listing exercise was carried out during February through March 2022 in Addis Ababa and during May through June 2022 in Somali Region.

Although a substantial number of refugees reside in Addis Ababa, they represent a small share of the population in this large metropolitan area, and previous survey efforts have struggled to reach sufficient numbers of respondents. To ensure that a large-enough sample would be obtained, in Addis Ababa the investigation used a sampling technique known as adaptive cluster sampling (ACS) to capture refugee households (Thompson 1990). The technique is considered useful for rare populations that live in clustered urban areas, but no study so far seems to have used ACS to study refugees or internally displaced persons (Eckman and Himelein 2022). Using the listing of households in the initial 150 clusters in Addis Ababa, those EAs in which refugees represented at least 10 percent of all households were identified, and a listing of all households in their neighboring EAs was conducted. This effort resulted in listing an additional 71 EAs identified as neighbors of the initial clusters. These additional EAs were then surveyed in the same manner as the initial EAs.

Survey work yielded a substantial sample of both host and refugee workers and households in all localities, including in Addis Ababa through the ACS method. The survey was administered in local languages using face-to-face interviews during April and May 2022 in Addis Ababa and during June and July 2022 in Somali Region by a team of local interviewers recruited and trained for this purpose. The survey resulted in a completed sample size of 4,405 households, of which 2,474 are host and 1,931 are refugee households. (Map 4.2 shows the location of respondent households in Ethiopia.) Furthermore, the survey resulted in a completed sample size of 3,901 individuals, of which 2,227 are hosts and 1,674 are refugees. Although the ACS approach proved very effective in Addis Ababa, not all aspects of refugees' labor market engagement could be characterized because of very low labor force participation. As in previous survey efforts, identifying a sufficient number of refugee households in Addis Ababa through PPS random sampling proved difficult. In the initially sampled EAs, 318 refugee households and 260 individual working-age respondents could be surveyed; the ACS approach yielded a far larger sample of 1,208 refugee households and 1,005 individual respondents. This larger ACS sample permits the characterization of some features of the labor market engagement of refugees that could not be analyzed in the PPS sample. Basic indicators that are easily observed, such as demographics, yield very similar summary statistics in the PPS and ACS samples.

MAP 4.2 Location of HHR-LMS respondent households, Ethiopia

a. Ethiopia

b. Addis Ababa

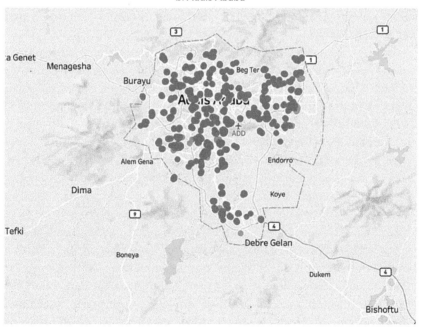

(continued)

MAP 4.2 Location of HHR-LMS respondent households, Ethiopia (*continued*)

c. Somali Region, Jijiga

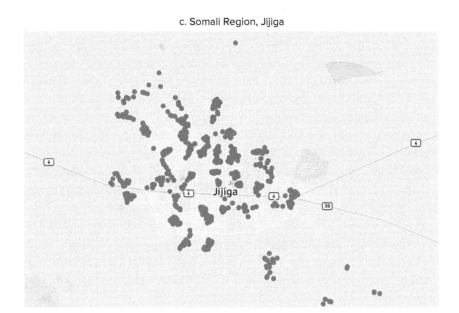

d. Somali Region, Kebribeyah

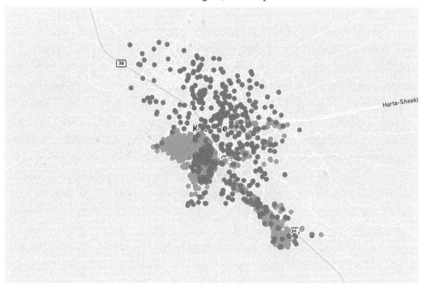

● Host household ● Refugee household

Source: Original maps for this report.

Questionnaires aimed to collect information on economic activity, socio-economic background, and the experience of displacement and the perceptions of displaced workers. The study team developed two structured questionnaires aimed at capturing information from both refugees and hosts. In summary, the survey can be thought of as a hybrid of a household survey with an income module, a labor market survey, and some modules related to the displacement experience and perceptions of the displaced. The first part of the questionnaire was administered to the head of the household and included question items on demographic profile, education, and labor market participation of all household members, as well as measures of the household's economic activity and its standard of living. The second part was administered to individual respondents and included survey modules related to their social background and skills, labor market participation and job characteristics, and their mobility history and social network; modules to assess social integration and perceptions of displacement as well as subjective well-being; and, finally, an experimental module designed to elicit framing effects on hosts' stated perceptions of refugees. The questionnaire development process included a pilot exercise to refine both the content of the questionnaire and field implementation procedures.

In Colombia, dedicated labor market data were collected for this report as part of a series of monitoring surveys, at a time that allows for consideration of the effect of a work permit initiative. The initiative collected data under the innovative Encuesta Pulso de la Migración (PM) series of phone surveys. The PM follows a subsample of respondents to the Gran Encuesta Integrada de Hogares (Large Integrated Household Survey, or GEIH), collected in 2021 by Colombia's National Administrative Department of Statistics (Departamento Administrativo Nacional de Estadística), or DANE (DANE 2018). Data were collected quarterly from mid-2021.[3] The third round of the survey was supported and designed by the World Bank in collaboration with DANE for the purposes of this report. It collected detailed labor market information on migrants, along with other dimensions of the effect of COVID-19 and job mobility. It was also timed to collect data about one year after the introduction of the Permiso de Permanencia Temporal (Temporary Protection Permit) work permit scheme to allow for an analysis of its impact. This sample of migrants surveyed in the PM includes about 12,500 individuals over the four rounds. The analysis in this chapter uses these data to show job outcomes for migrants and compare them with outcomes among the nearly 480,000 Colombians surveyed in the GEIH data collected in 2021.

To provide a comparative perspective on Jordan, this chapter uses two published data sets that trace job outcomes for Jordanians and for refugees. This analysis relies on existing secondary data to illustrate how patterns found in the primary data correspond to labor market features in Jordan. Both data sources cover labor market outcomes in some detail. Notably, although there is no single data set that provides a large and representative sample of both Jordanian and refugee workers, this investigation works with two surveys that were conducted a year apart and provide, in turn, such a sample for the two groups of workers. Thus, to describe labor market outcomes for Jordanians, the Jordan Labor Market Panel Survey (JLMPS) (OAMDI 2018) of 2016 is used; it provides a representative sample of about 28,000 Jordanians and is described in detail in chapter 3. To shed light on job outcomes for refugees, data collected in 2017 from a representative sample of nearly 41,000 Syrian refugees (the unpublished Survey of Syrian Refugees in Jordan provided by Fafo, henceforth SSRJ; described in Tiltnes, Pedersen, and Zhang 2019) are used. The observed patterns are cross-referenced with a third, more dated and smaller, data set that surveyed both hosts and refugees in 2014. Results are well-aligned in most instances; for conciseness, results from these additional data sets are reviewed in the following discussion only where there are differences worth noting.

The surveys conducted in Ethiopia and Uganda used the same questionnaire to facilitate comparison. Some of the same questions were also asked in the Colombia survey. The following analysis largely harmonizes indicators across all four settings, including the secondary data instrument used for Jordan; however, some differences remain and are discussed as appropriate.

Demographic profiles and displacement history

Key insights

Across the localities studied here, clear stylized patterns distinguish refugee households from those of hosts: refugee households tend to be larger, are more likely to be headed by women, and have younger household heads. These patterns are clearest in Ethiopia, Jordan, and Uganda, where those surveyed have fled violence. These characteristics potentially suggest both greater need for earned income and, thus, need for access to jobs, and greater vulnerability in the labor market because of the need to care for more household members, the lower wealth that tends to come with younger age, and gender differentials in skills and opportunities.

However, the nature of displacement and host country policies also have a bearing on household structure. Refugee households in Addis Ababa have a very different structure than do households in other localities that were surveyed in Ethiopia and Uganda, likely because of a restrictive resettlement policy that long limited the opportunity to move only to Eritrean households able to find an Ethiopian sponsor. As a consequence, demographics are suggestive of households composed of somewhat better-off exiles that are less likely to need earned income: they are smaller, are very likely to be headed by women, and have much younger household heads. Migrant households in Colombia reflect the demographics of people who have come to work, with younger households and fewer dependents.

The nationalities of refugees in the four localities in Ethiopia and Uganda illustrate that policy toward freedom of movement has a powerful impact on whether refugees can, in practice, sort into their preferred labor markets. Under Uganda's liberal regime, Kampala hosts an even mix of refugees of different nationalities, whereas policy narrowly limits who can resettle in Addis Ababa. At the same time, the nationalities of those who reside in the more remote refugee settlements show that geography still matters and limits refugee populations in some areas to those who fled neighboring countries.

Household composition and displacement history

In both localities in Uganda as well as in Jijiga in Ethiopia, refugee households are slightly larger, and women are more likely to head them. In Isingiro, Jijiga, and Kampala, refugee and host households have similar demographic structures, but with some clear differences. Refugee households are somewhat larger, with two additional members at the median in Jijiga and one additional member in the two Ugandan localities, as well as one additional working-age member at the median in each locality (table 4.1). Further, refugee household heads are slightly younger at the median, with similar gaps in Jijiga and Uganda (one to three years). A more pronounced difference is that refugee households are more likely to be headed by women than host households by a large margin (a difference of 13 percentage points and 12 percentage points in the two localities in Uganda, and 5 percentage points in Jijiga). In Kampala, refugee households are even slightly more likely to be headed by women than by men (52 percent). Previous studies in East Africa have found similar refugee household characteristics (Pape et al. 2021; Pape, Petrini, and Iqbal 2018; World Bank 2019). The high number of female-headed households might be due to split households, that is, men staying behind to fight, to continue to work, or to protect their belongings while the rest of the family flees; to men migrating onward to third countries for work; or to the male household head having died. All three differences can be interpreted as being related to households having fled violence, and may be correlated with both a greater need for engagement in the labor market and greater vulnerability.

In Jordan, refugee households are slightly larger than hosts', with typically one additional household member at the median. The share of household members who are of working age is somewhat higher among hosts (59 percent, compared with about 51 percent among refugees), and the share of women is lower. The household head's typical age is also much lower in refugee households, at 36 years of age at the median for refugees, compared with 46 years among hosts. Although the share of female household heads is low in both groups, it is substantially higher among refugees (about 18 percent of households) than hosts (about 9 percent of households). All these differences are consistent with the disruption of household structures through displacement. There are few differences in household structure between those residing in camps and those who live in urban areas (table 4.1).

In line with policy restrictions controlling mobility, refugee households in Addis Ababa typically are smaller than host households and are much more likely to be headed by women and younger people. Refugee households in Addis Ababa have at the median two fewer members than host households, including one fewer working-age member (table 4.1). They are almost twice as likely as host households to be headed by women: slightly more than one in three host households are female-headed, compared with two of every three refugee households (36 percent and 66 percent). Refugee household heads are also a decade younger at the median than their counterparts among hosts. These patterns are particularly noteworthy in the context of low labor market participation discussed later; they reinforce the impression of refugee households as somewhat better-off exiles in Addis Ababa.

In Colombia, displaced and host households are of similar size, in terms of both working-age members and dependents. However, household heads among migrants are much younger at the median, especially in urban areas, where the gap in median age is 13 years. By way of contrast with the other countries studied, it is host households that are somewhat more likely to be headed by a female. A DANE and Ladysmith (2021) study shows that Venezuelan men are more likely to migrate to Colombia for work than women, whereas women are more likely to move to reunite with family. Men might thus tend to move first and then women follow. These patterns are potentially in line with the fact that migrants are likely to flee economic hardship and may have made a conscious choice to migrate, at least at the beginning of the crisis, as opposed to situations in which people flee danger (table 4.1).

The national origin of refugees in the different localities is in line with geography but, in the case of Addis Ababa, is also driven by a policy that made it much easier for Eritreans to relocate from camps. Refugees in Addis Ababa overwhelmingly were born in Eritrea (98 percent; table 4.2), reflecting the policy framework in Ethiopia, which until recently allowed Eritreans to live out of camps only if they had someone who sponsored them. Those in Jijiga were overwhelmingly born in Somalia (75 percent), in line with the proximity of the camp to the border. About one in four of the camp residents who consider themselves to be displaced reports having been born in Ethiopia, reflecting the long-term nature of displacement causing some respondents to be among the second generation of refugees (and perhaps also reflecting the fluidity of national identities in the border area). Refugees in Isingiro come from countries that border

TABLE 4.1 Demographics of hosts, migrants, and refugees, case study countries

	HH members (median)	Working-age HH members (median)	Share of HH members in WAP (mean) (%)	Share of women among WAP (%)	Share of women among HH heads (%)	HH head age (median)	Share of refugees with documentation (%)
Ethiopia							
Addis Ababa, host	5	3	67	56	36	42	n.a.
Addis Ababa, refugees	3	2	74	59	66	32	69
Jijiga, hosts	7	3	48	53	55	40	n.a.
Jijiga, refugees	9	4	46	51	60	39	52
Uganda							
Kampala, hosts	4	2	66	56	39	38	n.a.
Kampala, refugees	5	3	67	54	52	36	74
Isingiro, hosts	6	2	49	52	21	45	n.a.
Isingiro, refugees	7	3	48	54	33	42	97
Colombia							
Urban, host	4	2	67	54	42	47	–
Urban, migrant	5	3	66	51	38	34	–
Rural, host	4	2	62	50	28	45	–
Rural, migrant	5	2	59	48	20	35	–
Jordan							
Urban, hosts	5	3	60	62	9	46	–
Urban, refugees	6	3	53	54	19	36	–
Rural, hosts	6	3	59	60	9	46	–
Rural, refugees	6	3	51	53	18	33	–
Camp, refugees	6	3	51	52	17	33	–

Source: Original table for this report based on data from JLMPS, SSRJ, GEIH, PM, HHR-LMS Ethiopia, and HHR-LMS Uganda. HH = household; n.a. = not applicable; WAP = working-age population; – = not available.

TABLE 4.2 Home country of the displaced, by study locality, Ethiopia and Uganda

Locality	Percent (%)
Ethiopia	
Addis Ababa	
Eritrea	97.8
Ethiopia	0.7
Somalia	1.6
Jijiga	
Ethiopia	24.9
Somalia	75.1
Uganda	
Kampala	
Burundi	4.0
Congo, Dem. Rep.	27.1
Eritrea	22.7
Ethiopia	5.6
Rwanda	2.1
Somalia	26.7
South Sudan	10.1
Uganda	0.5
Other	1.2
Isingiro	
Burundi	20.8
Congo, Dem. Rep.	61.0
Ethiopia	1.0
Rwanda	11.8
Somalia	4.2
Uganda	0.6
Other	0.6

Source: Original table for this report based on data from HHR-LMS Ethiopia, HHR-LMS Uganda, GEIH, and PM.

southern Uganda: 61 percent are from the Democratic Republic of Congo, 21 percent from Burundi, and 12 percent from Rwanda. Kampala hosts a much more mixed group of nationalities, in line with the city being for most refugees who live there the second locality in which they settle in Uganda: 27 percent are from the Democratic Republic of Congo, 27 percent from Somalia, 23 percent from Eritrea, and 10 percent from South Sudan. Uganda's liberal policy environment, which affords refugees freedom of movement, clearly allows for diverse groups of refugees to move to the capital, in contrast with Ethiopia's restrictive policy. However, geographic proximity still matters for refugees who remain in Isingiro in much the same way it does in Jijiga.

The reasons refugees left their home countries vary across the localities studied. Nearly all refugees in Isingiro (95 percent) and most in Jijiga (88 percent) and Kampala (82 percent) say that they fled conflict or persecution or received threats, whereas in Addis Ababa, only about one in four did (26 percent), and fewer among women (20 percent). Instead, refugees in Addis Ababa are most likely to say that they came for economic opportunities (40 percent among men and 27 percent among women) although, as shown in the section "Participation in the labor market and reliance on unearned income," activity rates among refugees are very low in the city. Others say that they came to reunite with their families (5 percent among men, and 37 percent among women) (table 4.3). The high share of refugees in Addis Ababa who say that they came for economic economic opportunities may seem in striking contrast with the other localities. However, it is worth recalling that most refugees in Addis Ababa are Eritrean nationals, and that the degree of government control of economic life in Eritrea creates pressures that resemble persecution. In this sense, the reasons for displacement among refugees in Addis Ababa may be more similar to those in other localities than it initially appears. Further, anecdotally, refugee families in Addis Ababa commonly depend on the remittances of relatives who move on to third countries (in line with the important role of foreign remittances in household income, also reported later), perhaps explaining how economic motives for displacement can coexist with low labor force participation rates. Venezuelan migrants in Colombia arguably have escaped similarly oppressive economic hardship. Among them, most (93 percent and 89 percent in urban and rural areas, respectively) say they fled economic instability, whereas a substantial minority (19 percent and 24 percent in urban and rural areas, respectively) say they fled insecurity (table 4.4). Still, even if most of them moved for economic reasons, the way they moved (in large numbers, arriving over a short period, and usually without having secured a job beforehand) sets their own labor market situation and their potential impact on hosts apart from typical labor migration.

Refugees in the two big cities are often relatively recent arrivals in their host communities and have previously lived elsewhere in the host country. Refugees settled in both Addis Ababa and Kampala have at the median been residents for four years, whereas those in Isingiro typically have been in the area longer, nine years at the median, and those who have found refuge in Jijiga report extremely long median residences of 31 years. Refugees in Addis Ababa overwhelmingly have lived elsewhere in Ethiopia: Addis Ababa is the first stop for only 22 percent of them, and 72 percent of them say that they previously lived in a refugee camp in Ethiopia, again in line with the policy environment, which has allowed limited opportunities for living outside of camps since 2010. About half of those in Kampala also report that they initially lived elsewhere in Uganda, including 15 percent who lived in settlements (table 4.4). By way of

TABLE 4.3   Reasons for displacement, by study locality, Ethiopia and Uganda

percent

Locality	Male	Female	Total
Ethiopia			
Addis Ababa			
Conflict	6.8	5.5	6.0
Received threats	1.2	1.1	1.2
Weather shocks	0.0	0.1	0.1
Business opportunity	40.4	26.5	31.8
Education	3.8	2.8	3.2
Health	1.0	4.7	3.3
Political persecution	25.0	13.3	17.7
Family reunion	5.3	36.6	24.7
Other	16.4	9.3	12.0
Jijiga			
Conflict	88.2	87.5	87.7
Weather shocks	0.5	0.0	0.2
Family reunion	0.0	0.4	0.2
Other	11.3	12.2	11.8
Uganda			
Kampala			
Conflict	66.4	67.5	67.1
Received threats	6.2	6.5	6.4
Business opportunity	4.8	2.7	3.6
Education	4.7	3.1	3.7
Health	0.7	3.0	2.0
Political persecution	9.1	7.8	8.3
Family reunion	2.1	5.1	3.9
Other	6.0	4.3	5.0
Isingiro			
Conflict	79.1	75.5	77.1
Received threats	8.0	9.2	8.7
Political persecution	8.9	9.0	8.9
Family reunion	0.8	1.9	1.4
Other	3.2	4.4	3.9

Source: Original table for this report based on data from HHR-LMS Ethiopia and HHR-LMS Uganda.

TABLE 4.4 Characteristics of displacement, by study locality, Ethiopia, Uganda, and Colombia

	Fled insecurity, conflict, repression, or threats (%)	Lived in a city in the home country (%)	Lived elsewhere in host country (%)	Residence time (years at median)	Lived in camp or settlement in host country (%)
Ethiopia					
Addis Ababa					
Men	33	57	75	4	68
Women	20	47	82	4	75
Jijiga					
Men	88	47	2	31	2
Women	87	43	2	31	1
Uganda					
Kampala					
Men	82	46	49	5	17
Women	82	60	42	4	13
Isingiro					
Men	96	15	28	10	22
Women	94	8	26	8	22
Colombia					
Urban					
Men	22	94	16	4	–
Women	16	92	18	4	–
Rural					
Men	30	86	31	4	–
Women	19	92	27	4	–

Source: Original table for this report based on data from HHR-LMS Ethiopia, HHR-LMS Uganda, GEIH, and PM.
Note: – = not available.

comparison, both urban and rural migrants in Colombia have been in the country for four years at the median, and relatively few report that they previously resided elsewhere in the country (table 4.4).

Participation in the labor market and reliance on unearned income

Key insights

Policy shapes the labor market participation of refugees but does not completely determine it. Even in highly informal labor markets such as Ethiopia's and Uganda's, policy restrictions on the labor market participation of refugees are clearly at least partially effective. Among the localities studied here, refugees are far more likely to work in markets with relatively liberal policy rules, both between countries and within Ethiopia, for example, comparing Jijiga with the more tightly regulated labor market in Addis Ababa. However, even in the more restrictive labor markets, a substantial number of refugees work—and, even in the less restrictive labor markets, refugees depend heavily on unearned income. Taken together, these patterns highlight the precarious position refugees find themselves in, even under different policy regimes.

Refugee households that draw upon earned and unearned income are consumers in local markets. In both Addis Ababa and Kampala, as in many other settings, refugee households do not rely on humanitarian assistance and participate directly in local markets for goods and services. This is true both among those whose main income comes from work and among those who rely on remittances or domestic family transfers. Refugees who receive cash-based assistance or food vouchers also directly participate in local markets. To hosts, the many refugee households that rely mostly on unearned income are chiefly consumers rather than competitors in the labor market, which may help explain gains for those working in agriculture and for hosts in urban areas in Ethiopia where labor force participation is low.

In the Ethiopian and Ugandan localities, refugees are far less likely than hosts to be active or employed, whereas their activity levels are similar in Colombia and in Jordan. Neither age structure, gender, school attendance, nor education levels account for this difference. Whereas the gap between activity levels among hosts and refugees is greater under Ethiopia's restrictive policy in Addis Ababa than it is in Kampala, the reverse is true for Jijiga and Isingiro. Perhaps surprisingly, in both middle-income countries, activity among refugees largely mirrors levels among hosts, despite the stark differences in labor market policies between Colombia and Jordan. At the same time, labor force participation among hosts and refugees in Jordan is much lower than that in Colombia.

Households that depend principally on unearned income can, in principle, still participate in the labor market: in some contexts, it may simply be that earned income is not sufficient to satisfy needs, and unearned income provides for most of them. However, in the labor markets studied here, the significant dependence on unearned income goes hand in hand with low levels of activity in the labor market. One important implication of this finding is that many refugee households are purely consumers in their host economies rather than competitors in the labor market. Another is that greater access to job opportunities could reduce the degree of outside assistance required, as has been acknowledged in policy discussions. In addition, the data show that displacement itself is the most obvious proximate reason of low activity among refugees, rather than, for instance, differences in demographics, education, or other characteristics.

Refugees' reliance on unearned income

About half of refugee households in Kampala have any earned income (48 percent), compared with virtually all host households (93 percent). Refugee households are more likely to rely on unearned income as their household's main revenue source (59 percent) than they are to rely on earned income (table 4A.1 in online annex 4A). Remittances from abroad matter the most by far as a source of unearned funds: more than two in five depend upon them (43 percent) (figure 4.1). For households that receive any unearned income, these funds are also often the most important income source: 95 percent of those who have any funds from such sources rely principally on them (table 4A.1 in online annex 4A). By contrast, host households rarely draw on unearned income as their most important income source (8 percent), though, again, unearned income is more often than not the principal revenue source when a household has any unearned income (78 percent of those who have any unearned income).

There are few obvious correlates of reliance on unearned income other than the fact that a household has been displaced. Although households with certain characteristics are more likely to rely on unearned income as their primary revenue, none of these differences comes close to accounting for the large gap between the displaced and their hosts with regard to dependence on unearned income. For instance, the share of people relying on unearned income is slightly higher among female-headed households and those with more education (both by 5 percentage points), perhaps reflecting traditional gender roles as well as reservation wages among the better-educated, without an additional differential between refugees and hosts (table 4.5). However, as is evident from table 4.5, a large gap between refugee and host households remains when these factors are accounted for (column (3)).

Even more than in Kampala, refugee households in Addis Ababa depend very heavily on remittances, and only one in seven has any income from work. About six in seven refugee households in Addis Ababa report that they have income from remittances (84 percent), compared with 5 percent among hosts (figure 4.2). Evidence from other contexts also finds that remittances allow refugees to move out of camps or settlements into cities. Remittances might be sent by family and friends who stayed back in their origin country or by those who moved to third countries (Vargas-Silva 2017). In contrast with households in the other localities, refugee households in Addis Ababa are very likely to rely primarily on these funds (96 percent of those who have unearned income, thus, 81 percent of all refugee households (figure 4.1). Only 19 percent of refugee households report that they have any income from work compared with 48 percent in Kampala, reflecting the restrictive labor market access regime. Within Ethiopia's restrictive labor market, the share is again markedly more depressed

FIGURE 4.1 Principal household revenue sources, hosts and refugees, Ethiopia and Uganda

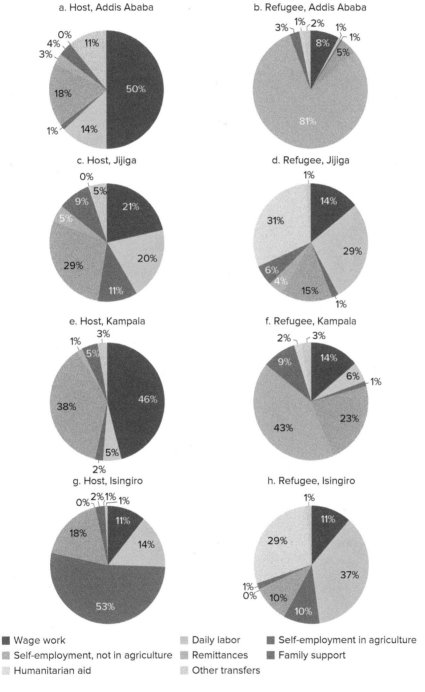

Source: Original figure for this report based on data from HHR-LMS Ethiopia and HHR-LMS Uganda.

TABLE 4.5 Correlates of reliance on unearned income, by study locality, Ethiopia and Uganda

Household with any unearned income	(1)	(2)	(3)	(4)	(5)	(6)
Ethiopia						
Addis Ababa						
Refugee	0.79*** (0.02)	0.82*** (0.04)	0.82*** (0.07)	-0.01 (0.06)		0.82*** (0.08)
Age	-0.03*** (0.01)	-0.03*** (0.01)	-0.03*** (0.01)	-0.03*** (0.01)	-0.03** (0.01)	-0.03*** (0.01)
Age²	0.00*** (0.00)	0.00*** (0.00)	0.00*** (0.00)	0.00*** (0.00)	0.00** (0.00)	0.00*** (0.00)
Female		0.01 (0.03)	-0.04 (0.06)	-0.04 (0.06)	0.00 (0.05)	0.04 (0.03)
Refugee × female		-0.04 (0.05)	0.03 (0.08)	0.02 (0.08)	0.02 (0.05)	-0.02 (0.05)
Education primary			-0.01 (0.06)	-0.01 (0.06)	0.02 (0.05)	0.02 (0.03)
Female × education			0.05 (0.07)	0.05 (0.07)	-0.05 (0.07)	
Refugee × female × education			-0.09 (0.09)	-0.09 (0.09)		
Birth country, Ethiopia				0.00 (0.00)		
Birth country, Eritrea				0.83*** (0.03)		
Birth country, Somalia				0.89*** (0.03)		
Birth country, Other				-0.11*** (0.02)		
Residence time					0.00 (0.02)	
Residence time²					-0.00 (0.00)	
Asset						0.01** (0.01)
Refugee × asset						-0.04** (0.02)
Refugee × asset²						-0.02** (0.01)
Constant	0.55*** (0.13)	0.54*** (0.13)	0.54*** (0.14)	0.54*** (0.14)	1.39*** (0.20)	0.54*** (0.12)
Observations	1,156	1,156	1,156	1,156	254	1,156
Jijiga						
Refugee	0.22*** (0.03)	0.24*** (0.05)	0.24*** (0.07)	0.28*** (0.08)		0.24*** (0.05)

(continued)

TABLE 4.5 Correlates of reliance on unearned income, by study locality, Ethiopia and Uganda *(continued)*

Household with any unearned income	(1)		(2)		(3)		(4)		(5)		(6)	
Age	-0.03***	(0.01)	-0.03***	(0.01)	-0.03***	(0.01)	-0.03***	(0.01)	-0.03**	(0.02)	-0.02***	(0.01)
Age²	0.00***	(0.00)	0.00***	(0.00)	0.00***	(0.00)	0.00***	(0.00)	0.00**	(0.00)	0.00***	(0.00)
Female			0.00	(0.03)	0.07*	(0.04)	0.07*	(0.04)	0.04	(0.09)	0.02	(0.03)
Refugee × female			-0.02	(0.06)	-0.10	(0.08)	-0.11	(0.08)			-0.01	(0.05)
Education primary					0.05	(0.04)	0.05	(0.04)	0.11	(0.11)	-0.02	(0.03)
Female × education					-0.14**	(0.06)	-0.14***	(0.05)	0.06	(0.14)		
Refugee × female × education					0.24*	(0.12)	0.24**	(0.12)				
Birth country, Ethiopia							-0.42	(0.35)				
Birth country, Somalia							-0.46	(0.36)				
Birth country, Other							0.50	(0.35)				
Residence time									-0.06*	(0.03)		
Residence time²									0.00**	(0.00)		
Asset											-0.00	(0.01)
Refugee × asset											-0.02	(0.02)
Refugee × asset²											0.00	(0.01)
Constant	0.59***	(0.13)	0.59***	(0.13)	0.58***	(0.14)	1.00***	(0.37)	0.91**	(0.39)	0.57***	(0.10)
Observations	1,671		1,671		1,671		1,671		428		1,671	

Uganda

Kampala and Isingiro

	(1)		(2)		(3)		(4)		(5)		(6)	
Refugee	0.51***	(0.03)	0.47***	(0.06)	0.56***	(0.14)	-0.01	(0.16)			0.55***	(0.07)
Age	-0.01*	(0.01)	-0.01*	(0.01)	-0.01	(0.01)	-0.01	(0.01)	-0.03	(0.02)	-0.02***	(0.01)
Age²	0.00	(0.00)	0.00	(0.00)	0.00	(0.00)	0.00	(0.00)	0.00	(0.00)	0.00***	(0.00)

(continued)

TABLE 4.5 Correlates of reliance on unearned income, by study locality, Ethiopia and Uganda (continued)

Household with any unearned income	(1)	(2)	(3)	(4)	(5)	(6)
Female		0.03 (0.02)	0.04 (0.03)	0.04 (0.03)	0.02 (0.16)	0.04* (0.02)
Refugee × female		0.08 (0.07)	0.02 (0.17)	−0.03 (0.12)	0.07	0.07 (0.05)
Education primary			0.05** (0.02)	0.05** (0.02)	−0.14 (0.16)	0.03 (0.03)
Female × education			−0.01 (0.04)	−0.00 (0.03)	0.09 (0.18)	
Refugee × female × education			0.06 (0.18)	0.05 (0.13)		
Birth country, Ethiopia				0.70*** (0.20)		
Birth country, Burundi				0.12 (0.15)		
Birth country, Congo, Dem. Rep.				0.29** (0.15)		
Birth country, Eritrea				0.90*** (0.13)		
Birth country, Rwanda				−0.01 (0.07)		
Birth country, Somalia				0.77*** (0.14)		
Birth country, South Sudan				0.77*** (0.15)		
Birth country, Other				0.10 (0.14)		
Residence time					−0.07*** (0.02)	
Residence time²					0.00*** (0.00)	
Asset						−0.00 (0.01)
Refugee × asset						0.01 (0.02)
Refugee × asset²						−0.00 (0.01)
Constant	0.26** (0.11)	0.24** (0.11)	0.19* (0.11)	0.16 (0.11)	1.56*** (0.35)	0.42*** (0.12)
Observations	1,380	1,380	1,380	1,380	558	1,380
Isingiro						
Refugee	0.30*** (0.03)	0.31*** (0.05)	0.17*** (0.04)	0.16 (0.13)		0.18*** (0.03)
Age	−0.01* (0.00)	−0.01** (0.00)	−0.01* (0.00)	−0.01** (0.00)	−0.02** (0.01)	−0.01* (0.00)

(continued)

TABLE 4.5 Correlates of reliance on unearned income, by study locality, Ethiopia and Uganda *(continued)*

Household with any unearned income	(1)	(2)	(3)	(4)	(5)	(6)
Age^2	0.00* (0.00)	0.00** (0.00)	0.00** (0.00)	0.00** (0.00)	0.00** (0.00)	0.00** (0.00)
Female		-0.00 (0.01)	-0.01 (0.01)	-0.01 (0.01)	0.13*** (0.05)	0.00 (0.01)
Refugee × female		-0.01 (0.06)	0.12** (0.05)	0.12** (0.05)		0.03 (0.03)
Education primary			-0.02 (0.01)	-0.02 (0.01)	0.28*** (0.10)	-0.01 (0.01)
Female × education			0.01 (0.02)	0.01 (0.02)	-0.32** (0.12)	
Refugee × female × education			-0.32*** (0.12)	-0.31*** (0.12)		
Birth country, Ethiopia				0.17 (0.27)		
Birth country, Burundi				-0.00 (0.13)		
Birth country, Congo, Dem. Rep.				0.06 (0.12)		
Birth country, Rwanda				-0.17 (0.12)		
Birth country, Somalia				0.23 (0.15)		
Birth country, Other				-0.06 (0.09)		
Residence time					-0.00 (0.01)	
Residence time^2					-0.00 (0.00)	
Asset						0.00 (0.00)
Refugee × asset						-0.08*** (0.02)
Refugee × asset^2						-0.02** (0.01)
Constant	0.14** (0.07)	0.14** (0.06)	0.15*** (0.06)	0.15*** (0.06)	0.64*** (0.21)	0.15* (0.08)
Observations	1,924	1,924	1,924	1,924	934	1,924

Source: Original table for this report, using HHR-LMS Ethiopia and HHR-LMS Uganda data.
* $p < .10$, ** $p < .05$, *** $p < .01$.

FIGURE 4.2 Household revenue sources (any revenue), hosts and refugees, Ethiopia and Uganda

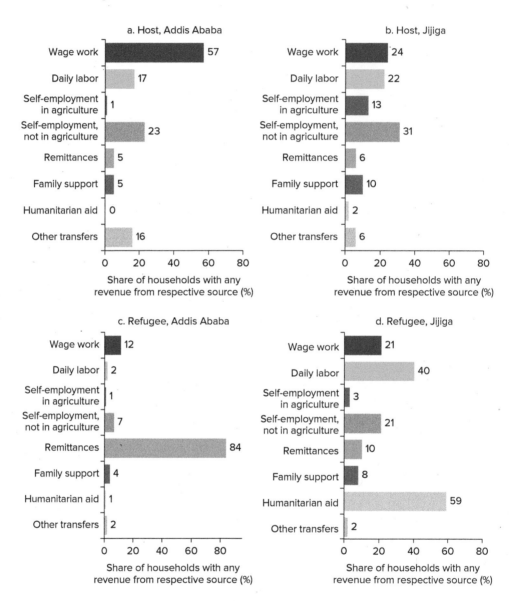

Source: Original figure for this report based on data from HHR-LMS Ethiopia.

in Addis Ababa than it is in Jijiga (where it is 76 percent), likely reflecting the additional difficulties of being active in the capital (figure 4.3). The impact of refugees on labor market outcomes of hosts in Addis Ababa thus occurs chiefly through the consumer and not directly through the labor market.

In both Isingiro and Jijiga, refugee households usually have some earned income, but about one in three still depends on unearned income (figure 4.3), chiefly from humanitarian aid. Unearned income plays a much less prominent role for refugee households in both localities. Most of them draw some income from humanitarian assistance (59 percent in Jijiga and 72 percent in Isingiro; refer to figures 4.2 and 4.4)—a benefit that is available only to residents of camps and, thus, plays no role among those who have resettled in the cities. In Isingiro, humanitarian assistance is nearly the sole source of unearned income for refugees; in Jijiga, some also receive domestic or international remittances (10 percent and 8 percent; refer to figure 4.2). However, most refugees in both localities have some earned income (76 percent in Jijiga and 82 percent in Isingiro), and up to two-thirds of refugee households say that their household's main livelihood comes from earned income (59 percent in Jijiga and 68 percent in Isingiro), suggesting either that there are attractive-enough activities available, including through access to land, or that aid

FIGURE 4.3 Household revenue sources, hosts and refugees, Ethiopia and Uganda

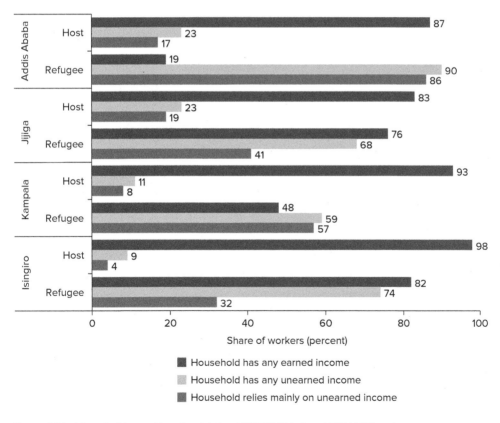

Source: Original figure for this report based on data from HHR-LMS Ethiopia and HHR-LMS Uganda.

FIGURE 4.4   Household reliance on unearned and earned income, hosts and refugees, Uganda

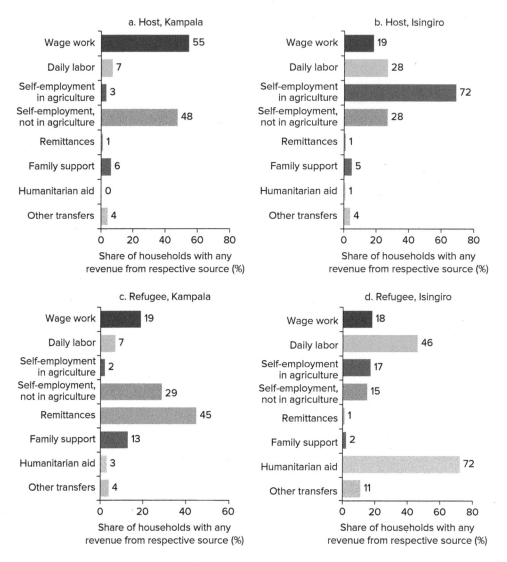

Source: Original figure for this report based on data from HHR-LMS Uganda.

does not fully satisfy their needs, or both (figure 4A.1 in online annex 4A and figure 4.3; refer to discussion of activities and incomes in the next section). Given the much more restrictive labor market rules for refugees in Ethiopia, it is remarkable that similar shares of households in the rural labor markets in both countries live on their own work. In Isingiro, although all refugee groups are more likely than hosts to draw upon unearned income, the share is more elevated among women, and even more so among men with at least primary education (table 4.5). Because, at the same time, wealthier households are less likely to rely on unearned income, the correlate with education may perhaps point to a reluctance to take lower-paying work.

Reliance on unearned income differs among displaced groups from different countries of origin. Across the localities studied in Ethiopia and Uganda, Eritrean and Somali nationals among refugees are much more likely to rely on remittances, with the share of households that rely on them often a multiple of the share among households of other nationalities (figures 4A.2 and 4A.3 in online annex 4A). There are some differences among other nationalities, but they are much smaller by comparison.

In Colombia and Jordan, reliance on unearned income reflects the degree of labor market access as well as the demographics of displaced households. Amid a restrictive labor market regime, most refugee households in Jordan relied on unearned income in 2017. Given the intense humanitarian support effort, it is little surprise that reliance on unearned income included virtually all refugees who lived in camps, in addition to most (86 percent) of those who resided in other areas. By comparison, about one in three host households reported that they received unearned transfers in 2014 (35 percent). More than two-thirds of households living in camps consider unearned income to be their main livelihood source (67 percent), in addition to 73 percent of those living in rural areas and 56 percent of those living in urban areas (figure 4.5). This finding compares to a bit more than one in four among hosts in 2014 (27 percent). By stark contrast, migrant households in Colombia are much less likely than host households to rely primarily on unearned income, with large gaps of 17 percentage points and 31 percentage points in urban and rural areas, respectively (figure 4.6). The low degree of dependence on unearned income among refugees in Colombia is again reflective of a population that has come to their host country to work and finds opportunities relatively easily. In both Colombia and Jordan, the percentage of those who rely on remittances is much lower than in Uganda and Ethiopia.

Low activity rates and dependence on unearned income

In the two low-income countries, participation and employment rates among hosts reflect the different characteristics of urban and rural labor markets, and, in the Somali Region, norms against female labor force participation. Participation of refugees in the labor market must be seen in the context of the level of activity among their hosts. The observed labor force participation and employment rates among hosts in the two low-income countries are largely in line with expectations. In the cities, participation is high (80 percent and 70 percent in Kampala and Addis Ababa, respectively), and employment rates are moderately high (69 percent and 60 percent, respectively) (table 4.6). In agriculturally dominated rural Isingiro, both participation and employment

FIGURE 4.5 Principal household revenue source, hosts and refugees, Jordan

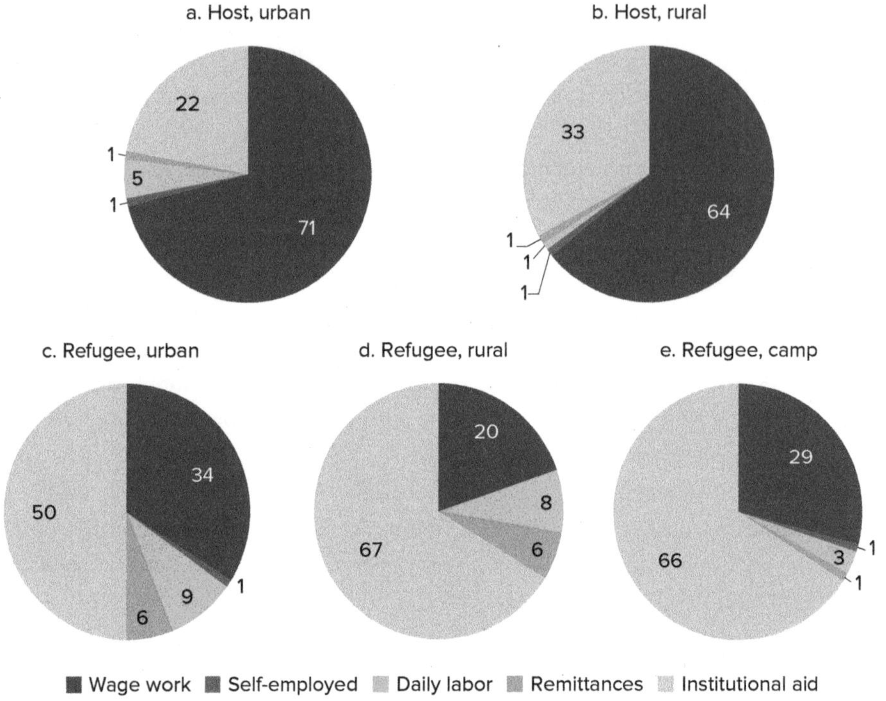

a. Host, urban

b. Host, rural

c. Refugee, urban

d. Refugee, rural

e. Refugee, camp

■ Wage work ■ Self-employed ▨ Daily labor ■ Remittances ▨ Institutional aid

Source: Original figure for this report based on data from JLMPS and SSRJ.

rates are very high (87 percent and 83 percent, respectively). In Jijiga, by contrast, both labor force participation and employment are sharply lower (57 percent and 41 percent, respectively), partially driven by far lower female activity in accordance with cultural norms (45 percent for female participation and 27 percent for female employment), and are more aligned with low labor market participation in neighboring Somalia (55 percent; World Bank 2021).

In both Ethiopia and Uganda, refugees are much less likely to be active and employed, especially in the urban labor markets. The labor force participation and employment rates of refugees show the same rural-urban divide and geographic pattern as are observed among hosts. However, refugees are drastically less likely to be active in the cities, with a margin of 23 percentage points and 35 percentage points in Kampala and Addis Ababa, respectively (table 4.6). The discrepancies in the employment rate are even larger: in Kampala, only slightly more than one in four refugees work (28 percent, a gap of more than 40 percentage points); in Addis Ababa, it is the rare exception for working-age

FIGURE 4.6 Principal household revenue source, hosts and migrants, Colombia

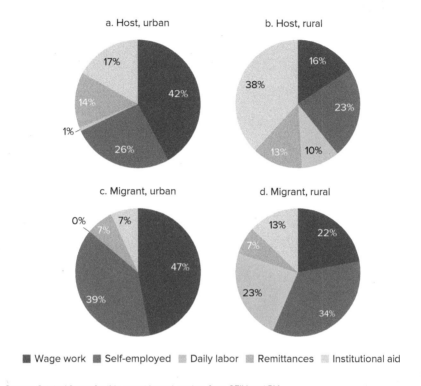

a. Host, urban

b. Host, rural

c. Migrant, urban

d. Migrant, rural

■ Wage work ■ Self-employed ■ Daily labor ■ Remittances ■ Institutional aid

Source: Original figure for this report based on data from GEIH and PM.

refugees to be employed (7 percent, a gap of more than 50 percentage points); for those who do work, employment is most commonly part-time. There are also sizable gaps in the rural localities, but the discrepancy is smaller in both participation (a 15 percentage point and an 8 percentage point gap in Isingiro and Jijiga, respectively) and employment (21 percentage points and 8 percentage points, respectively) (table 4.6).[4]

In the low-income labor markets, demographics do not explain why refugees participate less; large gender gaps affect hosts and refugees equally, although wealthier refugees in the cities may be better able to afford to wait for a good job. In the Ethiopian and Ugandan localities, worker characteristics relate in similar ways to activity levels among hosts and refugees, with the possible exception of wealth perhaps allowing urban refugee workers to afford to wait for a better job.

- *Gender matters greatly for activity levels, but does not drive the gap between hosts and refugees.* In the cities and in Jijiga, women in both groups are much less likely than men to participate, but there is no additional significant gender gap among refugees (table 4.7). In Isingiro, there is no gender gap among

TABLE 4.6 Basic labor market outcomes, hosts and refugees, Ethiopia and Uganda

	Labor force participation (%)	Employment rate (%)	Hours per week (median among the employed)	Days per month (median among the employed)
Ethiopia				
Addis Ababa, total host	70	60	45	24
Addis Ababa, total refugee	35	7	10	22
Jijiga, total host	57	41	40	24
Jijiga, total refugee	49	33	48	25
Addis Ababa				
Host, male	85	76	46	24
Host, female	59	48	45	25
Refugee, male	41	12	12	26
Refugee, female	32	4	8	12
Jijiga				
Host, male	73	60	40	22
Host, female	45	27	40	26
Refugee, male	68	49	50	24
Refugee, female	38	24	28	25
Uganda				
Kampala, total host	80	69	49	26
Kampala, total refugee	57	28	36	25
Isingiro, total host	87	83	36	25
Isingiro, total refugee	72	62	35	20
Kampala				
Host, male	90	84	56	26
Host, female	74	61	48	26
Refugee, male	71	36	36	25
Refugee, female	47	23	30	25
Isingiro				
Host, male	87	82	40	25
Host, female	86	83	36	25
Refugee, male	70	60	36	21
Refugee, female	73	64	35	20

Source: Original table for this report based on data from HHR-LMS Ethiopia and HHR-LMS Uganda.

TABLE 4.7 Correlates of labor force participation, by study locality, Ethiopia and Uganda

Ethiopia

Addis Ababa

Labor force participation	(1)		(2)		(3)		(4)		(5)		(6)	
Refugee	-0.32***	(0.09)	-0.42***	(0.07)	-0.59***	(0.10)	-0.68***	(0.22)			-0.49***	(0.10)
Age	0.07***	(0.01)	0.06***	(0.01)	0.06***	(0.01)	0.06***	(0.01)	-0.03	(0.06)	0.05***	(0.01)
Age^2	-0.00***	(0.00)	-0.00***	(0.00)	-0.00***	(0.00)	-0.00***	(0.00)	0.00	(0.00)	-0.00***	(0.00)
Female			-0.22***	(0.03)	-0.33***	(0.06)	-0.33***	(0.06)	0.10	(0.24)	-0.24***	(0.03)
Refugee × female			0.16	(0.15)	0.28	(0.19)	0.28	(0.19)			0.07	(0.06)
Education primary					-0.08*	(0.04)	-0.08*	(0.04)	0.37*	(0.20)	0.02	(0.04)
Female × education					0.13*	(0.07)	0.13*	(0.07)	-0.22	(0.30)		
Refugee × female × education					-0.14	(0.25)	-0.14	(0.25)				
Birth country, Eritrea							0.11	(0.19)				
Birth country, Ethiopia							0.00	(.)				
Birth country, Somalia							-0.09	(0.19)				
Birth country, Other							0.07***	(0.02)				
Residence time									-0.06	(0.06)		
Residence time^2									0.00	(0.00)		
Asset											-0.01	(0.01)
Refugee × asset											-0.01	(0.02)
Refugee × asset^2											-0.01	(0.01)
Constant	-0.51***	(0.15)	-0.21	(0.17)	-0.14	(0.17)	-0.14	(0.17)	0.93	(1.01)	-0.09	(0.15)
Observations	2,259		2,259		2,259		2,259		254		1,156	

(continued)

TABLE 4.7 Correlates of labor force participation, by study locality, Ethiopia and Uganda *(continued)*

Jijiga

Labor force participation	(1)		(2)		(3)		(4)		(5)		(6)	
Refugee	-0.07**	(0.04)	-0.04	(0.04)	-0.15**	(0.06)	-0.15*	(0.08)			-0.11**	(0.05)
Age	0.06***	(0.01)	0.06***	(0.01)	0.05***	(0.01)	0.05***	(0.01)	0.06***	(0.02)	0.06***	(0.01)
Age²	-0.00***	(0.00)	-0.00***	(0.00)	-0.00***	(0.00)	-0.00***	(0.00)	-0.00***	(0.00)	-0.00***	(0.00)
Female			-0.27***	(0.03)	-0.34***	(0.05)	-0.34***	(0.05)	-0.25***	(0.09)	-0.30***	(0.03)
Refugee × female			-0.03	(0.07)	0.12	(0.09)	0.12	(0.09)			-0.01	(0.05)
Education primary					-0.12**	(0.05)	-0.12**	(0.05)	-0.02	(0.10)	-0.04	(0.03)
Female × education					0.09	(0.07)	0.09	(0.07)	-0.18	(0.12)		
Refugee × female × education					-0.33***	(0.12)	-0.33***	(0.12)				
Birth country, Ethiopia							-0.15***	(0.04)				
Birth country, Somalia							-0.15**	(0.07)				
Birth country, Other							-0.62***	(0.06)				
Residence time									0.02	(0.04)		
Residence time²									-0.00	(0.00)		
Asset											-0.00	(0.01)
Refugee × asset											0.00	(0.02)
Refugee × asset²											-0.00	(0.01)
Constant	-0.43***	(0.15)	-0.25	(0.15)	-0.12	(0.16)	0.03	(0.17)	-0.32	(0.43)	-0.22*	(0.11)
Observations	1,671		1,671		1,671		1,671		428		1,671	

(continued)

TABLE 4.7 Correlates of labor force participation, by study locality, Ethiopia and Uganda (continued)

Uganda

Kampala

Labor force participation	(1)		(2)		(3)		(4)		(5)		(6)	
Refugee	-0.21***	(0.03)	-0.16***	(0.05)	-0.16	(0.13)	0.17	(0.18)			-0.37***	(0.07)
Age	0.05***	(0.01)	0.05***	(0.01)	0.05***	(0.01)	0.05***	(0.01)	0.02	(0.01)	0.04***	(0.01)
Age²	-0.00***	(0.00)	-0.00***	(0.00)	-0.00***	(0.00)	-0.00***	(0.00)	-0.00	(0.00)	-0.00***	(0.00)
Female			-0.16***	(0.03)	-0.16***	(0.06)	-0.16***	(0.06)	-0.13	(0.13)	-0.17***	(0.03)
Refugee × female			-0.10	(0.06)	-0.20	(0.16)	-0.19	(0.16)			-0.03	(0.05)
Education primary					-0.03	(0.04)	-0.03	(0.04)	0.12	(0.10)	-0.01	(0.04)
Female × education					0.00	(0.07)	0.00	(0.07)	-0.09	(0.14)		
Refugee × female × education					0.13	(0.18)	0.16	(0.17)				
Birth country, Burundi							-0.07	(0.12)				
Birth country, Congo, Dem. Rep.							-0.12	(0.12)				
Birth country, Eritrea							-0.55***	(0.12)				
Birth country, Ethiopia							-0.46**	(0.18)				
Birth country, Rwanda							0.09	(0.08)				
Birth country, Somalia							-0.36***	(0.12)				
Birth country, South Sudan							-0.73***	(0.13)				
Birth country, Other							-0.27	(0.21)				
Residence time									0.04***	(0.02)		
Residence time²									-0.00*	(0.00)		

(continued)

179

TABLE 4.7 Correlates of labor force participation, by study locality, Ethiopia and Uganda (continued)

Labor force participation	(1)		(2)		(3)		(4)		(5)		(6)	
Asset											-0.02**	(0.01)
Refugee × asset											-0.07***	(0.02)
Refugee × asset²											-0.00	(0.01)
Constant	-0.11	(0.17)	-0.00	(0.17)	0.03	(0.17)	0.05	(0.18)	0.01	(0.23)	0.12	(0.13)
Observations	1,380		1,380		1,380		1,380		558		1,380	
Isingiro												
Refugee	-0.13***	(0.03)	-0.14**	(0.06)	-0.01	(0.05)	-0.01	(0.12)			-0.10***	(0.04)
Age	0.04***	(0.01)	0.04***	(0.01)	0.04***	(0.01)	0.04***	(0.01)	0.05***	(0.01)	0.04***	(0.00)
Age²	-0.00***	(0.00)	-0.00***	(0.00)	-0.00***	(0.00)	-0.00***	(0.00)	-0.00***	(0.00)	-0.00***	(0.00)
Female			-0.01	(0.03)	0.02	(0.04)	0.02	(0.04)	-0.07	(0.05)	-0.02	(0.02)
Refugee × female			0.01	(0.06)	-0.08	(0.06)	-0.08	(0.06)			-0.04	(0.03)
Education primary					0.04	(0.04)	0.04	(0.04)	-0.25***	(0.10)	0.03	(0.02)
Female × education					-0.05	(0.06)	-0.05	(0.06)	0.09	(0.12)		
Refugee × female × education					0.12	(0.14)	0.12	(0.14)				
Birth country, Burundi							-0.03	(0.12)				
Birth country, Congo, Dem. Rep.							-0.02	(0.11)				
Birth country, Ethiopia							-0.18	(0.25)				

(continued)

TABLE 4.7 Correlates of labor force participation, by study locality, Ethiopia and Uganda *(continued)*

Labor force participation	(1)	(2)	(3)	(4)	(5)	(6)
Birth country, Rwanda				0.13 (0.11)		
Birth country, Somalia				−0.15 (0.14)		
Birth country, Other				0.20*** (0.08)		
Residence time					−0.01 (0.01)	
Residence time^2					0.00 (0.00)	
Asset						0.02** (0.01)
Refugee × asset						−0.05* (0.03)
Refugee × asset^2						−0.00 (0.01)
Constant	0.12 (0.13)	0.13 (0.13)	0.12 (0.13)	0.12 (0.13)	−0.07 (0.19)	0.23** (0.09)
Observations	1,924	1,924	1,924	1,924	934	1,924

Source: Original table for this report based on data from HHR-LMS Ethiopia and HHR-LMS Uganda.
* $p < .10$, ** $p < .05$, *** $p < .01$.

either hosts or refugees, which suggests that, despite the significant barriers to participation women face, refugee women are not further disadvantaged.

- *Higher education is in some localities associated with less activity among refugees, but less so when wealth is considered.* As is common, those with better education (at least primary) are somewhat less likely to participate in the labor force in the cities, with no additional difference among refugees. In Isingiro, there is no difference in participation by education group among hosts, but a large difference (24 percentage points) among refugees, possibly suggesting that better-educated workers find a matching activity less easily or are better able to afford a search. Because the gap narrows when wealth is considered, affordability might be playing a greater role than difficulty in finding a match. Conversely, in Jijiga, the education gap is observed only among hosts.

- *Wealth among refugees correlates with inactivity in Kampala and perhaps in Addis Ababa, but not in the rural localities.* As is also common in cities in low-income countries, in Addis Ababa and Kampala, members of wealthier households are less likely to participate, with a large additional effect among refugees in Kampala and a weak one in Addis Ababa. In Isingiro, wealth is positively correlated with participation among hosts, and only weakly negatively correlated among refugees; it does not correlate with activity among either group in Jijiga. In the data, the causal relationship between activity and wealth can go both ways, of course; however, one consistent reading of the evidence is that it may suggest that wealthier refugees in Kampala can better afford to queue for scarce good jobs; in rural areas, wealth accrues from activity.

A different level of employment before displacement may explain some of the gaps in activity but may also reflect the impact of conflict. Refugees in Addis Ababa and Kampala who were of working age before being displaced report that their employment rates at home were higher than in the host country, but less than the employment rates among hosts. In both cities, there is a very large gap between home employment rates of refugees and the employment rates among hosts—27 percentage points in both localities (table 4.8). This pattern may seem to suggest that the low employment rates among refugees in their host communities are not purely driven by the consequences of displacement but potentially also by the characteristics of displaced workers (other than the ones observed in the data and considered in the analysis in table 4.7). However, an important alternative explanation is that conflict in the home country may have depressed activity before the refugee workers left. The patterns in Isingiro and Jijiga are still different. As noted, although the employment rate among refugees is lower than among hosts, the gap is narrower. What is more, in Isingiro, the employment rate is also above the rate among refugees in their home countries, among both men and women.

TABLE 4.8 Refugees' employment rate at home and in host country, by study locality, Ethiopia and Uganda

percent

	Employment among refugees in host country	Employment among refugees at home	Employment among hosts
Ethiopia			
Addis Ababa			
Men	13	49	76
Women	4	23	48
Jijiga			
Men	32	20	60
Women	24	9	27
Uganda			
Kampala			
Men	36	52	84
Women	23	35	61
Isingiro			
Men	67	53	82
Women	67	55	83

Source: Original table for this report based on data from HHR-LMS Ethiopia and HHR-LMS Uganda.

In the two low-income countries, being in school does not explain the inactivity rates among refugees, and most inactive refugees live in households that rely on unearned income, far more so than among hosts. Refugees who are of working age but inactive overwhelmingly live in households that rely principally on unearned income. This is true of most refugees in Addis Ababa and Kampala (92 percent and 81 percent, respectively), and about half in Jijiga and Isingiro (51 percent and 49 percent, respectively) (table 4.9). Among the unemployed, the shares are similarly high. This level of reliance on unearned income is far above the level among hosts. Conversely, refugees who are not employed are similarly likely as nonemployed hosts to be in school (table 4.9). Accounting for age and gender, working-age refugees in Addis Ababa and Jijiga are much less likely to be in school than their hosts (8 percentage points and 4 percentage points, respectively). In Isingiro, refugees are more likely to be in school (10 percentage points), but this effect is largely due to different age distributions. In Kampala, there is no correlation. In summary, these findings suggest that refugees are not only more likely to be inactive but also more likely to be truly idle.

TABLE 4.9 Share of those with unearned income and workers in school, by employment status, Ethiopia and Uganda

percent

a. Ethiopia				b. Uganda			
	Host	Refugee	Total		Host	Refugee	Total
Addis Ababa				**Kampala**			
Unearned income				*Unearned income*			
Employed	7	20	7	Employed	3	14	3
Unemployed	34	100	36	Unemployed	25	71	36
Out of labor force	23	92	24	Out Labor Force	15	81	28
Total	15	93	15	**Total**	8	59	13
In school				*In school*			
Employed	14	10	14	Employed	9	7	9
Unemployed	17	7	17	Unemployed	19	16	19
Out of labor force	27	11	27	Out of labor force	30	26	29
Total	18	10	18	**Total**	14	18	15
Jijiga				**Isingiro**			
Unearned income				*Unearned income*			
Employed	8	18	8	Employed	1	19	4
Unemployed	21	50	23	Unemployed	4	58	30
Out of labor force	25	51	26	Out of labor force	5	49	23
Total	17	40	18	**Total**	1	31	9
In school				*In school*			
Employed	15	5	14	Employed	2	2	2
Unemployed	17	11	17	Unemployed	11	3	7
Out of labor force	26	24	26	Out of labor force	17	26	21
Total	20	16	20	**Total**	4	9	6

Source: Original table for this report based on data from HHR-LMS Ethiopia and HHR-LMS Uganda.
Note: HH = household.

The Colombian and Jordanian labor markets differ greatly, both in their openness to refugees (as argued earlier) and in the activity level among hosts; however, in both countries, refugees and hosts are similarly likely to be employed. The Jordanian labor market shows very low labor force participation and employment rates (39 percent and 32 percent, respectively),[5] partially because of minimal participation among women (17 percent and 11 percent, respectively) (table 4.10). (Low participation can also be read as reflecting discouragement.) Participation and employment in Colombia are at levels more typical of middle-income economies (70 percent and 61 percent, respectively) (table 4.10). Venezuelan migrants in Colombia are slightly more likely to be active than their hosts, and about as likely to be employed. This finding is in line with expectations, given the openness of the labor market and the partially economic nature of displacement. At the same time, employment rates of Venezuelan migrants in Colombia are less than what they were at home, with particularly large gaps among women. By contrast, given the

TABLE 4.10 Basic labor market outcomes of hosts and refugees, urban and rural, Colombia and Jordan

percent

a. Colombia			b. Jordan		
	Labor force participation rate	Employment rate		Labor force participation rate	Employment rate
National			*National*		
Host	70	61	Host	39	32
Refugee	75	62	Refugee	38	29
Urban			*Urban*		
Host	72	61	Host	40	33
Refugee	75	62	Refugee	37	28
Rural			*Rural*		
Host	65	60	Host	37	29
Refugee	71	61	Refugee	33	24
Women			*Camp*		
Host	58	48	Refugee	42	32
Refugee	59	46	*Women*		
Men			Host	17	11
Host	83	74	Refugee	9	5
Refugee	90	76	*Men*		
			Host	63	55
			Refugee	69	56

Source: Original table for this report based on data from GEIH, JLMPS, PM and SSRJ.

restrictiveness of labor market access in Jordan, it is perhaps surprising that both participation and employment rates in that country are very similar among refugees as they are among hosts (38 percent for participation and 29 percent for employment), but this has to be understood in the context of a much lower level of activity among hosts in Jordan than in Colombia. Among men, refugees are more active than hosts, whereas activity among refugee women is even lower than among host women (9 percent participation and 5 percent employment), further widening the gender gap. More surprisingly, activity is slightly higher among refugees living in camps than among those who have settled elsewhere.

Sources of earned income, vulnerable employment, and earnings

Key insights

Where refugees work, their activities show clear patterns of limited choices due to lack of assets and other access obstacles—which in turn, for hosts creates a specific pattern of competition and opportunities. Access to jobs for refugees is not only about formal rules but also about the productivity of job opportunities that are available to them in practice. Thus, even in the more liberal labor markets studied here, refugees are less likely to hold wage jobs in those labor markets where such employment plays an important role for hosts, and to be self-employed where this kind of work is a chief income source for hosts. For refugee households, the question is whether they can access productive kinds of jobs; for hosts, the implication is that there will be more competitive pressure in certain parts of the labor market, as well as potential opportunities, for instance, through the availability of daily laborers.

In more and less restrictive labor markets alike, vulnerable work as daily laborers plays a greater role for refugees than for their hosts. Refugees are, across different contexts, more likely than their hosts to rely on daily labor, which is true in the low-income labor markets in this analysis. In these labor markets, a key consideration is that, with low assets, refugees face greater barriers to establishing self-employed activities (refer to the section "Savings, asset wealth, and loss of assets through displacement"). It also holds, however, in both middle-income economies: in Colombia and Jordan, daily labor partially replaces more regular salaried work as a source of income for refugee households. In these labor markets, where hosts have substantial access to formal sector jobs, refugees are also much more likely than their hosts to be informally employed.

Employment patterns suggest that refugees have significant difficulty in working as self-employed farmers in rural areas and in obtaining wage work in urban areas. These patterns may point to the different barriers refugees face in the two types of labor markets: barriers to accessing land and capital sufficient for independent farming in the rural zone, and to competing for a limited number of wage jobs in the city. Refugees find very little work as self-employed farmers in either Colombia or Uganda, despite the liberal policy environments in the two labor markets. This pattern may suggest that, even with good labor market access, poor asset ownership or limited de facto access to land can create significant barriers for refugees in accessing one of the main types of job opportunities.

Except in Colombia, refugees in the countries studied here earn lower incomes than hosts across most or all activity types. As argued, although policy influences the degree to which refugees participate in the labor market, they work under both more liberal and more restrictive conditions. Similarly, it is also true that, although the policy environment matters for the quality of work refugees find, they tend to face worse outcomes along some dimensions in all labor markets studied here. Other than in Colombia, these worse outcomes are most directly reflected in lower earnings and greater reliance on daily labor. In the low-income labor markets studied here, as well as in Jordan, refugees report substantially lower earnings than hosts, with gaps as large as half of the median earnings among hosts. The picture is somewhat nuanced in the two big-city labor markets: in both Addis Ababa and Kampala, only refugees who do paid work for others earn less, whereas those in self-employment have similar typical incomes (although, as shown in the next section, access to self-employment is itself constrained). An exception is refugee workers in Colombia, who report typical incomes similar to those of their hosts—although much more often they find themselves in informal work.

Sources of earned income for refugees and hosts

In Ethiopia and Uganda, job types among hosts are typical of urban and rural labor markets in low-income economies. In the two urban centers, wage work is the main source of earned income for about half of all host households (50 percent and 60 percent, respectively, in Kampala and Addis Ababa), and it is also the main livelihood source for most of those households that report any income from wage work. (This study further discusses that a correlate of this fact is that wage work accounts for a much smaller share of individual workers' jobs.) In Kampala, self-employment outside of agriculture accounts for most other earned income (42 percent); in Addis

Ababa, daily labor and nonagriculture self-employment have roughly simi-lar importance (17 percent and 22 percent, respectively) (refer to figure 4.7). In Isingiro, a productive agricultural area, about half of all households pri-marily rely on self-employed agriculture activities (55 percent); most others have their main activity in other self-employment (18 percent) or daily labor (15 percent), and only one in nine draws their principal income from wage work (11 percent). Jijiga's climate is far less favorable for agriculture, so that only one in seven jobs (14 percent) is in self-employed agriculture. Self-employment in other activities is the most common type of job (29 percent), and paid work for others employs about half of all workers (27 percent in wage work and 25 percent in daily labor).

Refugee households rely much less on wage work and farming to generate a livelihood, and daily labor plays a more important role, sometimes alongside nonagriculture self-employment. Refugee households differ from their hosts not only in reliance on unearned income but also in the type of work they undertake to earn incomes. Refugee households in Kampala are far less likely to look to wage work for their household's livelihood (32 percent, compared with 50 percent among hosts), and far more likely to draw from nonagriculture self-employment and daily labor (figure 4.7). Activity shares in Addis Ababa also differ, with greater refugee engagement in self-employment, but these gaps are far smaller than the very wide discrepancy in the level of reliance on unearned income. Refugees in rural Isingiro district are much less likely to have their main activity in agriculture self-employment than their hosts (15 percent and 55 percent, respectively), and base their livelihoods much more heavily on daily labor. As discussed later, poor access to capital and constraints to finding land to farm may both contribute to this pattern. Taking into account the different role of agriculture in Jijiga, a similar pattern holds there—refugees are much less likely to be self-employed in agriculture (by a difference of 12 percentage points) or other activities (10 percentage points), and far more likely to be day laborers (figure 4.7).

In Colombia and Jordan, refugee households are also less likely to rely on wage employment and more likely to draw most income from daily labor or self-employed activities. Self-employment is a minor source in household livelihoods among hosts in Jordan, and it plays virtually no role for refugee households. Thus, only 1 percent of Jordanian households derive most income from self-employment (figure 4.8). Among refugees, fewer than 1 percent of households do, so that nearly all work is paid work for others. This pattern is in line with the significant obstacles refugees are known to face in start-ing business activities in Jordan. At the same time, refugee households are much more likely to rely on daily labor than hosts, and much less likely to be able to draw upon wage work, with particularly large differentials in rural labor markets (25 percentage points, compared with 15 percentage points in

FIGURE 4.7 Principal household revenue source among those who rely on earned income, hosts and refugees, Ethiopia and Uganda

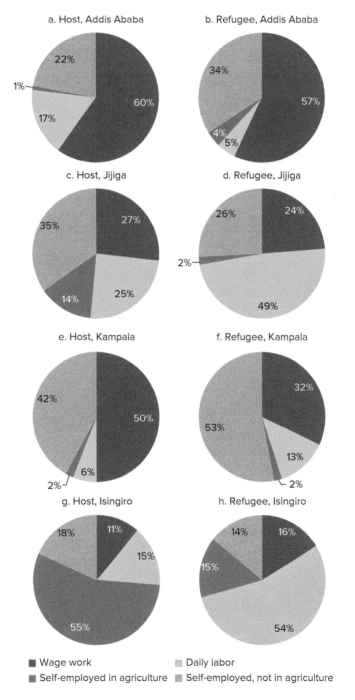

Source: Original figure for this report based on data from HHR-LMS Ethiopia and HHR-LMS Uganda.

FIGURE 4.8   Principal household revenue source among those who rely on earned income, hosts and refugees, Jordan

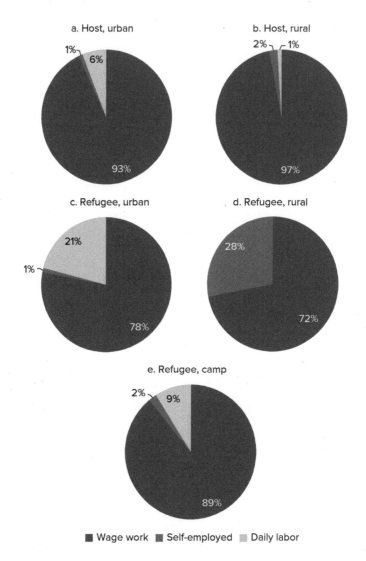

Source: Original figure for this report based on data from JLMPS and SSRJ.

urban areas). In Colombia's open labor market, host and migrant households rely on similar activity types, with slightly more emphasis on wage employment among migrants. Migrants are instead somewhat more likely to rely on self-employment in urban areas and much more likely to rely on daily labor in rural settings. The difference is modest, with differentials of 8 percentage points and 9 percentage points, respectively (figure 4.9).

FIGURE 4.9 Principal household revenue source among those who rely on earned income, hosts and migrants, Colombia

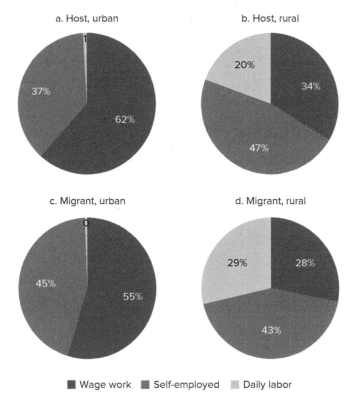

a. Host, urban

37%
62%

b. Host, rural

20%
34%
47%

c. Migrant, urban

45%
55%

d. Migrant, rural

29%
28%
43%

■ Wage work ■ Self-employed ■ Daily labor

Source: Original figure for this report based on data from GEIH and PM.

Active refugees and vulnerable jobs

Across contexts, patterns in the types of jobs refugee workers hold reflect limited choices and a greater dependence on vulnerable work. It may seem implicit that, if refugee households rely more on certain activities than do their host counterparts, refugee workers are also going to be more likely to work in these activities. However, the two need not go hand in hand: even if refugee and host workers have similar activity profiles, households could differ in their reliance on certain activities because the relative earnings from these activities diverge. This analysis shows that refugee and host workers indeed differ in their level of engagement in different activities. Across contexts, there is a clear indication of constrained choices, with lower participation in independent farming in labor markets where such work employs a significant number of workers among hosts and, in most cases, higher dependence on daily labor in labor markets where paid work for others is most common. In Colombia and Jordan, where formal sector work plays a significant role, refugees are far less likely to have these formal sector jobs.

In the rural localities in low-income countries, refugees are much less likely to be self-employed in agriculture; instead, they work as daily or casual laborers. Thus, whereas about half of all host nationals among workers in Isingiro are self-employed in agriculture as their principal activity (52 percent) (figure 4.10), only about one in seven refugees farms independently (14 percent). Refugees are also less likely than hosts to be self-employed outside of agriculture. Instead, most employed refugees work for others (70 percent), most often as daily or casual laborers (58 percent), compared with one-fourth of hosts (26 percent).

FIGURE 4.10 Share of workers, by type of work, hosts and refugees, Ethiopia and Uganda

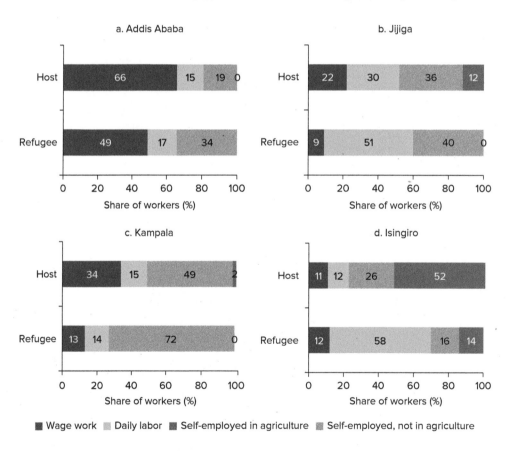

Source: Original figure for this report based on data from HHR-LMS Ethiopia and HHR-LMS Uganda.
Note: ACS = adaptive cluster sampling.

Accounting again for the lesser importance of agriculture in Jijiga, hardly any refugees are independent farmers, compared with one in nine hosts (12 percent). Most of the refugees who work for others have casual forms of employment (51 percent). However, self-employment outside of agriculture plays a much more pronounced role than in Isingiro.

In the cities in Ethiopia and Uganda, refugees are less likely than hosts to be wage-employed, and rely more on self-employment outside of agriculture. In contrast to the rural localities, refugees in Kampala and Addis Ababa are more likely than their hosts to be self-employed, and they are substantially less likely to be wage workers. The difference is large in Kampala, where one in three hosts has a wage job, compared with one in eight refugees (34 percent and 13 percent, respectively) (figure 4.10). Among the few working refugees in Addis Ababa, wage work still accounts for about every other job, but with a 17 percentage point differential with hosts in the share of wage work. The distinct activity patterns in urban and rural areas may point to different barriers refugees face in the two localities: barriers to accessing land and capital large enough for independent farming in the rural zone, and barriers to competing for a limited number of "good" wage jobs in the city.

Venezuelans settled in rural Colombia are similarly disengaged from self-employment in agriculture, despite the fact that the activity provides many jobs to Colombians. Thus, among hosts in rural labor markets, more than one in three work for their own account in agriculture (40 percent), but hardly any Venezuelan migrants do (7 percent) (figure 4.11). Combining all types of employment, the agriculture sector provides far fewer jobs for refugees in rural areas than for hosts (30 percent, compared with 60 percent) (figure 4A.5 in online annex 4A). Wage work largely makes up the gap (44 percent among migrants, compared with 22 percent among hosts). It is of interest that this similarity emerges between Colombia and the two low-income countries despite the big gap in the level of development, and that the pattern obtains in Colombia and Uganda, two of the labor markets most open to refugees. This finding suggests that, even with good labor market access, poor asset ownership and, in certain cases, limited de facto access to land (discussed further in the section "Characteristics of employment in different sectors") can create significant barriers for refugees in accessing one of the main types of job opportunities.

As noted, paid work for others is the norm for employed workers in Jordan, both among hosts and refugees (figure 4.12). However, there is a very pronounced difference in the types of work refugees and hosts do. Among hosts, regular wage work is by far the most common (74 percent), particularly in rural labor markets (91 percent). As is intuitive in a labor market with rather restrictive access for refugees, displaced workers are

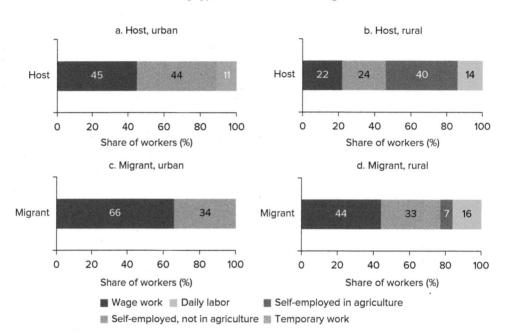

FIGURE 4.11 Share of workers, by type of work, hosts and migrants, Colombia

Source: Original figure for this report based on data from GEIH and PM.

much more likely to have temporary employment (47 percent, compared with 5 percent among hosts) or be in daily labor (21 percent, compared with 6 percent among hosts). Those in camps are particularly likely to have temporary jobs, and those residing in rural communities outside of camps are particularly often day laborers (42 percent). Although temporary workers have occupations similar to those in more regular wage employment, the share of blue-collar occupations is higher, and this difference is even more pronounced among those in daily labor.

Refugee workers in Colombia and Jordan are much more likely than hosts to be in informal jobs. In Colombia's and Jordan's middle-income labor markets, formality of employment is a meaningful proxy for the precariousness of employment. In this important dimension, refugees work in jobs that are less secure than those that host workers hold, an outcome that is particularly obvious in Jordan (table 4.11), where wage workers among refugees are less than half as likely to have a written contract than wage workers among hosts (16 percent and 40 percent, respectively). Very few are entitled to participate in social security (6 percent), whereas more than half of wage workers among hosts did in 2014 (58 percent, 2014 data). As noted earlier,

FIGURE 4.12 Share of workers by type of work, hosts and refugees, Jordan

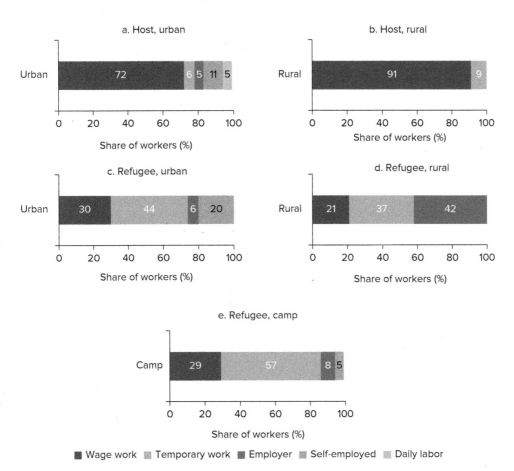

a. Host, urban

b. Host, rural

c. Refugee, urban

d. Refugee, rural

e. Refugee, camp

■ Wage work ▨ Temporary work ■ Employer ▨ Self-employed ▨ Daily labor

Source: Original table for this report baed on data from JLMPS and SSRJ.

TABLE 4.11 Formality of employment, urban, rural, and camp, by host and refugee, Jordan

percent

	Urban		Rural		Camp	
	Host	Refugee	Host	Refugee	Refugee	Total
Formal	65	7	82	0	47	67

Source: Original table for this report based on data from JLMPS and SSRJ.

refugees are also more likely to be temporary workers or daily laborers, and they more often say that they work in unpleasant or unhealthy conditions (by margins of 11 percentage points and 7 percentage points, respectively). In Colombia, despite only a slight difference in the prevalence of daily labor between the two groups, migrants are much less likely to have formal employment in urban areas (overall 19 percent, compared with 42 percent among hosts) (table 4.12).

Refugees' likelihood of holding vulnerable jobs before displacement

A comparison of the type of job before and after displacement suggests that refugee workers largely conform to the type of jobs available to refugees in their new localities. In Kampala, where self-employment is predominant, not only do 82 percent of those who were self-employed at home remain so, but self-employment also provides the jobs of three-quarters of those who were doing paid work for others at home (75 percent) and nearly all of those who were in agriculture (93 percent) (table 4.13).[6] (In Addis Ababa, the few refugees who remain employed most commonly stay in the type of job they previously held.) In Isingiro, there is a shift into daily labor among those who previously held other types of jobs—in connection with the shift out of agriculture reported above. About one in four refugee workers in Jijiga changed their type of work, notably workers who were previously self-employed in agriculture and now engage in daily work or self-employment outside of agriculture.

Venezuelan migrants in Colombia often switched to informal jobs, but many former daily laborers also report having found more stable work. A substantial number say that they changed their type of work (39 percent and 50 percent) (table 4.14). This notably includes the great majority (70 percent) of former *jornaleros* (daily workers), who switched to more regular employment or

---

TABLE 4.12 Formality of employment, urban and rural, host and migrant, urban and rural, Colombia

percent

	Urban		Rural		
	Host	Migrant	Host	Migrant	Total
Formal	42	19	14	19	36

Source: Original table for this report based on data from GEIH and PM.

TABLE 4.13 Type of job at home and in the host country, by study locality, Ethiopia and Uganda

Percent

a. Ethiopia

Job at home	Job in host country		
	Paid work for others	Daily labor	Self-employed, not in agriculture
Addis Ababa			
Paid work for others	66	12	22
Daily labor	16	84	0
Self-employed, not in agriculture	11	5	84
Total	39	12	49
Jijiga			
Self-employed, not in agriculture	0	0	100
Self-employed in agriculture	0	75	25
Total	0	40	60

b. Uganda

Job at home	Job in host country			
	Paid work for others	Daily labor	Self-employed, not in agriculture	Self-employed, agriculture
Kampala				
Paid work for others	8	17	75	n.a.
Daily labor	5	57	38	n.a.
Self-employed, not in agriculture	5	14	82	n.a.
Self-employed in agriculture	7	0	93	n.a.
Total	6	20	74	n.a.
Isingiro				
Paid work for others	8	52	32	8
Daily labor	7	82	5	6
Self-employed, not in agriculture	4	36	43	17
Self-employed in agriculture	9	56	9	25
Total	7	54	21	18

Source: Original table for this report based on data from HHR-LMS Ethiopia and HHR-LMS Uganda. Differences from shares shown in Figure 4.10 arise because information on employment before displacement is not available for all respondents.
Note: n.a. = not applicable.

TABLE 4.14 Job mobility and transitions of Venezuelan migrants in Colombia, by gender

percent

Gender	Changed industry between home and now	Became informal between home and now	Changed Industry between first Job in Colombia and now	Have PEP?	Changed industry between before PEP and now	Became employed between before PEP and now	Became unemployed between home and now	Changed ToW between before home and now	Changed ToW between first Job in Colombia and now	Changed ToW between before PEP and now
Male	64	71	28	17	38	19	8	46	38	0
Female	51	78	20	16	34	5	48	71	41	0
Total	60	73	25	16	37	8	22	50	39	0

Source: Original table for this report based on data from GEIH and PM.
Note: PEP = Permiso Especial de Permanencia (Special Permanence Permit); ToW = type of work.

self-employment (table 4.15) (in urban areas, fully 87 percent made this switch, perhaps partially explaining the attractiveness of Colombia's urban labor markets to migrants). Conversely, very few of those who were employers in República Bolivariana de Venezuela were able to continue with this type of work (less than 1 percent), with most switching to regular paid work or self-employment. Those who held formal sector jobs in República Bolivariana de Venezuela are also very likely to now have informal sector jobs (73 percent, implying an overall informality rate of 80 percent among migrants) (table 4.16). The introduction of the Permiso Especial de Permanencia (Special Permanence Permit, or PEP) may have favored transition from work as jornaleros into more regular employment (51 percent of those formerly in daily labor) and self-employment (46 percent) (table 4.17).

TABLE 4.15   Type of work in República Bolivariana de Venezuela and in Colombia, Venezuelans only

percent

Type of work in República Bolivariana de Venezuela	Type of work in Colombia						
	Wage work	Self-employed	Self-employed in agriculture	Temporary	Daily labor	Employer	Other
Employed	67	29	0	1	2	1	1
Self-employed	43	50	0	0	3	0	3
Daily labor	58	12	0	0	30	0	0
Employer	58	42	0	0	0	1	0
Total	58	36	0	0	3	1	2

Source: Original table for this report based on data from GEIH and PM.

TABLE 4.16   Formality in República Bolivariana de Venezuela and in Colombia, Venezuelans only

percent

Formality in República Bolivariana de Venezuela	Formality in Colombia	
	Informal	Formal
Informal	88	12
Formal	73	27
Total	80	20

Source: Original table for this report based on data from GEIH and PM.
Note: Data from a recall period of seven days.

TABLE 4.17 Type of work in Colombia before the implementation of the PEP in 2017, compared to 2021, Venezuelans only

percent

Type of work in 2017	Type of work in 2021						
	Employed	Self-employed	Temporary	Daily labor	Employer	Other	Total
Employed	84	15	0	0	0	1	100
Self-employed	30	67	0	1	0	1	100
Daily labor	51	46	0	2	0	0	100
Employer	0	72	0	0	28	0	100
Total	64	34	0	0	1	1	100

Source: Original table for this report based on data from GEIH and PM.
Note: This table compares the type of work in Columbia, for Venezuelans only, before the implementation of PEP in 2017, compared to results from a survey conducted in 2021. Data from a recall period of seven days. PEP = Permiso Especial de Permanencia (Special Permanence Permit).

Lower revenue from job activities for refugees

Refugee workers in Isingiro and Jijiga report much lower revenue than hosts across different types of activities; those in Kampala report similar revenue from self-employment, but not from paid work for others. Host country nationals in the two cities report typical (median) revenues of US$55–US$58 per month, or US$2.75–US$3.00 per day, assuming full-time work (table 4.18). Hosts in Isingiro can typically expect US$42 per month, or US$2 per day if work is full time. These are typical daily incomes in low-income economies. Hosts in Jijiga report much higher median earnings of US$105 per month, or US$5 per day, which is an elevated level of median earnings, perhaps partially reflecting much lower activity levels.[7] There are large gender gaps in earnings. In addition, among workers in Isingiro and Jijiga, a very pronounced gap is seen between the typical incomes of refugees and hosts, with refugees typically earning about half of what hosts can expect, across all activities. This difference is consistent with significant competition among refugees for paid work, alongside lower capacity to invest in self-employment. In Kampala, such a gap is observed only among those who do wage work or daily labor, suggesting that, in addition to having difficulties accessing paid work, refugees also have to settle for lower-paid positions (table 4A.6 in online annex 4A). (Correlates of income from wage work and self-employment are explored further in this section.)

There is a wide earnings differential between hosts and refugees in Jordan, but migrants in Colombia earn similar amounts as hosts. At the median, refugees in Jordan earned the equivalent of US$277 per month,

TABLE 4.18 Revenue from different types of activities, hosts and refugees, case study countries

	Revenue from main activity (median US$)	Observations	Revenue from wage work (median US$)	Observations	Revenue from daily labor (median US$)	Observations	Revenue from self-employment outside of agriculture (median US$)	Observations	Revenue from agricultural self-employment (median US$)	Observations
Ethiopia										
Addis Ababa, host	58	629	68	450	39	89	58	90	–	0
Addis Ababa, refugee	58	79	48	50	48	15	485	14	78	0
Jijiga, host	105	350	87	88	116	115	126	124	78	23
Jijiga, refugee	58	172	58	24	68	85	58	63	–	0
Uganda										
Kampala, host	55	377	69	147	28	73	55	152	277	5
Kampala, refugee	55	114	67	26	17	25	55	63	–	0
Isingiro, host	42	593	42	81	28	90	40	175	55	247
Isingiro, refugee	17	484	20	57	17	340	22	79	28	8
Colombia										
Urban, host	273	219,274	285	114,154	240	885	180	104,235	–	–
Urban, migrant	279	2,389	271	1,297	270	588	150	1,075	–	–
Rural, host	150	22,322	273	5,616	216	3,162	114	13,544	–	–
Rural, migrant	240	130	270	68	270	43	150	54	–	–
Total	270	244,115	273	121,135	225	4,678	150	118,908	–	–
Jordan										
Urban, hosts	522	3,657	522	3,450	367	210	–	–	–	–
Urban, refugee	282	1,183	324	912	212	277	–	–	–	–
Rural, host	494	1,029	494	1,003	244	26	–	–	–	–
Rural, refugee	212	46	282	26	212	20	–	–	–	–
Camp, refugee	219	275	226	257	212	19	–	–	–	–
Total	508	6,190	522	5,648	356	552	–	–	–	–

Source: Original table for this report based on data from JLMPS, SSRJ, GEIH, PM, HHR-LMS Ethiopia, and HHR-LMS Uganda.
Note: – = not available.

compared with US$508 among hosts, almost double (table 4.18).[8] The difference is especially appreciable at the lower end of the distribution: whereas one in four refugees in the bottom quartile earns no more than US$100 per month, among hosts, one in four in the bottom quartile earns no more than US$300. The difference with hosts is also higher among refugees living in camps and rural areas than among those who settled in urban areas. By contrast, income for urban migrants in Colombia is only slightly less than that of hosts across a range of activities (table 4.18). (The relatively limited number of migrants in rural areas may have higher median incomes than their hosts, but the sample size is small in the data.) Previous analyses using earlier rounds of the same survey data found much larger income gaps (Carranza et al. 2022).

The four low-income-country labor markets differ in whether observable characteristics of refugees and the types of jobs they have explain the earnings differential. The regression analysis in table 4.19 asks whether differences in the share of women among refugee workers, in education, or in the kind of work respondents do account for some of the observed gaps in earnings. Findings vary across localities. However, in all four labor markets, although women earn far less than men at the median, there is no significant additional gender gap. In Isingiro, the earnings gap for refugees is observed whether or not workers and job characteristics are considered, suggesting that refugee workers face difficulties regardless of their profile and the work they do. In line with a limited range of labor market choices for refugees, the earnings gap is larger among better-educated workers who have completed at least primary education. Indeed, whereas such workers among hosts enjoy an earnings premium, better-educated refugees do not earn more than their less-qualified peers. In Jijiga, conversely, worker and job characteristics largely account for the disparity in earnings. Finally, there is no overall gap in earnings in either Addis Ababa or Kampala, but refugees earn weakly less when worker or job characteristics are accounted for.

TABLE 4.19 Correlates of revenue, Ethiopia and Uganda

Revenue (ln) (median, US$)	(1)	(2)	(3)	(4)	(5)
Addis Ababa					
Refugee	0.00 (20.07)	0.00 (75.76)	0.00 (295.78)	−27.91 (203.33)	−38.76 (153.99)
Female		−29.07*** (5.29)	−19.38*** (5.09)	−19.38*** (4.55)	−19.38*** (5.43)
Refugee × female		−9.69 (75.99)	−19.38 (80.42)	−19.38 (15.83)	19.38 (54.44)
Education primary			29.07*** (4.81)	30.23*** (4.10)	19.38*** (6.25)
Refugee × education			0.00 (317.21)	27.91 (208.27)	29.07 (85.72)
Self-employed, nonagriculture				12.79 (11.23)	
Refugee × self-employed, nonagriculture				394.19 (407.83)	
Trade					0.00 (0.00)
Food					−5.81 (10.29)
Care					−9.69 (18.86)
Clothing					1.94 (10.69)
Manual labor					−9.69 (9.23)
Manual technical services					9.69 (15.47)
Public					19.38 (13.58)
Refugee × trade					0.00 (.)
Refugee × food					5.81 (85.12)
Refugee × care					−9.69 (91.60)
Refugee × clothing					36.82 (109.48)
Refugee × manual labor					116.28 (232.58)

(continued)

203

TABLE 4.19 Correlates of revenue, Ethiopia and Uganda *(continued)*

Revenue (ln) (median, US$)	(1)	(2)	(3)	(4)	(5)
Refugee × manual technical services					-9.69 (129.10)
Refugee × public					406.98 (.)
Constant	58.14*** (3.14)	77.52*** (4.33)	48.45*** (4.13)	47.29*** (4.04)	48.45*** (10.01)
Observations	709	709	709	709	709
Jijiga					
Refugee	-46.51*** (11.96)	-19.38 (32.85)	0.00 (44.11)	19.38 (37.82)	0.00 (483.30)
Female		-73.64*** (9.75)	-58.14*** (11.14)	-58.14*** (8.74)	-58.14*** (13.49)
Refugee × female		15.50 (.)	0.00 (171.04)	-19.38 (73.53)	19.38 (70.98)
Education primary			19.38 (11.91)	29.07*** (10.76)	19.38 (12.67)
Refugee × education			-38.76 (96.75)	-48.45 (31.07)	-19.38 (30.11)
Self-employed, nonagriculture				48.45*** (9.72)	
Self-employed, agriculture				31.01*** (10.61)	
Refugee × self-employed, nonagriculture				-29.07 (125.55)	
Refugee × self-employed, agriculture				0.00 (.)	
Trade					0.00 (17.65)
Food					29.07* (15.42)
Clothing					9.69 (28.58)
Manual labor					0.00 (18.85)

(continued)

TABLE 4.19 Correlates of revenue, Ethiopia and Uganda *(continued)*

Revenue (ln) (median, US$)	(1)		(2)		(3)		(4)		(5)	
Manual technical services									-19.38	(23.64)
Public									38.76	(32.21)
Refugee × trade									-19.38	(490.36)
Refugee × food									-48.45	(1655.75)
Refugee × clothing									-9.69	(.)
Refugee × manual labor									-0.00	(489.00)
Refugee × manual technical services									-38.76	(.)
Refugee × public									-96.90	(501.74)
Constant	104.65***	(7.37)	135.66***	(7.04)	116.28***	(10.26)	96.90***	(7.90)	116.28***	(14.95)
Observations	524		524		524		524		524	
Kampala										
Refugee	0.00	(10.89)	-41.60*	(21.24)	-19.41	(19.69)	-19.41	(15.15)	-22.19	(55.01)
Female			-27.73***	(9.38)	-27.73**	(10.97)	-27.73**	(11.87)	-27.73***	(7.20)
Refugee × female			41.60	(25.40)	27.73	(21.74)	27.73	(17.03)	30.51	(37.46)
Education primary					22.19***	(7.03)	22.19***	(6.85)	19.41**	(8.00)
Refugee × education					-8.32	(18.42)	-13.87	(16.02)	-8.32	(44.58)
Self-employed, nonagriculture							0.00	(7.72)		
Self-employed, agriculture							221.88	(173.59)		
Refugee × self-employed, nonagriculture							5.55	(15.14)		

(continued)

205

TABLE 4.19 Correlates of revenue, Ethiopia and Uganda (continued)

Revenue (ln) (median, US$)	(1)	(2)	(3)	(4)	(5)
Refugee × self-employed, agriculture				0.00 (.)	
Trade					0.00 (.)
Food					5.55 (10.06)
Care					−13.87 (12.98)
Clothing					13.87 (13.66)
Manual labor					5.55 (10.56)
Public					69.34*** (24.26)
Refugee × trade					0.00 (.)
Refugee × food					38.83 (47.50)
Refugee × care					27.73 (.)
Refugee × clothing					−13.87 (30.50)
Refugee × manual labor					8.32 (52.08)
Refugee × public					−27.73 (.)
Constant	55.47*** (5.19)	83.20*** (8.43)	61.02*** (11.48)	61.02*** (11.95)	49.92*** (10.80)
Observations	492	492	492	492	492
Isingiro					
Refugee	−24.96*** (3.22)	−19.41*** (3.62)	−19.41*** (6.44)	−11.09* (5.67)	−22.19*** (5.85)
Female		0.00 (5.22)	−13.87** (5.69)	−13.87** (5.42)	−9.01* (5.15)

(continued)

TABLE 4.19 Correlates of revenue, Ethiopia and Uganda *(continued)*

Revenue (ln) (median, US$)	(1)	(2)	(3)	(4)	(5)
Refugee × female		-8.32 (6.09)	5.55 (6.39)	5.55 (6.05)	3.47 (5.58)
Education primary			13.87*** (4.34)	13.87*** (5.01)	20.11*** (4.37)
Refugee × education			-13.87*** (5.07)	-16.64*** (5.67)	-22.88*** (5.33)
Self-employed, nonagriculture				8.32 (6.18)	
Self-employed, agriculture				22.19*** (6.54)	
Refugee × self-employed, nonagriculture				0.00 (9.40)	
Refugee × self-employed, agriculture				-8.32 (17.83)	
Trade					-18.72*** (3.62)
Care					-27.04* (15.67)
Manual labor					-22.88*** (7.23)
Refugee × trade					15.95*** (5.29)
Refugee × care					27.04 (24.53)
Refugee × manual labor					20.11*** (7.52)
Constant	41.60*** (2.83)	41.60*** (2.60)	41.60*** (5.80)	33.28*** (5.17)	44.38*** (5.47)
Observations	1,081	1,081	1,081	1,081	1,081

Source: Original table for this report based on data from HHR-LMS Ethiopia and HHR-LMS Uganda.

* $p < .10$, ** $p < .05$, *** $p < .01$.

Savings, asset wealth, and loss of assets through displacement

Key insights

Refugees have less capital, lower savings, and more debt. Across contexts, refugees report lower asset wealth than their hosts, sometimes by very wide margins of up to two standard deviations of an index of asset wealth. In addition, there are large gaps between the share of refugee and host households who report any savings, and refugee households are, in most settings, more likely to carry debt. Despite their high borrowing activity, however, refugees report poorer access to formal lending, even relative to the modest level of such access to finance among hosts. Taken together, these facts suggest that refugees face considerable additional barriers to establishing self-employed activities, a key source of jobs and incomes, particularly in low-income labor markets.

With savings hard to accumulate, bringing some assets when first displaced is potentially very important, but few refugees have had a chance to do so. In low-income countries, accumulating savings is a slow and difficult process for anyone, and the evidence here suggests that refugees in the Ethiopian and Ugandan localities build savings even more slowly than do hosts. The ability to bring some of one's hard-won assets with the household when first seeking refuge may have decisive implications for the prospects of thriving in future job activities. However, few refugees are able to bring savings, even if those who were able to do so typically brought significant amounts relative to savings of host families.

Lower wealth for refugees across contexts

Among host country nationals in Uganda and Ethiopia, about two in five report that their household has any savings in three localities: 41 percent in Kampala and Isingiro, and slightly more in Addis Ababa (46 percent) (table 4.20). In Jijiga, only about one in eight has savings. The amounts saved are equivalent to one month's revenue in the two Ugandan localities and in Jijiga. Households in Kampala have US$55 in both median savings and median monthly revenue, and households in Isingiro, US$42. The few Ethiopian households in Jijiga that report having any savings say that they have saved US$97 at the median, close to the monthly median income of US$105. Host households in Addis Ababa record higher median savings of US$116, or equivalent to two months' median revenue.

In Isingiro, Jijiga, and Kampala, refugees have lower asset wealth than hosts, and by far the largest discrepancy between the two groups occurs in Isingiro.[9] Across all three localities, refugees are much less likely to have any savings: hosts are between three and six times more likely to report having funds set aside. In Kampala, those refugees who have savings report higher median

TABLE 4.20 Household asset ownership at survey time, hosts and refugees, Ethiopia and Uganda

	Asset index (median)	Asset and housing index (median)	Has any savings? (%)	Amount of savings (median US$)	Observations with savings data	Has any debt? (%)	Has any debt with formal lender? (%)	Amount of debt (median US$)	Observations with debt data
Ethiopia									
Addis Ababa, host	0.05	0.05	46	116	509	11	53	969	142
Addis Ababa, refugee	-0.95	-0.37	39	39	392	10	12	155	98
Jijiga, host	-0.35	-0.22	13	97	94	29	45	194	359
Jijiga, refugee	-0.79	-0.97	2	155	6	56	51	194	382
Uganda									
Kampala, host	-0.16	-0.58	41	55	244	32	31	139	336
Kampala, refugee	-0.31	0.81	15	97	41	39	15	222	294
Isingiro, host	0.26	0.23	41	42	430	60	28	100	679
Isingiro, refugee	-1.72	-1.71	11	11	103	81	13	36	787

Source: Original table for this report based on data from HHR-LMS Ethiopia and HHR-LMS Uganda.

values than their hosts, whereas the level of savings is minimal among those in Isingiro (and there are too little data available to assess levels in Jijiga). At the same time, refugees are more likely to carry debt, especially in Jijiga; those in Uganda are at the same time less likely to borrow from formal lenders. In sum, therefore, there is a substantial wealth gap between refugees and their hosts. In turn, this wealth gap suggests that refugees can be expected to find it significantly harder to invest in self-employed activities.

In Addis Ababa, refugee households also report substantially lower asset wealth,[10] with a difference of one standard deviation at the median (table 4A.2 in online annex 4A). The gap is less wide if housing characteristics are included. However, the difference in their ability to save and access capital is not as clearly distinct from hosts as it is in the other localities, in line with other evidence that characterizes refugees in Addis Ababa as somewhat better off. Although similar shares of households have savings and debt among hosts and refugees, refugees save far smaller amounts (about one-third of what hosts save, at the median) and borrow much lower amounts (about one-sixth as much). Refugees are much less likely to borrow from formal lenders.

Asset ownership is also much lower among migrants in Colombia and refugees in Jordan than among their hosts, and many Venezuelans explain that they used savings to fund their exodus. Notwithstanding the different contexts, the displaced in both Colombia and Jordan report far lower asset wealth than their hosts. The divide is particularly wide in Jordan, with gaps of two standard deviations of the asset index among urban residents and of three standard deviations among those in rural areas. Further, among migrants in Colombia, a plurality say that they either used savings (30 percent) or sold assets (32 percent) to fund their emigration (figure 4.13). However, migrant households in Colombia are more likely than hosts to say that they save, by substantial margins (5 percentage points and 8 percentage points in urban and rural labor markets, respectively). One could conjecture that this pattern may be in keeping with the low dependency rate among migrant households and the potential need to send remittances to family members who may have remained at home and potentially fund their journey out of República Bolivariana de Venezuela.[11]

Loss of savings from displacement

Few refugees in Ethiopia and Uganda say that they were able to take money when they were displaced, particularly those in Jijiga and Isingiro, among whom very few were able to bring funds (table 4.21). The gap between households that fled danger and those displaced for other reasons is large, with the latter much more likely to have brought funds. In Isingiro, the few households that were able to take funds often brought meaningful amounts: the median of US$111 is equivalent to about half a year's median earnings, and 10 times the median savings among those who have any money set aside (too little data are available in Jijiga to

FIGURE 4.13 Strategies used to migrate to Colombia

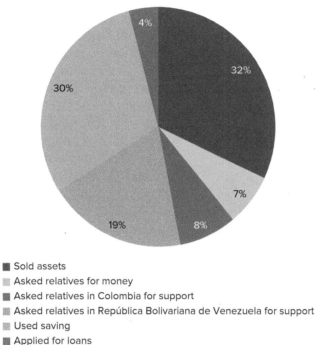

- Sold assets
- Asked relatives for money
- Asked relatives in Colombia for support
- Asked relatives in República Bolivariana de Venezuela for support
- Used saving
- Applied for loans

Source: Original table for this report based on data from GEIH and PM.
Note: Further results available in table 4A.3 in online annex 4A.

assess amounts). Those in the two capitals were substantially more likely to have brought funds (table 4.21), likely reflecting self-selection: better-off refugees may be more likely both to have moved to the cities where no humanitarian support is available and to have brought funds. Thus, compared to refugees in Isingiro, a higher share of refugees in Kampala brought money with them (a 16 percentage point differential), and those in Kampala were more likely to have brought far higher amounts, nearly US$600 at the median, or almost a year's median revenue among refugees in Kampala and six times the median savings. Those in Addis Ababa are even more likely to have brought funds (30 percentage points more likely), perhaps because refugees who could obtain sponsorship to move to the capital were also better off before displacement or better able to liquefy assets. However, they also typically report having taken surprisingly modest amounts—US$39 at the median, a bit less than a month's income (among the few refugees who work), or about half of median savings.

Refugees in the Ethiopian and Ugandan localities who fled conflict are less likely to report that they brought assets with them when they first arrived in the host country. In Kampala, there is a distinct correlation between whether refugees left because of acute security concerns and whether they were able to bring any funds when they fled. Among those who left for security reasons, one in eight brought funds (12 percent) and 1 percent sold assets to prepare, but among others, more than one in four did (28 percent), and 7 percent sold assets. In the other localities, the correlation points in the same direction, but is much weaker (table 4.21).

In line with low current wealth among refugees, very few refugees who owned homes, land, or productive assets in their home country say that they were able to sell before fleeing. Refugees in Jijiga are quite unlikely to say that they owned property or productive assets before displacement (9 percent), perhaps partially because of the very long time most have resided in Ethiopia. Among those in Addis Ababa, one in five say they owned assets (18 percent), followed by one in four in Kampala (24 percent). Among those displaced to Isingiro, slightly more than half owned assets (56 percent), in line with a much higher share of refugees who lived in rural areas before displacement (table 4.22). Properties were most commonly a home and farmland. Among those in Isingiro, livestock was also relatively common (28 percent). Across all four localities, among those who owned property or a significant asset, very few say they were able to sell before they left—a maximum of one in six in Addis Ababa and fewer in the other localities.

TABLE 4.21 Correlates of having brought funds when first displaced, by study locality, Ethiopia and Uganda

	Brought funds (%)	Sold assets (%)	Observations
Ethiopia			
Addis Ababa			
Displaced for other reasons	31	1	194
Displaced for security reasons	26	3	61
Jijiga			
Displaced for other reasons	3	0	49
Displaced for security reasons	2	0	485
Uganda			
Kampala			
Displaced for other reasons	28	7	81
Displaced for security reasons	12	1	464
Isingiro			
Displaced for other reasons	9	3	56
Displaced for security reasons	7	3	858

Source: Original table for this report based on data from HHR-LMS Ethiopia and HHR-LMS Uganda.

TABLE 4.22 Refugees' ownership of assets at home and in current country by type of asset, Ethiopia and Uganda

percent

	Any major assets	House	Place of business	Vehicle or equipment	Land	Livestock
Owned assets at home						
Addis Ababa	18	14	2	3	5	2
Jijiga	9	8	2	1	4	4
Kampala	24	21	5	8	10	3
Isingiro	56	49	5	8	40	28
Sold assets before displacement						
Addis Ababa	3	2	0	1	0	0
Jijiga	0	0	0	0	0	0
Kampala	2	1	1	1	0	1
Isingiro	3	1	0	1	2	2
Still owns assets at home						
Addis Ababa	11	9	0	2	2	1
Jijiga	2*	1	0	0	0	0
Kampala	11	10	3	5	5	2
Isingiro	3	2	0	1	2	1

Source: Original table for this report based on data from HHR-LMS Ethiopia and HHR-LMS Uganda.

At the same time, few consider that they still own their property in their home country. For instance, of the 40 percent in Isingiro who owned land, only 2 percent hold this belief.

Having brought funds when first displaced is often associated with greater wealth at survey time and with investment in self-employment, though the patterns are not fully consistent. Self-employment is a dominant type of employment among hosts in the low-income labor markets, and establishing self-employed activities takes an investment. Therefore, the question becomes whether the limited extent to which refugees were able to bring savings is consistent with the difficulty in establishing productive business activities. There is some corroborating evidence of such a link, but it is not fully consistent. Thus, among refugees in Jijiga and Kampala, having brought funds with them when displaced is weakly associated with higher asset ownership at survey time (table 4.23). Outside of Addis Ababa, having taken savings is also at least weakly correlated with investment in self-employed activities. In Jijiga—where this type of self-employment plays a greater role—there is a positive association between bringing savings and

TABLE 4.23 Correlation of current outcomes with asset ownership on arrival, Ethiopia and Uganda

	(1) Asset index		(2) Asset index		(3) Self-employed, nonagriculture		(4) Self-employed, nonagriculture		(5) Self-employment investment (US$)		(6) Self-employment own investment (US$)		(7) Self-employment income (US$)	
Addis Ababa														
Brought funds at arrival	0.34	(0.36)	2.49	(2.95)	0.18	(0.29)	0.00	(0.01)						
Brought funds × self-employed			-2.64	(2.99)										
Self-employed			1.50	(2.12)										
Female	-0.22	(0.46)	-0.56	(1.56)	0.21	(0.24)	-0.00	(0.01)						
Education	1.02***	(0.28)	0.22	(12.90)	-0.58*	(0.28)	-0.02	(0.03)						
Age	0.15	(0.11)	-1.32	(0.78)	-0.09	(0.15)	0.01	(0.01)						
Age²	-0.00	(0.00)	0.02	(0.02)	0.00	(0.00)	-0.00	(0.00)						
Observations	258		19		19		258							
Jijiga														
Brought funds at arrival	0.45	(0.47)	0.84	(0.72)	0.41**	(0.20)	0.37**	(0.18)	121.61	(143.13)	107.13	(64.89)	-89.06	(0.00)
Brought funds × self-employed			-0.40	(.)										
Self-employed			-0.03	(0.26)										
Female	-0.06	(0.13)	-0.20	(0.26)	0.42***	(0.09)	0.03	(0.03)	-49.72	(72.86)	7.83	(58.66)	-64.35*	(36.45)

(continued)

TABLE 4.23 Correlation of current outcomes with asset ownership on arrival, Ethiopia and Uganda (continued)

	(1) Asset index		(2) Asset index		(3) Self-employed, nonagriculture		(4) Self-employed, nonagriculture		(5) Self-employment investment (US$)		(6) Self-employment own investment (US$)		(7) Self-employment income (US$)	
Education	0.18	(0.13)	0.20	(0.33)	0.04	(0.08)	-0.01	(0.03)	40.97	(142.77)	51.61	(69.93)	-3.48	(79.76)
Age	-0.05*	(0.03)	-0.07	(0.08)	-0.01	(0.02)	0.02***	(0.01)	-18.44	(22.12)	10.30	(13.05)	5.84	(6.79)
Age²	0.00*	(0.00)	0.00	(0.00)	0.00	(0.00)	-0.00**	(0.00)	0.23	(0.27)	-0.11	(0.16)	-0.07	(0.08)
Observations	542		158		158		542		60		60		51	
Kampala														
Brought funds at arrival	0.83	(0.62)	3.78	(2.97)	0.20	(0.12)	0.11	(0.09)	88.10*	(51.01)	-5.44	(20.63)	-13.93	(19.78)
Brought funds × self-employed			-2.98	(3.76)										
Self-employed			-0.13	(0.43)										
Female	0.45*	(0.23)	1.19***	(0.38)	0.22**	(0.09)	-0.03	(0.05)	23.48	(75.24)	-4.12	(72.84)	2.64	(26.51)
Education	1.06***	(0.26)	1.90***	(0.37)	0.46***	(0.09)	0.12***	(0.04)	-8.26	(64.14)	46.62**	(18.68)	11.06	(19.23)
Age	0.02	(0.09)	-0.27**	(0.11)	0.03	(0.04)	0.03	(0.02)	-37.96	(44.24)	-23.88	(36.85)	-15.75	(12.13)
Age²	-0.00	(0.00)	0.00***	(0.00)	-0.00	(0.00)	-0.00	(0.00)	0.52	(0.59)	0.35	(0.47)	0.25	(0.17)
Observations	553		155		155		553		84		80		61	

(continued)

TABLE 4.23 Correlation of current outcomes with asset ownership on arrival, Ethiopia and Uganda *(continued)*

	(1) Asset index		(2) Asset index		(3) Self-employed, nonagriculture		(4) Self-employed, nonagriculture		(5) Self-employment investment (US$)		(6) Self-employment own investment (US$)		(7) Self-employment income (US$)	
Isingiro														
Brought funds at arrival	0.07	(0.30)	0.17	(0.41)	−0.13**	(0.05)	−0.08***	(0.03)	23.89	( )	97.30***	(25.55)	111.94	(94.96)
Brought funds × self-employed			−1.06*	(0.63)										
Brought funds × self-employed, agriculture			−0.26	(1.98)										
Self-employed			0.35*	(0.21)										
Agricultural worker			0.64***	(0.17)										
Female	0.00	(0.12)	0.02	(0.13)	0.05	(0.03)	0.02	(0.02)	−100.97*	(51.20)	−31.30	(25.56)	−18.53*	(9.45)
Education	0.64***	(0.12)	0.63***	(0.16)	0.25***	(0.05)	0.11***	(0.03)	−12.34	(23.47)	−0.69	(3.63)	−5.27	(4.12)
Age	−0.02	(0.03)	0.02	(0.04)	0.00	(0.01)	0.01**	(0.00)	2.06	(7.15)	3.03***	(0.96)	−0.49	(2.03)
Age^2	0.00	(0.00)	−0.00	(0.00)	−0.00	(0.00)	−0.00*	(0.00)	−0.02	(0.09)	−0.04***	(0.01)	0.01	(0.03)
Observations	915		598		598		915		100		100		73	

Source: Original table for this report based on data from HHR-LMS Ethiopia and HHR-LMS Uganda.

Note: In all columns except columns (1) and (4), the sample is restricted to households that are active in the job market. In columns (1) and (4), inactive households are included.
* $p < .10$, ** $p < .05$, *** $p < .01$.

engagement in self-employment outside of agriculture; in Isingiro, there is a negative correlation. In no locality is there a correlation with earnings among those who are active in agriculture, perhaps suggesting that savings from home help in the initial establishment of activities, but do not suffice to raise refugees' productivity above common levels.

Asset wealth of refugees rises (at least weakly) less with age than among hosts and rises slowly with residence time, which may point to difficulty in making capital investments. Households generally accumulate asset wealth over time, a process that can enable them to invest in income-generating activities. In cross-sectional data, one way to measure this effect—even though imperfectly—is to consider the level of wealth in households with younger and with older household heads. For hosts, the relationship between the age of household heads and asset wealth is readily apparent in figures 4.14 and 4.15.

FIGURE 4.14   Asset ownership, by age and residence time, Ethiopia

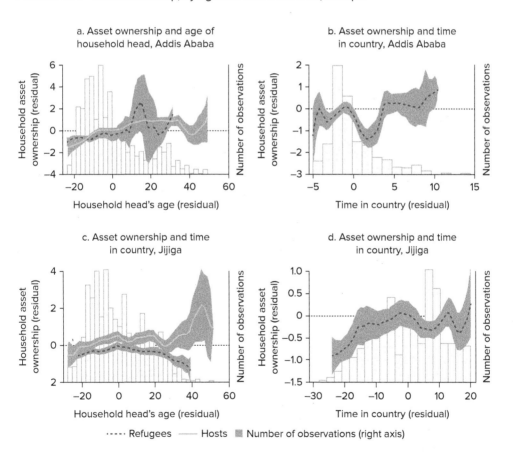

Source: Original figure for this report based on data from HHR-LMS Ethiopia.
Note: The relationship is shown as a local polynomial with its confidence interval. The overlaid histogram shows the number of observations.

FIGURE 4.15   Asset ownership, by age and residence time, Uganda

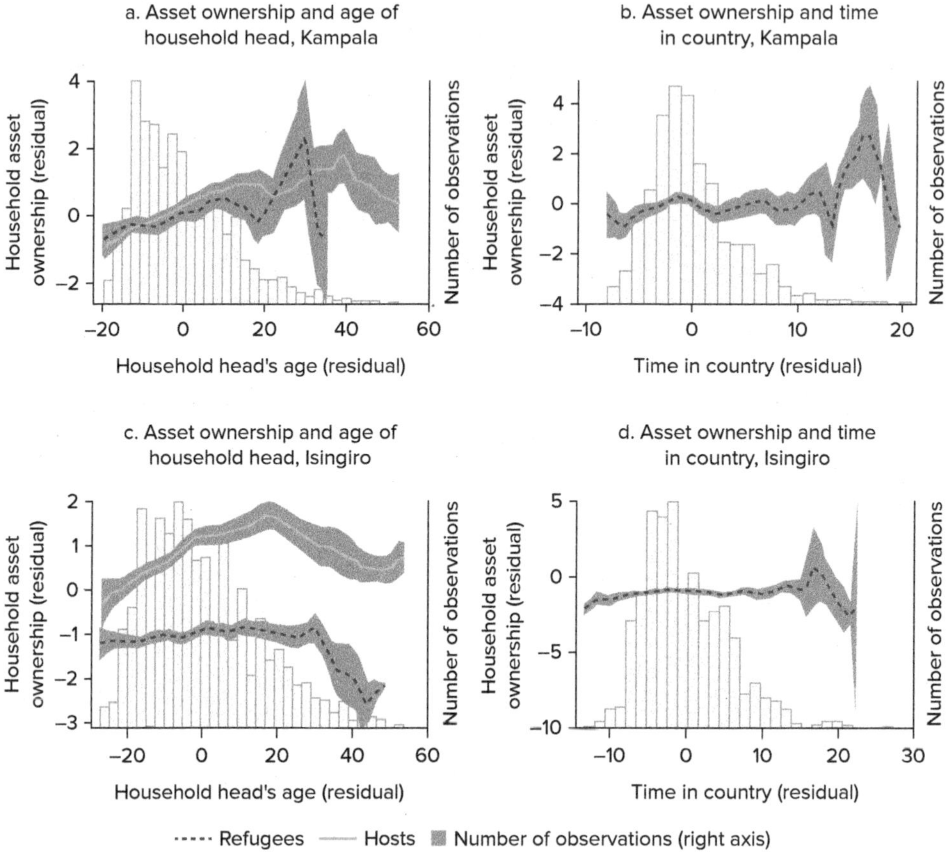

a. Asset ownership and age of
household head, Kampala

b. Asset ownership and time
in country, Kampala

c. Asset ownership and age of
household head, Isingiro

d. Asset ownership and time
in country, Isingiro

····· Refugees ——— Hosts ■ Number of observations (right axis)

Source: Original figure for this report based on data from HHR-LMS Uganda.
Note: The relationship is shown as a local polynomial with its confidence interval. The overlaid histogram shows the number of observations.

Regression analysis shows that, across all localities, asset wealth among hosts is expected to rise by about 0.1–0.4 standard deviation with each 10-year increase in the head's age.[12] Among refugee families, there is also a gradient in age, but the increase is (at least weakly) smaller in each of the localities. This weak gradient in age is particularly pronounced in Isingiro and Jijiga, where there is essentially no expected increase in ownership with age among refugees, compared with a 0.17 standard deviation and a 0.09 standard deviation incline, respectively, among hosts per decade of age in the linear specification. (As shown in figure 4A.4 in online annex 4A, there is little difference among refugees of different nationalities with regard to the relationship between age and asset accumulation. Only figures for Isingiro and Kampala are shown because the refugee populations in Addis Ababa and Jijiga are largely drawn from a single nationality.) The data are cross-sectional, and allow for multiple interpretations of the pattern. However, the finding is certainly consistent with the low revenues refugees can typically expect in Isingiro. It is also consistent with a failure to accumulate assets over time in the manner typical of households in low-income countries and, certainly, an inability to accumulate assets at a higher rate that might compensate for the loss of assets that usually comes with displacement. These patterns raise the question of whether refugee households will also face greater barriers to establishing over time the more rewarding activities households attempt to diversify into.

Skills and skill match

Key insights

The localities studied here show that the relative levels of education and skills between hosts and refugees can vary widely between labor markets. Similarly, although language does not pose a barrier to refugee communities that share a language with their hosts across borders, Addis Ababa, Isingiro, and Kampala provide examples of refugee populations among whom language is a significant barrier.

In labor markets with a narrow range of economic activities, the concept of skill complementarity and substitutability may not have the same explanatory power as in more diversified markets. Although skills profiles in the Ethiopian and Ugandan labor markets are somewhat complementary, activities are not highly diversified, so that host and refugee workers inevitably find themselves in the same sectors. The types of skills that hosts and refugees highlight are not dissimilar, but there is a certain distinction between the most common top skills, suggesting a certain level of complementarity. However, the economic activities in the labor markets in question are not very diversified, and the skills of both groups of workers overlap to a substantial degree. If they were to pursue their top skills, refugees would expect to find themselves competing with a significant number of hosts, and vice versa.

Skills match surprisingly well but may have less bearing on job quality in low-income labor markets than they do in higher-income economies. With some exceptions, refugees and hosts in Ethiopia and Uganda report similarly good skill matches, and the overlap between top skills and current activities is similar (and substantial) for both groups. This is not to say that skills always match, especially for women, but there is little additional gap for refugees. The evidence from Colombia and Jordan is similar. It is possible, however, that even where the "overall" activity apparently matches, the fit of the concrete tasks refugees carry out may be less good. Recall also that refugees in the study localities tend to have lower revenues (except for Colombia) and work more precarious jobs. In labor markets with relatively few common activities, these dimensions may have a greater bearing on job quality than skill matches.

Education and practical skills

In both urban areas and in Jijiga, working-age refugees have similar education levels as their hosts (table 4.24). In the urban areas, most have at least primary education, and nearly all are literate. In Isingiro, refugees lag far behind their hosts, with a differential of 18 percentage points in primary education and 21 percentage points in literacy. The share of workers with vocational or business training is also similar across localities—with the exception of Kampala, where refugees are less likely to have such training. Although refugees thus may not face an obvious disadvantage because of their education with the exception of Isingiro, language is an important barrier in all labor markets except Jijiga, where virtually all refugees and hosts speak Somali. Even when a relatively lax definition of community languages is applied to include those spoken by at least 20 percent of hosts in the respective labor market, between three-quarters and one-third of refugees in Addis Ababa, Isingiro, and Kampala do not speak a community language well, limiting their opportunities in the labor market. Existing literature shows across different contexts that refugees who speak the local language are more likely to be employed (Schuettler and Caron 2020). How important language is as a constraint will vary between skill levels and sectors.

The labor markets in Jordan and Colombia differ radically in the relative educational attainment of hosts and refugees. Refugees in Jordan report far lower educational achievement than hosts, with few educated beyond the

TABLE 4.24   Education and skills, hosts and refugees, Ethiopia and Uganda

percent

	More than primary education	Literate	Vocational or business training	Has professional skill	Speaks community language
Ethiopia					
Addis Ababa, host	79	90	28	76	96
Addis Ababa, refugee	88	97	29	46	65
Jijiga, host	46	56	5	62	98
Jijiga, refugee	41	52	6	42	99
Uganda					
Kampala, host	85	93	32	86	99
Kampala, refugee	85	95	20	72	51
Isingiro, host	50	71	15	87	99
Isingiro, refugee	32	50	14	71	27

Source: Original table for this report based on data from HHR-LMS Ethiopia and HHR-LMS Uganda.

primary level (6 percent, compared with 58 percent among hosts; table 4.25), and fewer than one in ten with at least secondary education (2 percent, compared with 31 percent among hosts). By contrast, Venezuelan migrants have similarly high educational achievement as their hosts, with at least two in four household heads in both urban areas (51 percent and 67 percent, respectively), and in rural areas (49 percent and 55 percent, respectively) having at least completed secondary school (table 4.26).

In all low-income localities, professional skills are rarer among refugees than among hosts. Although education levels diverge only in specific localities, hosts are substantially more likely across all four localities in Ethiopia and Uganda to report that they have a specific professional skill, with a gap of 14 percentage points to 30 percentage points (table 4.24). By far the largest differential is observed in Addis Ababa, where fewer than half of refugees report having a specific skill, compared with three of four host workers (46 percent and 76 percent). Regression analysis shows that, with the exception of Isingiro, some of this gap is due to a different gender and age structure among refugees, but gaps of 14 percentage points and 25 percentage points remain, controlling for demographic factors (table 4.27).

TABLE 4.25 Education level, hosts and refugees, Jordan

percent

Education level	Urban, host	Urban, refugee	Rural, host	Rural, refugee	Camp, refugee
Primary	42	94	47	95	95
Secondary	25	5	22	3	4
Postsecondary	33	2	31	1	1
Total	100	100	100	100	100

Source: Original table for this report based on data from JLMPS and SSRJ.

TABLE 4.26 Education levels, hosts and migrants, Colombia

percent

Education level	Urban, host	Urban, Migrant	Rural, host	Rural, Migrant
None	2	2	7	4
Primary	14	22	36	38
Secondary	51	67	49	55
University	33	9	9	4
Total	100	100	100	100

Source: Original table for this report based on data from GEIH and PM.

TABLE 4.27   Correlates of reporting any professional skill, Ethiopia and Uganda

	Ethiopia				Uganda			
	(1)		(2)		(3)		(4)	
Has Skills	Addis Ababa		Jijiga		Kampala		Isingiro	
Refugee	−0.25***	(0.08)	−0.21***	(0.05)	−0.14***	(0.05)	−0.15***	(0.06)
Female	−0.10***	(0.03)	−0.25***	(0.03)	−0.10***	(0.03)	0.01	(0.03)
Refugee × female	0.02	(0.10)	0.05	(0.07)	0.02	(0.06)	−0.01	(0.07)
Age	0.06***	(0.01)	0.04***	(0.01)	0.04***	(0.01)	0.03***	(0.01)
Age²	−0.00***	(0.00)	−0.00***	(0.00)	−0.00***	(0.00)	−0.00***	(0.00)
Constant	−0.33**	(0.15)	0.03	(0.16)	0.25*	(0.15)	0.26**	(0.13)
Observations	2,259		1,671		1,380		1,924	

Source: Original table for this report based on data from HHR-LMS Ethiopia and HHR-LMS Uganda.
* $p < .10$, ** $p < .05$, *** $p < .01$.

The kinds of skills refugees and hosts report in Addis Ababa and Kampala are not dissimilar. However, fewer refugees than hosts report that their best skills are in business, and more report that they specialize in personal services such as driving or care (table 4.28).

In both rural areas, fewer refugees than hosts report that their skills are in agriculture; in Jijiga, many refugees report that business is their top skill. Both hosts and refugees in Isingiro are by far most likely to have skills in agriculture (59 percent among hosts and 46 percent among refugees), followed by business skills (15 percent and 10 percent). Refugees are, however, much more likely than hosts to have specific skills outside of these two activities (44 percent and 26 percent, respectively), potentially reflecting their more diverse professional backgrounds. These higher skill levels are, however, not because refugees have an urban background: the share of refugees who previously lived in a city is low in Isingiro (one in nine refugees, compared with about half in the other three localities), and reporting a skill other than agriculture or business correlates negatively with having lived in a city before. In Jijiga, there is a similar gap in skills in agriculture, but refugees are notably more likely to say that their skills are in business (44 percent, compared with 25 percent among hosts).

Indications of skill matches

In Uganda, workers among hosts and refugees have largely similar experiences in whether their most recent work fits their skills at least "to some extent."

TABLE 4.28 Self-reported top skill (conditional on reporting any), hosts and refugees, Ethiopia and Uganda

percent

a. Ethiopia	Host	Refugee	b. Uganda	Host	Refugee
Addis Ababa			*Kampala*		
Business	26	8	Business	34	26
Food	10	6	Food	13	13
Care	3	35	Care	9	15
Driving	11	8	Driving	3	10
Construction	4	5	Construction	4	1
Cleaning	7	1	Cleaning	5	1
Education	3	8	Education	5	2
Agriculture	1	0	Agriculture	2	1
Other	35	30	Other	24	29
Total	100	100	**Total**	100	100
Jijiga			*Isingiro*		
Business	25	44	Business	15	10
Food	7	3	Food	2	1
Care	2	3	Care	4	6
Driving	12	8	Driving	3	4
Construction	6	12	Construction	2	3
Cleaning	4	3	Cleaning	0	7
Education	3	4	Education	4	3
Agriculture	13	3	Agriculture	59	46
Other	28	20	Other	12	19
Total	100	100	**Total**	100	100

Source: Original table for this report based on data from HHR-LMS Ethiopia and HHR-LMS Uganda.

In Kampala, the shares are nearly the same, just above two-thirds (table 4.29); in Isingiro, the share among both groups is close to three-quarters. Among host workers in Addis Ababa, the share is virtually the same as in Kampala, at 66 percent. Among refugees in Addis Ababa, most say that there is a match between their activity and skill (89 percent), but recall that very few refugees in the city work. However, in Jijiga, where activity is slightly higher, a similarly high share of refugees feel that their skills match their activity (85 percent), again a higher share than among hosts. Because the question about skills match is worded to also ascertain the most recent work of currently inactive workers, it is unlikely that the good apparent skills match among refugees reflects discouragement

TABLE 4.29 Hosts and refugees reporting that their activity matches their skills at least "to some extent," by activity, Ethiopia and Uganda

percent

a. Ethiopia				b. Uganda			
	Host	Refugee	Total		Host	Refugee	Total
Addis Ababa				*Kampala*			
Business	61	81	61	Business	64	74	65
Food	66	74	66	Food	62	85	63
Care	59	94	60	Care	69	70	69
Driving	82	84	82	Driving	72	64	70
Construction	84	100	84	Construction	88	100	89
Cleaning	41	100	41	Cleaning	60	58	60
Education	85	96	86	Education	84	7	81
Agriculture	0	81	1	Agriculture	68	100	68
Other	67	83	67	Other	66	62	66
Total	66	89	66	**Total**	67	68	67
Jijiga				*Isingiro*			
Business	72	80	73	Business	63	72	64
Food	50	45	50	Food	50	60	52
Care	82	100	82	Care	38	68	49
Driving	72	99	73	Driving	96	43	82
Construction	72	86	73	Construction	77	80	78
Cleaning	49	74	50	Cleaning	60	31	36
Education	86	94	86	Education	92	73	89
Agriculture	78	100	79	Agriculture	79	83	80
Other	73	94	74	Other	81	66	76
Total	72	85	72	**Total**	76	72	75

Source: Original table for this report based on data from HHR-LMS Ethiopia and HHR-LMS Uganda.

among those who could not find a matching activity. Rather, the pattern is consistent with a relatively satisfactory skill match among refugees who work, by the standard of what hosts experience.

There are limited differences across activity types in whether workers feel their skills are being used. However, because of the potential of agriculture to provide jobs at substantial scale, those in agriculture—both hosts and refugees—are quite likely to feel that there is a fit. Regression analysis confirms that, across the four localities, refugees do not have a worse overall skill match than hosts, controlling for demographics; women report at least a weakly poorer fit than men, but not differentially so among refugees (table 4.30).

TABLE 4.30 Correlates of refugees reporting that activity matches skills at least "to some extent," Ethiopia and Uganda

Match in skills	(1)		(2)		(3)	
Ethiopia						
Addis Ababa						
Refugee	0.23***	(0.03)	0.21***	(0.04)	0.54***	(0.10)
Female			−0.05	(0.04)	−0.04	(0.04)
Refugee × female			0.03	(0.06)	0.02	(0.06)
Age			−0.01	(0.01)	−0.01	(0.01)
Age²			0.00	(0.00)	0.00	(0.00)
Some primary education					0.19*	(0.11)
Completed primary					0.24**	(0.10)
Secondary education or more					0.23**	(0.10)
Refugee × some primary					−0.21*	(0.12)
Refugee × primary					−0.35***	(0.12)
Refugee × secondary or more					−0.34***	(0.10)
Constant	0.66***	(0.02)	0.90***	(0.22)	0.65***	(0.25)
Observations	1,081		1,081		1,081	
Jijiga						
Refugee	0.14***	(0.04)	0.19***	(0.05)	0.03	(0.07)
Female			0.01	(0.05)	−0.03	(0.05)
Refugee × female			−0.13	(0.09)	−0.03	(0.08)
Age			0.01	(0.01)	0.00	(0.01)
Age²			−0.00	(0.00)	0.00	(0.00)
Some primary education					−0.11	(0.07)
Completed primary					−0.14*	(0.08)
Secondary education or more					−0.14**	(0.06)
Refugee × some primary					0.21**	(0.09)
Refugee × primary					−0.05	(0.14)
Refugee × secondary or more					0.27***	(0.08)
Constant	0.72***	(0.02)	0.57**	(0.22)	0.78***	(0.24)
Observations	746		746		746	
Uganda						
Kampala						
Refugee	0.01	(0.04)	0.04	(0.06)	0.08	(0.19)
Female			−0.10**	(0.04)	−0.07*	(0.04)
Refugee × female			−0.06	(0.08)	−0.09	(0.08)

(continued)

TABLE 4.30 Correlates of reporting that activity matches skills at least "to some extent," Ethiopia and Uganda *(continued)*

	(1)		(2)		(3)	
Age			0.02	(0.01)	0.01	(0.01)
Age²			−0.00	(0.00)	−0.00	(0.00)
Some primary education					−0.04	(0.14)
Completed primary					−0.19	(0.14)
Secondary education or more					0.02	(0.13)
Refugee × some primary					0.09	(0.21)
Refugee × primary					0.15	(0.20)
Refugee × secondary or more					−0.10	(0.18)
Constant	0.67***	(0.02)	0.44**	(0.22)	0.54**	(0.26)
Observations	1,006		1,006		1,006	
Isingiro						
Refugee	−0.04	(0.03)	−0.03	(0.05)	0.14*	(0.08)
Female			−0.04	(0.03)	−0.04	(0.03)
Refugee × female			0.00	(0.06)	−0.02	(0.06)
Age			0.01	(0.01)	0.01	(0.01)
Age²			−0.00	(0.00)	−0.00	(0.00)
Some primary education					0.09	(0.06)
Completed primary					0.09	(0.06)
Secondary education or more					0.06	(0.07)
Refugee × some primary					−0.20**	(0.08)
Refugee × primary					−0.25**	(0.11)
Refugee × secondary or more					−0.17*	(0.09)
Constant	0.76***	(0.02)	0.51***	(0.15)	0.45***	(0.16)
Observations	1,519		1,519		1,519	

Source: Original table for this report based on data from HHR-LMS Ethiopia and HHR-LMS Uganda.
* $p < .10$, ** $p < .05$, *** $p < .01$.

In the cities in Ethiopia and Uganda, there is no difference in how refugees with different education levels view their skill match, but outcomes vary in the two rural localities. In Isingiro, refugees without any formal education report a substantially better fit than their peers among hosts (14 percentage points), whereas among workers with any higher schooling level, refugees report a substantially worse fit (a 17 percentage point to 25 percentage point differential, depending on the level of education), perhaps because of the predominance of work in agriculture. In Jijiga, better-educated hosts feel they have a worse match, whereas better-educated refugees feel their skills are being used better.

Despite difficult conditions, refugees in Jordan overwhelmingly say that their work fits their skills to some degree. More than nine in ten employed refugees in Jordan say that their current job is in line with their professional training (94 percent), despite the low pay and challenging conditions they encounter at work (table 4.31; refer also to table 4.32). Similarly, few refugees in camps (14 percent), and hardly any living outside of camps, say they changed jobs to have a better match with qualifications (6 percent in urban areas). Instead, better pay and better working conditions are by far the most commonly cited reasons (61 percent and 18 percent, respectively) (table 4.33). Refugees and hosts are similarly likely to say that their work requires technical skills, although hosts are much more likely to report that they use literacy, math, or computer skills in their work, in line with a higher propensity of refugees to work in basic occupations.

TABLE 4.31 Alignment of refugees' current job with professional training, urban and rural, Jordan

percent

Is your current job in line with your training?	Urban, refugee	Rural, refugee	Camp, refugee	Total
Yes	95	92	91	94
No	5	8	9	6
Total	100	100	100	100

Source: Original table for this report based on data from JLMPS and SSRJ.

TABLE 4.32 Satisfaction with match between qualifications and current position, urban and rural, Jordan

percent

How satisfied are you with regard to the match between your qualifications and current position?	Urban, refugee	Rural, refugee	Total
Fully dissatisfied	2	1	2
Rather dissatisfied	6	2	6
Neither satisfied, nor dissatisfied	5	3	5
Rather satisfied	48	51	48
Fully satisfied	39	42	39
Total	100	100	100

Source: Original table for this report based on data from JLMPS and SSRJ.

TABLE 4.33 Refugees' main reason for wanting a different job, urban and rural, Jordan

percent

What is the main reason you want a different job?	Urban, refugee	Rural, refugee	Camp, refugee	Total
More in line with qualifications	6	1	12	7
Better pay	61	52	63	61
Shorter work hours	4	0	5	4
More flexible work hours	1	0	0	0
Current work cannot be combined with responsibilities	0	0	2	1
Better working conditions	19	40	10	18
Less tiresome work	8	2	6	7
Shorter travel time	1	4	2	1
Other	1	0	0	0
Total	100	100	100	100

Source: Original table for this report based on data from JLMPS and SSRJ.

Among both refugees and hosts, skills and sector of employment often match, but for both groups, there may be task mismatches even when the larger activity type fits. A mapping of skills against current activities shows roughly similar patterns for both hosts and refugees in Isingiro, Jijiga, and Kampala, the three localities with a sufficient sample size to carry out the analysis. First, skills and activities often match. For instance, 94 percent of hosts and 92 percent of refugees who are most well-versed in agriculture work in the sector in Isingiro, and 86 percent (80 percent) and 77 percent (70 percent) of those in Kampala (Jijiga) who prefer cooking and catering work in food-related business (tables 4A.5 and 4A.7 in online annex 4A). Second, because some activities are very common, they provide the main job for a substantial number of workers with different top skills, which is most clearly the case in agriculture in Isingiro. For example, in this locality, 45 percent of hosts and 18 percent of refugees who report tailoring as their top skill say that they primarily work in agriculture, as do 18 percent of workers in both groups who prefer trading. Because this pattern affects hosts and refugees alike, it most likely reflects limited market opportunities rather than barriers to refugees that obviate skill matches. It is noteworthy that, as tables 4A.8 and 4A.9 in online annex 4A show, respondents who say that there is no match between their skills and activity often do jobs that appear to match their skills. For instance, about half of host workers (51 percent) and a quarter of refugee workers (26 percent) in Isingiro who complain about a poor match say that their top skill is in agriculture and that they also work in agriculture. This finding may suggest that, although workers find jobs in the sectors they are familiar with, their tasks within these sectors do not fully match their skills; as noted, however, this situation does not seem to affect refugees differently from hosts.

Venezuelan migrants in Colombia commonly changed their sector of activity after migrating (table 4.34), but are less likely to have changed what they do since they arrived in Colombia (table 4.35). Like the patterns in the four labor markets in low-income countries, relatively few migrants in Colombia say that they would like to change their job because of a skill mismatch (7 percent in rural areas and 11 percent in urban areas) (table 4.36). This statement is true even though very few say that they were able to get any professional qualifications accepted in Colombia (5 percent in rural areas and 7 percent in urban areas). Venezuelan migrants are more likely than not to say that they currently work in a different sector of the economy now than they did before leaving República Bolivariana de Venezuela (60 percent in urban areas and 70 percent in rural areas). Sector

TABLE 4.34 Industry of job in República Bolivariana de Venezuela and in Colombia, Venezuelans only

percent

Industry in República Bolivariana de Venezuela	Industry in Colombia			
	Agriculture	Manufacturing	Commerce	Services
Agriculture	1.4	40.9	8.1	49.6
Manufacturing	0.6	21.2	22.7	55.5
Services	8.3	27.8	21.2	42.7
Total	6.9	26.8	21.4	45.0

Source: Original table for this report based on data from GEIH and PM.
Note: Data from a recall period of seven days.

TABLE 4.35 Industry of job before and after the PEP in Colombia, Venezuelans only

percent

Industry of job before PEP	Current industry			
	Agriculture	Manufacturing	Commerce	Services
Agriculture	84.7	10.5	0.0	4.9
Manufacturing	0.0	59.0	12.5	28.5
Commerce	0.0	19.0	34.4	46.6
Services	0.1	14.3	7.5	78.1
Total	1.3	26.5	14.8	57.4

Source: Original table for this report based on data from GEIH and PM.
Note: Data from a recall period of seven days. PEP = Permiso Especial de Permanencia (Special Permanence Permit).

TABLE 4.36 Ability to use skills from República Bolivariana de Venezuela in Colombia

percent

	Has validated degree	Reasons jobs not validated			Practices skills with permit	Wants to change job because of mismatch in skills
		Lack of knowledge	Lack of documents	Lack of money		
Urban						
Male	7	22	31	36	5	12
Female	8	21	42	25	3	10
Total	7	22	37	30	4	11
Rural						
Male	0	27	33	18	5	8
Female	8	29	43	22	4	7
Total	5	28	39	20	5	7

Source: Original table for this report based on data from GEIH and PM.
Note: Degrees for doctors, engineers, and other professionals must be validated by the Colombian Ministry of Education.

changes notably include a shift from services into agriculture among those who settled in rural areas and, conversely, shifts from agriculture into manufacturing and services for those who now reside in towns and cities. There are far fewer shifts between the sector of a migrant's first job in Colombia and their present job, with the notable exception of a number of workers who were first in agriculture but moved to urban areas and out of the sector. Finally, the introduction of the PEP work permit program may have been associated with a modest shift from manufacturing and commerce jobs into work in other service sectors.

In the localities in Ethiopia and Ugandan, typical incomes vary little across most common activities, and skill matches may have less bearing on job quality than type of work and ability to invest. In the Ethiopian and Ugandan labor markets studied here, a relatively small number of activities account for most jobs. Across these activities, typical (median) incomes are relatively similar, with few exceptions. For instance, in Kampala, five of the seven activities that employ at least 5 percent of all workers have median monthly incomes between US$42 and US$55 (table 4.37). The two activities that yield substantially higher incomes are transportation (US$139 median monthly income), which requires significant capital, and education (US$97 median monthly income), which requires much more specialized training. Similar patterns apply in the other localities, with transportation and public services the only activities that pay much better. It is worth asking whether, in labor markets with such little variation in typical incomes across activities, skill matches may matter less for job quality than, for instance, the type of work or one's ability to invest in activities.

TABLE 4.37   Median income in different activities, hosts and refugees, Ethiopia and Uganda

US dollars per month

a. Ethiopia	Host	Refugee	b. Uganda	Host	Refugee
Addis Ababa			*Kampala*		
Trade	58	39	Trade	55	42
Food	39	48	Food	42	83
Care	58	39	Care	42	55
Clothing	48	48	Clothing	55	42
Manual labor	39	116	Manual labor	51	42
Manual technical services	58	58	Transportation	139	80
Transportation	81	485	Education	97	–
Public sector work	87	58	Other	83	17
Other	78	48	**Total**	55	55
Total	58	58	*Isingiro*		
Jijiga			Agriculture	42	18
Agriculture	66	116	Trade	28	14
Trade	87	58	Care	33	19
Food	87	58	Manual work	28	14
Clothing	97	116	Other	55	42
Manual labor	116	116	**Total**	42	17
Manual technical services	97	58			
Transportation	174	58			
Other	105	52			
Total	105	58			

Source: Original table for this report based on data from HHR-LMS Ethiopia and HHR-LMS Uganda.
Note: – = not available.

Characteristics of employment in different sectors

Key insights

Beyond any earnings differentials, paid employment for refugees tends to be more precarious than for hosts: it is more likely to be daily work, and less likely to be formal. Refugee workers are also more likely to be concentrated in a limited set of sectoral activities, even in the two open labor markets, perhaps pointing to networks or perceptions that narrow the range of job opportunities. Finally, refugees are obviously restricted from working in the public sector, an important source of good salaried jobs.

In many respects, self-employment in Ethiopia and Uganda looks similar for hosts and refugees, but refugees contend with additional obstacles and tend to have lower revenue. In these two countries, whereas most self-employed workers rely on savings or loans from family and friends, only hosts ever borrow from formal lenders. Self-employment is important in creating jobs for others than the one who runs the activity, but refugees who run business activities are much more likely to hire only family workers. Hosts and refugees share key business concerns—access to funding, finding customers, and transporting goods—but refugees face additional obstacles that reflect the harshness of the business environment for them.

There are significant obstacles for refugees to engage effectively in agriculture, even in Uganda. Isingiro's labor market revolves around agriculture, and Uganda's generous policy, in principle, gives refugees access to land. However, significant obstacles clearly remain in practice. Thus, whereas hosts are overwhelmingly active in the sector as independent farmers, refugees are far more likely to be paid helpers, reflecting barriers to accessing either funding or land, or both. In addition, those refugees who farm independently typically have much smaller plots and are less likely to produce for the market, again suggesting similar barriers. Jijiga's economy relies much less on agriculture, but Ethiopian workers do reasonably well in the sector, and it is plausible that some refugees could find meaningful employment there as well if fewer obstacles existed.

Wage work and daily labor

The shares of hosts and employees active in wage work and daily labor vary widely among the four Ethiopia and Ugandan labor markets that are the focus of this analysis. To facilitate a consistent analysis across localities, this section therefore does not carry through the distinction between more regular waged work and more casual daily labor; instead, it considers both jointly as two forms of "paid work for others," by comparison with the other ubiquitous forms of jobs in self-employment. Refugees and hosts who work for others tend to separate by nationality, with refugees engaging in more precarious work and more often working for households or smaller businesses. Across localities, there are common patterns in the characteristics of paid employment among refugees and their hosts, though they are not equally strong everywhere. Four observations stand out:

- *First, refugees and hosts both tend to work within their own nationality group in wage work.* Host country nationals tend to work for other host nationals (between 84 percent and 98 percent outside of Jijiga), whereas only 35–36 percent among refugees in Uganda work for host nationals, along with 66–71 percent in Ethiopia—despite the fact that, outside of Jijiga, the number of refugees who hire any workers is small (discussed later in this section) (table 4.38).

TABLE 4.38 Characteristics of wage work, hosts and refugees, Ethiopia and Uganda

	Works for business, not household (%)	Works for host national (%)	Most workers at workplace are refugees (%)	Has written contract (%)	Daily labor (%)	Number of workers at workplace (median)	Observations
Ethiopia							
Addis Ababa, host	68	95	1	54	11	12	591
Addis Ababa, refugee	50	66	36	16	6	3	72
Jijiga, host	57	68	1	24	53	6	213
Jijiga, refugee	42	71	24	7	82	12	112
Uganda							
Kampala, host	74	84	4	36	19	5	278
Kampala, refugee	72	35	51	4	36	4	62
Isingiro, host	60	98	1	24	33	4	194
Isingiro, refugee	20	36	96	2	58	2	433

Source: Original table for this report based on data from HHR-LMS Ethiopia and HHR-LMS Uganda.

Similarly, in all localities, significant shares of refugee workers say that most others at their workplaces are refugees, including 96 percent of refugees who work for other employers in Isingiro, whereas hardly any host workers do.

- *Second, in Jijiga, significant shares of workers, both among hosts and among refugees, work for businesses owned by refugees.* Jijiga stands apart from the other localities in that a substantial share of not only refugees (29 percent) but also hosts (32 percent) work for businesses run by refugees, in line with the greater importance of trade and engagement of refugees in operating businesses that maintain relationships with neighboring Somaliland and Somalia.

- *Third, in addition to drawing lower wages, refugees also tend to work under more tenuous conditions.* Hardly any have a written contract—between 2 percent and 16 percent—compared with 24 percent to 54 percent of all host wage workers (table 4.38). Across localities, refugees are nearly twice as likely as hosts to be daily laborers (with the exception of Addis Ababa, where few hosts and few refugees say they have this kind of work).

- *Fourth, other than in Kampala, refugees are much less likely to work for businesses than for individual employers or households.* The differential ranges from 40 percentage points in Isingiro to 15 percentage points in Jijiga. Similarly, refugee workers in Isingiro at the median report that there are two workers in their workplace, compared with four among host nationals, whereas refugees and hosts in Addis Ababa report three and twelve, respectively (table 4.38). Given the association between productivity and both working for established businesses and working for larger businesses, this small size is likely to be a correlate of the low wages earned by refugees.

Refugees who do wage work or daily labor are more concentrated in some common activities than hosts. For instance, the two most common wage work activities among refugees in Kampala—commerce and food-related business—account for 52 percent of all wage work, compared with 21 percent for the two most common activities among hosts, and only 16 percent of refugees work in activities that do not employ at least 5 percent of wage workers, compared with 35 percent among hosts (figure 4.16). In Isingiro, the range of activities among both groups is limited, but farming and manual labor account for fully 84 percent

FIGURE 4.16   Sector of wage employment, hosts and refugees, Ethiopia and Uganda

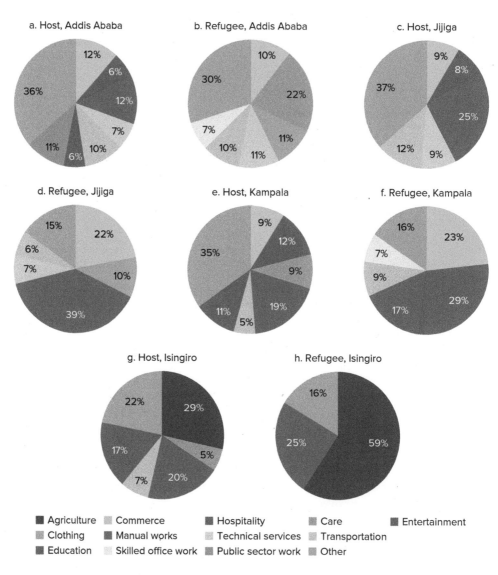

Source: Original figure for this report based on data from HHR-LMS Ethiopia and HHR-LMS Uganda.

of refugees, compared with 49 percent of hosts. In Jijiga, wage work among refugees is heavily concentrated in manual labor and trade, which together account for 61 percent of paid employment. The pattern also holds in urban Colombia, where the leading three activities in wage work among migrants—commerce, hospitality, and manufacturing—together account for two-thirds of all wage jobs (69 percent), compared with about half among hosts (54 percent) (figure 4.17). However, wage work in rural areas among hosts is greatly concentrated in agriculture, whereas migrants are quite likely to also be active in construction. In Jordan, refugees are also substantially more likely to be active in agriculture, and less likely to work in services outside of commerce (figure 4.18).[13]

Refugees in Jordan are much more likely to be active in basic occupations than their hosts. Among refugees, crafts, basic activities in services, and elementary occupations account for 85 percent of all employment. Among hosts, these activities employ 49 percent of all workers. At the same time, refugees in urban areas are much more likely to be working in manufacturing (28 percent, compared with 14 percent of hosts in urban areas), and far less likely to be

FIGURE 4.17   Industry of wage employment, hosts and migrants, Colombia

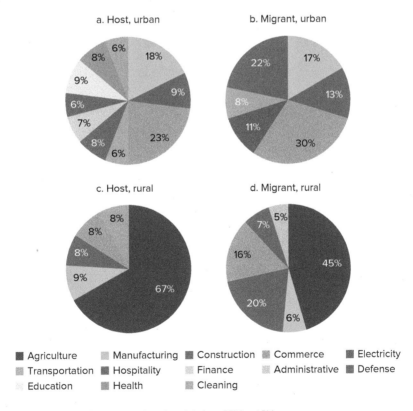

a. Host, urban

b. Migrant, urban

c. Host, rural

d. Migrant, rural

Legend: Agriculture · Manufacturing · Construction · Commerce · Electricity · Transportation · Hospitality · Finance · Administrative · Defense · Education · Health · Cleaning

Source: Original table for this report based on data from GEIH and PM.

FIGURE 4.18   Industry of wage employment, hosts and refugees, Jordan

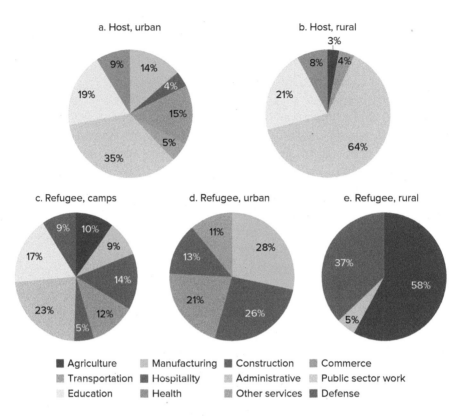

Source: Original table for this report based on data from JLMPS and SSRJ.

active in services outside of commerce (25 percent, compared with 61 percent) (figure 4A.6 in online annex 4A). A high percentage of hosts work in the public sector, which is not accessible to refugees.

The fact that refugees cannot compete for public sector jobs in some labor markets is clearly reflected in wage work statistics. Thus, whereas Ethiopia's large public sector accounts for 11 percent of all wage employment among hosts in Addis Ababa, it provides only 2 percent of wage jobs for the displaced (figure 4.19). More broadly, although the public education and health sectors employ 12 percent and 19 percent of host wage workers in Kampala and Isingiro, they employ no refugee wage workers in the study sample in Kampala and 2 percent in Isingiro (figure 4.20).

Self-employment outside of agriculture

Self-employment is a key source of jobs for refugees and hosts alike in the low-income labor markets studied here. As noted, refugees in Kampala are highly reliant on self-employment outside of agriculture. In Addis Ababa and

FIGURE 4.19 Wage employment in the public sector and in education and health, hosts and refugees, Ethiopia

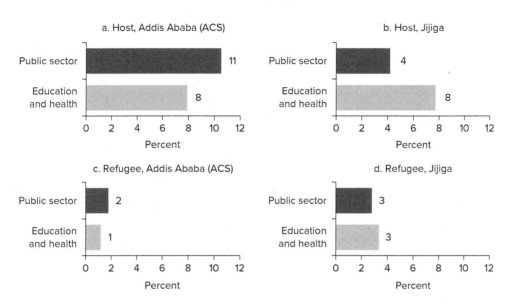

Source: Original table for this report based on data from HHR-LMS Ethiopia and HHR-LMS Uganda.
Note: ACS = adaptive cluster sampling.

FIGURE 4.20 Wage employment in the public sector and in education and in health, hosts and refugees, Uganda

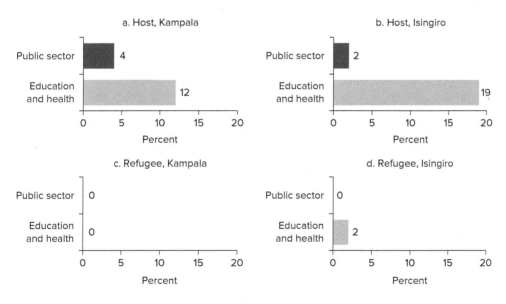

Source: Original table for this report based on data from HHR-LMS Ethiopia and HHR-LMS Uganda.

Jijiga, self-employment also plays an important role compared with other forms of employment, whereas relatively few refugees in Isingiro rely on their own self-employed activities outside of agriculture (16 percent) (table 4.39). However, although self-employment outside of agriculture accounts for 34 percent of all refugee jobs in Addis Ababa, given the low overall labor force participation rate, data are too sparse to reliably characterize self-employed activities. There is therefore little further information on refugee's independent activities in Addis Ababa's labor market that can be discussed in the following section (table 4.39).

The self-employed activities of hosts and refugees in Jijiga and Kampala are alike in many characteristics that are known to correlate with productivity. However, refugees are less likely to report recent growth in their business. Refugees in all localities are much less likely than hosts to report that they have sought funding to expand their activities over the two years preceding the survey (table 4.39). Those in Uganda are also much less likely to say that their profits have increased over the past two years (with similarly low shares in Jijiga). However, in Jijiga and Kampala, it is striking that refugees are about as likely as hosts to report that they operate their activity from a place of business other than their home and that they have been in business for longer than five years. Both are meaningful measures of the degree to which an activity is established and, often, a correlate of productivity. In Isingiro, the patterns are less clear: refugees are slightly more likely to have a separate place of business, but about

TABLE 4.39 Characteristics of self-employment outside of agriculture, hosts and refugees, Ethiopia and Uganda

	Self-employed (%)	Operating more than five years (%)	Has separate place of business (%)	Has business license (%)	Has sought funding for expansion (%)	Profit up past two years (%)	Start-up Investment (median US$)	Start-up borrowing? (%)	Start-up borrowing (median US$)
Ethiopia									
Addis Ababa, host	19	47	29	52	14	9	97	37	194
Jijiga, host	36	26	24	27	15	7	155	40	194
Jijiga, refugee	40	26	24	2	7	9	194	24	194
Uganda									
Kampala, host	49	23	29	25	28	33	139	42	139
Kampala, refugee	72	30	31	16	11	13	83	21	166
Isingiro, host	26	42	18	27	18	32	83	31	166
Isingiro, refugee	16	20	22	13	11	17	55	53	111

Source: Original table for this report based on data from HHR-LMS Ethiopia and HHR-LMS Uganda.

half as likely to have a license or to have operated for more than five years, and a far smaller share of refugees are self-employed.

In Colombia, self-employed migrants and hosts report that their self-employed activities have similar profits. Migrants are less likely to be running a formal activity, but the share is very low among hosts as well (table 4.40). However, hosts and refugees alike commonly characterize self-employment as a fallback in the absence of wage work opportunities (40 percent), reflecting necessity rather than opportunity entrepreneurship, though some also emphasize the independence of this kind of work (23 percent) (figure 4.21).

TABLE 4.40 Characteristics of self-employment, hosts and migrants, Colombia

	Profit (median) (US$)	Duration at least three years (%)	Frequently work in self-employment (%)	Own business (%)	Formal business (%)	Self-employment size (1–4 employees)	Number of people who help in own business (median)	Self-employment work hours per week (median)
Urban, host	180	n.a.	84	41	14	2.35	1	48
Urban, migrant	150	24	79	31	1	–	–	–
Rural, host	108	n.a.	85	22	1	1.78	1	40
Rural, migrant	150	21	80	32	6	–	–	–
Total	150	24	84	37	9	2.23	1	48

Source: Original table for this report based on data from GEIH and PM.
Note: n.a. = not available; – = not available.

FIGURE 4.21 Reasons for being self-employed, urban and rural, hosts and migrants, Colombia

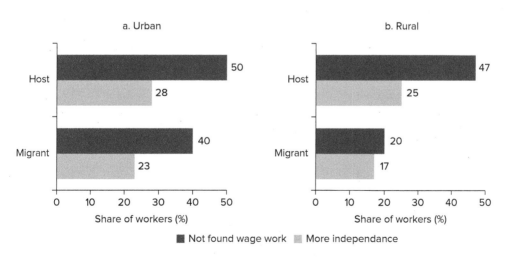

Source: Original table for this report based on data from GEIH and PM.
Note: Reasons mentioned by at least 20 percent of either group.

Self-employed hosts across the four localities say that, at the median, it took them the equivalent of about two to three months' median revenue to establish their self-employed activities (table 4.39). Among them, 30–40 percent say that they borrowed some of this amount. Of the amount, self-employed hosts in Kampala and Addis Ababa say they funded about 40 percent themselves and borrowed the remainder, with much less borrowing in Isingiro and much more in Jijiga. The workers' own investment in Isingiro and Kampala is close to the median household savings; in Addis Ababa and Jijiga, it is substantially below. Overall, the patterns of financing suggest a meaningful, if entirely informal, degree of access to finance.

Refugees in Uganda invest less than hosts in starting their self-employed activities, both in absolute terms and relative to median revenue, whereas those in Jijiga invest more (table 4.39). In both Isingiro and Kampala, refugees say that they invested about a third less than hosts in setting up their activity (with median investment amounting to 66 percent and 60 percent of the value among hosts) (table 4.39). In both localities, this amount corresponds to roughly one-and-a-half months' median revenue, which is less than the value of hosts' investments relative to their revenues. Notably, however, those in Jijiga invested more than their hosts. Among self-employed refugees, the share of borrowers is lower with the exception of Isingiro, where half of all self-employed refugees borrowed. Those who do borrow, however, draw significant amounts, between US$100 and US$200 at the median, or about twice the median start-up investment in Kampala and Isingiro (and about the same amount in Jijiga). Notably, many self-employed refugees in Isingiro borrow, and they borrow significant amounts—but, at the same time, relatively few workers are self-employed (16 percent), potentially pointing toward a degree of self-selection. These patterns suggest that, outside of Isingiro, refugees in the low-income labor markets studied encountered substantial barriers in funding their self-employment activities through their own savings and casual borrowing, with likely consequences for both the ability to start activities and the level of ambition of the latter. There is also an impression that those who were able to begin activities may typically have managed to make meaningful investments, perhaps leading to the absence of a pronounced gap in self-employment earnings.

As is common in low-income economies, workers who have their own business activities chiefly draw upon their own savings in setting up and running their activities, followed by borrowed funds from family or friends. This holds true in the four sample localities concerning start-up funding, funding for expansion, or unexpected costs over the year preceding the survey, or sources considered for hypothetical future expenses (table 4A.10 in online annex 4A). However, two additional observations come to light. First, whereas borrowing from official lenders plays a small role among hosts, it plays barely any among refugees. For instance, in Isingiro, 62 percent of hosts and 75 percent of refugees say that they would expect to cover an unexpected expense with their own funds, remittances, or funds borrowed from family or friends, while 26 percent and 6 percent, respectively, say they would expect to borrow from banks, microfinance lenders, or cooperatives (known as Savings and Credit Cooperative Organization, or SACCOs). Second, although remittances play a very small role among refugees in establishing their activities in Uganda, they are by far the most common source of start-up funding for those in Addis Ababa and play some role among those in Jijiga.

Migrants in Colombia cite the difficulty of obtaining a loan from formal lenders by far the most frequently as the reason why they have not begun a business activity (87 percent) (figure 4.22). Regarding difficulties in beginning self-employed work, migrants most commonly point to the fact that they do not have a work permit, or to the difficulty of finding customers.

FIGURE 4.22   Reasons for difficulties in creating a business, urban and rural, Venezuelans in Colombia

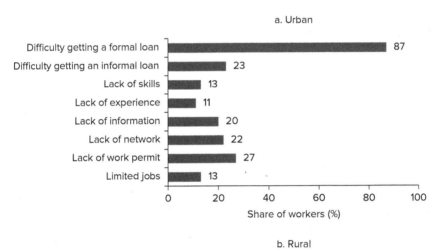

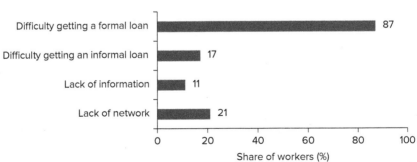

Source: Original table for this report based on data from GEIH and PM.
Note: Reasons mentioned by at least 10 percent of respondents.

Self-employed activities in Ethiopia and Uganda are in commerce, food, and basic services, with a significant degree of specialization among refugee groups. Among self-employed activities of host country nationals, commerce is most common in each locality, and accounts for 30–44 percent of all activities (figure 4.23). Hospitality and basic personal services account for most of the remainder, as is common in low-income economies. Commerce plays a large role among the activities of refugees as well, with the exception of Addis Ababa. However, by way of contrast to hosts, there are some distinct specialties among

FIGURE 4.23   Sector of self-employed activity, hosts and refugees, Ethiopia and Uganda

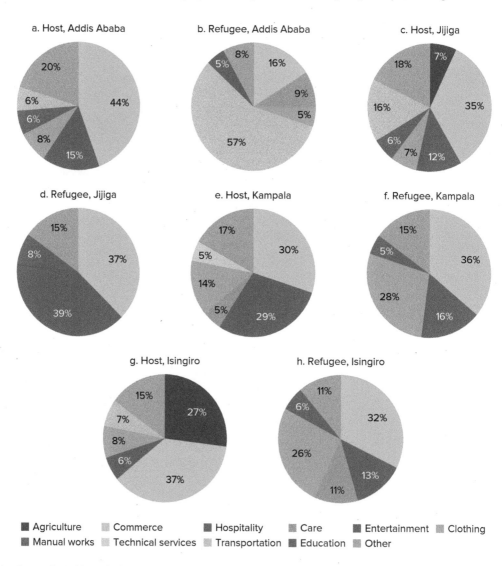

Source: Original figure for this report based on data from HHR-LMS Ethiopia and HHR-LMS Uganda.

the kinds of business activities refugees undertake, though it is not clear that they are systematic. In Addis Ababa, more than half of self-employed refugees work in transportation (57 percent), far more than among either hosts in Addis Ababa or refugees in Kampala. In both Kampala and Isingiro, more than one in four refugees are active in clothing (28 percent and 26 percent, respectively). In Jijiga, hospitality is the dominant activity (39 percent). (Colombia has no comparable patterns of specialization, and Jordan has so little self-employment among refugees that a comparison is not practicable.)

Outside of Jijiga, about one in every three self-employed hosts employs additional workers (from 26 percent in Kampala to 34 percent in Addis Ababa), and 12 percent to 19 percent employ workers from outside the owner's household (table 4.41). Hosts in Jijiga are a bit less likely to employ others (20 percent do so), and much more rarely employ those from outside their household (6 percent do so). On average, each self-employed worker among hosts in Kampala creates one more job, and each five create between them four jobs for workers from outside the household. Self-employed hosts in Addis Ababa and Isingiro create somewhat fewer jobs (seven for every ten self-employed workers), including three jobs for nonhousehold members for every ten self-employed workers; total employment created in Jijiga is lower. (For comparison, in Colombia, one self-employed worker at the median employs one other worker.)

Self-employed refugees also provide significant work for others from within their households, but are less likely to hire workers from outside the household. Across the two Ugandan localities, self-employed refugees provide more employment for other household members than do self-employed hosts (table 4.41). In Kampala, the difference is particularly pronounced, with nearly twice as many household members employed per self-employed worker. In the Ethiopian localities, self-employed refugees employ fewer household members, but still create a substantial number of jobs, employing one additional worker for every five primary operators, compared with one for every three among hosts. At the same time, the share of refugees who hire nonhousehold members is lower than among hosts, and those who employ nonhousehold labor hire fewer workers. Again, there is a remarkable difference between the two countries: those in Uganda still hire about one non-family worker for every seven to eight self-employed activities, whereas in the two Ethiopian labor markets, there is hardly any hiring from outside the household.

With the partial exception of Kampala, where the self-employed hire workers from outside of their own household, they tend to hire their compatriots. Hosts say that between 77 percent and 91 percent of those they hire share their nationality (table 4.41). Refugees outside of Kampala say that they hire very few host nationals—2 percent in Isingiro and 10 percent in Jijiga (with too little data for Addis Ababa). Kampala is a partial exception: about two in five workers hired by refugees are Ugandan nationals (39 percent). Among hosts, this pattern is partially to be expected, given that the host population is much larger

TABLE 4.41 Employment created by self-employed workers, hosts and refugees, Ethiopia and Uganda

	Has any employees (%)	Number of employees (mean)	Number of employees (median)	Has any HH employees (%)	Number of HH employees (mean)	Number of HH employees (median)	Has any non-HH employees (%)	Number of non-HH employees (mean)	Number of non-HH employees (median)	Share of employees who are hosts (%)	Observations
Ethiopia											
Addis Ababa, host	34	0.71	2	19	0.33	2	19	0.38	1	77	728
Addis Ababa, refugee	12	0.20	2	12	0.20	2	0	0.00	–	–	88
Jijiga, host	20	0.47	2	14	0.33	2	6	0.13	2	91	410
Jijiga, refugee	14	0.23	2	14	0.22	2	1	0.01	1	10	197
Uganda											
Kampala, host	26	0.99	2	14	0.20	1	14	0.80	2	88	556
Kampala, refugee	31	0.53	2	25	0.38	1	6	0.15	2	39	162
Isingiro, host	27	0.71	2	20	0.40	2	12	0.31	2	84	831
Isingiro, refugee	20	0.70	2	17	0.58	2	7	0.12	2	2	617

Source: Original table for this report based on data from HHR-LMS Ethiopia and HHR-LMS Uganda.
Note: HH = household; – = not available.

than the refugee workforce. Among refugees, it is perhaps more clearly indicative of affinity for workers of the owner's nationality.

Entrepreneurs among hosts complain most about poor access to capital, competition, low demand, and transportation. Self-employed hosts in all four localities echo each other's concerns about finding customers, funding their activities, and transporting goods. Hosts in Kampala are most concerned about competition (32 percent) and low demand (27 percent), followed by poor access to capital (19 percent) (figure 4.24). Similarly, in Addis Ababa, low demand (33 percent) and access to capital (28 percent) stand out. Those in Jijiga are by far the most concerned about low demand (50 percent), followed by access to capital, transportation, and competition. In Isingiro, difficulties are led by transportation obstacles (34 percent) and the related issue of poor market access. Poor access to capital (32 percent) and low demand (31 percent) follow.

Refugee entrepreneurs have similar top concerns as self-employed hosts; however, they report additional challenges. In Kampala, the second most frequently cited obstacle is police harassment (22 percent compared with 13 percent among hosts), and they are much more likely to worry about discrimination (16 percent compared with 3 percent). In Isingiro, 17 percent are concerned about poor freedom of movement (compared with 2 percent among hosts); conversely, land access and quality and climate shocks are a lesser concern for them (not surprisingly, given the lack of engagement in agriculture). Conversely, refugees in Jijiga are particularly worried about climate shocks (34 percent compared with 12 percent for hosts), perhaps in line with much higher engagement among refugees in food-related business activities.

Self-employment in agriculture

Among the localities studied in Ethiopia and Uganda, only in Isingiro does agriculture employ a sufficiently large share of refugees to allow for detailed analysis. Unsurprisingly, agriculture is a very small employer of both hosts and refugees in the two major cities; statistics are omitted here. As noted earlier, although agriculture does offer employment to refugees in both Isingiro and Jijiga, most of this employment is paid work for others. Because of the much more prominent role of the sector in Isingiro compared with Jijiga, only Isingiro has a sufficient sample size of independent refugee farmers to allow for an analysis of comparative performance in this kind of activity.

Agriculture is a very large employer for both hosts and refugees in Isingiro; however, whereas hosts are normally self-employed farmers, refugees mostly work for others. As is to be expected in a rural low-income area with favorable agro-climatic conditions such as Isingiro, agriculture is the largest sector of employment of both hosts (65 percent) and refugees (55 percent) (table 4.42). However, the types of jobs workers from the two groups usually hold are clearly different. For hosts, the norm is to be independent farmers: they are about

FIGURE 4.24 Main obstacles in self-employed activity, hosts and refugees, Ethiopia and Uganda

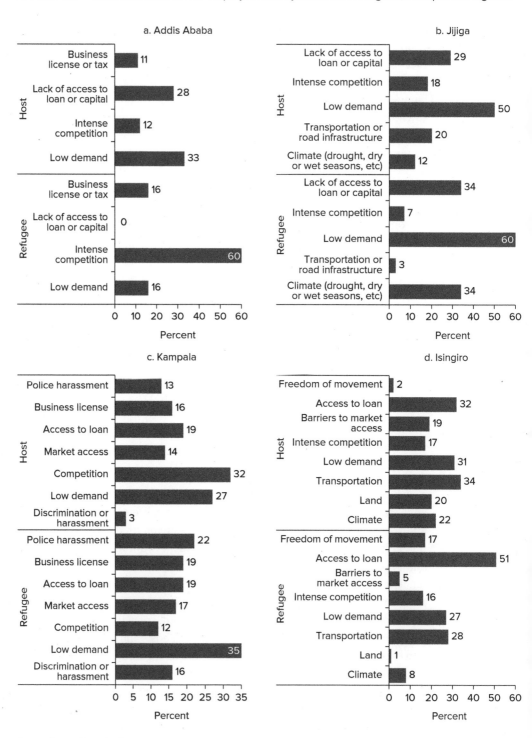

Source: Original figure for this report based on data from HHR-LMS Ethiopia and HHR-LMS Uganda.

246

TABLE 4.42 Profile of work in agriculture, hosts and refugees, Ethiopia and Uganda

	Self-employed in agriculture (%)	Among households that are self-employed in agriculture						
		Works for others in agriculture (%)	Land area (hectares) (median)	Owns land (%)	Works in livestock (%)	Works for market (%)	Sells and trades (%)	Profit up after one year (%)
Ethiopia								
Jijiga, host	14	2	2.0	92	47	31	60	0
Jijiga, refugee	1	1	–	–	100	100	0	0
Uganda								
Isingiro, host	59	6	2.5	65	4	34	36	8
Isingiro, refugee	14	41	1.0	64	0	4	36	2

Source: Original table for this report based on data from HHR-LMS Ethiopia and HHR-LMS Uganda.
Note: – = not available.

10 times more likely to work for their own account than to be employed by others (59 percent and 6 percent). The reverse is the case for refugees. Whereas one in seven refugee workers in Isingiro is a self-employed farmer (14 percent), refugees far more commonly work on someone else's farm—two in five workers do so (41 percent), or about three times as many as those who own a farm. As noted earlier, this stark distinction could speak to difficulties in accessing sufficient quality land, to a lack of capital, or both. (In Jijiga, independent farming is a much less important employer for hosts, but it is again true that refugees are much less likely to have a similar activity.)

More recent arrivals in Isingiro cultivate far less land than those whose families arrived earlier. For instance, among those whose families have been residents less than 10 years, 4 percent farm, and 2 percent farm their own land, compared with 10 percent and 6 percent among those whose households arrived 10 to 19 years ago, and 29 percent and 21 percent among those who arrived even earlier (table 4.43). Figure 4.25 illustrates this pattern. (Household residence time correlates with workers' age, and it is possible that younger workers have a lesser propensity to work in agriculture, regardless of land availability. However, patterns of land use look similar when the effect of the worker's age is accounted for; the simple relationship is shown in figure 4.25 for readability.)

Although few refugees are self-employed independent farmers, it is no less common for those who do this kind of work to farm their own plots: two-thirds of both hosts and refugees do (table 4.42). However, the area of refugee farms is typically much smaller than that cultivated by hosts—1.0 hectare compared with 2.5—at the median. The degree of market orientation of agricultural production is in line with the area farmed. Only one in three farmers among hosts

TABLE 4.43 · Land use and ownership by refugees in Isingiro, by household residence time in Uganda

Minimum household residence time (years)	Area farmed (median) (hectares)	Area farmed (mean) (hectares)	Share of workers farming any land (%)	Share of workers farming own land (%)
0	1	0.82	4	2
10	1	1.30	10	6
20	1	3.39	29	21

Source: Original table for this report based on data from HHR-LMS Uganda.

FIGURE 4.25 Land use and ownership among refugees in Isingiro, by time of arrival in Uganda

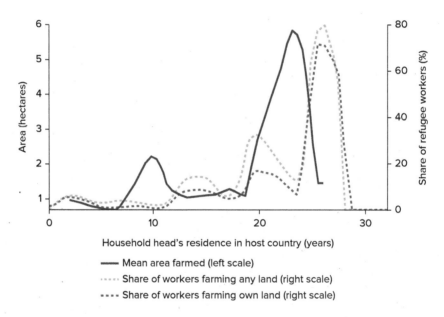

Source: Original table for this report based on data from HHR-LMS Uganda.

likely to present a real obstacle. The data on revenue among independent refugee farmers in Isingiro are insufficient for studying associations with access to factors of production. However, as is intuitive, among hosts, farming a greater area, owning land, and producing for the market are associated with higher reported revenues. Thus, producing mainly for the market is associated with an in Isingiro reports producing only or mainly for the market (34 percent), but few (12 percent) are purely subsistence farmers (table 4.44). By contrast, refugees are much less likely to produce mostly or only for the market (4 percent), and most are subsistence farmers (62 percent). It is useful to note, however, that those refugees who sell any of their products are as likely as hosts to sell to traders, suggesting that refugees have opportunities to work with aggregators in accessing markets. Very few independent farmers in either group say that their profits have increased in the past year (8 percent and 2 percent in Isingiro; table 4.42), far fewer than among the self-employed in other activities.

Among hosts, land ownership and market orientation are associated with higher revenue, so that limited access to land and markets among refugees is

TABLE 4.44   Farmers' sales of products, hosts and refugees, Ethiopia and Uganda

percent

	Host	Refugee	Total
In general, are the products obtained from your agricultural activities for sale?			
Ethiopia			
Jijiga			
Only for sale or barter	7	100	7
Mainly for sale or barter but partly for own or HH use	24	0	24
Mainly for own or HH use but partly for sale or barter	53	0	53
Only for own or HH use	16	0	16
Total	100	100	100
Uganda			
Kampala			
Only for sale or barter	65	–	–
Mainly for sale or barter but partly for own or HH use	7	–	–
Mainly for own or HH use but partly for sale or barter	19	–	–
Only for own or HH use	9	–	–
Total	100	–	–
Isingiro			
Only for sale or barter	2	0	2
Mainly for sale or barter but partly for own or HH use	32	4	30
Mainly for own or HH use but partly for sale or barter	55	34	53
Only for own or HH use	12	62	15
Total	100	100	100

Source: Original table for this report based on HHR-LMS Ethiopia and HHR-LMS Uganda.
Note: HH = household; – = not available.

increment in income of nearly 40 percent, and owning land of 36 percent—both more than either the difference in earnings between women and men who farm for a living or the difference between farmers with and without complete primary education. The association of income with area farmed is statistically strong, but nearly negligible in magnitude, with the difference between the 25th and 75th percentile in area farmed associated with a mere 1 percent difference in income.

About one in four Ugandan farmers in Isingiro employs other workers, most often their compatriots; hardly any refugee farmers employ workers. Among hosts, 23 percent of self-employed farmers employ any labor from outside their households, but very few refugee farmers do (3 percent) (table 4.45). Those who do employ any workers hire a significant number—five longer-term employees at the median. They offer lodging on farms to about half of their workers (52 percent). More than four of every five workers hired are Ugandan nationals (84 percent, including 93 percent of those lodged on farms). (However, refugee workers account for only 20 percent of the overall workforce in Isingiro.) Farmers who employ workers at the median say they pay their longer-term workers US$42 per month, or about US$2 per day assuming full-time work; they believe that the going rate for daily labor is US$1, a very low rate even in a low-income context, and perhaps indicative of the significant labor supply available.

Although too few refugees in Jijiga farm to allow for a characterization of their work, reviewing the characteristics of host farmers is instructive. Agriculture is a much less important employer for hosts in Jijiga than it is in Isingiro, and livestock accounts for half of employment (table 4.42). Neither pattern is surprising, given the agro-climatic difference. It is, however, noteworthy that hosts who are in agriculture in Jijiga do reasonably well: their median revenues are lower than those in wage work or other self-employed activities; however, at US$78 per month, they exceed median earnings for refugees in both other types of activities. What is more, Ethiopian farmers in the labor market have a number of characteristics associated with productivity: they almost always farm their own land (92 percent), are about as likely to mainly produce for the market as farmers in Isingiro (31 percent), and are more likely than not to sell to traders (60 percent). Although few of the refugees settled in Jijiga worked in agriculture in their home country, it still stands to reason that the sector could be a source of appealing employment for some refugees; however, the restrictive policy environment makes engagement very difficult.

TABLE 4.45 Workers employed in agricultural activities, hosts and refugees, Ethiopia and Uganda

	Has any employees (%)	Has any FT employees (%)	Has any PT employees (%)	Number of all employees (median)	Number of FT employees (median)	Number of PT employees (median)	Share of FT workers who are hosts (%)	Share of PT workers who are hosts (%)	Median wage paid (US$)	Going rate for daily labor (US$/day)	Share of FT workers offered lodging (%)	Share of hosts among lodgers (%)
Ethiopia												
Addis, host	–	–	–	–	–	–	–	–	–	–	–	–
Addis, refugee	–	–	–	–	–	–	–	–	–	–	–	–
Jijiga, host	5	0	5	1	–	1	–	66	–	6	–	–
Jijiga, refugee	0	0	0	–	–	–	–	–	–	–	–	–
Uganda												
Kampala, host	52	22	49	15	5	13	100	100	139	4	100	100
Kampala, refugee	–	–	–	–	–	–	–	–	–	–	–	–
Isingiro, host	23	10	18	5	5	3	83	84	42	1	52	93
Isingiro, refugee	3	1	2	2	2	2	0	0	0	1	0	–

Source: Original table for this report based on data from HHR-LMS Ethiopia and HHR-LMS Uganda.
Note: FT = full-time; PT = part-time; – = not available.

Conclusion

Interactions between host and refugee workers and their different profiles and histories shape labor market outcomes.

Refugee households are in a precarious position that compels them to look for work even under restrictive policy rules. In the study localities, refugee households share some traits that are associated both with a great need to be active in the labor market and with vulnerability: they have a greater number of household members, younger household heads, and more women among household heads. As a consequence, although access rules for labor markets make a difference for the degree of participation, even in the more restrictive labor markets, substantial numbers of refugees work.

The way refugees engage in the labor market is shaped by a loss of assets, particularly in economies where self-employment is key. Compared with their hosts, refugees have less capital, lower savings, and more debt, often by wide margins in the economies studied here. Refugees in the Ethiopian and Ugandan localities in this investigation build savings even more slowly than hosts. Thus, the ability to bring some savings with the household when first displaced may have a significant influence on the prospects of thriving in future job activities—but few refugees can bring such savings. Refugees therefore face considerable additional barriers to establishing and growing self-employment activities, a serious constraint in the many economies where most jobs depend on such activities. Policy attention to refugees' access to capital is needed.

Support to refugees needs to consider the obstacles posed by a lack of assets, poor access to land, and other barriers that limit refugees' choices. In lower-income labor markets, policy requiring work permits can limit refugees' access to wage jobs, but it is not the only or even the most important factor that determines access to jobs for refugees. In the localities studied, a lack of savings and assets limits the ability of refugees to succeed in self-employment, and limited availability of land makes farming a difficult activity to access. Refugees are thus less likely than hosts to hold wage jobs in labor markets where such jobs are the main type of work, and are less likely to be self-employed in labor markets where self-employment is the mainstay of hosts. Conversely, across contexts, refugee workers are more likely than their hosts to rely on daily labor. In addition, except in Colombia, refugee workers have substantially lower incomes than their peers. Policy choices thus need to be based in the reality that a rather vulnerable group of workers needs to be supported.

Even under liberal labor market regimes, many refugees rely at least partially on unearned income, thus expanding market demand without greater labor market competition. Substantial numbers of refugee households depend on unearned income and are consumers in local markets without participating in labor markets, even in economies with more liberal labor market access. For host workers, these refugees are potential customers but not likely competitors for jobs. It is constructive for policy to ask how it can support host workers in seizing the opportunities that the resulting increase in demand presents.

The issue of skill complementarity between refugees and hosts may be a lesser priority in lower-income economies, but language can be a significant barrier. The relative levels of education and skills between hosts and refugees vary quite widely between the labor markets studied here. However, it is notable that, with a few exceptions, refugees and hosts report similarly good skill matches, which arguably may be expected in labor markets with a relatively narrow range of activities and broad skill groups. However, policy should carefully investigate whether there are potential skill complementarities that are not as readily measured, for instance, relating to specific tasks within broader occupations. In addition, in some of the labor markets analyzed, language is a barrier for a significant number of refugees, an issue that deserves policy attention.

Notes

1 | Datasets and documentation are available in the World Bank's Microdata Library, https://microdata .worldbank.org/index.php/home.

2 | In Kampala, an additional sample was collected using an adaptive cluster sampling (ACS) technique. This report does not use the data obtained through this process in Kampala, but uses data collected through the same approach in Addis Ababa (Data description). Starting with the listing of households in the initial 150 clusters in Kampala, those EAs that had a share of refugees among households of 10 percent or more were identified and a listing of all households in their neighboring EAs was conducted. This resulted in listing an additional 49 clusters that are identified as neighbors to these initial clusters.

3 | Round 1 in July and August 2021; round 2 in October and November 2021; round 3 in January and February 2022; and round 4 in March and April 2022.

4 | Unemployment rates in low-income countries are generally low and concentrated among urban educated workers; few others can afford to queue for jobs and instead have to engage in low-productivity job activities rather than remaining unemployed. Unemployment rates among hosts—11 percent in Addis Ababa and Kampala, 4 percent in Isingiro—reflect this reality (table 4A.4 in online annex 4A), whereas Jijiga stands somewhat apart in reporting a higher unemployment rate (16 percent). The analysis finds the same urban-rural gap among refugees, but the displaced are again more likely to be unemployed than their hosts.

5 | There is a small gap between the participation and employment rates as measured in the 2016 labor market survey and the International Labour Organization's modeled data, which show a labor force participation rate of 42 percent and employment rate of 34 percent for the same year. In both instances, activity levels are very low, however.

6 | Note that activity shares reported here differ from the breakdown of all current activities among refugees in figure 4.8. Information on prior employment in the home country is available for only a subset of refugee workers, particularly those in in Jijiga, where many refugees were displaced long ago.

7 | Regression analysis pooling all four localities in the low-income countries shows that this difference is not explained by demographics.

8 | Incomes in Jordan were measured for hosts and refugees one year apart; however, given the magnitude of the observed difference in median earnings, it is unlikely that a change in overall earnings between survey rounds substantially influences findings.

9 | Although those residents in Kampala typically live in better housing than hosts (reflected in a higher value of an asset and housing index), the reverse is true in the two rural localities.

10 | The asset indexes are the result of principal component analyses on physical assets owned by the household. The housing index, by contrast, includes elements of the house, including quality, owned by the respondents.

11 | Unfortunately, data in Jordan do not provide for a productive comparison of savings, given that the concept is defined very narrowly as savings held in bank accounts in survey data for hosts (which 3 percent report having); in surveys covering refugees, it is more appropriately defined to include ownership of gold jewelry and other common informal saving modalities.

12 | Results from linear specifications shown for tractability; with a quadratic in age, the relationship has a curvature that reflects an inverse relationship in households with very old household heads, but results reflecting differences between hosts and refugees are qualitatively similar.

13 | As noted elsewhere, work permits are available to refugees in Jordan for work only in some sectors, though refugees do, in practice, work informally in a broad range of activities.

References

Carranza, Eliana, William David Wiseman, Andreas Eberhard-Ruiz, and Ana Lucia Cardenas Martinez. 2022. *Colombia Jobs Diagnostic: Structural Challenges for the Creation of More and Better Jobs.* Washington, DC: World Bank.

DANE (National Administrative Department of Statistics of Colombia). 2018. *Gran Encuesta Integrada de Hogares (GEIH).* Government of Colombia. https://www.datos.gov.co/Estad-sticas-Nacionales /Gran-Encuesta-Integrada-de-Hogares-GEIH/mcpt-3dws.

DANE (National Administrative Department of Statistics of Colombia) and Ladysmith. 2021. *Poblacion migrante venezolana en Colombia, un panorama con enfoque de genero.* Technical Report. Bogota. https://www.dane.gov.co/files/investigaciones/notas-estadisticas/jul-2021-nota-estadistica -poblacion-migrante-venezolana-panorama-con-enfoque-de-genero.pdf.

Eckman, Stephanie, and Kristen Himelein. 2022. "Innovative Sample Designs for Studies of Refugees and Internally Displaced Persons." In *Migration Research in a Digitized World: Using Innovative Technology to Tackle Methodological Challenges,* IMISCOE Research Series, edited by Steffen Potzschke and Sebastian Rinken, 15–34. Cham: Springer International Publishing. doi:10.1007/978-3-031-01319-5_2.

OAMDI (Open Access Micro Data Initiative). 2018. *Labor Market Panel Surveys (LMPS).* http://erf.org.eg /data-portal/.

Pape, Utz Johann, Theresa Beltramo, Jededia Fix, Florence Nimoh, Ibrahima Sarr, and Laura Abril Ríos Rivera. 2021. "Understanding the Socioeconomic Differences of Urban and Camp-Based Refugees in Kenya: Comparative Analysis Brief 2018 Kalobeyei Settlement, 2019 Kakuma Camp, and 2020–21 Urban Socioeconomic Surveys." World Bank, Washington, DC.

Pape, Utz Johann, Benjamin Petrini, and Syedah Aroob Iqbal. 2018. *Informing Durable Solutions by Microdata: A Skills Survey for Refugees in Ethiopia.* Washington, DC: World Bank.

Schuettler, Kirsten, and Laura Caron. 2020. "Jobs Interventions for Refugees and Internally Displaced Persons." Working Paper, World Bank, Washington, DC. https://openknowledge.worldbank.org /handle/10986/33953.

Thompson, Steven K. 1990. "Adaptive Cluster Sampling." *Journal of the American Statistical Association* 85 (412): 1050–59.

Tiltnes, Age, Jon Pedersen, and Huafeng Zhang. 2019. The Living Conditions of Syrian Refugees in Jordan. Fafo-Report 2019:04. Oslo: Fafo. https://www.fafo.no/en/publications/fafo-reports/the-living -conditions-of-syrian-refugees-in-jordan.

Vargas-Silva, Carlos. 2017. "Remittances Sent to and from the Forcibly Displaced." *Journal of Development Studies* 53 (11): 1835–48.

World Bank. 2019. "Informing the Refugee Policy Response in Uganda: Results from the Uganda Refugee and Host Communities 2018 Household Survey." World Bank, Washington, DC.

World Bank. 2021. "Somalia Country Economic Memorandum: Towards an Inclusive Jobs Agenda." World Bank, Washington, DC.

Special Topic 2. The Role of Perceived Labor Market Competition in Shaping Attitudes toward Refugees

Issue

Among other factors discussed in this report, perceptions and attitudes can matter for the performance of refugees in the labor market. As shown in the preceding chapters, a number of issues influence the way refugees are active in the host labor market, including the economic structure of the host economy, comparative characteristics of hosts and refugees as workers, asset ownership, access to capital, and the legal environment. In addition, however, the attitudes hosts have toward refugees as labor market participants, and their perceptions of refugees that shape these attitudes, are likely also to matter for refugees' job outcomes and therefore, for impacts on hosts (refer to, for instance, Loiacono and Silva Vargas 2019).

Attitudes are liable to influence labor market outcomes for refugees both directly and indirectly. They have a plausible direct bearing on whether hosts will hire refugees to work for them, whether they will buy from refugees, whether they integrate them into networks through which information flows, and whether they will lend to them (whether formally or informally). Further, attitudes indirectly shape labor market outcomes for refugees insofar as they shape support for changes in the policy environment that determine economic opportunities for refugees.

In turn, attitudes and perceptions may depend on whether hosts and refugees compete in the labor market or provide opportunities for one another. Competition for employment is the basic reality of the labor market, along with competition for business in labor markets where most jobs are in self-employment. However, working lives also shape identity, and there can be feelings of recognition or kinship among those with shared experiences. Therefore, hosts' attitudes toward refugees can plausibly be assumed to relate to whether they view them neutrally, as colleagues, as competitors, as a source of demand, or some combination. Attitudes will arguably depend most directly upon hosts' subjective beliefs about competition, and these attitudes may be shaped by the actual experience of competition (conversely, by the experience of additional business from refugees), but they may equally be formed on the basis of secondhand information or preconceptions.

As part of the data collection for this study, an experiment was conducted to assess hosts' attitudes toward refugees (as well as attitudes of other groups in the labor market toward each other), conditional on whether groups were described, or "framed," to respondents as being potential labor market competitors. This special topic section summarizes some key results from a working paper commissioned for this report (Bousquet et al., 2024) that analyzes the outcomes of the experiment.

Methods and data

Experimental data were collected in surveys in two urban and two rural labor markets in Ethiopia and Uganda described in detail in chapter 4.

The experimental section of the surveys first provided respondents with a short narrative describing a fictional same-gender character struggling to find a job. Two key characteristics of this fictional character were randomly changed, namely, whether they were described as being a host national or a refugee, and whether they were described as having the same occupation as the respondent or a different occupation. If a different occupation was chosen, it was selected to still roughly match the respondent's skill level. Respondents were then asked a set of six questions about the degree to which (on a five-point Likert scale) they would like to interact with the fictional character in a social, private, or work setting; responses were summarized into an index of prejudice using an established method (Anderson 2008).

Sample narrative that randomly provides a different framing regarding occupation

"[AIDA/ROBERT] is a [Ugandan/ refugee living in Uganda OR of same nationality as refugee respondent]. [She/He] (has lived in Uganda [her/his] entire life and) moved to [Isingiro district/Kampala] five years ago. [She/He] has been working as a [OCCUPATION: Same occupation as respondent/ different occupation] for a long time so [she/he] has a lot of experience in [her/his] occupation. [She/He] also speaks many Ugandan local languages and English very well. [She/He] enjoys working in this profession and would recommend [her/his] friends to work in the same sector. But while being a [OCCUPATION O: Same occupation as respondent/ different occupation] fulfills [her/him], [she/he] is sometimes very tired after work. Due to difficult circumstances, [she/he] has to change jobs while keeping [her/his] current profession. So far, [she/he] has struggled finding a job."

The experiment's design provides a clear framework for assessing whether nationality/legal status and perceived competition, separately or jointly, influence attitudes. Based on the data collected, statistical methods were then used to assess (H1) whether there are prejudicial attitudes between hosts and refugees regardless of occupation, (H2) whether the level of prejudice is greater or lower when respondents think of interacting with anyone (host or refugee) who has the same occupation they do—and are thus more alike, but also potential competitors—and (H3) whether the effect of having the same occupation is different when host and refugee respondents are thinking of refugees and hosts, respectively. Random assignment of "nationality" and "occupation" of the fictional character implies that any difference in the attitudes respondents express is purely because they were prompted to think of interaction with someone who is more or less like them with regard to these two characteristics.

Results

Across the four labor markets studied, host workers show prejudicial attitudes toward refugees only when they share the same occupation (table ST2.1). It is perhaps remarkable that, when data from the four labor markets are pooled, hosts express no reservations about interacting with refugees who are described to them as having a different occupation from their own. (Isingiro district stands out as the only locality where hosts hold such reservations.) However, when refugees are described as having the same occupation, there is a marked negative bias. The difference is 0.25 standard deviation from the index. The index, in turn, has a standard deviation of 1.0, and effects below 0.2 are generally considered "small" effects in the literature (refer to, for example, Muller 1989). By way of contrast, hosts actually have more favorable attitudes toward their co-nationals if they are described to the respondent as holding the same occupation they do, perhaps indicating a greater feeling of kinship with those who have a similar work experience.

Hosts in Jijiga and Kampala show no adverse perceptions of refugees who are described to them as being, implicitly, potential labor market competitors. A prejudicial attitude is observed only in the other two labor markets, Addis Ababa and Isingiro district. As discussed in chapter 4, very few refugees in Addis Ababa work. Thus, the prejudicial attitudes expressed are likely to be linked to potential competition rather than to the actual experience of competing with refugees. (The displaced population in Addis Ababa had risen sharply in the months preceding data collection, perhaps leading to heightened fears of future competition.) In Isingiro, respondents among hosts are most commonly independent farmers, whereas refugees in agriculture overwhelmingly are hired workers. To the degree that host respondents are aware of this difference, the fact that they view refugees active in agriculture more negatively than others suggests that there may be some perceptions of competition, whether because of concerns over the demand for land from refugees or because laborers contribute through their work to greater competition in output markets.

There is no corresponding bias among refugees toward hosts who share their occupation; in some localities, refugees view their hosts more positively than they view their fellow refugees. In none of the four labor markets studied does thinking of a fictional host character who shares their occupation significantly worsen refugees' stated readiness to interact. When data from all localities are pooled, there is also no difference in how refugees view their hosts, as compared with fellow refugees. However, in the two rural labor markets in Isingiro district and Jijiga, refugees view their hosts significantly more positively than they view others who have been displaced (on average across occupation groups), which may suggest either appreciation for hosts or potential grievances toward fellow refugees in the camp-like living environments in the two localities. Given that in both localities refugees show lower levels of prejudice toward fellow refugees than hosts show toward other hosts, it is perhaps more compelling to view refugees' preference for hosts as a sign of appreciation or readiness to integrate.

TABLE ST2.1 Estimates for the pooled index of prejudice, Ethiopia and Uganda

Treatment variable	(1) Host		(2) Refugee	
OLS and margins				
Regression coefficients				
α1: OutGroup (1) versus InGroup (0)	0.03	(0.06)	−0.09	(0.13)
α2: Same (1) versus Different (0) Occupation	−0.17***	(0.06)	−0.01	(0.14)
H3: OutGroup × Same Occupation	0.25***	(0.08)	−0.04	(0.17)
Average effects in the population				
H1: OutGroup (1) versus InGroup (0)	0.16***	(0.04)	−0.11	(0.08)
H2: Same (1) versus Different (0) Occupation	−0.04	(0.04)	−0.03	(0.10)
Observations	2,949		1,738	
Mean	−0.01		0.06	
Addis Ababa				
Regression coefficients				
α1: OutGroup (1) versus InGroup (0)	−0.24*	(0.13)	0.19	(0.20)
α2: Same (1) versus Different (0) Occupation	−0.34***	(0.11)	−0.33	(0.27)
H3: OutGroup × Same Occupation	0.50***	(0.17)	0.10	(0.30)
Observations	841		197	
Average effects in the population				
H1: OutGroup (1) versus InGroup (0)	−0.00	(0.08)	0.22	(0.18)
H2: Same (1) versus Different (0) Occupation	−0.09	(0.08)	−0.29	(0.18)
Observations	841		197	
Mean	−0.16		−0.67	
Jigija				
Regression coefficients				
α1: OutGroup (1) versus InGroup (0)	0.15	(0.11)	−0.33	(0.23)
α2: Same (1) versus Different (0) Occupation	−0.09	(0.11)	0.02	(0.16)
H3: OutGroup × Same Occupation	−0.05	(0.16)	−0.23	(0.20)
Observations	570		300	
Average effects in the population				
H1: OutGroup (1) versus InGroup (0)	0.12*	(0.07)	−0.43**	(0.20)
H2: Same (1) versus Different (0) Occupation	−0.12	(0.09)	−0.09	(0.14)
Observations	570		300	
Mean	0.08		0.17	

(continued)

TABLE ST2.1 Estimates for the pooled index of prejudice in Ethiopia and Uganda *(continued)*

Treatment variable	(1) Host		(2) Refugee	
Kampala				
Regression coefficients				
α1: OutGroup (1) versus InGroup (0)	−0.01	(0.13)	−0.17	(0.19)
α2: Same (1) versus Different (0) Occupation	−0.12	(0.11)	−0.03	(0.24)
H3: OutGroup × Same Occupation	0.09	(0.17)	0.41	(0.34)
Observations	685		539	
Average effects in the population				
H1: OutGroup (1) versus InGroup (0)	0.04	(0.08)	0.02	(0.14)
H2: Same (1) versus Different (0) Occupation	−0.07	(0.09)	0.17	(0.21)
Observations	685		539	
Mean	0.06		0.33	
Isingiro				
Regression coefficients				
α1: OutGroup (1) versus InGroup (0)	0.30***	(0.11)	−0.18	(0.12)
α2: Same (1) versus Different (0) Occupation	−0.01	(0.11)	−0.04	(0.12)
H3: OutGroup × Same Occupation	0.24*	(0.14)	−0.06	(0.17)
Observations	853		702	
Average effects in the population				
H1: OutGroup (1) versus InGroup (0)	0.43***	(0.09)	−0.21**	(0.08)
H2: Same (1) versus Different (0) Occupation	0.10	(0.07)	−0.07	(0.08)
Observations	853		702	
Mean	0.02		0.01	

Source: Adapted from Bousquet et al., 2024.
Note: Weighted regressions. The analysis uses the Anderson (2008) index. Standard errors clustered at the level of primary sampling units. All the models include the same control variables. Controls include age, gender, household size, education, employment status, country of residence, and urban/rural areas. OLS = ordinary least squares.
* $p < .10$, ** $p < .05$, *** $p < .01$.

Implications

Hosts' preoccupation with competition from refugees matters for attitudes toward displaced groups. Supportive attitudes from hosts are important to the well-being of refugees and to their success in building good lives while living in displacement. The evidence shown here suggests that, to foster positive attitudes, addressing concerns about actual or potential competition in the labor market is important. Notably, this logic does not hold among refugees: it is not the case that any concern over competition shapes their views of their hosts.

Both development investments in host communities and promoting contact with, and information about, refugees could help lessen adverse views. Policy discourse increasingly acknowledges the importance of providing job support to host communities alongside the displaced. The results shown here suggest that this approach may indeed be helpful in mitigating one of the key drivers of adverse perceptions. However, results also suggest that worries about competition can shape perceptions even when there is little actual competition. Therefore, further experiments are needed to identify the best approaches to shape perceptions. Emerging evidence suggests that promoting contact between hosts and refugees, providing information about refugees, stressing commonalities with hosts or directly encouraging hosts to empathize with refugees by imagining themselves being in a similar situation can change perceptions in some settings. A full discussion of the existing evidence related to these interventions is provided in chapter 5. Although the experiment conducted for this report did not investigate the effect of describing refugees to hosts as potential customers, further research could ask whether the demand created by refugees could act as a counterbalance to worries about labor market competition.

References

Anderson, Michael L. 2008. "Multiple Inference and Gender Differences in the Effects of Early Intervention: A Reevaluation of the Abecedarian, Perry Preschool, and Early Training Projects." *Journal of the American Statistical Association* 103 (484): 1481–95.

Bousquet, Julie, Anna Gasten, Mark Marvin Kadigo, Jean-Francois Maystadt, and Colette Salemi. 2024. "Does perceived labor market competition increase prejudice between refugees and their local hosts? Evidence from Uganda and Ethiopia." Background paper written for this report. World Bank, Washington, DC.

Loiacono, Francesco, and Mariajose Silva Vargas. 2019. "Improving Access to Labor Markets for Refugees: Evidence from Uganda." International Growth Center Report C-43445-UGA-1. https://www .theigc.org/sites/default/files/2019/10/Loiacono-and-Vargas-2019-final-paper_revision.pdf.

Muller, Keith. 1989. *Statistical Power Analysis for the Behavioral Sciences*. Technometrics, 31(4), 499–500.

5. Conclusion

Introduction

This report seeks to address important knowledge gaps relating to the impact of forced displacement on jobs in host communities. Research on the impacts of hosting refugees has grown markedly over the past years, and effects in host labor markets have received significant attention. However, knowledge gaps remain. This report addresses some of these important gaps, including the dearth of comparative assessments of impacts across economies with different labor market characteristics and policy regimes and the lack of comparative studies of changes in work permit regimes. Further, these gaps relate to the relative absence of detailed analysis of market interactions between refugees and hosts and their comparative outcomes in the same labor markets. Finally, the report seeks to contribute to the understanding of how perceptions of job competition shape attitudes toward refugees.

The growing evidence base now allows host countries to more confidently manage the participation of displaced workers for the benefit of hosts as well as refugees. With a better understanding of how displacement changes local job outcomes, decision-makers in host countries and international partners can more confidently assess each context and make policy choices that respond to the situation at hand. Policies that aim to improve outcomes for both displaced groups and their hosts are both pragmatic and ethically appealing. As this report shows, it is encouraging that such policies are likely to be within reach across a diverse range of settings.

This chapter provides guidance on how to conduct labor market analysis to inform policy regarding refugee participation, reviews policy options, and identifies important areas for future work. Based on the evidence provided in this report, this concluding chapter seeks to provide some tools to help in formulating effective policies. First, it discusses what lessons emerge from the investigation that can help guide labor market analysis to better understand the context with the goal of informing refugee policy. Second, it reviews possible policy tools for better job outcomes for both hosts and refugees, discusses the evidence on their performance, and provides suggestions on when such tools are likely to be a good fit. Finally, it highlights remaining gaps that should be addressed to further strengthen the knowledge base for policy.

How labor market analysis can support better jobs policy for hosts and refugees

Policy addressing the integration of refugee workers needs to be grounded in labor market analysis. The goal of analysis is to understand the job outcomes of refugees and the likely impact of their participation in the economy on job outcomes for hosts under different policy choices. Such analysis can draw upon a growing range of evidence, much of which is reviewed in this report. However, the evidence needs to be interpreted in light of local labor market conditions. The following sections set out lessons on how to conduct such an analysis, and figure 5.1 summarizes the proposed approach. The analysis should ask what hosts' current jobs look like; how hosting refugees is likely to change the labor market, both through the contribution refugees make to market demand and through their engagement as workers (given policy and other constraints); and what adaptations hosts may make. With assessments of these questions in hand, the analysis can then consider policy options to improve hosts' and refugees' job outcomes.

Analysis can be grounded in the conceptual models of the impact of hosting refugees reviewed in chapter 1 of this report. Theory discusses a range of possible conduits through which hosting refugees affects the local economy. Still, as a practical matter, in many economies, there are likely to be two primary conduits for impacts: (1) the contribution of refugees to demand for goods and services, and (2) the effect on labor supply that arises from their labor market participation. In some cases, refugees may bring physical and human capital with them that allows them to become entrepreneurs, thereby directly affecting labor demand.

If analysis is to support policy that benefits hosts and refugees, realism about labor market conditions and likely impacts is critical. An important function of analysis is to test expectations and concerns about the potential job impacts of

FIGURE 5.1 An analytical approach to assessing the impact of forced displacement on jobs for hosts

GUIDING CONSIDERATIONS

- Assess opportunities, not just competition.
- Be realistic about the kinds of jobs hosts currently rely on, and do not overlook informal and casual work.
- Keep in mind that many refugees will work even in restrictive environments, but many will be inactive even in permissive ones.
- Do not underestimate the potential for change in local markets, but do not overestimate the potential for change in the overall economy.

KEY QUESTION	ANALYTICAL STEPS
What kinds of jobs do hosts rely on?	• Consider all income-generating activities, not just full-time, waged, or formal work. • Basic indicators include income level, sector of work, type of work, and level of engagement. • Disaggregate for significant labor market groups: gender, age, urban and rural localities, and localities that host large and smaller numbers of refugees.
What is the likely impact of displacement on local market demand for goods and services?	• How important is the number of refugees relative to local market size? • To what degree will refugees participate in the market (assess mobility and ability to access markets, reliance on food aid, access to earned and unearned income and savings)? • Distinguish between traded and nontraded goods and services. • Are local markets in refugee-hosting areas integrated or likely to be supplied by local producers?
How are refugees likely to engage in the labor market?	• Remember that self-employment is, in many developing economies, likely to be a key type of job. • Consider jobs refugees may look for by assessing job profiles in home countries, jobs other migrant groups take, and jobs hosts with similar profiles take. • Consider constraints, such as de facto policy restrictions, capital access as a constraint on self-employment, and language barriers. Consider skill matches with common jobs in the host country. • Consider the scale of the likely shift in labor demand relative to the size of the labor market.
What constraints do hosts face in seizing opportunities and adapting to competition?	• What are the barriers to benefiting from additional market demand, including poor access to capital, land scarcity, poor availability of inputs, and competition from imports? • What are the barriers to adapting to greater competition: for example, capital constraints, skills, barriers to mobility, and information?

CONSIDER HOW DIFFERENT POLICY CHOICES WOULD CHANGE THE PICTURE

Source: Original figure for this report.

hosting refugees. As this report argues, such discussions are quite commonly guided by misconceptions, for instance, about the kinds of jobs most hosts rely on, about the level of labor market participation by refugees in the absence of a welcoming policy, or about the contribution refugees make to market demand. For policy to be more effective, analysis needs to be realistic at each step.

Understand the baseline for jobs for hosts

The tools of jobs analysis are well-honed, and a good picture can be shaped by focusing on income, sector and type of work, and the level of labor market engagement. The set of indicators used in this report can provide a good basic understanding of jobs; these indicators consist of income levels, the sector of work (often usefully disaggregated into agriculture, manufacturing, construction, commerce, and other services), the type of work (self-employed and household activities, wage work, and daily labor), and the level of engagement (participation and time at work).

Understanding the impact of forced displacement in developing countries requires thinking broadly about jobs. In line with the World Bank's *World Development Report 2013: Jobs,* analysis should consider a broad concept of "jobs" (World Bank 2013). In some economies, a job is thought of as paid work for others, an activity that is full-time and of which most workers have only one, as well as an activity that workers carry out for a formal business and that is itself formalized. However, this is not the reality in most developing countries. Self-employment and household work are often more common than paid work for others. What paid work there is may be more akin to daily labor than to waged work. Workers do several jobs at different times of the year, and households may work together on some activities but not on others. Most activities are informal. For instance, as shown in previous chapters, in Uganda's Isingiro district, wage work accounts for only one in nine jobs held by hosts; in Kampala as well, far more Ugandan workers rely on self-employment than hold a waged job. Even in Colombia, with its far higher income level, wage work accounts for less than half of all urban jobs, and more than half of the wage jobs are informal. To understand the impact of displacement, analysis must consider all such activities. What matters is to follow the World Development Report's definition and consider jobs to be all "activities that generate actual income, monetary or in kind, and do not violate fundamental rights and principles at work" (World Bank 2013, 66).

Impacts are not the same for all groups of workers, and analysis must be based on an understanding of how groups that account for a significant share of workers differ in the activities they rely on. This report emphasizes that, even when mild or even positive overall effects occur in host communities, some groups of workers may benefit and others may experience losses. Analysis must be informed by an assessment of the job profiles of different groups of workers.

The dimensions of disaggregation used in this report include gender, age (young workers and others), urban and rural residence, and localities that host large numbers of refugees and those that host fewer.

Understand the potential for refugees to add to demand in local markets

Policy discussions of the job impacts of displacement understandably focus on the potential risks of greater labor market competition. To balance this analytical tilt, it may be useful for analysis to begin by assessing opportunities, which are likely to arise initially through an increase in market demand for goods and services. (However, although higher labor supply poses a competitive challenge for host workers, it may offer opportunities for host employers, especially in combination with higher market demand.)

Analysis should consider the scale of additional demand relative to local markets. This additional demand will depend on the number of refugees, the degree to which they are likely to receive assistance and which form this assistance might take (cash, vouchers, or in kind), their ability to earn incomes, and their ability to draw upon other unearned income sources. Chapter 4 provides vivid examples of how such income sources vary across displacement settings. Thus, remittances play a very large role for refugees in both Addis Ababa and Kampala; aid is a major source of livelihoods for refugees in Jordan; and migrants in Colombia largely rely on earned income. A critical further consideration is whether markets, particularly in the food sector, are highly integrated, so that incremental demand will be satisfied by trade, or are more segmented, so that local producers are likely to benefit. At the same time, analysis also needs to bear in mind that, if the higher demand cannot be met, either through trade or increased local production, prices are likely to increase, at least in the short term, which negatively affects nonproducers. In addition, in some situations, opportunities may arise through the physical and human capital refugees bring. Data on these factors can often be collected with limited effort.

Ask how refugees' participation is likely to change labor market opportunities for hosts

Gather information on what kinds of jobs refugees are likely to look for. Refugees must begin their working lives anew in host communities. Although the constraints they face are important in shaping labor market choices (discussed in the following paragraphs), it is important to ask what jobs refugees may look for, given the chance. Insights into this question can come from refugees' job profiles before displacement. Another perspective comes from jobs other migrants are taking, and a final approach is to ask what kinds of jobs hosts with similar profiles do.

Understand the constraints refugees are likely to face in restarting their working lives, whether as a result of policy or other obstacles. Understanding the impediments refugees face can begin with policy obstacles, notably barriers to mobility; legal or customary prohibitions against acquiring land or owning a business without a local partner; restrictions on working, even in the informal sector; and, in labor markets where there is significant formal work, restrictions to accessing such jobs (perhaps with sectoral restrictions) and barriers to acceptance of qualifications. Restrictions can be placed on refugees' participation in the labor market even where most hosts work in informal jobs (Zetter and Ruaudel 2016). Although a focus on such barriers is justified, it is important not to lose sight of two constraints that will be critical in many localities—first, language barriers, which can limit access to most types of paid work for others; and, second, access to capital, a critical constraint to most common types of self-employment (commerce, hospitality, transportation, and so on) with the exception of some personal services (household aide, porter, and the like). Chapter 4 reviews a range of indicators that matter in assessing refugees' access to capital, including household savings and assets, the ability of refugees to bring funds with them when displaced, and the use of different sources of financing (keeping in mind that, even among hosts, informal borrowing from family and networks may be the most common way to fund the expenses associated with self-employment). Skill matches should also be considered; however, as this report shows, analyzing skill matches is sometimes best done in a simple way that takes into account the kinds of activities that provide most jobs. For instance, it may be informative to determine whether refugees displaced into rural farming areas are by background farmers or, for instance, herders or traders.

Consider the scale of the shift in labor demand. With some exceptions, even large refugee inflows tend to be modest in size relative to the overall labor force (see chapter 2). However, they can be large both to certain groups of host workers who compete closely with refugees and relative to the local labor force in localities that host large numbers of refugees. Some simple calculations can provide insights into how the likely scale of participation by refugee workers measures up against the size of the labor market in given localities and occupations.

Understand the scope for adaptation

What constraints do hosts face in adapting to competition and seizing opportunities? Based on the job profiles of hosts and an understanding of the likely change in opportunities and competition, the next question is what constraints hosts contend with in adapting to both. With regard to seizing additional market demand (as well as additional labor), the constraints may relate to land scarcity, the availability of inputs, the lack of capital, competition from imports (as noted, in highly integrated food markets, the additional local demand may not translate into greater opportunity for local producers), and regulations that might restrain responses to increased demand, for instance, in the housing sector. Constraints related to adapting to greater competition in certain labor markets are more likely to relate to mobility and to lack of capital and skills to change to different business activities.

What policy choices can benefit both? Following an assessment of the likely impact on host communities, analysis can then consider policy choices to help improve job outcomes for both refugees and hosts. Such policy options are discussed in detail in the following section.

Policy implications

Policies for better job outcomes for hosts

International assistance to host communities can make a key contribution to seizing opportunities and cushioning impacts. Although this report cannot isolate the impact of aid from the international community on job outcomes for hosts, the relatively benign overall impacts come in the context of significant assistance. Funding for refugees and host communities makes up a sizable part of bilateral development assistance (12 percent) (Hesemann, Desai, and Rockenfeller 2021; World Bank 2023).[1] Such spending is likely to have important cushioning effects. Simulations, for example, show the positive impacts of cash transfers in Rwanda on areas around camps (Taylor et al. 2016).

Distributional changes demand policy attention even where displacement or work permit schemes cause few changes in overall employment outcomes for hosts. The four countries studied in this report all experienced substantial refugee inflows but little change in aggregate earnings, participation, and unemployment. Similarly, the estimated effects of large work permit schemes on jobs for hosts are limited. However, there are larger and more significant welfare gains for some groups of workers and adverse effects on others, notably in the short term. Policy makers should direct their attention toward assisting workers who encounter disruption. Quick and effective support is critical to welfare, fairness, social stability, and, ultimately, to sustaining policies to help refugees rebuild their livelihoods. The labor market analysis described previously can help identify groups that are likely to be negatively affected. Policy makers should then monitor whether such impacts materialize and how they might change over time.

With support from the international community and economywide mild or positive effects, concrete policy measures can be adopted to compensate host workers who experience worse job outcomes. The absence of economywide adverse effects from hosting refugees and granting work permits should not blind policy makers to the fact that some groups of workers may face greater labor market competition. However, limited or even positive aggregate effects suggest that policy makers can focus on compensating those affected, help them adapt, and boost overall demand for labor where competition has increased. Continued international support is also important; it is legitimate to ask whether the overall effects of hosting refugees would have been negligible or even positive without the aid and government investments the countries studied here benefited from.

The arrival of displaced workers presents opportunities that deserve as much policy attention as concerns about labor market competition. Public discourse tends to focus on the potential adverse effect on jobs for hosts. Far less attention addresses opportunities arising from the arrival of additional consumers and from the aid and investment that often accompany refugee flows. This report's analysis shows the potential for large gains in host communities. Policy should not only seek to limit potential harm to hosts but also consider how best to help workers and businesses take advantage of new opportunities.

To seize these opportunities, policy makers need to establish a favorable environment and use aid and investments wisely for hosts and refugees alike. A positive business and investment climate, available infrastructure, and access to finance are key elements that allow firms to exploit the opportunities created by a refugee inflow. In addition, policy makers can specifically support refugees' creation of firms, which not only generate income for refugees themselves but also employ others. In addition to providing a constructive general environment, specific obstacles that refugees might face with regard to access to finance need to be addressed (Schuettler and Caron 2020). Legally allowing refugees to create businesses also assists with the creation and growth of formal firms, as the example of Colombia shows (Bahar, Cowgill, and Guzman 2022). Policy makers should seek to provide aid and government investments in a way that can also benefit hosts. Uganda, and more recently Ethiopia and Jordan through their compacts, directly links support for refugees to support for host communities. An example showing long-term gains for hosts, even after refugees returned, is provided in Tanzania, thanks to infrastructure built after the refugee inflow and the related permanent decrease in transportation costs (Maystadt and Duranton 2019).

More particularly, structural changes in host communities reflect a "move toward opportunity" that policies should seek to support. Analysis of the type of work and industry shows that host workers make significant efforts to adapt to the arrival of refugee workers. Overall, there is an impression of a move toward sectors and activities likely to experience increased demand and less competition. Policy can seek to facilitate such shifts, which, in low-income countries, will often mean supporting self-employed workers to make small investments to change their activities. In higher-income economies, moving toward opportunity is likely to involve capital support and access to finance for firms as well as an improved investment climate, particularly in sectors where new opportunities arise, and training opportunities for workers.

In addition, the agriculture sector is often well-positioned to provide additional opportunities for host communities. Across the four countries analyzed, multiple indicators suggest that agriculture workers in host communities benefit from an influx of refugees. It is intuitive that refugees increase demand for food, and that opportunities for producers arise in food markets that are not fully integrated. Policy should consider investment needs that would help local communities benefit from such opportunities. At the same time, the food sector can also help employ refugees.

Policy options with which to directly support the mobility of host community workers are available. Further, supporting worker geographic mobility can help facilitate adaptation. Policy makers need to look at areas such as affordable housing, transportation costs, minimum wages adapted to the cost of living, incentives set through existing social benefits, information frictions, and discrimination against internal migrants when aiming to encourage such internal migration (World Bank 2008).

Cash transfers are a tested tool with which to cushion changes and make space for adaptation. Even small disruptions in the working lives of workers with low incomes and few assets pose a serious challenge. At the same time, disruptions are common, and the arrival of displaced workers is far from the only issue. Cash transfers have emerged as a reliable tool for adjusting to and recovering from disruptions, and would be a good fit for many host communities, particularly in lower-income economies. Even if transfers are intended to help workers weather greater competition, they are also likely to be useful to others in seizing new market opportunities. Higher-income developing economies can consider delivering such assistance through more formal channels, such as unemployment insurance. However, even in such economies, it is important to consider whether such channels will reach the groups of workers likely to experience the most competition from refugees or to have new opportunities worth pursuing.

Training can help hosts when skills are the binding constraint (which is often not the case). Some evidence from middle- and high-income countries shows that, in the wake of a refugee inflow, "occupational upgrading" sometimes happens among hosts, that is, hosts shift toward higher-skilled occupations that command higher incomes. Such occupational upgrading might happen because new job opportunities arise in the area caused by the inflow of refugees, because hosts have skills that complement those of refugees, or because hosts decide to acquire additional skills to compete less directly with refugees. In principle, training can support occupational upgrading. However, in lower-income economies and other settings with weak labor demand and limited access to capital for self-employment, investigating whether skills are the actual binding constraint preventing hosts from seizing new opportunities is critical. Training alone will not improve job outcomes when there is little demand for wage workers or scant access to capital to fund activities.

More liberal refugee labor market policies do not worsen aggregate outcomes for hosts, but policy makers need to take into account how such policies are likely to change distributional effects. The two countries in this study with more liberal refugee policies do not show worse outcomes than those with more restrictive policies. The introduction of work permit programs does not lead to substantial adverse effects on hosts, as this report shows. Economic theory suggests that empowering refugee workers to choose their activities more freely is likely to lead to economywide gains. Still, all policy choices affect distributional outcomes, and more or less liberal policy regimes will affect different groups differently. Policies that restrict refugees' access to formal jobs will increase competition for vulnerable workers in the informal sector; in countries issuing work permits to refugees, labor market competition may shift toward formal jobs. Liberalizing access to land or capital may increase competition among self-employed workers but may lessen competition among daily laborers. To limit distributional effects, policies should aim to minimize negative impacts on the most vulnerable workers. In practice, however, the political economy in each country is likely to define whose interests will be better protected.

Policies for better job outcomes for refugees

Characteristics of the host labor market are critical to informing effective policies to help refugees take advantage of labor and product market demand. Conditions vary enormously in host labor markets, notably with differences in income level and between urban and rural areas. Refugee support must carefully take into account the types of activities that have demand for labor and for self-employment, and sectors in need of product supply. For instance, programs to promote access to formal jobs are more likely to be meaningful in urban or higher-income labor markets with more demand for wage workers. In agricultural areas, access to land and capital is critical. Elsewhere, focusing on barriers to self-employment might be most beneficial.

Skill matches may play a role in helping refugees improve their livelihoods, but perhaps not in obvious ways, so policies need to be based on careful assessments. The relative level of skills among hosts and refugees may vary widely. Refugee skill gaps may not be based on having less education; they could—as in this study—be due to the lack of language or practical skills. Further, because most jobs in lower-income labor markets are in a small number of common activities, skill matches may be less relevant than in higher-income markets. Policy makers must determine whether refugees are well-equipped to find a niche among workers who carry out common activities. In addition, the capacity to invest may be more important to success than skills match. Evidence shows that training programs that are not combined with the provision of cash or access to finance are not very likely to be successful, at least in the short term and in low-income settings (Barberis et al. 2022; Schuettler and Caron 2020). Where refugees do not speak the language, language training might help them fare better in the labor market, as evidence from European high-income countries shows (Arendt and Bolvig 2020; Auer 2018; Bailey et al. 2022; Foged, Hasager, and Peri 2022; Foged et al. 2022; Foged and van der Werf 2023; Lochmann, Rapoport, and Speciale 2019).

Policies need to alleviate the substantial capital constraints refugees face that limit their ability to succeed in self-employment and their ability to search for better jobs. Both displacement itself and barriers to earning good incomes disadvantage refugees in building capital, including in low-income economies where accumulating savings is already very difficult. Capital constraints are a severe obstacle in labor markets where self-employment is the key economic activity. They also limit the ability of refugees to wait and invest in searching for better jobs and take more risks when setting up an economic activity. Policies should seek to alleviate these capital constraints. Gaining an understanding of what viable avenues exist for refugees to access capital is crucial. For instance, in markets where even hosts rarely borrow outside their families, borrowing may be especially hard for refugees. Cash transfers have a successful track record in helping refugees rebuild assets, at least while the programs are ongoing (Schuettler and Do 2023). Emerging evidence on economic inclusion programs for refugees, which combine cash with additional interventions, shows promising results longer term and with regard to productive assets and economic activities (Andrews et al. 2021; Heisey, Sánchez, and Bernagros 2022). In a middle-income country such as Jordan, regular cash transfers can also help attenuate liquidity constraints and allow refugees to search for better jobs (Caria et al. 2024).

In labor markets with significant formal employment and vigorous labor demand, work permits are an important tool for promoting better outcomes for refugees. Although policy attention to the repercussions of work permits on hosts is warranted, refugees quite obviously stand to benefit substantially from work permit programs, especially where having a work permit gives a refugee a realistic chance of obtaining a higher-earning, formal job with better working conditions. Evidence from high-income countries shows lasting positive impacts on the labor market outcomes of refugees who were more quickly allowed to work (Marbach, Hainmueller, and Hangartner 2018; Slotwinski, Stutzer, and Uhlig 2019).

Even in labor markets with little demand for formal workers, work permits can empower refugee workers by providing a potent and visible signal that they have a right to work, thus not limiting them to jobs in which they are less likely to be detected while working, thereby promoting their bargaining power and reducing their vulnerability. In economies where informality and self-employment are common, this signaling may be the most important function of a work permit scheme. In Jordan, for example, some refugees employed outside of agriculture still requested permits for work in agriculture (which were more flexible and easier to obtain than permits for work in other sectors) (Ait Ali Slimane and Al-Abbadi 2023). Thus, policy makers should seek additional ways of sending the same message, for instance, by creating programs in which permits are easy to obtain and not tied to formal work, or through government communications campaigns targeting workers and employers. In addition, because work permits alone are unlikely to facilitate job access in such labor markets, policy needs to target other obstacles refugees face in lower-income economies, such as access to land and capital for self-employment activities.

Policy needs to address worries about labor market competition that shape adverse views toward displaced workers and negatively affect their job outcomes. Supportive attitudes from hosts are important to the well-being of refugees and to their success in building lives while living in displacement. The findings in this report suggest that addressing concerns about actual or potential labor market competition is critical. Policy discourse increasingly acknowledges the importance of providing job support to host communities alongside the displaced, but worries about competition can shape perceptions even when there is little actual competition.

Interventions promoting contact, perspective taking, and information, as well as public investments that benefit hosts, seem most promising in influencing attitudes toward refugees. A growing literature shows that interventions can sometimes succeed in positively influencing attitudes toward refugees and other migrants (Schuettler and Do 2023). Extended or imagined contact seems to be more effective than other interventions (Paluck et al. 2021), but which conditions need to be fulfilled is still unclear, the medium- to longer-term impacts still need to be studied and more experiments run in low- and middle-income countries (Zhou and Lyall 2022). Interventions providing personal narratives and encouraging hosts to empathize with refugees by imagining themselves in a similar situation, as well as stressing commonalities, find positive but not always significant or large impacts (Adida, Lo, and Platas 2018; Alan et al. 2021; Audette et al. 2020; Dinas, Fouka, and Schläpfer 2021; Lazarev and Sharma, 2017; Rodríguez Chatruc and Rozo, 2024). Providing factual information alone can help in some settings (Grigorieff, Roth, and Ubfal 2020; Haaland and Roth 2020; Lergetporer, Piopiunik, and Simon 2021) but is less likely to change attitudes that have already formed (Alesina, Armando, and Stantcheva 2023; Barrera et al. 2020; Hopkins, Sides, and Citrin 2019). In addition to specific interventions, social transfers and other public investments resulting from the refugee inflow that benefit hosts might positively impact host attitudes (Baseler et al. 2023; Kreibaum 2016; Lehmann and Masterson 2020; Valli, Peterman, and Hidrobo 2019; Zhou, Grossman, and Ge 2023). Notwithstanding the substantial progress, important research questions still need to be answered to more effectively inform policy.

Priorities for future work

This report seeks to analyze the interactions and comparative outcomes of hosts and refugees in the same labor markets by illustrating a range of channels through which displacement affects job outcomes for hosts. However, some important channels deserve dedicated attention in future work. First, there is a need for an effective study of the role of aid to host communities in accounting for the relatively benign overall impacts found in this study and the broader literature. Such a study would face both data and methodological constraints, but its potential contribution is high. Second, although labor market competition as a consequence of hosting displaced workers receives much emphasis, the effect on market demand and related opportunities remains relatively understudied. An analysis is needed that accounts for differences in market integration and the degree to which different goods and services are traded. Third, this report illustrates the importance of access to capital for both hosts and refugees who depend on self-employed activity. Capital is clearly a critical conduit, and further study is warranted. Finally, although data on hosts' and refugees' networks were collected for this report, the impact of such networks could not yet be analyzed.

Although this report presents some evidence on distributional impacts, some further questions are worth asking. This study considers the impact of displacement on a broad set of different groups of workers, including those living in poverty and those at a higher consumption level. It also seeks to provide some perspective on whether there are different impacts in communities that host particularly large numbers of refugees. However, a wide agenda remains. The impact of displacement—not only on average outcomes but also on the income distribution (whether by modeling a one-number index of inequality or studying incomes at different percentiles)—could be modeled. Further, the data used in this report were only moderately well-suited to studying differential effects in localities that host high numbers of refugees. This spatial aspect of distributional effects is worth pursuing.

The experiment conducted for this study suggests that further investigating the relationship between job competition and perceptions, and asking how open-mindedness can best be promoted, would be worthwhile. Although much work has been done on hosts' perceptions of refugees, the experimental evidence provided here remains to date the only explicit study of the link between such perceptions and both actual competition for jobs and the anticipation or fear of such competition in a low-income country setting. Policy will benefit from a more solid understanding of the answers to these questions. Further, there is an important need to understand what jobs-related policies and investments can promote openness toward refugees. Such policies could include not only material support to hosts alongside refugees but also communications campaigns or policies that visibly shift the position of refugees in the labor market and provide them with a degree of legitimacy.

Further study is needed to assess the longer-term effects of work permit policies and the impact of allowing refugees to move freely. This study shows that, in three work permit schemes, legally opening (parts of) the labor market did not have large negative impacts on hosts in the short run. Simultaneously, in the one case in which refugees' outcomes were studied, there were large benefits. Further studies should seek to understand how these impacts evolve over time, for hosts and for refugees. In addition, the question of whether those who obtained work permits earlier after arrival have better outcomes over time than those who had to wait longer would be worth pursuing. Such studies exist for high-income but not for low- and middle-income countries (Marbach, Hainmueller, and Hangartner 2018; Slotwinski, Stutzer, and Uhlig 2019). In addition, it has been argued that the ability to move and settle where economic opportunities are is more important for refugees than legal access to the labor market, notably in low- and middle-income countries. Future research should seek to provide empirical evidence of this observation.

Data collection for this report has aimed to allow for a better understanding of the interactions between refugees and hosts in the labor market, but panel data would provide additional insights. Panel data following refugees and hosts over time in the same labor market could form the basis for the analysis of a broad set of important questions while more rigorously identifying causal impacts. Panel data would also help provide a better understanding of how interactions between refugees and hosts evolve. In addition, it could be informative to compare refugee characteristics with origin country household survey data to understand selection effects better.

Note

1 | Please note, however, that the official development assistance numbers include spending on refugees in high-income countries.

References

Adida, Claire L., Adeline Lo, and Melina R. Platas. 2018. "Perspective Taking Can Promote Short-Term Inclusionary Behavior toward Syrian Refugees." *Proceedings of the National Academy of Sciences* 115 (38): 9521–26.

Ait Ali Slimane, Meriem, and Shereen Al-Abbadi. 2023. "Six Years after the Jordan Compact: The Effect of Labour Market Policies on Syrians' Economic Integration." *Forced Migration Review.* https://www.fmreview.org/sites/fmr/files/FMRdownloads/en/issue71/aitalislimane-alabbadi.pdf.

Alan, Sule, Ceren Baysan, Mert Gumren, and Elif Kubilay, "Building Social Cohesion in Ethnically Mixed Schools: An Intervention on Perspective Taking," *The Quarterly Journal of Economics*, November 2021, 136 (4), 2147–2194.

Alesina, Alberto, Armando, Miano, and Stefanie Stantcheva. 2023. "Immigration and Redistribution." *The Review of Economic Studies* 90 (1): 1–39, https://doi.org/10.1093/restud/rdac011.

Andrews, Colin, Aude de Montesquiou, Inés Arévalo Sánchez, Puja Vasudeva Dutta, Sadna Amaranayake, Janet Heisey, Timothy Clay, and Sarang Chaudhary. 2021. *The State of Economic Inclusion Report 2021: The Potential to Scale.* Washington, DC: World Bank.

Arendt, Jacob Nielsen, and Iben Bolvig. 2020. "Early Labor Market Entry, Language Acquisition and Labor Market Success of Refugees." Danish Center for Social Science Research, Copenhagen. https://pure.vive.dk/ws/files/4974591/Early_labor_market_entry_language_acquisition_and_labor_market_success_of_refugees_A_sikret.pdf.

Audette, Nicole, Jeremy Horowitz, and Kristin Michelitch. 2020. "Personal Narratives Reduce Negative Attitudes toward Refugees and Immigrant Outgroups: Evidence from Kenya," Working Paper 1-2020. Nashville: Center for the Study of Democratic Institutions, Vanderbilt University.

Auer, Daniel. 2018. "Language Roulette—The Effect of Random Placement on Refugees' Labour Market Integration." *Journal of Ethnic and Migration Studies* 44 (3): 341–62.

Bahar, Dany, Bo Cowgill, and Jorge Guzman. 2022. "The Economic Effects of Immigration Pardons: Evidence from Venezuelan Entrepreneurs." Working Paper 30624, National Bureau of Economic Research, Cambridge, MA.

Bailey, Michael, Drew M. Johnston, Martin Koenen, Theresa Kuchler, Dominic Russel, and Johannes Stroebel. 2022. "The Social Integration of International Migrants: Evidence from the Networks of Syrians in Germany." Working Paper 29925, National Bureau of Economic Research, Cambridge, MA.

Barberis, Virginia, Laura Brouwer, Jan von der Goltz, Timothy Hobden, Mira Saidi, Kirsten Schuettler, and Karin Seyfert. 2022. *Cost-Effectiveness of Jobs Projects in Conflict and Forced Displacement Contexts*. Washington, DC: World Bank.

Barrera, Oscar, Sergei Guriev, Emeric Henry, and Ekaterina Zhuravskaya. 2020. "Facts, Alternative Facts, and Fact Checking in Times of Post-Truth Politics." *Journal of Public Economics* 182: 104123.

Baseler, Travis, Thomas Ginn, Robert Hakiza, Helidah Ogude-Chambert, and Olivia Woldemikael. 2023. "Can Redistribution Change Policy Views?" Working Paper 645, Center for Global Development, Washington, DC.

Caria, Stefano, Maximilian Kasy, Simon Quinn, Soha Shami, and Alex Teytelboym. 2024. "An Adaptive Targeted Field Experiment: Job Search Assistance for Refugees in Jordan." *Journal of the European Economic Association* 22(2): 781–836, https://doi.org/10.1093/jeea/jvad067.

Dinas, Elias, Vasiliki Fouka, and Alain Schläpfer. 2021. "Family history and attitudes toward out-groups: Evidence from the European refugee crisis." *The Journal of Politics* 83 (2): 647–661.

Foged, Mette, Linea Hasager, and Giovanni Peri. 2022. "Comparing the Effects of Policies for the Labor Market Integration of Refugees." Working Paper 30534, National Bureau of Economic Research, Cambridge.

Foged, Mette, Linea Hasager, Giovanni Peri, Jacob Nielsen Arendt, and Iben Bolvig. 2022b. "Language Training and Refugees' Integration." *Review of Economics and Statistics* 1–41.

Foged, Mette, and Cynthia van der Werf. 2023. "Access to Language Training and the Local Integration of Refugees." *Labour Economics* 84: 102366.

Grigorieff, Alexis, Christopher Roth, and Diego Ubfal. 2020. "Does Information Change Attitudes toward Immigrants?" *Demography* 57 (3): 1117–43.

Haaland, Ingar, and Christopher Roth. 2020. "Labor Market Concerns and Support for Immigration." *Journal of Public Economics* 191: 104256.

Heisey, Janet, Inés Arévalo Sánchez, and Alexi Bernagros. 2022. *Working for Inclusion: Economic Inclusion in Contexts of Forced Displacement*. Washington, DC: World Bank.

Hesemann, J., H. Desai, and Y. Rockenfeller. 2021. "Financing for Refugee Situations 2018–19." OECD Publishing, Paris.

Hopkins, Daniel J., John Sides, and Jack Citrin. 2019. "The muted consequences of correct information about immigration." *The Journal of Politics* 81 (1): 315–320.

Kreibaum, Merle. 2016. "Their Suffering, Our Burden? How Congolese Refugees Affect the Ugandan Population." *World Development* 78: 262–87.

Lazarev, Egor and Kunaal Sharma. 2017."Brother or Burden: An Experiment on Reducing Prejudice Toward Syrian Refugees in Turkey." *Political Science Research and Methods* 5 (2), 201–219.

Lehmann, M. Christian, and Daniel T. R. Masterson. 2020. "Does Aid Reduce Anti-Refugee Violence? Evidence from Syrian Refugees in Lebanon." *American Political Science Review* 114 (4): 1335–42.

Lergetporer, Philipp, Marc Piopiunik, and Lisa Simon. 2021. "Does the Education Level of Refugees Affect Natives' Attitudes?" *European Economic Review* 134: 103710.

Lochmann, Alexia, Hillel Rapoport, and Biagio Speciale. 2019. "The Effect of Language Training on Immigrants' Economic Integration: Empirical Evidence from France." *European Economic Review* 113: 265–96.

Marbach, Moritz, Jens Hainmueller, and Dominik Hangartner. 2018. "The Long-Term Impact of Employment Bans on the Economic Integration of Refugees." *Science Advances* 4 (9).

Maystadt, Jean-Francois, and Gilles Duranton. 2019. "The Development Push of Refugees: Evidence from Tanzania." *Journal of Economic Geography* 19 (2): 299–334.

Paluck, Elizabeth Levy, Roni Porat, Chelsey S. Clark, and Donald P. Green. 2021. "Prejudice Reduction: Progress and Challenges." *Annual Review of Psychology* 72: 533–60.

Rodríguez Chatruc, Marisol and Sandra V. Rozo. 2024. "In Someone Else's Shoes: Reducing Prejudice Through Perspective Taking." *Journal of Development Studies* 170.

Schuettler, Kirsten, and Laura Caron. 2020. "Jobs Interventions for Refugees and Internally Displaced Persons." World Bank, Washington, DC.

Schuettler, Kirsten, and Quy-Toan Do. 2023. "Outcomes for Internally Displaced Persons and Refugees in Low and Middle-Income Countries." Policy Research Working Paper 10278, World Bank, Washington, DC.

Slotwinski, Michaela, Alois Stutzer, and Roman Uhlig. 2019. "Are Asylum Seekers More Likely to Work with More Inclusive Labor Market Access Regulations?" *Swiss Journal of Economics and Statistics* 155: 1–15.

Taylor, J. Edward, Mateusz J. Filipski, Mohamad Alloush, Anubhab Gupta, Ruben Irvin Rojas Valdes, and Ernesto Gonzalez-Estrada. 2016. "Economic Impact of Refugees." *Proceedings of the National Academy of Sciences* 113 (27): 7449–53.

Valli, Elsa, Amber Peterman, and Melissa Hidrobo. 2019. "Economic Transfers and Social Cohesion in a Refugee-Hosting Setting." *Journal of Development Studies* 55 (Suppl. 1): 128–46.

World Bank. 2008. *World Development Report 2009: Reshaping Economic Geography*. Washington, DC: World Bank.

World Bank. 2013. *World Development Report 2013: Jobs*. Washington, DC: World Bank.

World Bank. 2023. *World Development Report 2023: Migrants, Refugees, and Societies*. Washington, DC: World Bank. https://live.worldbank.org/events/world-development-report-migrants-refugees-societies.

Zetter, Roger, and Héloïse Ruaudel. 2016. "Refugees' Right to Work and Access to Labor Markets—An Assessment." World Bank Global Program on Forced Displacement (GPFD) and the Global Knowledge Partnership on Migration and Development (KNOMAD) Thematic Working Group on Forced Migration, KNOMAD Working Paper, World Bank, Washington, DC.

Zhou, Yang-Yang, Guy Grossman, and Shuning Ge. 2023. "Inclusive Refugee-Hosting Can Improve Local Development and Prevent Public Backlash." *World Development* 166: 106203.

Zhou, Yang-Yang, and Jason Lyall. 2024. "Prolonged Contact Does Not Reshape Locals' Attitudes toward Migrants in Wartime Settings: Experimental Evidence from Afghanistan." *American Journal of Political Science*. https://doi.org/10.1111/ajps.12862.